A CULTURAL HISTORY OF THE SEA

VOLUME 3

A Cultural History of the Sea
General Editor: Margaret Cohen

Volume 1
A Cultural History of the Sea in Antiquity
Edited by Marie-Claire Beaulieu

Volume 2
A Cultural History of the Sea in the Medieval Age
Edited by Elizabeth Lambourn

Volume 3
A Cultural History of the Sea in the Early Modern Age
Edited by Steve Mentz

Volume 4
A Cultural History of the Sea in the Age of Enlightenment
Edited by Jonathan Lamb

Volume 5
A Cultural History of the Sea in the Age of Empire
Edited by Margaret Cohen

Volume 6
A Cultural History of the Sea in the Global Age
Edited by Franziska Torma

A CULTURAL HISTORY
OF THE SEA

IN THE EARLY
MODERN AGE

VOLUME 3

Edited by Steve Mentz

BLOOMSBURY ACADEMIC
LONDON • NEW YORK • OXFORD • NEW DELHI • SYDNEY

BLOOMSBURY ACADEMIC
Bloomsbury Publishing Plc
50 Bedford Square, London, WC1B 3DP, UK
1385 Broadway, New York, NY 10018, USA

BLOOMSBURY, BLOOMSBURY ACADEMIC and the Diana logo are
trademarks of Bloomsbury Publishing Plc

First published in Great Britain 2021
This edition first published in Great Britain 2024

Copyright © Bloomsbury Publishing, 2021

Steve Mentz has asserted his right under the Copyright,
Designs and Patents Act, 1988, to be identified as Editor of this work.

Cover image © Chart of Europe, Africa, and Asia – Eastern hemisphere (modified), and
Chart of North America and South America with Greenland in the upper right corner –
Western hemisphere (modified) Courtesy of the John Carter Brown Library

All rights reserved. No part of this publication may be reproduced or transmitted
in any form or by any means, electronic or mechanical, including photocopying,
recording, or any information storage or retrieval system, without prior
permission in writing from the publishers.

Bloomsbury Publishing Plc does not have any control over, or responsibility for,
any third-party websites referred to or in this book. All internet addresses given
in this book were correct at the time of going to press. The author and publisher
regret any inconvenience caused if addresses have changed or sites have
ceased to exist, but can accept no responsibility for any such changes.

Every effort has been made to trace copyright holders and to obtain their permissions
for the use of copyright material. The publisher apologizes for any errors or omissions and
would be grateful if notified of any corrections that should be incorporated in future reprints
or editions of this book.

A catalogue record for this book is available from the British Library.

A catalog record for this book is available from the Library of Congress.

ISBN: HB: 978-1-4742-9903-9
       Set: 978-1-4742-9910-7
       PB: 978-1-3504-5118-6
       Set: 978-1-3504-5130-8

Series: The Cultural Histories Series

Typeset by Integra Software Services Pvt. Ltd.
Printed and bound in Great Britain

To find out more about our authors and books visit www.bloomsbury.com
and sign up for our newsletters.

CONTENTS

LIST OF ILLUSTRATIONS	vii
GENERAL EDITOR'S PREFACE *Margaret Cohen*	xii
Introduction *Steve Mentz*	1
1 Knowledges *Christopher L. Pastore*	25
2 Practices *John B. Hattendorf*	53
3 Networks *Dan Brayton*	83
4 Conflicts *Dyani Johns Taff*	105
5 Islands and Shores *Debapriya Sarkar*	135
6 Travelers *Josiah Blackmore*	157
7 Representations *James Seth*	179

8	Imaginary Worlds *Lowell Duckert*	205

NOTES 226
BIBLIOGRAPHY 235
NOTES ON CONTRIBUTORS 258
INDEX 261

ILLUSTRATIONS

i.	*Wright-Molyneux Map*	xvi
0.1	Sir Francis Drake, with a map of his circumnavigation, from *Franciscus Dracus nobiliss eques Angliae aetatis suae* XXXXVI. Cologne, 1596	14
0.2	Treatment of slaves on Martinique, from Francois Froger, *Relation d'un voyage* … London: M. Gillyflower, 1698. Plate following p. 120	15
0.3	Hurricane strikes land, from *Naaukeurige versameling der gedenk-waardigste* … Leiden: Door Pieter Vander Aa, 1707. Fold-out plate following p. 12, vol. 3	16
0.4	"The Tobacco Plant," from Jonathan Carver, *Travels through the Interior Parts of North-America*. London: William Richardson, 1779. Plate following p. 522	18
0.5	The maritime globe, from Pedro Cubero Sebastian, *Peregrinacio del Mundo* … Naples: Carolos Porsile, 1682. Engraved title page	19
0.6	Frontispiece, from Luís vaz de Camões, *The Lusiad, or, Portugals Historicall Poem*, 1655	21
1.1	Imaginary islands and apocryphal creatures lurked just beyond the limits of oceanic knowledge. Here, somewhere west of Mediterranean Sea, St. Brendan lands on the back of a sea monster between the imaginary St. Brendan's and Fortunate Islands.	

"St. Brendan and the Whale Island," from Honorius Philoponus, *Nova Typis Transacta Navigatio* (Linz: Wolfgang Kilian, 1621), plate following p. 10   29

1.2 The caravela redonda and its hybrid lateen and square-rigged sail plan was an important form of technology that helped usher in the age of exploration. "Oceanica Classis," from Carlo Verardi, *In Laudem Serenissimi Ferdinandi Hispania[rum] Regis, Bethicae [et] Regni Granatae* (Basel, Switzerland: Johann Bergname de Olpel, 1494), verso of leaf [36]   33

1.3 Innovations in navigational technique created new oceanic knowledge. This allegorical representation of the navigational arts shows four women holding a pair of dividers and plumb line (*bottom left*), a ship's rudder (*top left*), a map and dividers (*top right*), and an astrolabe and dividers (*bottom right*). The two on the left look down into the sea, while the women on the right contemplate the earth and the heavens. "Art of Navigation," from Antonio de Ulloa, *Relacion Historica del Viage a la American Meridional...* (Madrid: Antonio Marin, 1748), frontispiece   37

1.4 Natural knowledge about the sea was often produced during the search for riches and by the people who conducted the work. Here, Native American and/or African divers labor in the seventeenth-century Venezuelan pearl fishery. "Perlen Fischerey," from Christoph Vielheuer, *Gründliche Beschreibung Fremder Materialien und Specereyen Ursprung, Wachssthum, Herkommen und Deroselben Natur und Eigenschafften* (Leipzig: Johann Fritzsche, 1676), plate following p. 176   41

1.5 The establishment of the Royal Society in 1660 initiated a more systematic approach to the study of marine natural history. Sir Hans Sloane (1660–1753) was a particularly careful observer of oceanic nature, in this case depicting coral-encrusted ship planks and silver coins and the sailed jellyfish that evoked the Portuguese caravela, which in English came to be called the Man o' War. "Nummus Argenteus Hispanicus, Cuj Lapis Astroites Innascitur, ab Eodem Naufragio Expiscatus... [and] Urtica Marina Soluta, Purpurea, Oblonga, Cirrhis longissimis," from Sir Hans Sloane, *A Voyage to the Islands Madera, Barbados, Nieves. S. Christophers and Jamaica: With the Natural History of the Herbs and Trees, Four-footed Beasts, Fishes, Birds, Insects, Reptiles, &c. of the Last of Those Islands* (London: Printed by B.M. for the author, 1707)   43

ILLUSTRATIONS ix

1.6 During the early modern period the contest for empire encouraged the creation of new oceanic legal regimes. If at least a modicum of law and order reigned in metropolitan waters, violence often held sway "beyond the line." Here, the notorious New England pirate Edward Low executes an adversary while his crew watches. [Edward Low Shoots a Man], from Daniel Defoe, Historie der Engelsche Zee-Roovers (Amsterdam: Hermanus Uytwerf, 1725), plate following p. 590   49

2.1 Theodor de Bry, *Petits Voyages* (Frankfurt, 1601)   57

2.2 Pierre Garcie, called Ferrande, *The rutter of the sea: with the hauens, rodes, soundings, kenning, windes, floods and ebbes ...* (London, 1567)   58

2.3 John Davis, *The Seaman's Secrets* (London, 1595)   59

2.4 John Seller, *Practical navigation; or an introduction to that whole art* (London, 1680)   62

2.5 F. Dassié, *L'Architecture navale* (Paris, 1677)   67

2.6 Hans Staden, *Warhaftige Historia* (Marburg, 1567)   75

2.7 *Librio di Consolato* (Venice, 1539)   78

2.8 Hugo Grotius, *De Mari Liberio* (Leiden, 1633)   79

3.1 *Ptolemaic World Map*, 1482   87

3.2 Johannes Stabius, *World Map*, 1515   93

3.3 Hessel Gerritsz, *Chart of the Pacific*, 1622   99

4.1 Plate from Jerónimo Corte-Real, *Sucesso do Segundo Cerco de Diu* (Lisbon, 1574), p. 35r   110

4.2 Plate from Jerónimo Corte-Real, *Sucesso do Segundo Cerco de Diu* (Lisbon, 1574), p. 165v   112

4.3 First page of the *Sejarah Melayu* manuscript. British Library, Or.16214, f.1r   114

4.4 Georgio Vasari, *Battle of Lepanto: Fleets Approaching Each Other* (Sala Regia, Vatican Palace, 1572)   117

4.5 Georgio Vasari, *Battle of Lepanto: Fleets Engaging* (Sala Regia, Vatican Palace, 1572)   118

4.6	Marcus Gheeraerts, Portrait of Queen Elizabeth I (Armada Portrait), *c*. 1588. Oil on panel	121
4.7	"A Pyigyimon boat, which consists of two conjoined gilded boats, with a seven-tired roof (pyatthat). There are two separate dragon-headed hulls, while on the bow are figures of a garuda (mythical bird) and a naga (mythical dragon), with Sakka (a celestial king and the ruler of Tavatimsa heaven) standing between them." Caption by Annabel Gallop, British Library blog post November 21, 2018, https://blogs.bl.uk/asian-and-african/2018/11/beautiful-burmese-barges-and-boats.html. British Library, Or. 14005, f. 1	129
5.1	Abraham Ortelius, *Map of Utopia*	139
5.2	Abraham Ortelius, *Map of Bohemia,* from *Theatrum orbis terrarium*	140
5.3	Abraham Ortelius, *Map of Cyprus and Inset Map of Lemnos,* from *Theatrum orbis terrarium*	140
5.4	Richard Norwood, *Map of Bermuda*, made after his survey of the island in 1616, published in 1626	143
5.5	George Sandys, *A Relation of a Journey Begun an: Dom*, 1610	151
6.1	Panoramic view of Lisbon in 1622—the shipyard is at the far left—from João Baptista Lavanha, *Viagem da Catholica Real Magestade del Rey D. Filipe II. N.S. ao Reyno de Portvgal e rellação do solene recebimento que nelle se lhe fez*	164
6.2	The gods ordain Vasco da Gama's journey to India, from Manuel de Faria e Sousa, *Lvsiadas de Lvis de Camones / Principe de los poetas de España*, vol. 1 (1639)	166
6.3	Illuminations of ships of the fleet of Francisco de Almeida, first Portuguese viceroy of India, from *Livro de Lisuarte de Abreu*	168
6.4	Portrait of Vasco da Gama, from *Livro de Lisuarte de Abreu*	169
6.5	Sea nereids supporting and steering Gama's ship, from *Os Lusíadas*, edited by Miguel Rodrigues (1772)	172
6.6	Woodcut of shipwreck, from *Naufragio e lastimoso sucesso da perdiçam de Manoel de Sousa de Sepulueda, & Dona Lianor de Sá sua molher & filhos …* (1594)	174

ILLUSTRATIONS xi

7.1	Caravaggio, *Narcissus*, *c*. 1597–9	180
7.2	Rembrandt Van Rijn, *Christ in the Storm on the Sea of Galilee*, 1633	183
7.3	Vittore Carpaccio, *The Legend of St Ursula*, 1497–8	189
7.4	Hendrick Cornelisz Vroom, *A Number of East Indiamen off the Coast*, *c*. 1600–1630	192
7.5	Joos de Momper, *River Landscape with Hunt*, *c*. 1600	194
7.6	*Americae sive quartae orbis partis nova et exactissima descriptio*, 1562	197
8.1	Other Worlds. Photograph by Viktor Lyagushkin	209
8.2	*Septentrionalium Terrarum Description*, 1606	211

GENERAL EDITOR'S PREFACE

MARGARET COHEN

Over the past thirty years, oceanic studies has emerged in the humanities as a leading interdisciplinary field. It owes its importance to its capacity to give an account of globalization spanning millenia that is robustly cross-cultural. As this new field has taken shape, it has both incorporated and revised an earlier generation of scholarship, which attended to maritime transport, naval warfare, and global exploration, often within a framework of national history. Contributions of oceanic studies range across scales: from showing how maritime transport and marine resources join separated lands into waterbased regions to resurrecting how a meeting on a beach between societies never before in contact could create intractable structures of domination to revealing the impact of a single photograph from outer space of the earth as a blue planet. Today, oceanic studies aims to tell the stories of all who have traveled the seas: professionals, adventurers, passengers, forced migrants—and animals.

Further, this emerging field recognizes that the seas are a rich realm for the imagination, all the more so given the paradoxical tension between their remoteness for many people and yet their life-sustaining importance. It is telling that a poet, the Nobel prize-winning Derek Walcott, has penned the memorable phrase, "The Sea is History."[1] At the same time, the imagination of the seas is not purely fanciful but rather takes shape in relation to located marine environments and how humans practice them, leading humanists to engage the reality of the physical world. When modern oceanography and marine biology took shape in the nineteenth century, these sciences established the oceans as nonhuman natural realms, despite their prehistory in mixed, practical knowledge conjoining environmental curiosity with the pursuit of power and wealth. Since this disciplinary cleavage, the sea has time and time again shown us the need to recognize its existence for and with humans, as well as in itself.

In the twenty-first century, the importance of the sea in world-defining developments, including second-wave globalization, postcolonial conflict and climate change, has become so evident that its social and cultural reality cannot be ignored. In the words of Franziska Torma, volume editor of *The Global Age*, such developments have "forced us to 'think science and humanities' together, because science provides data and humanities 'translate' them into social and academic interpretation; this opens up historical perspective on the oceans from antiquity to the present" (Franziska Torma, personal communication, May 2020). Whether drawing on nautical archaeology resurrecting sunken cities and shipwrecks, or using scientific research about the impact of climate change on coastal communities, oceanic studies is taking the lead among humanities fields in pursuing this urgent, if vexed, disciplinary crossing.

In editing *A Cultural History of the Sea*, I have been fortunate to work with volume editors who have made major contributions to setting the agenda of oceanic studies in its twenty-first-century form. Taken together, their expertise encompasses the oceans of the globe, notably the Mediterranean, the Indian Ocean, the Atlantic, and the Pacific and includes the history of science and the environment as well. We have launched our project from our institutional homes in transatlantic universities, even as we mark our starting point at once to acknowledge and brush against the grain of Western-oriented perspectives. Further, readers will see that the abstraction Western itself fractures when subjected to the pressure of water-based movement and seafaring practices. Thus, maritime travel creates far-flung contact zones across thousands of kilometers, which cannot be reduced to the orientation of the West, even if Western Europe may have been a point of departure. These contact zones are characterized by extreme social complexity, which modify those whom they involve, and the importance of the physical environment in such contact zones creates yet another set of considerations. The demands of sea-oriented life, moreover, unmoor those who work on ships to the point where they may be a culture unto themselves, unnervingly apart for their societies, due to such factors as the rigors of shipboard living and the multicultural *habitus* even on vessels enforcing the routes of empire.

Our interest in conveying the heterogeneous histories that meet on the sea extends to the themes we have chosen for our series' organization. A unique feature of the Bloomsbury *Cultural History* series is to devise eight chapter headings for each volume that can run from antiquity to the present. These headings address culture understood in its expansive, anthropological sense: as designating the diverse realms of practices organizing the structures of a society. In the case of the seas, important aspects include but are not limited to war, technology, and trade at sea, scientific knowledge, as well as myth and imagination. We defined our themes in a fashion that would enable contributors to present a democratic history. Thus, for example, we framed histories of "War and Empire," at sea as "Conflicts," to take account of the many scales of violent struggles at sea, including frames of state-supported navies, non-state actors, and the violence of shipboard life, ranging from mutinies to treatment of passengers and transport of the enslaved. Or thus, we reframed the theme "Science and Technology," as "Knowledges," to provide an opportunity to include knowledge beyond the strict boundary of science. Such knowledge ranges from philosophical speculation in classical antiquity to sea knowledge and practice outside Western paradigms.

In organizing the chapters, we have respected conventional Western historical periodization, which has been shaped by events on land. At the same time, readers will find within the volumes chapters that take up the question of whether such periodization stops at shore, due to the previously mentioned pressures of a sea perspective on concepts whose operations are focused toward the land. Thus, the history of Egyptian seafaring and contacts with other cultures of the Mediterranean basin traverses the land-based periodization of this particular culture, traditionally understood in terms of its ruling dynasties, from Greek prehistory through the classical period and into Roman times, roughly the second millennium BCE to the first century CE. Within the modern era, to take the example of a single technology, the years from 1769 to 1989 form one period in the history of navigation, although this epoch runs across three volumes in the series. In 1769, British engineer John Harrison perfected a chronometer that would keep accurate time over a long traverse. With the ability to compare noon during a ship's traverse and noon at an arbitrarily defined starting point—it became the Greenwich Meridian by convention— navigators could finally establish their longitude while a ship was sailing, a development that would vastly improve safety at sea, even if it took decades to expand beyond naval circles. Celestial navigation would remain the best practice for establishing a ship's location until the invention of the global positioning system (GPS) in the third quarter of the twentieth century, which could be dated to 1989, when the US Department of Defense launched a satellite system that would become GPS, replacing with the touch of a few buttons the arduous calculations needed for celestial navigation.

Another dimension to the specificity of sea-based periodization is the timescale of the oceans as a physical environment. For eons marine history moved at a geological pace, but in the age of the Anthropocene we are learning about the human impact on a realm of the planet long considered an inexhaustible resource and a vast power beyond human reach. Such an impact can occur within a person's lifetime, as is the case, for example, with melting ice caps at the poles, which have drastically diminished in satellite visualizations, dating back to 1979 (Starr 2016).[1] This impact in turn is affecting societies, from Indigenous inhabitants of the Arctic to farmers around the world, who depend on weather patterns disrupted by global warming. Yet further entangling human and geological timescales at sea, melting ice caps open up new shipping routes through the Arctic, which present potential for a greater human footprint there.

The global consequences of polar ice melt exemplify how a sea perspective reorients terrestrial units of geographical analysis, which is the case not only for the oceans as an environment but also for the oceans as an arena of human practice. Chapters across the series reveal how state-drawn borders may be less important for cultures at sea than fluid spaces defined by natural features, and how islands or coasts eccentric from the perspective of land-based history may play an outsized, formative role in a nation's oceanic ambitions. Further, sea transport produces states that are at once joined under the same flag yet are also territorially disconnected, with unique and uniquely difficult administrative features. Yet another challenge, at the lexical level, is that when we try to express oceanic phenomena with language from the land, we reach to unsatisfactory imagery that impedes understanding. A good example today is the great "garbage patch" of pollution in the Pacific Ocean. The figure of a "patch" misleadingly limits its reach and does not capture the microscopic pervasion of plastic in sea water.

The seas are vast expanses, whose study drives home the point that any research is necessarily fragmentary and located. Contributors to these volumes include established and emerging voices, who have written chapters that are original research around our central themes rather than summaries of secondary literature. Volume editors have encouraged their contributors to present their insights in whatever way they thought would best bring out the originality of their topic and suit their disciplinary expertise. Some have used the narrative of a survey. Others have taken a single event as their canvas, whether the event is exemplary or tellingly anomalous. Yet others have spun out their questions at the scale of one marine environment.

Such flexibility is also important because "the sea" of our series' title is not one thing. Rather, the saltwater element is culturally constructed and imagined in widely different ways, depending on who is engaging with it and to what ends. This range is evident as well in the rich imagery accompanying the chapters, which is another feature of the *Cultural History* series. Thus, readers will see how in antiquity, the sea was never represented directly but rather suggested metonymically on frescoes and vases, with depictions of fish, ships, or mythological sea creatures. Grand seascapes, exhibiting the ocean as a theatre of awe, in contrast, compelled audiences in Enlightenment and Romantic eras. One constant across centuries are practical charts, which have used a variety of methods, shaped by different epistemes and environments, to find and mark paths across the waters, all nonetheless sharing an aim of safety. To draw a parallel between navigating vast, and in many cases, untracked waters and emergent areas of scholarship: as readers constellate the diverse subjects and approaches collected in this series, I hope they will gain a better understanding of the abiding, pervasive human interface with the seas as well as recognize new and future directions for oceanic studies.

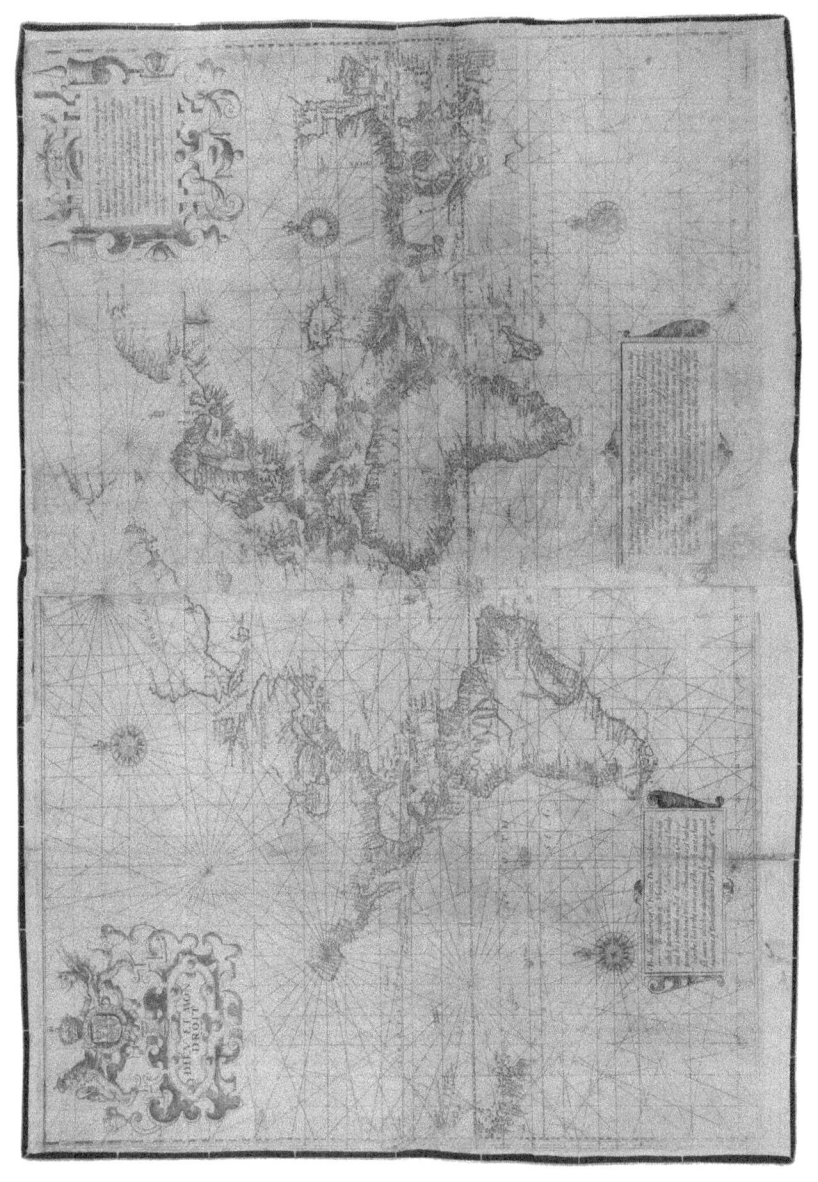

FIGURE 1 *Wright-Molyneux Map*. © Wikimedia Commons (public domain).

Introduction

Wet Globalization: The Early Modern Ocean as World-System

STEVE MENTZ

The early modern period witnessed the rapid growth of maritime voyaging across and between the major global ocean basins. The period expanded but by no means inaugurated long-haul oceanic exploration, colonization, and trade. It developed regular interconnections between multiple regional systems into the first fully global maritime network in human history. Earlier historical periods had seen expansive sea travel, including some interoceanic routes. The monsoon system of the Indian Ocean had been an active trade network for a millennium before the arrival of Vasco da Gama's fleet in 1499 CE. The famous Chinese Admiral Zeng He led a series of voyages between the Pacific and Indian basins in the fifteenth century. Lief Erikson crossed the North Atlantic and founded a relatively short-lived settlement in Vinland around 1000. A determined minority of scholars continues to argue for occasional contact between the Americas and Afro-Eurasia before Columbus.[1] But the sudden burst of ocean crossings and transoceanic trade and settlement that followed the voyages of da Gama, Columbus, and many other European mariners in the decades around 1500 CE drove major changes in the ecological and economic world-systems. The physical and cultural integration of the globe by sea, a process that I call "wet globalization," had massive consequences for the early modern world.[2] In material and cultural ways, early modern mariners created the globalized world we live in today.

This volume contains a series of eight essays that will explore the cultural changes driven by the early modern oceanic turn. As scholarship in the "blue humanities" has been arguing in recent years, the human–ocean relationship has always been a major driver of material and cultural history.[3] The early modern period, with its global oceanic expansion and rapid succession of circumnavigations after Francis Magellan's fleet returned to Spain without its admiral in 1522, occupies a crucial transitional moment in oceanic history. Driven by an initial focus on European ships, this analysis of early modern globalization cannot entirely avoid Eurocentrism. Thinking about the nonhuman Ocean as co-contributor to the structures and dislocations of wet globalization, however, helps dethrone capital-M Man from his supposedly dominant position. The physical space that modern oceanographers call the World Ocean can contextualize the puny mariners who splash across and through it. Early modern global voyages had massive consequences for human and nonhuman populations around the world, but the story of the early modern sea is hardly one of conquest or discovery. Rather, wet globalization narrates a series of catastrophes and a collection of practical and ideological responses to catastrophe. The period teems with human evil and cruelty, including crucial early stages of the horrific crimes of colonialism and the slave trade. An Ocean-centered view shows, however, that figures such as Columbus were nowhere near as domineering as titles such as "Admiral of the Ocean Sea" fantasized. The physical geography of the oceans structured all voyages in the age of sail. Columbus's voyages to the New World, it seems important to remember, simply followed the downwind paths of prevailing winds and the Canary and North Equatorial ocean currents. His ships arrived in the Bahamas because they could not have arrived anywhere else.

Many of the supposedly new inventions of the European Renaissance, from the purported "invention of the human" to such innovations as capitalism, the nation-state, and interiority, are neither new nor exclusive to this period in world history. But while knowledge and experience of maritime travel has been central to human cultures as long as historical and prehistorical evidence allows us to trace, the oceanic turn on a global scale largely begins in the fifteenth century. The long history of interactions with the world ocean is always structured through the attempts of tiny humans to conceptualize the planet-sized expanse of the great waters. The global thinking pioneered by early modern sailors engaged with the paradoxical physical binary that continues to define human–ocean relations today:

1. The sea is a hostile environment in which humans cannot live.
2. The sea makes possible long-haul transportation of objects around the globe.

The human relationship with the sea always oscillates between these two poles. During the period of European culture known as the early modern period or the Renaissance, the global balance shifted in the direction of transportation: no European ships are known to have circumnavigated the globe before 1522, but by the end of the sixteenth century, at least three ships, and perhaps a bit over a hundred persons, had accomplished the feat. These ships and sailors represent a tiny fraction of the humans engaged in oceanic trade and travel in this period, but they had an outsized impact on global history.

The early modern sea was a contested space, especially after long-haul voyages revealed the planetary scale of the World Ocean. In arguing for a conception of the early modern sea that emphasizes global movements both economic and ecological, wet globalization engages with several existing ways of thinking about the sea that provide helpful context. To help explain these ideas, I will use catchphrases from modern writers as touchstones. The cultural history of the early modern ocean includes glimpses of what would become postcolonial, Romantic, and antislavery schools of ocean thinking.

1. **The Sea is (postcolonial) history**: Derek Walcott's great poem "The Sea is History" from 1979 (2007: 137–9) posits a Caribbean-centered rereading of Atlantic history, retelling the Western origin narrative from Genesis through the Renaissance to Emancipation through the master-narrative of the slave trade. "It's all subtle and submarine," he writes, asking us to rethink history with the sea as its center. Wet globalization takes inspiration from Walcott's Atlantic-based critique to imagine a planet-wide oceanic theory of historical change.
2. **"The Sea is slavery"**: The British-Guyanese poet and novelist Fred D'Aguiar transforms Walcott's "history" into a narrower focus on the Atlantic slave trade in the opening line of his novel, *Feeding the Ghosts* (1997). Taking up the infamous story of the slave ship *Zong*, from which living Africans in the process of being transported to the New World were tossed into the sea to later collect insurance money, D'Aguiar underlines the relationship between economic expansion and violence. His dramatic focus on the way oceanic movements facilitated the transatlantic slave trade helps reinforce the centrality of maritime culture to the violence that birthed modernity.
3. **The Sea is Romanticism**: W.H. Auden (1950) also provides a poetic vision of the sea in history, but he places Romantic poetry rather than the slave trade at the center. I have argued previously that Auden's claim that the Romantic poets "invented" the modern sense of the sea is overstated, particularly since so many of Auden's examples are from Shakespeare (Mentz 2015: 50n179). His sense that Romantic visions of fathomless deeps dominate oceanic writings from Melville and Byron casts an intriguing backward shadow on any investigation of pre-Romantic maritime writings.

While my focus on globalization might seem to tread too close to the Great Man-school distortions of Eurocentric histories of explorers and conquistadors, a posthuman approach emphasizes that the most consequential passengers on these circumnavigational ships were not once-iconic and now morally disreputable elite European men such as Columbus, Vasco da Gama, and Sir Francis Drake, whose human legacies of slavery, imperialism, and piratical bloodshed are problematic enough. Alongside pirates and slavers, European ships carried Afro-Eurasian diseases and nonhuman animals, including plague, malaria, smallpox, and many other destructive illnesses. The hemispheres also exchanged through these voyages animal and plant populations, with American crops such as potatoes, maize, and cassava thriving in Afro-Eurasia, and European animals such as the horse insinuating themselves into American cultural lives.[4] I have recently argued that the term "Columbian Exchange" through which this process has been described should be retired in favor of the more impersonal "ecological globalization," but no matter what you call it, the ecological mixing of the Americas with Afro-Eurasia had drastic global environmental effects (2015: esp. ix–xxiii). Emphasizing "wet globalization"— the construction and integration of salt-water routes connecting nearly all of the planet's land masses—marks the period 1450–1750 as among the most environmentally consequential and disastrous in the history of the human race.

This introduction will frame the chapters that follow in this volume by sketching three alternative theories of early modern globalization. The recent analysis of earth systems scientists Simon L. Lewis and Mark A. Maslin (2018) posits that the early modern reintegration of the Americas with the ecosystems of Afro-Eurasia created a "New Pangea" that represents the most consequential turn in ecological history since the invention of agriculture. In contrast to Lewis and Maslin's purportedly objective vision, I proffer the powerful critique of radical geographer Kathyrn Yussof, whose short volume *A Billion Black Anthropocenes or None* (2018) brings race and gender into the geological conversation. These two alternate explorations of geological history both contrast with the German philosopher Peter Sloterdijk's theory of "spherology," as developed across the three sprawling volumes of the *Spheres* trilogy (Vol. 1 1998, English 2011; Vol. 2 1999, English 2014; Vol. 3 2004, English 2016). Sloterdijk argues that the global circumnavigations of the early modern period represent a crucial literalization of intellectual and geographical history. For Sloterdijk, the transformation of the ancient trope of the sphere into geographic reality inaugurates the modern period. Together, Sloterdijk's ideology critique, Yussof's racially informed analysis, and Lewis and Maslin's geophysical history provide conceptual bases through which to understand oceanic globalization in the early modern period. These sections will be followed by brief explorations of six keywords that provide windows onto the maritime history of the period. A speculative conclusion gestures briefly toward the poetics of the encounter with the alien ocean.

THE NEW PANGEA: LEWIS AND MASLIN'S *THE HUMAN PLANET*

When the supercontinent Pangea fractured and began to drift into distinct continents 750 million years ago, the ecosystems of the newly separated land masses began to diverge from one another.[5] For much of subsequent history, there was only limited contact between the massive land mass on which homo sapiens first evolved, Afro-Eurasia, and the distant ecosystems of the Americas. During the most recent Ice Age, which ended nearly 12,000 years ago, water levels were low enough that many animals, including humans, traveled across the land bridge connecting Siberia to North America. But after the ice melted and the seas rose, the separation of the ecospheres became closer to absolute. Birds crossed the oceans, a small number of Viking ships crossed the North Atlantic around 1000 CE, and the range of maritime exploration of Pacific Island cultures remains difficult to determine precisely. But in broad terms, the living networks and human ecologies of the Americas remained separate from those of the larger connected landmass of Afro-Eurasia between the dawn of history and the late fifteenth century. During many thousands of years, animal, plant, viral, and human ecologies on each side of the Atlantic and Pacific basins developed in isolation from each other. The over-familiar date of 1492 fingers Columbus at the start of the new era of ecological globalization that reintegrated these ecological systems, but the arrival of the Portuguese fleet led by Vasco da Gama in India in 1499 also marked a key east-facing node in what would soon develop into a global maritime network of trade, violence, colonization, and eventually empire. In the phrase of earth systems scientists Lewis and Maslin, the period scholars call the "early modern" period witnessed the creation of a "New Pangea" (2018: 166) that relinked the ecologies and economies of the once-sundered continents.

Many different names have been proposed for the period in which European sailors took to the World Ocean, encircled the globe and began to occupy the global spaces of World History. The environmental historian Alfred Crosby (2003) influentially proposed the term "Columbian Exchange" in 1972, inaugurating a tradition that would treat Christopher Columbus's voyages to the Americas as the essential first step in global transformation. Crosby's focus, however, was on an ecological process not a man. He examined the physical interweaving of the living and nonliving networks of the sundered parts of Pangea, the Americas and Afro-Eurasia. Bringing these ecosystems back together, he observed, pushed unlike systems into becoming increasing like each other. "That trend toward biological homogeneity," Crosby writes, "is one of the most important aspects of the history of life on this planet since the retreat of the continental glaciers" (3). Charles C. Mann, whose two works of global ecohistory, *1491: New Revelations of the Americas before Columbus* (2005) and *1493: Uncovering the New World Columbus Created* (2011), have done much to communicate the consequences of Crosby's vision, emphasizing the "role of *exchange*, both ecological and economic" in what was "not … the discovery of a New World, but its creation" (2011: xxiv, emphasis in original). Marxist eco-historian Jason W. Moore has emphasized how the development of frontier capitalism during the early modern period gave rise to a "world-ecology"

(2015: 3) of appropriation and exploitation. "Capitalism," Moore argues, became during this period above all "a way of organizing nature" (3, 78) Historians of the period between 1400–1800 CE also use categories like "early modernity," and the older Eurocentric term "Renaissance" to describe a process of cultural expansion that can also be accurately named "first globalization," to borrow Geoffrey C. Gunn's (2003) description of the worldwide trade network that arose after 1500 CE. An older historical tradition referred in Eurocentric terms to the "discovery of the oceans" after the voyages of the 1480s and 1490s to Asia and the New World (Parry 1974). In an almost certainly vain effort to avoid canonizing individuals, I have suggested that we omit Columbus and instead describe this period as "wet globalization" because its crucial technology was the ocean-going ship and its anti-fundamental environment the ocean.

In describing "wet globalization," I like the phrase "offshore trajectory" because those words emphasize that the process relies upon navigation on and global movements of salt water. Sea travel connected humans, nations, empires, and religions—not to mention plants, animals, viruses, and ecosystems. Globalization operates now and has always operated through sea routes, from the Spanish silver trade that linked the Pacific coast of the Americas to the Philippines to China in the sixteenth century, through efforts underway in the summer of 2018 by Russian container ships to open the Northwest and Northeast passages through no-longer-icebound Arctic waters. Even though today most individuals, at least most relatively wealthy individuals, travel the globe by air, the goods that comprise the global economy still travel by ships, in standard-sized containers. Shifting our attention from firm ground to the unstable fluid covering most of our planet's surface emphasizes that many events in the ages of discovery and empire emerged through forces and encounters that were largely beyond the control of individual humans, even those well-known figures who have been canonized as "discovers" or "explorers." It may be too late at this point to rename the "Columbian Exchange" with less focus on one man, though one of my arguments for "wet globalization" is the way the phrase captures the impersonal nature of the forces at work during this period. The World Ocean, with its interwoven patterns of currents and prevailing winds, drove the populations of the separated continents back together. No single mariner, nation, or community fueled those voyages by themselves. The New Pangea floats on the ocean.

For Lewis and Maslin, in their earth systems science perspective, wet globalization in the early modern period marks a new phase in anthropogenic climate change. This period, they argue, fixes the Anthropocene and the origins of the modern world ecosystem. In nominating the year 1610 as the "Orbis Spike," a "Golden Spike" marker inaugurating the Anthropocene, they emphasize the more-than-human consequences of this moment in human history:

> In Earth systems terms it is the last globally cool moment before the long-term warmth of the Anthropocene, and the key moment after which Earth's biota becomes progressively globally homogenized ... thereby setting Earth on a new evolutionary trajectory. (2018: 318)

The scientists choose 1610 as an observed minimum for carbon levels following the collapse of New World populations and consequent afforestation. Carbon levels would subsequently increase rapidly, and so far uninterruptedly, after industrialization and global population growth. While as a humanities scholar who believes that human meaning requires stories, I remain suspicious of all magic dates, their nomination of 1610 makes a valuable contrast to Columbus's 1492. For Lewis and Maslin, the age of Man begins as an age of death: historical estimates of the death rate of Native American populations estimate that at least 70 percent of the pre-Contact population, and perhaps as high as 90 percent, died within the first 150 years after the arrival of Europeans and the viruses that sailed with them (156). Total human casualties during the period of Contact and early colonization range from 50 to 76 million. It was on a decimated American continent that early European settlers planted their flags: "The arrival of Europeans in America probably killed about 10 per cent of all humans on the planet over the period 1493 to 1650" (158). The decimation of American populations in the early modern period holds up a horrific mirror in which we can glimpse worst-case scenarios of large-scale climactic disruption today. Lewis and Maslin demonstrate that transoceanic travel during the early modern period marks the key moment when human actions dramatically reshaped our environment on a planetary scale:

> The 1610 Orbis Spike marks the beginning of today's globally interconnected economy and ecology, which set Earth on a new evolutionary trajectory. [...] In narrative terms, the Anthropocene began with widespread colonialism and slavery: it is a story of how people treat the environment and how people treat each other. (13)

The World Ocean flowed with the blood of Native Americans in the years after Contact, and soon after the drowned bodies jettisoned by the Middle Passage would further stain the waters.

From the red waters of conquest, slavery, and settlement emerged the new ecological order of globalization. The material and symbolic centrality of two genocides—the disease- and conquest-driven extermination of Native Americans, and the brutal displacement of the transatlantic slave trade—locates early modernity under an oceanic cloud. Martinican poet and theorist Édouard Glissant suggests that the slave ship and the Caribbean waters into which African bodies were thrown capture the hard birth of something new in the world:

> This boat is your womb, a matrix, and yet it expels you. This boat: pregnant with as many dead as living under sentence of death. (1997: 6)

The multiplicity that the poet-theorist names *Relation* launches itself out from the womb of the Middle Passage. As the historian Marcus Rediker has shown in his award-winning *The Slave Ship: A Human History* (2007), the ocean-going ships that transported human cargo from African into the New World created global modernity. The living and dead with whom the ships were "pregnant," in Glissant's term, formed the crucible of the global economy and ecology that would define the modern era. Rediker cites W.E.B. DuBois's well-known observation that the slave trade was the "most magnificent drama in the last thousand years of human history" (348). Rediker's expertise as maritime historian shows in detail how that tragic drama relied on the practice of transoceanic navigation. The history of the Middle Passage, Rediker concludes, contains at its heart the inchoate "terror" (354) experienced below decks of the slave ship. Around that ship, managing its buoyancy and its direction, a maritime culture steered the world into a new phase of globalization.

Any consideration of wet globalization guides our attention inevitably toward the slave trade, as if drawn gravitationally by the forces of cruelty and world-changing evil. The devastation and upheaval wrought by nonhuman agents during the era of wet globalization, in particular the Afro-Eurasian diseases that devastated Native American humans whose bodies lacked antibodies to counter them, may have killed a larger number than did the slave trade—but the moral blindness of the slaver exposes the fundamental inhumanity to fellow humans that was the harbinger of first globalization. As Lewis and Maslin observe, the choice of any a hinge-point in the long arc of ecological history leading to the Anthropocene amounts to a narrative choice. Their choice of 1610 and the wet ecological globalization that brought forth the violent birth of the New Pangea emphasizes human cruelty as well as unintended ecological consequences as drivers of climate change. On a fundamental physical level, the ultimate cause of this global catastrophe was the salt-water substrate on which this cruelty floated, across which those viruses and bacteria traveled to the New World, by means of which the separated ecosystems remerged into a single global system.

The devastating consequences of wet globalization for the New World included the political collapse of major Native American polities in Mexico, Peru, and elsewhere. The cultures that later arose in the Americas, first as European colonies and later as independent nations, developed as ocean-centric states. Maritime passages to and from Europe and Asia dominated the trade in goods such as sugar, rum, tobacco, and indigo. The human consequences of living inside this global system include a particular obsession with human liberty. As the historian Edmund Morgan has observed, "the growth of freedom experienced in the American Revolution depended more than we would like to admit on the enslavement of more than 20 percent of us at that time" (1975: x). Morgan emphasizes not just the material contributions of slave labor—the slaves that built the White House—but also the ideological gymnastics required to justify a slave-holding nation dedicated to human liberty.

The omnipresence of maritime slavery in the early modern New World also generated a particular freedom-story known as *marronage*. The fantasy of escaping from slavery to build a free society became historical fact in innumerable locations across the New World. These maroon communities included such disparate groups as the *cimarones* in Panama with whom Sir Francis Drake made an anti-Spanish alliance in 1580s, to assorted larger groups that mixed with Native Americans in the Caribbean, Suriname, French Guinea, and other locations. As detailed by anthropologists Richard and Sally Price, the Saramanka maroon communities of Suriname maintain today a complex African-and-American hybrid social and linguistic culture.[6] Maroon peoples in the Americans are not as evident on the global stage as the descendants of European settlers, but the fantasy of marronage—of taking flight into liberty—represents an essential dream of the New World.

To maroon one's way from slavery to freedom represents an individual effort to cast oneself into the sea of history but also swim by one's own power. As the philosopher Neil Roberts has recently written in his book *Freedom as Marronage*, this action "is a multidimensional, constant act of flight" (2015: 9). In Roberts's view, flight-into-marronage captures "modernity's underside" (23, citing Enrique Dussel). Building on Glissant's writings on freedom and marronage in the Caribbean, Roberts develops a "marronage philosophy [that] runs counter to the idea of fixed, determinate endings" (174). For Roberts, the unfixedness of marronage rejects Kantian philosophical ideas of freedom and autonomy—but in a saltier key, unfixedness suggests a maritime connection. Acts of flight, escape, and radical difference speak to Roberts's critique of Enlightenment political philosophy, but they also speak to the destabilizing process of exchanging solid ground for liquid sea. Glissant describes the birth of global modernity through the contrast between the Mediterranean, "an inner sea surrounded by lands," and the fracturing Caribbean, "a sea that explodes the scattered lands into an arc" (33). In this "sea that diffracts" (33), human culture assumes maritime multiplicity.

Wet globalization links the flight into radical freedom described by Glissant and Roberts with the resuturing of the global ecology into a "New Pangea" described by Lewis and Maslin. This premodern Anthropocene—the world humans have built, intentionally and not, from the late fifteenth century forward—relies on and is unimaginable without the structural movement and violence of the sea.

RETHINKING OUR HUMAN PLANET: YUSSOF'S *A BILLION BLACK ANTHROPOCENES OR NONE*

Lewis and Maslin present a persuasive scientific description of the changing nature of the earth system, but their analysis cries out for what critical geologist Kathryn Yussof calls "a redress to the White Geology of the Anthropocene" (2018: xi). The default tendency to assume a collective Anthropos who normatively appears white, male, and in possession of political power has long been an object of critique in Anthropocene studies. Alternative names for the geologic have now appeared, from Capitalocene to Trumpocene. (I work through nearly two dozen distinct 'cenes in my recent minigraph, *Break Up the Anthropocene*, 2019.) Yussof's analysis stands out both because she is herself a geologist and because she juxtaposes her own professional discourse with a historicist analysis of blackness, drawn from Critical Race Theory, Éduoard Glissant, and especially from black feminist poets and theorists including Audre Lorde, Dionne Brand, Sylvia Wynter, Saidya Hartman, and others. While for Lewis and Maslin, the "human" in *The Human Planet* is a category that requires no explanation, Yussof turns to race and the development of racialized thinking in early modernity as an example of "the problem of humanism and *its exclusions*" (2018: 14, emphasis in original). To reread the Anthropocene from inside the hold of the slave ship makes the scientific view from above seem overly simplistic.

In addressing Lewis and Maslen's proposed Orbis Spike of 1610 among other Golden Spike possibilities, Yussof reads all the magic dates as "dubious origins" (23). She cites the work of Fred Moten and S. Harvey in conceptualizing an "undercommons" comprised of black and brown bodies that suffer the "environmental effects of colonization and industrialization" (28). Remembering the undersong of human suffering enables Yussof to recast the discourse of geo-thinking. She notes that Lewis and Maslen do refer to the slave trade, and to colonial violence, but these facts, which to her are central to the Anthropocene's formation, are "quickly acknowledged and then passed over" (29). She instead requires a thorough recasting of geology itself: "Geology as a mode of embodied thinking remains restricted, unable to acknowledge the excess of this praxis in either world or subject-making dimensions" (29). In place of the relatively bloodless truisms of earth systems science as currently practiced, Yussof models an "insurgent geology" (87) that attends to human truths and histories of injustice.

The inspiration for Yussof's insurgency comes from black feminist scholarship and in particular Hartman's dream of a "black geophysics crafted in the indices of fungibility and fugitivity, an aesthetics made in the provisional ground of slavery and its continuing afterlives" (87). Part of the force of Yussof's argument surges from the radical juxtaposition of humanist critique and geological analysis. She explores biography, art, poetry, and other genres that take stock of the formation of black subjectivity during and after the early modern period. Her aim to "decolonize the Anthropocene" takes shape in what she terms "geo-Poethics" (104). Taking the poetry-ethics coinage from the work of Denise Silva, Yussof affixes the tag "geo-" to connect the science of geology to the humanist radical practice of black feminism. She recognizes that the discourse she calls "White Geology" is not easily displaced or modified. But she insists that "rather than seeing Blackness as [only] biopolitical, we might see it as a geopolitical act in the division of flesh and earth through the grammar of the inhuman" (107). With this geological understanding of blackness in mind, she seeks in her short book "a grammar of geology for the storm next time" (107). By refusing "the white overburden of geology that has secreted its excess into every pore of the earth" (108), Yussof suggests the alternative possibility of "embrac[ing] [our] intimacies with the inhuman" (107). Her "insurgent geology for the end of the world" would open up "the possibility of other worlds, not marked by anti-Blackness, where the inhuman is a relation, no long an appendage of fungibility" (107–8). Her effort to connect lived human suffering with the narratives of deep geological time recasts the 1610 Anthropocene as marking the cultural instantiation of blackness as well as bending the global carbon curve. By placing Yussof's radical critique alongside Lewis and Maslen's technocratic discourse, wet globalization acquires a human as well as planetary face.

THEORIES OF GLOBALIZATION: PETER SLOTERDIJK'S "SPHEROLOGY"

The tension between Lewis and Maslen's global view and Yussof's social justice critique becomes even clearer when considered alongside a different theoretical and abstract exploration of early modern oceanic globalization. The controversial German theorist Peter Sloterdijk makes a series of typically hyperbolic statements about the symbolic force he believes that the globe or sphere has during the totality of Western intellectual history. Sloterdijk's pivotal volume *Globes*, volume II of his *Spheres* trilogy, opens with this expansive claim:

> If one had to pinpoint the dominant motif in the metaphysical era of European thought in a single word, it could only be "globalization." The affair between occidental reason and the world-whole unfolded and exhausted itself in the sign of the geometrically perfect round form, which we still label with the Greek "sphere" and even more widely the Roman "globe." […] Globalization or sphereopoeiesis on the grandest scale is the

fundamental event of European thought, which for two and a half thousand years has not ceased to provoke radical changes in human thinking and living conditions. ([1999] 2014: 45–6)

The strain between globalization as a mathematical and philosophical concept, which Sloterdijk notes "preceded its terrestrial variety by over two thousand years" (31), and globalization as historical experience, reached a climax during the years after European sailors began encircling the earth's curved surface in the late fifteenth and sixteenth centuries. "The pure sphere in thinking-as-circumspection-in-the-unanimous," Sloterdijk continues, "becomes a critique of empirical, imperfect, un-round reality" (49). The circumnavigational voyages that followed in Magellan's wake put spherical idealism in messy, wet, and dangerous contact with lived experience.

In an extension of this thesis, *In the World Interior of Capitalism*, Sloterdijk further argues that the "waterworld" discovered by sixteenth-century geographers provides an often unacknowledged basis for modern thought (2013: 40). In the shift from "the metaphysicists" of the geometric sphere to the "geographers and seafarers" of the global ocean (21), Sloterdijk locates the strongly anti-idealist and practical cast of early modern thinking about maritime globalization. The key figure in this analysis is Antonio Pigafetta, keeper of the logbook for Magellan and Elcano's first circumnavigation. Pigafetta recognized the extent of the Pacific in a seemingly innocent phrase in his journal:

For three months and twenty days … we did not suffer any storm. (41)

The vastness of that time and space, roughly 110 days, in Sloterdijk's view, marks this period's essential change in world history. The vastness of the Pacific made the size of the spherical global physical to early modern sailors. In this moment, Europeans encountered a literal articulation of the globe they had been theorizing since antiquity. In this "oceanographic reversal," the waters of the Pacific become more important to Sloterdijk's conception of early modernity than the silver mines of Bolivia, spice islands of Indonesia, or thriving marketplaces of China. Recognizing by painful and scurvy-infected experience the vast dimensions of the World Ocean, early modern sailors were the essential actors of wet globalization.[7] The turn to oceanic rather than terrestrial substrates would recreate the ways people thought about early modern cultural exchange, conflict, and colonialism. The conditions of early modern maritime life forced a harsh turn away from philosophical abstraction and toward the practicalities of survival, as Margaret Cohen's (2012: 15–58) deft analysis of seventeenth-century maritime guidebooks has shown. The habits of thinking and action she calls (following Joseph Conrad) "craft," and that I call (following Homer) "metis" represent an embodied response to maritime disorientation.[8] Sloterdijk calls this laboring-and-thinking "maritime reason" (2013: 88); I have elsewhere described human-sized aspects of the technical interface between mortal bodies and the world ocean through the metaphor "swimmer poetics" (2012: 586–92). This particular cast of thought, while in no sense new to early modernity, shows itself through the entanglement of maritime experience and intellectual labor. The wet globalization that defined the European experience of the global Renaissance serves to define the poles of global maritime culture from roughly 1550 to 1750. On the one hand, this period saw Europe's first globalizing voyages and colonies, with all the attendant economic dislocation, cultural disruption, and ecological catastrophes that followed that process. On the other hand, the process was incessantly wet, dependent upon the hand-labor of sailors as well as head-work of poets, geometers, and other educated figures. Bringing the wet back into our sense of the global and globalizing helps reconnect visionary sphereology to lived physical experience.

KEYWORDS

The following six keywords frame this volume's global narrative about the oceanic movements of humans and the creatures and cultures that accompanied them on a planetary scale. Even combining these terms with the book's eight substantial chapters will not manage to cover all elements of global maritime experience in the early modern period. Most notable among the things we lack space and expertise to explore here but which form important parts of the larger story are greater attention to the experiences and knowledges of Indigenous Americans and Pacific Islanders. Critical discourses that emerge from attention to women, queer desire, and gender nonconforming minorities also merit attention during this era of global maritime expansion, only some of which these areas receive here. Scholarship in these areas is rich and thriving; this volume is able to present just a selection.

Circumnavigation

The circumnavigations of this period started and ended in western Europe. Magellan's fleet left Seville with five ships in 1519, and returned to Spain in 1522 under the command of Juan Sebastian Elcano after Magellan's death. Drake's flagship *The Golden Hind* left Plymouth in 1577 and returned in 1580. In 1586, Cavendish's ship *Desire* left with two other vessels to sail around the globe. His flagship returned in 1588, nine months faster than his compatriot Drake. In arguing that these familiar stories are central to the early modern sea, I emphasize the many ships that foundered, not the few that made it home. I am less interested in the commanders than the ships and the crews, in particular the changing composition of the sailors over the course of these multiyear voyages. Five ships set sail under the command of Ferdinand Magellan from Seville in 1519, but only one, the *Victoria,* returned to Spain in

FIGURE 0.1 Sir Francis Drake, with a map of his circumnavigation, from *Franciscus Dracus nobiliss eques Angliae aetatis suae* XXXXVI (Cologne, 1596). © Courtesy of the John Carter Brown Library at Brown University.

1522, under the command of Elcano. Sir Francis Drake left Plymouth in 1577 with a fleet of five ships, and that number increased by one after he captured a Portuguese merchant ship near the Cape Verde Islands (Figure 0.1). The ship's captain, Nuno da Silva, joined Drake's company and presumably aided the fleet through his experience of South American navigation. By the time they returned to Plymouth in 1580, Drake's command was down to one ship, the *Golden Hind*, and only fifty-nine men. Thomas Cavendish launched the next English circumnavigation attempt with only three ships from Plymouth in 1586, but like Drake and Elcano his fleet was reduced to one when he returned to English in 1588, shaving nine months off Drake's time.

Slavery

The transatlantic slave trade began in the early sixteenth century with the first voyages from Africa to Brazil by Portuguese slavers. Other European nations

FIGURE 0.2 Treatment of slaves on Martinique, from Francois Froger, *Relation d'un voyage …* (London: M. Gillyflower, 1698). Plate following p. 120. Courtesy of the John Carter Brown Library at Brown University.

quickly followed, with French, Spanish, Dutch, and English vessels joining in the rapidly growing trade (Figure 0.2). Recent scholarship, including the pioneering work of John Thornton, has explored the ways that European slave traders engaged with and distorted the existing system of slavery in early modern West Africa.[9] Literary scholarship, including influential scholarship by Kim Hall (1996b) and Ayanna Thompson (2011) as well as newer works by Urvashi Chakrabarty (2016) and Amberdeen Dadabhoy (2020), has begun to consider the centrality of the slave system to English, European, and global contexts. Vincent Caretta's work on Olaudah Equiano (2005), among other Atlantic abolitionists in the eighteenth century, provides a useful model for reconsidering the transatlantic maritime networks that structure and make possible the growth of both slavery and cultural responses to it. Further work remains to be done, in particular on the late sixteenth- and seventeenth-century growth of the slave trade.

Hurricanes

Hurricanes are New World storms, which had perhaps never been encountered by European mariners before the late fifteenth century.[10] The Carib word

FIGURE 0.3 Hurricane strikes land, from *Naaukeurige versameling der gedenkwaardigste …* (Leiden: Door Pieter Vander Aa, 1707). Fold-out plate following p. 12, vol. 3. © Courtesy of the John Carter Brown Library at Brown University.

hurucan entered European languages early in the sixteenth century, with reports of voyages to the Caribbean (Figure 0.3). These storms very rarely reach even the Irish and British island outposts off the European continent. Created inside the North Atlantic Gyre, these storms usually form off the west coast of Africa. They gain force as they circulate westward into the warm waters of the Caribbean before either turning north toward the Gulf of Mexico or northeast up the North American coastline. Eventually the storms turn out to sea, where they usually weaken before they can circulate all the way back east to the Azores, the British isles, or the European continent. As Peter Hulme ([1985] 1986: 93) has observed, these storms represented a radically new weather pattern for European explorers in the early modern period. The integration of the native Caribbean word "hurricane" into Spanish, French, and English epitomizes the arrival of New Word meanings into Old World systems.

American plants

New World plants, from potatoes to tomatoes, transformed the Old World's agricultural system. As Edward Maclean Test recently observes in *Sacred Seeds: New World Plants and Early Modern English Literature* (2019), the cultural influence of New World plants on Europe was massive. Test reads the famous case of tobacco alongside less familiar New World products including amaranth, guaiac, and the cochineal insects that accompanied the Mexican nopal (prickly pear) cacti, which were used to make red dye. Test claims that when humans colonized the New World, "plants colonized the Old World" (188). The case of tobacco (Figure 0.4), which by the 1530s become a major trade commodity and a major driver of the emerging African slave trade, remains the most notorious, but other plants, including the humble potato, also had global impacts during this period.

Maps

Among the many important maritime maps of the early modern period, I focus on the *Wright-Molyneux Map*, which is printed on the cover of this volume. This map appeared in print for the first time in the third volume of Richard Hakluyt's massive compendium of maritime histories, the *Principal Navigations* of 1599–1600. This book's cover shows a composite of the two separate "eastern" and "western" pages that make up Wright's map. The map is named "Wright-Molyneux," because Wright took his images of landforms and coastlines from the globes of English cartographer Emery Molynuex. The essential features of Wright's map, however, are not Molyneux's curved lines that represent coastlines but the many straight lines that Wright drew across the surface of the ocean. Wright's map was made in response to Gerard Mercator's 1569 visual projection of a global map onto a flat plane surface.

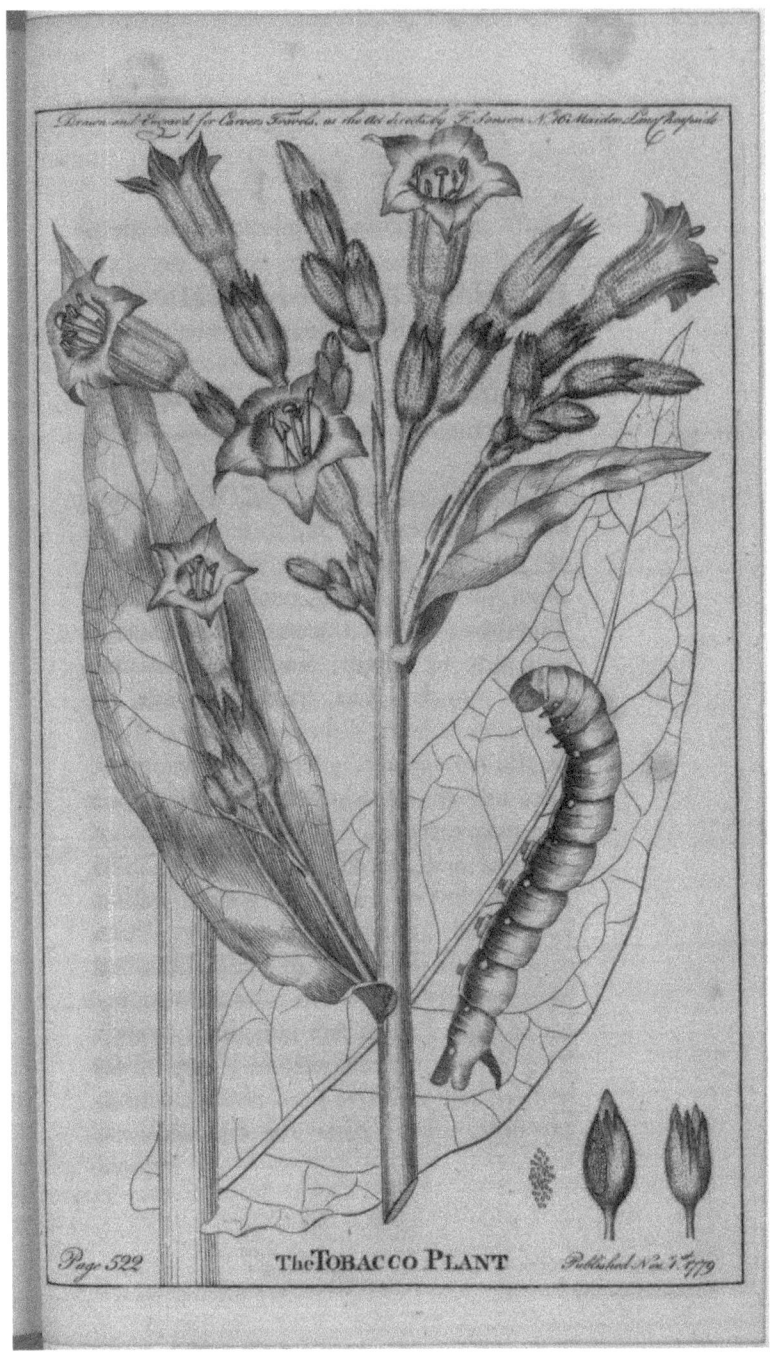

FIGURE 0.4 "The Tobacco Plant," from Jonathan Carver, *Travels through the Interior Parts of North-America* (London: William Richardson, 1779). Plate following p. 522. © Courtesy of the John Carter Brown Library at Brown University.

FIGURE 0.5 The maritime globe, from Pedro Cubero Sebastian, *Peregrinacio del Mundo* ... (Naples: Carolos Porsile, 1682). Engraved title page. © Courtesy of the John Carter Brown Library at Brown University.

Wright provided a mathematical extension of Mercator's images, which were being promoted for their special value to navigation. The essential features of the map for navigators—the mathematical proofs—were also previewed in Wright's small pamphlet of 1599, *Certaine Errors in Navigation*. The reason Wright's map is crucial for the history of navigation is that it is the first two-dimensional European map to represent the three-dimensional globe with mathematical accuracy. With the precise numerical formulae and tables included in *Certaine Errors,* Wright supplements Mercator's and Molyneux's images. By combining the tables and the images, Wright produced the first flat plane map that, if used to travel across the Atlantic, gets you where you want to go. As Wright notes early in *Certaine Errors* (1599), attempts to plot a course by a plane map of the globe without Wright-Mercator corrections could lead to navigation being off by 150–200 leagues on a voyage from the West Indies to the Azores; that amounts to about 500 miles, far enough to miss the islands entirely. Wright himself was more mathematician than voyager, though he did make at least one trip by sea, to the Azores in 1589 (Apt 2004). His authorship of the accurate charts of the Azores that appear on the final pages of *Certaine Errors*, which include navigationally useful rhumb lines, seems to be his primary contribution to Drake's voyage. He notes in his "Preface to the Reader" that on returning to Ushent, an island off the coast of Normandy, from the Azores "we were comme within sight of that Island, when by account of the ordinary chart we should haue beene 50 leagues short of it" (1599: sig. ¶¶1 [unpaginated]). Noting that wise sailing masters did not trust charts, Wright sought to build a better map through mathematics. (For a less mathematical image of the globe, see Figure 0.5.)

Wright's short book of 1599 presents his mathematical proof and the techniques for creating the 1600 map. Wright's innovation was producing mathematical formulae to calculate rhumb lines, the straight radial lines that appear all over the ocean in Wright's charts. These lines preserve a constant angle with respect to all the north–south meridians of longitude that they cross. To preserve this angle and represent directions accurately on the curved surface of the earth, the map distorts the size of geographic land masses in high northern or southern latitudes. Mercator's map began this process visually, but Wright's mathematical formulae provided a way to calculate numerically the rhumb lines that the printed map shows on the page. Lloyd Brown's summary in *The Story of Maps* does not seem hyperbolic: "Edward Wright's *Certaine Errors* may properly be considered the first practically correct treatise on navigation and in most respects it marked the turning point in scientific chart construction" (1949: 138). The map's deliberate inaccuracies of geographic size, which make a small island such as Iceland appear nearly as large as Spain, and Greenland almost as large as Africa, make it possible to portray direction across global spaces with accuracy. To sail on a spherical globe requires superimposing complex mathematical systems upon the map.

Poetic Manuscripts

FIGURE 0.6 Luís vaz de Camões, *The Lusiad, or, Portugals Historicall Poem* (1655). Frontispiece. © Courtesy of the John Carter Brown Library at Brown University.

The preeminent maritime narrative poem of early modern Europe was the epic *Os Lusiados*, written in Portuguese by Luís vaz de Camões (Figure 0.6). The manuscript of Camões's ten-canto poem has its own story of oceanic immersion, in which it was carried to shore from a wrecked ship off the Mekong Delta in modern Vietnam by its shipwrecked author in 1559. The only contemporary evidence we have for this now-legendary feat are a few stray references in Camões's own poem, but if we believe the poetry, the legend, and some scraps of documentary evidence, Camões may well have been shipwrecked off the Mekong in 1559. According to his elliptical account in *The Lusiads* (1997: 10:128), later published in Lisbon in 1572, the poet was recalled from the Far East to Goa following an "unjust mandate," for which he would be jailed in Goa in 1561. Despite losing all his possessions in the wreck, he preserved the draft of the poem that would become the epic of the modern Portuguese nation:

> The wet and ship-wrackt SONG receive shall *Hee*
> Which in a lamentable plight shall swim
> From Sholes and Quicksands of tempestuous *Sea*,
> (The dire effect of *Exile*) when on *Him*
> Is executed the unjust Decree:
> Whose repercussuive Lyre shall have the Fate
> To be *renowned* more then *Fortunate*.
> (Camões 1655: 10.128.2–8; p. 218)

The poet's melodramatic self-presentation, which shows him persecuted by unjust magistrates while also being buffeted at sea, contrasts with the "sweet dexterity" of his verse. *The Lusiads* becomes not only the epic of the Portuguese maritime nation, which put Vasca da Gama's first voyage to India in 1497 to 1499 in the central place of the epic hero, but also the transfigured product of a shipwrecked sailor's wet pen.

The possibly fictional account of the shipwrecked genesis of Camões's poem highlights the intimacy of this canonical literary figure with maritime travel and disaster. Camões was not a mariner, but his life was defined through transoceanic travel. Earlier in the epic, he describes himself, again in perfectly conventional terms, as storm tossed:

> Sometimes committed to *Sea*'s rolling Tow'rs,
> Sometimes to bloody dangers *Marteale*! [...]
> Now scapt, with my life onely, which hung by
> A single Thrid (even *that* a load too great):
> That 'tis no less a wonder, I am here,
> Then JUDA'S *King*'s new lease of fifteen yeere.
> (Camões 1655: 7.79.5–6; 7.80.5–8; p. 152)

The echoes of Odysseus's travails are exact, but they are also historicized, as the Renaissance epic transforms the solitary classical sailor into an emblem of an early modern maritime nation. Poems and salt water combine in Camões's imagination to define the poles of his wayward life: he endures oceanic dislocation to deliver a poem that makes the ocean into a force that writes for Portugal a heroic destiny.

The shipwreck of Camões's vessel off the Mekong Delta in 1559 provides a taste of the unreliable nature of long-haul maritime voyages during this period. As Josiah Blackmore has argued (2002: 44), shipwreck produced in early modern Portuguese culture a "counter-historiography" of maritime empire, celebrating its achievements while also emphasizing its fragility. The image of Camões in the surf with his manuscript combines both triumph and risk.

CONCLUSION: ALIEN OCEAN AND THE ECOPOETICS OF SHIPWRECK

These keywords and analyses of the early modern global system emphasize how oceanic travel generated historically new experiences and ideas during the early modern age. My hope in this introduction has been to emphasize the immense human shock of encountering the massive alien space of the world ocean. In particular the Pacific, so much larger even than the Atlantic and Indian Oceans, strained human limits. I will close by recalling the particular combination of intimacy and pain that marks the human encounter with the oceans. We love those waters, and they drown us. I hope that this volume can elucidate the relationship between those things.

CHAPTER ONE

Knowledges

Constructing the Early Modern Ocean, 1450–1700

CHRISTOPHER L. PASTORE

Both a seasoned sailor and committed scholar, Christopher Columbus compiled knowledge about the ocean by corroborating hard-won experience with stories and printed accounts of exploration and world geography. According to Columbus's son Ferdinand, who sailed with and later wrote a biography of his father, Columbus, who had a hunch that one could sail west from Europe to Asia, had interviewed numerous sailors who had ventured great distances onto the "western seas." One Portuguese pilot told Columbus that at sea he had found a piece of carved wood drifting before a persistent western wind. Columbus's brother-in-law, Pedro Correa, had discovered several large "canes" that had been driven by the wind toward European shores "from some neighbouring islands or perhaps from India" (Columbus 1959: 48). Pine trunks, the people of the Azores attested, were sometimes washed upon their shores "after the wind had blown for a long time from the west." In one instance, they had also discovered several "covered boats or canoes" as well as the bodies of two men "with broad faces and different in appearance from the Christians" (49). Ocean currents, Columbus believed, hinted that something existed somewhere beyond the horizon.

These accounts seemed to confirm those speculations penned by classical and medieval scholars that Columbus had carefully collected. Pliny, for instance, had asserted that wood washed from distant shores formed large island-like rafts at sea. Seneca had claimed that in India a type of floating stone sometimes formed drifting islands. Columbus also looked to St. Brendan, who had noted that there were islands beyond Cape Verde and the Azores. He referenced charts that showed the island of "Antilla," which, the Portuguese surmised, could have been the fabled "island of the Seven Cities" (Casas 1957: 76–8). By corroborating his notes with published works, Columbus became a seminal figure in the production of oceanic knowledge during the age of exploration. Naturally, he was selective about his sources, placing far greater emphasis on those that supported his goal of finding a westward route to Asia. His son and biographer then curated Columbus's notes in an effort to secure a Crown pension for his family (Columbus 1959: 20–1). But a closer look at Columbus's methods and observations nevertheless reveals the possibilities and limits of oceanic knowledge production and circulation during the early modern period. Realities mingled with mythologies. Textual sources conversed with local lore and observation. And all of it was poured through the filters of memory and time.

Between roughly 1450 and 1650, European knowledge of oceanic navigation, geography, and natural history expanded dramatically. After 1439, Gutenberg's printing press promoted the efforts of compilers, including Columbus and his contemporaries, and led to the publication of maps, chronicles of exploration, treatises on marine technology and practice, and colonial promotional materials on an unprecedented scale. As Michel Foucault posited, a careful reading of Renaissance literature revealed what he believed was an abrupt epistemological shift by which mythologies gave way to more empirical ways of knowing (Foucault 1973). Dorinda Outram has criticized Foucault's assumption that these structural changes were universal, pointing out that natural history production was very different in the Anglo-Irish and Anglo-American contexts, whereby natural historians "aimed to give a unified account of human and natural activity within a particular region" (Outram 1997: 467). Knowledge production, in other words, varied widely from place to place. But it also drew from the past at the same time it marked a break from it. As Brian Ogilvie has shown, Renaissance naturalists often corroborated their observations with accounts from classical antiquity, thereby melding humanism, empiricism, and theology. In turn, they created new cultures and economies of natural philosophy and ultimately a new "science of describing" (Ogilvie 2006: 10–17). These new ways of interpreting the natural world extended to the ocean. As this chapter will argue, the sheer volume of maritime books that were produced during the Renaissance ushered in a new age of ocean literacy, one in which knowledge of the sea, once reserved to those who worked it, became integral to Europe's commercial and religious expansion. In other words, "craft," or what both novelist Joseph Conrad and literary scholar Margaret Cohen have identified as a seaman's special skills and capacity for cool reason, was, in time, committed to print (Cohen 2010: 15–58). When oceanic sensory experience—how it looked, smelled, felt, tasted, and sounded in all conditions—was placed on the page, mythologies conversed with new realities, which circulated among a growing reading audience, reshaping wider conceptions of the sea. So sought after was this knowledge that as European nations vied for access to it, they remade the legal regimes that had long governed them and the ocean itself. As this chapter will show, the early modern period witnessed a profound expansion of oceanic knowledge that redefined the precincts of geography, natural history, and the law. In sum, the spread of ocean literacy helped foster a new awareness of the global.

OCEAN GEOGRAPHIES

The European Renaissance inherited an understanding of global geography that melded classical and Christian conceptions of space. For the Greeks, the earth consisted of an island *Orbis Terrarum,* a circular landmass bounded by the river *Oceanus,* which gave rise to the universe. Named after the Titan Oceanus, the river extended indefinitely, "forming a region beyond the boundaries of earth" (Romm 1992: 23, 16). Chaotic, lawless, and impassible, the ocean lay outside the limits of civilization. When Alexander the Great hoped to sail overseas in search of new lands, his advisor, Artemon, warned that the ocean marked "the boundary of nature" and the "origin of the gods." So sacred was the sea that he warned Alexander that "its water is too holy to be crossed by ships" (25–6). While some ancients argued that the Nile flowed from Oceanus into the Mediterranean Sea, or *Thalassa,* Herodotus rejected that claim outright. "They *say* that the Ocean runs around the whole earth," he wrote, "but they don't *show* any evidence for it" (34). Others, including, most notably, Strabo, depicted the earth island as indented by small seas or gulfs. Ptolemy went so far as to call the ocean river concept "fallacious." The acknowledgement that the seas surrounded, penetrated, and partitioned the land existed alongside the concept of a world-circling ocean through the medieval period (Lewis 1999: 191).

Medieval thinkers adapted these ideas to Judeo-Christian cosmologies. According to the book of Genesis, on the second day God separated the waters of the sea from the waters of the sky. He then gathered the waters to "let the dry land appear" (Gen. 1:9 [NRSV]). Terrestrial spaces were human and celestial and oceanic spaces divine. So steeped in religious thought were medieval conceptions of space that, as John Kirtland Wright has argued, medieval geography could be more accurately described as "geosophy." (1947: 11–12). Maps reflected this religious outlook. For instance, many *mappae mundi*—whether those that adhered to the geometric T and O formats or others that attempted to depict the undulating contours of the world's known continents and their coasts—frequently placed Jerusalem at the center, a spiritual hub from which the spokes of Europe, Asia, and Africa radiated (Gillis 2004: 5–18). The oceans surrounded, penetrated, and ultimately partitioned the earth island in ways that conveyed religious conviction and consolidated political power (Harley 2002: 56). Even if many of these medieval maps were more reflections of Christian allegory than depictions of geographic space, they nevertheless played important roles in the creation of new ocean imaginaries. The Latin translation and then circulation of Ptolemy's *Geography* around 1406 marked one of the most important breakthroughs in European geographic knowledge. Ptolemy divided the globe into a 360-degree sphere onto which lines of latitude and longitude provided a coordinate system for mapping the earth. Ptolemy's ideas introduced more quantitative conceptions of global space, providing the means to produce maps that far surpassed medieval *mappae mundi* and point-to-point portolan charts (Parry 1963: 11–13). Nevertheless, the creation of geographic knowledge during the early modern period relied heavily on hard-won experience. Breakthroughs in geographic theory were important, but the shape of the sea was drawn from the decks of ships, with new bits and pieces of information added to maps as new lands were discovered.

Islands served as essential elements in the growing body of oceanic knowledge. As John Gillis has attested, islands "provide metaphors that allow us to give shape to a world that would otherwise be formless and meaningless" (2004: 1). As imaginary spaces, islands provided psychological permanence amidst chaos and confusion. Bathed by a divine sea, they opened access to the spiritual world (Hirsch 1995: 4). For pre-Christian Europeans islands served as important sites of divine connection. Medieval Christians later adopted these sacred landscapes, reshaping them to meet their material and spiritual needs. For example, sometime between the sixth and eighth centuries CE, a monastic community of monks came to inhabit the rocky shores of Skellig Michael off the west coast of Ireland. High above the Atlantic's pounding surf, they built their beehive stone huts in which they prayed in partial isolation. The waters west of Ireland, which lay at the margins of Europe, were rumored to hold many more islands as well. By the tenth century CE mapmakers began to populate those seas with imaginary lands. St. Brendan's Islands, the Fortunate Islands, Hy Brasil, and Ultimate Thule, among others, appeared on medieval maps, but as geographic knowledge of the seas increased, those islands migrated to the new margins of an expanding Atlantic, and in some cases Pacific, world. The islands of St. Brendan, for instance, moved from somewhere west of Ireland toward the Mediterranean (see Figure 1.1). Once plantations had been established at Madeira and the Canary Islands, St. Brendan's island continued to migrate westward so that by the sixteenth century it appeared somewhere off the coast of Newfoundland (Gillis 2004: 51–4). Similarly, for the ancient Romans Ultimate Thule was believed to be somewhere north of Britain, perhaps among the Faeroe or Shetland Islands.

FIGURE 1.1 Imaginary islands and apocryphal creatures lurked just beyond the limits of oceanic knowledge. Here, somewhere west of the Mediterranean Sea, St. Brendan lands on the back of a sea monster between the imaginary St. Brendan's and Fortunate Islands. St. Brendan and the Whale Island, from Honorius Philoponus, *Nova Typis Transacta Navigatio* (Linz: Wolfgang Kilian, 1621), plate following p. 10. © Courtesy of the John Carter Brown Library at Brown University.

Some early medieval geographers imagined another Thule in Asia and others somewhere in the northeast Atlantic near Norway. But as Europeans spread across the Atlantic, Ultimate Thule migrated before them, first to Iceland, then to Greenland, then on to Vinland, always looming just beyond the limits of geographic knowledge (Cassidy 1963).

As material places, islands also served as steppingstones across which oceanic knowledge was conveyed. Beginning in the Levant, the islands of the Mediterranean served as important sites of sugar production. As Europeans extended their reach into the Atlantic and south along the coast of Africa, islands served as important commercial and imperial outposts. As the demand for sugar in Europe increased, planters pushed farther west in search of new land for cultivation. They settled the Azores, Madeira, Canary, and Cape Verde Islands and then sailed farther south into the Gulf of Guinea where they established plantations close to sources of slave labor on Fernando Po, Principe, Annobon, and Sao Tome. The Spanish created a sugar hub of the Canary Islands and the Portuguese of Madeira. By the end of the fifteenth century, Columbus had ventured west from the Canaries to the Caribbean, and Pedro Cabral had landed in Brazil. As Philip Curtin (1998) has shown, the European expansion into America was not simply the start of something new.

Rather, it was the end of a very old process of plantation expansion among the islands of the Atlantic world.

As the plantation complex stretched across the equatorial Atlantic, fishermen sailed west across the boreal Atlantic. Much of the demand for fish was driven by religious food rules, which mandated abstinence from meat on specified holy days. The number of days per year that banned meat increased over time, so that by the fourteenth century, Catholics were abstaining from meat for nearly half of the calendar year. Although Europeans consumed mostly freshwater fish until about 1000 CE, erosion caused by plow agriculture and the proliferation of dams along the rivers of continental Europe destroyed fish habitat, leading to declining catches and encouraging fishermen to turn to the sea (Fagan 2006: 147, 94, 99). Fishermen targeted salt-water species with increasing effort to meet the growing demand. Archeological remains suggest that by the fourteenth and fifteenth centuries, between 60 and 80 percent of all fish eaten were salt-water species (Roberts 2007: 26). Fishermen pushed farther over the horizon in search of larger fish and more abundant stocks, hauling their catches back to European markets. As Richard Hoffman (2001) has shown, the long-distance trade in preserved fish, alongside those in cattle and grain during the late medieval period, ushered in patterns of food consumption by which people began eating outside of their ecosystems. In consequence, consumers often overlooked or ignored "the social and environmental costs" of acquiring food from distant frontiers. "Ecological relationships," Hoffman concluded, "faded from the view of especially urban consumers, replaced in their consciousness by economic links" (155). With new forms of oceanic knowledge came new patterns of environmental indifference.

If the ocean was peripheral to plantation agriculture—merely a space for transporting labor, sugar, and equipment—the sea was the primary location of fish production, and this shaped the ways it was understood. Although there is no evidence that fishermen had visited Newfoundland before John Cabot's 1497 voyage to the New World on behalf of the English, it is possible that fishermen had ventured into those waters but kept that knowledge to themselves. But after reports of Cabot's voyage spread, the waters near Newfoundland were increasingly filled with Europeans. They found fish in abundance there, but they also noticed that, except for a few endemic species including, most notably, the horseshoe crab, the boreal Atlantic in America was quite similar to that of Europe. They saw the same cod, hake, and flounder. The rocks were covered in mussels and crawling with clawed lobsters. The beaches, fringed with Spartina grass, seemed similar to those of the North Sea. Indeed, the incessant screeching of gulls was all too familiar. Although sixteenth- and seventeenth-century commentators marveled at the abundance of marine life, they nevertheless saw similar creatures. As W. Jeffrey Bolster (2008, 2012) has argued, when one imagines the boreal Atlantic as a continuous ecosystem stretching from the North Sea to North America, the waters near Newfoundland, Nova Scotia, and the Gulf of Maine seemed less a threshold into a New World and more the western edge of the Old.

The encounter with America fundamentally challenged European cosmography (O'Gorman 1961: 127–37). In keeping with Christian millenarian conceptions of world geography, America represented more the "recovery" of ancient biblical lands than the discovery of something new (Gillis 2004: 43). If a "new world" was created, it was in Europe, as the proponents of a more secular Renaissance humanism reimagined Christendom in terms of the European continent (Lewis and Wigen 1997: 25). Throughout the sixteenth century some European geographers were reluctant to acknowledge America as something distinct from existing geographic models that imagined Europe, Africa, and Asia lumped together onto one world island. But knowledge of a new continent populated by humans and reachable by ocean voyage effectively fractured the *Orbis Terrarum*. "The Greek notion of a unitary human terrain," explained Martin Lewis and Kären Wigen, "was dissembled into its constituent continents, whose relative *isolation* was now ironically converted into their defining feature" (26). By the seventeenth century, a consensus among geographers had been reached: America was its own entity, one separated by broad swaths of oceanic space. In sum, oceanic exploration and commercial expansion during the fifteenth and sixteenth centuries fundamentally challenged contemporary conceptions of geographic space. What had been a unified Earth island had been shattered into a global archipelago. And this forced geographers to rethink the oceanic spaces that flowed among this new constellation of landmasses. Indeed, for the first time the ocean was integrated into the *Orbis Terrarum* (O'Gorman 1961: 128).

No longer a barrier, the ocean was reimagined as a bridge that connected a much larger world filled with new possibilities. This transformed the way humans imagined their place in the universe. If, as Edmundo O'Gorman has argued, life on the *Orbis Terrarum* had been a "cosmic jail," the discovery of America allowed "man [...] to picture himself as a free agent in the deep and radical sense of possessing unlimited possibilities in his own being, and as living in a world made by him in his own image and to his own measure." As Renaissance mapmakers incorporated America into their new cartographic visions of the globe, the ocean no longer represented an undifferentiated void that confined human ambition but instead constituted distinct bodies of water that provided corridors of connectivity. On all accounts, this newly defined terraqueous globe, one in which a network of continents was punctuated by specific ocean basins, celebrated human potential (O'Gorman 1961: 68–9, 129, 131–2).

What had once been a timeless, undifferentiated barren became during the Renaissance imbued with a sense of place. Naming the oceans gave them new significance by connecting them with adjacent lands and the people who inhabited them. For instance, in 1570 Abraham Ortelius identified an "Ethiopian Ocean" in the South Atlantic and a "Mar del Nort" in the North Atlantic. But he also marked the existence of an "Oceanus Britannicus" and an "Oceanus Deucaledonius," or Scottish Ocean. Farther to the east he marked the "Sea of India" and in what is now the Pacific a "Mar del Sur." Other cartographers similarly identified a "South Sea" or "Pacific Sea," the northeastern most reaches of which were sometimes referred to as the "Oceanus Occidentalis," or Western Ocean. Dutch maps marked the western rim of the Pacific as the "Oceanus Cinensus," or Chinese Ocean. Even as maps began to label an "Atlantic Ocean" west of Europe in the seventeenth century, most sailors referred to that space as the "Western Ocean" as well (Lewis 1999: 198–203). Sailing thousands of kilometers, sailors systematically knitted together new oceanic networks (Parry 1974: viii). Narrative accounts and printed maps added shape to the sea. As knowledge of ocean geography expanded, the sea gained new meaning.

NAVIGATIONAL KNOWLEDGE

Breakthroughs in ocean technology made the seas more accessible. Although, during the early fifteenth century the Chinese had built a fleet of large, ocean-going vessels, which they sent across the Indian Ocean, Red Sea, and Persian Gulf, they soon determined the costs of long-distance voyaging was not worth the effort, thereby limiting China's trade to Southeast Asia (Parry 1974: 22; Fagan 2012: 162–4). But in producing some of the most technologically advanced sailing vessels in the Renaissance world, Europeans soon expanded their global footprint.

The fifteenth-century Portuguese caravel marked an important innovation in ocean travel. With a steady wind drawing on carefully trimmed sails, an attentive helmsman could steer his caravel to within 30 degrees of the wind. Framed in oak and planked in cork, caravels had a fine bow, narrow beam, and a sweeping lateen rig, making them swift and highly maneuverable (Russell 2000: 227–8). Likely drawing less than 1.8 meters of water, they were shallow-drafted vessels that after running aground could be floated off obstructions by simply shifting the weight of the cargo (Parry 1974: 29). The lateen, triangular fore-and-aft sails had likely originated somewhere in west Asian waters, possibly in the eastern Mediterranean, Persian Gulf, or western Indian Ocean, and separately in Oceania, most likely somewhere in the Indonesian archipelago (Campbell 1995). Although its ancient origins remain elusive, the lateen rig had by the eleventh century made its way across the Mediterranean to Iberia's Atlantic coast, soon becoming the standard sail plan across the region (Parry 1963: 58). Lateen-rigged caravels could also be mounted with multiple masts that sometimes carried square-rigged sails, which allowed them to run before

FIGURE 1.2 The *caravela redonda* and its hybrid lateen and square-rigged sail plan was an important technology that helped usher in the age of exploration. "Oceanica Classis," from Carlo Verardi, *In Laudem Serenissimi Ferdinandi Hispania[rum] Regis, Bethicae [et] Regni Granatae* (Basel: Johann Bergname de Olpel, 1494), verso of leaf [36]. © Courtesy of the John Carter Brown Library at Brown University.

the wind more efficiently. Although recent scholarship has questioned the importance of the lateen rig to Atlantic expansion, the sail plan was certainly adapted to many forms of commercial activity. Perhaps the lateen rig drove oceanic exploration, or perhaps it was simply one of several technological innovations at the time (Campbell 1995: 23). But it certainly played an important role in shaping what J.H. Parry called the "age of reconnaissance" (1963: 58).

Over the course of the fourteenth century, square-rigged vessels increasingly drove ocean exploration. Although square-rigged vessels had long been favored among the waters of northern Europe, they began to migrate south into the Mediterranean. Square-rigged vessels could carry more sails, which could be more easily configured to maximize sailing ability according to the wind conditions, but they were far more limited in their ability to sail upwind than caravels. Through trial and error, Mediterranean sailors had, by the fifteenth century, figured out how to combine square- and lateen-rigged sails on their boats. These hybrid sail plans, which came to be known as *caravelas redondas*, were soon adopted across Europe (see Figure 1.2). Shipbuilders began adding masts, so that some ocean-going vessels had three or four, often with at least one lateen-rigged sail, commonly placed near the stern, effectively functioning like a wind rudder to complement the steering rudder that extended below the waterline (Parry 1974: 152).

These new technologies allowed sailors to venture over longer distances. Although knowledge of Africa had trickled into Europe by the beginning of the fourteenth century, it was not until the middle of the fifteenth that European explorers began to describe the sub-Saharan coast with some precision. By the early 1440s several Portuguese captains had explored the Atlantic coast of the Sahara Desert. In 1455 and 1456, Venetian navigator Alvise da Cadamosto established for Portugal a foothold along the Senegal River, producing, likely several years later, "the first original account to have survived of a voyage into the regions opened up by European enterprise at the dawn of modern overseas expansion" (Crone 1937: xxiv; Parry 1974: 114). Diogo Cão explored the Congo River, and Bartholomeu Dias ventured around the southern tip of Africa and into the Indian Ocean. Portuguese stories, both real and apocryphal, piqued the curiosity of others, including Christopher Columbus, who compiled them in notebooks. By the second half of the fifteenth century Iberian caravels were frequenting the Azores, Madeira, Cape Verde Islands, and the Canaries and had extended their reach into the Gulf of Guinea (Curtin 1998: 18–25). They developed systems for returning to Iberian ports, sailing the *volta do mar*, which led them across the northeast trade winds and out to sea and then back to Europe before the prevailing westerlies (Edwards 1992; Russell 2000: 228). Once those patterns were in place, the possibility of venturing even farther became a reality.

As the promises of ocean exploration became clear, navigational knowledge grew increasingly valuable. Columbus's first voyage to America in 1492 sparked the search for alternative routes to Asia among Spain's European rivals. In 1497 Vasco da Gama led a fleet of Portuguese ships around Africa to India. Entering England into the scramble for overseas acquisitions, John Cabot made for Newfoundland in the same year. He relied heavily on experiential knowledge acquired from his Bristol sailors, some of whom had made voyages to the west in search of fish. Leaving Bristol aboard the *Matthew* on May 22, Cabot sailed along the west coast of Ireland to Dursey Island in County Cork, and then sailed in a southwesterly direction until he made landfall in eastern Nova Scotia just over a month later. He coasted east to northern Newfoundland and then returned, first making landfall along the Breton Coast and then sailing north to Bristol. Soon after, on August 10 or 11, Cabot made his way to London and reported the success of his voyage (Quinn 1974: 94–6). Word spread rapidly, for he told stories of his journey to the Venetian Lorenzo Pasqualigo (1497: 95–96), who sent a letter on August 23 to his brothers Alvise and Francesco. In that letter, he explained that "That Venetian of ours [Cabot]" had by sailing 700 leagues to the west discovered "the country of the Grand Khan." News of his discoveries was dispatched to the Duke of Milan in August with more details forthcoming in December ("News Sent from London to the Duke of Milan, August 24, 1497": 96–7). In January a London Merchant named John Day sent a description (Day to "the Grand Admiral [Christopher Columbus]" 1497: 98–9) of the voyage to a correspondent who was most likely Christopher Columbus. In sum, news of the discovery spread quickly, and soon after the number of voyages to Newfoundland, sponsored by England, Spain, France, and Portugal, increased.

Knowledge of new lands, people, and commercial opportunities combined with the grim recognition that many of these voyages ended in tragedy, affirmed the importance of refining navigational methodology. Most navigators used some form of dead reckoning to calculate their positions at sea. By measuring speed and time (with a sand glass), they could calculate distance. Particularly gifted navigators might construct a chart as the voyage unfolded. Others might carry published maps while acknowledging the extent to which they often lacked geographic precision. Navigators could also calculate latitude in the Northern Hemisphere by measuring the angle to the pole star. The farther north one sailed, the larger the angle; the closer to the equator one sailed, the smaller the angle. Using a compass, one could also calculate a rough semblance of direction. When sailing east to west, or vice versa, a navigator could correct his compass heading by maintaining a constant angle with the pole star. By the mid-sixteenth century navigators were traveling with quadrants, astrolabes, or cross staffs, all of which provided a means to measure the angle between the horizon and Polaris (Parry 1974: 156–9).

As ocean-going commerce expanded so too did the demand for navigational knowledge. By the sixteenth century navigational handbooks called "rutters" began to circulate across Europe (Morison 1974: 174). In an effort to write a more practical manual on navigation for English sailors, William Bourne, one of London's most prolific mathematical writers, published *A Regiment for the Sea* in 1574 (Harkness 2007: 122). Although he lacked a university education, Bourne had gained plenty of practical knowledge by talking with sailors, by serving as a garrison gunner, and by running barges between London and his hometown of Gravesend near the mouth of the Thames (Turner 2004). His writing reflected his pragmatic approach to oceanic instruction. "Navigation," Bourne wrote, "is an Art teaching how to direct our course in the Sea, to any place assigned … having consideration how to preserve the Ship in all … changes of weather … to bring the Ship safe unto the port assigned, and in the shortest time" (1574: 7). Bourne's book provided instruction on how to use the astrolabe and the cross staff, for he explained that a ship's master "aught to be sober and wise," and must "govern his company well." But to instill confidence in his crew, he continued, a competent shipmaster must understand the tides, how to avoid obstructions, how to use navigational instruments, and he must "have capacitie to correct those instruments" to produce accurate navigational calculations (8). In his 1578 *A Booke Called the Treasure for Traveilers* Bourne asked simply, what could be more important for travelers than "to know the distances from place to place … & how to make a Plat or Carde for any country"? He lamented that he knew "a great number of persons" who had traveled over great distances but "have not known unto what quarter of the world the place is, that they have been." His book proposed methods for navigation but also for calculating the size and weight of objects on land and at sea. He also examined the processes by which natural features, such as marshes, rivers, cliffs, and ocean currents, had formed (preface [3], chs. 4–5). Ultimately, his was no abstract exposition on navigational mathematics. Rather, by showing what the sea was made of and how it worked, he advanced a utilitarian definition of seamanship that placed "the physical in dialogue with the rational" (Mentz 2015: 79). For Bourne, oceanic knowledge remained practical at its core.

In their ability to connect the sailor's craft with head knowledge, instrument makers played an important role in expanding navigational know-how. Elizabethan London, and particularly its western end and Lime Street neighborhoods, became a veritable "jewel house" of navigational instrumentation and practice (Harkness 2007). Following the Spanish Armada's failed invasion of England in 1588 the market for mathematical instruction, particularly that for navigation, increased dramatically. But over time, as Deborah Harkness has shown, mathematical books evolved into technical manuals "as laborious arithmetical calculation and painstaking geometrical mensuration were being effaced by instrumentation" (2007: 104, 133, 137). For instance, in 1597

FIGURE 1.3 Innovations in navigational technique created new oceanic knowledge. This allegorical representation of the navigational arts shows four women holding a pair of dividers and plumb line (*bottom left*), a ship's rudder (*top left*), a map and dividers (*top right*), and an astrolabe and dividers (*bottom right*). The two on the left look down into the sea, while the women on the right contemplate the earth and the heavens. "Art of Navigation," from Antonio de Ulloa, *Relacion Historica del Viage a la American Meridional...* (Madrid: Antonio Marin, 1748), frontispiece. © Courtesy of the John Carter Brown Library at Brown University.

William Barlow published his *Navigator's Supply*, which described the latest navigational equipment in painstaking detail. He described how compasses were constructed both in Europe and in Asia, warned shipmasters to pay careful attention to what they were purchasing, and made a concerted effort to impress upon instrument makers the importance of their craft. He even went so far as to advocate that those "such as exactly make them, should be rewarded and esteemed accordingly" (Barlow 1597: B3). Barlow described the use of a compass as well as the quadrant and pantometer, both devices used for measuring angles. He also explained their "severall most necessarie uses thereof upon sea or land," including the calculation of variation, or the angular difference between true and magnetic north (E2). He described how to calculate latitude and how to use a traverse board, an instrument used to keep track of speed, time, and heading while navigating by dead reckoning, and then transferring that information onto a "carde," or chart (F3, H2–H5) (see Figure 1.3).

Barlow's efforts and those of others, he believed, were making the art of navigation at sea more accessible. For in recent years he had seen even those of "meane capacitie" learn the art of Navigation. With only a "willing minde," a "sufficient Instructour," and "fitte Instruments," he avowed, just about anyone could "in one moneths space attaine unto great contentment of knowledge" (Barlow 1597: K2). In his 1596 treatise on navigational instrumentation, John Balgrave explained that his intention "was that every man should have the furniture of this Astrolabe" (C). So determined was he to make the astrolabe accessible to a wide audience that he left paper templates with his publisher William Matts on Fleet Street so that his readers could build the instrument on their own (Harkness 2007: 139).

Government policy also shaped the production of navigational knowledge. For the English and the Dutch, who operated under crown-chartered companies, exploration and the publication of navigational information was decentralized and largely privatized. But Spanish and Portuguese efforts were controlled by the state. The Casa de Contratación in Seville and the Casa da Índia in Lisbon controlled cartographic knowledge, licensed pilots, and oversaw most aspects of colonial trade. They required navigators to keep a ship's log noting the weather and keeping track of notable coastal features. These logs were then submitted to the Casa upon a ship's return (Morison 1974: 474–5). If in some cases, the consolidation of navigational knowledge limited its circulation, Spain's ability to train its pilots under the tutelage of some of Europe's most experienced navigators, including Amerigo Vespucci and Sebastian Cabot, was greatly admired by its neighbors (Parry 1963: 96).

Although books, instruments, and administrative practice surely bolstered navigational capabilities, the divine still maintained ultimate control of the early modern oceans. William Barlow was careful to remind his readers that sailors went to sea at God's pleasure, explaining at the end of his *Navigator's Supply* that there is no "other Arte, wherein God sheweth his divine power so manifestly, as in yours; permitting unto you certain Rules to work by, and increasing them from time to time, growing still onwards toward perfection, as the World doth toward his end." Man's ability to traverse the world's oceans was improving. But, he warned his readers, God "alone is the Lord of the Seas, that all stormes and tempestes doe but fulfill his will and pleasure, and that all the waves of the Sea are continually at his commaundement" (Barlow 1597: 13).

A healthy fear of God—and of the sea itself—accompanied most ocean voyages during the age of exploration. As Steve Mentz has shown, the specter of shipwreck loomed large in the early modern imagination. If the Renaissance has been long praised as an age of human progress, Mentz showed that shipwreck "qualifies Renaissance triumphalism" (2015: xxviii). Sinking ships dampened the spirit of improvement. And ultimately, shipwreck showed that despite the human quest for a more rational understanding of the natural world, God still held considerable sway at sea. Indeed, the shift toward empirical ways of understanding natural ocurrences such as storms and waves was slow and irregular, less a clear break from the past and more a process of "wet fragmentation" (Mentz 2014: 80–2). Old forms of oceanic understanding dissolved into new ways of knowing.

One of the most profound changes during the Renaissance was the development of a new planetary consciousness. Around-the-world voyages that followed the lead of Magellan who circumnavigated the globe between 1519 and 1522, established enduring patterns of global interaction that we are still laboring to navigate today. As Joyce Chaplin (2012: xxi) has shown, the Renaissance endeavor to send ships around the world crystallized the belief that humans can create "technologies and political alliances to dominate the planet." Recognizing that during the 250 years following Magellan more than half of the sailors who ventured around the globe died, circumnavigation has also made us painfully aware that "the planet could simply shrug us off." That tension between human ambition and nature's limitations spurred the quest for new forms of oceanic knowledge.

OCEANIC NATURAL HISTORY

If early modern thinkers had determined where the ocean was and how to cross it, they also wanted to know what was in it. During the sixteenth century, natural history developed into a discipline, and natural philosophers looked to classical sources in efforts to reconstruct knowledge of plants, animals, minerals, and medicine. "By drawing creatively on the past," explained Brian Ogilvie, "Renaissance naturalists shaped a new field within the humanist idiom of restoration" (2006: 89). Drawing, most notably, from the works of Aristotle, who is widely considered the first writer to "treat natural history as an intellectual pursuit," Renaissance humanists systematically compiled observations about the natural world with the goal of explaining what they saw and why it occurred. Although natural history took many forms and did not convene a coherent community of investigators, it nevertheless developed into a new literary genre, one that "privileged empirical experience over theory" and that championed a "concern for the particular" over the scholastic preoccupation with universals (Ogilvie 2006: 93, 99, 115–16).

But the ocean resisted the type of systematic investigation that had been applied to terrestrial environments. By the fifteenth century, natural historians had made great strides in describing and illustrating various plants and medicinal herbs. By the sixteenth century, they had compiled a growing collection of samples and established specimen gardens across Renaissance Europe. By the seventeenth century natural history networks expanded as the Dutch and English extended their commercial empires in competition with Spain and Portugal (Ogilvie 2006: 210). But comparatively little attention was paid to the natural history of the sea. Those who plied the oceans as explorers, fishermen, merchant mariners, and naval seamen knew the most about it (Deacon 1971: 23). Although during the medieval period scholars had taken great pains to explain how tides functioned, most early modern marine knowledge was firmly rooted in ancient ideas (39). Into the seventeenth century, explained W. Jeffrey Bolster (2006: 592n21), "most … Englishmen simply took the ocean for granted. It was a highway, barrier, and fishing ground, but not a political space to be ruled, a subject for naturalists' inquiries, or a playground."

If early modern natural historians had given the sea short shrift, explorers and missionaries nevertheless laid the foundations for a natural history of the ocean. Spanish voyagers provided some of the first descriptions of oceanic nature in the New World. Columbus described numerous seabirds and witnessed sea turtles in such abundance that he feared the ship would run aground on them. Near Hispaniola, while on his second voyage, Columbus engaged in what could have been the first New World seal hunt. His men caught fish, supposedly by tethering a line to a lamprey, which after attaching itself to a host, was reeled in, thereby recovering both fish in the process. This story drew skepticism, as did, no doubt, Columbus's claim that in January 1493 near Hispaniola he had seen three mermaids. But it was his account of finding pearls that piqued contemporary curiosity, including that of Vincente Yañez Pinzón, who while searching for pearls along the north coast of South America between 1499 and 1500 discovering the Amazon estuary (De Asúa and French 2005: 2–4, 13).

In the generation that followed, New World observers created even more comprehensive natural histories. For example, Bernardino de Sahagún traveled to Mexico in 1529 and, drawing from Aztec knowledge, published vivid descriptions of plants and animals, including fish, in his *General History*

FIGURE 1.4 Natural knowledge about the sea was often produced during the search for riches and by the people who conducted the work. Here, Native American and/or African divers labor in the seventeenth-century Venezuelan pearl fishery. "Perlen Fischerey," from Christoph Vielheuer, *Gründliche Beschreibung Fremder Materialien und Specereyen Ursprung, Wachssthum, Herkommen und Deroselben Natur und Eigenschafften* (Leipzig: Johann Fritzsche, 1676), plate following p. 176. © Courtesy of the John Carter Brown Library at Brown University.

of the Things of New Spain. Francisco Fernandez de Oviedo, who after sailing to New Spain in 1514 published his *General and Natural History of the Indies* in 1535. After traveling to Peru in 1570 José de Acosta published his *Natural and Moral History of the Indies* in 1590. They all included the study of plants and animals, including marine birds, fish, and other creatures. Like other early modern natural histories, their observations were often curated to complement classical sources, but the authors nevertheless filled their works with both their own observations and practical knowledge gleaned from Native Americans, thereby adding new ideas to the existing pool of oceanic understanding (De Asúa and French 2005: 42–3, 62–74, 76–85) (see Figure 1.4).

In Europe these fragments of oceanic information were subjected to new forms of organization. Over the course of the sixteenth and early seventeenth centuries, several notable chroniclers began to compile the growing body of knowledge about the sea. Although they were far more bookish than salty, the chroniclers nevertheless made new knowledge about the sea accessible. The Italian historian Peter Martyr, for instance, penned some of the first accounts of the European encounter with the New World. He included coastal maps, described giant sea turtles, and recounted a particularly curious story of a domesticated manatee in New Spain (De Asúa and French 2005: 58). English chroniclers Richard Hakluyt and Samuel Purchas compiled still more sea stories. So influential were Hakluyt's *The Principall Navigations, Voiages, Traffiques and Discoueries of the English Nation* (1589–1600) and Purchas's *Pilgramage of Samuel Purchas* (1613) and *Hakluytus Posthumus, or Purchas his Pilgrimes* (1625) that they made a strong case for English expansion into the New World (De Asúa and French 2005: 130–1; Mancall 2007).

Natural history, a branch of natural philosophy that espoused observation, systematic inquiry, and narrative description, was particularly well suited to the skill sets held by physicians. As a result, the study of natural history thrived in European medical schools, particularly in Leiden, Paris, and London (Cook 1996: 99–100). A professor of medicine in Montpellier, Guillaume Rondelet produced one of the most important sixteenth-century studies of marine life in his *Libri de piscibus marinis* (1554–5). Several years later in 1558 Conrad Gessner published the fourth volume of his *Historia animalium,* which though it borrowed heavily from earlier works, including Rondelet's, placed particular emphasis on fish (Kusukawa 2016: 306). Physicians were also important contributors to the first scientific societies, including the Royal Society in London, established in 1660 (Cook 1996: 103–4). President of the Royal College of Physicians and one of the Royal Society's most notable members (and president from 1727 to 1741), Sir Hans Sloane was such a devoted natural history collector that his cabinet of curiosities formed the foundation of the British Museum (Delbourgo 2017) (see Figure 1.5).

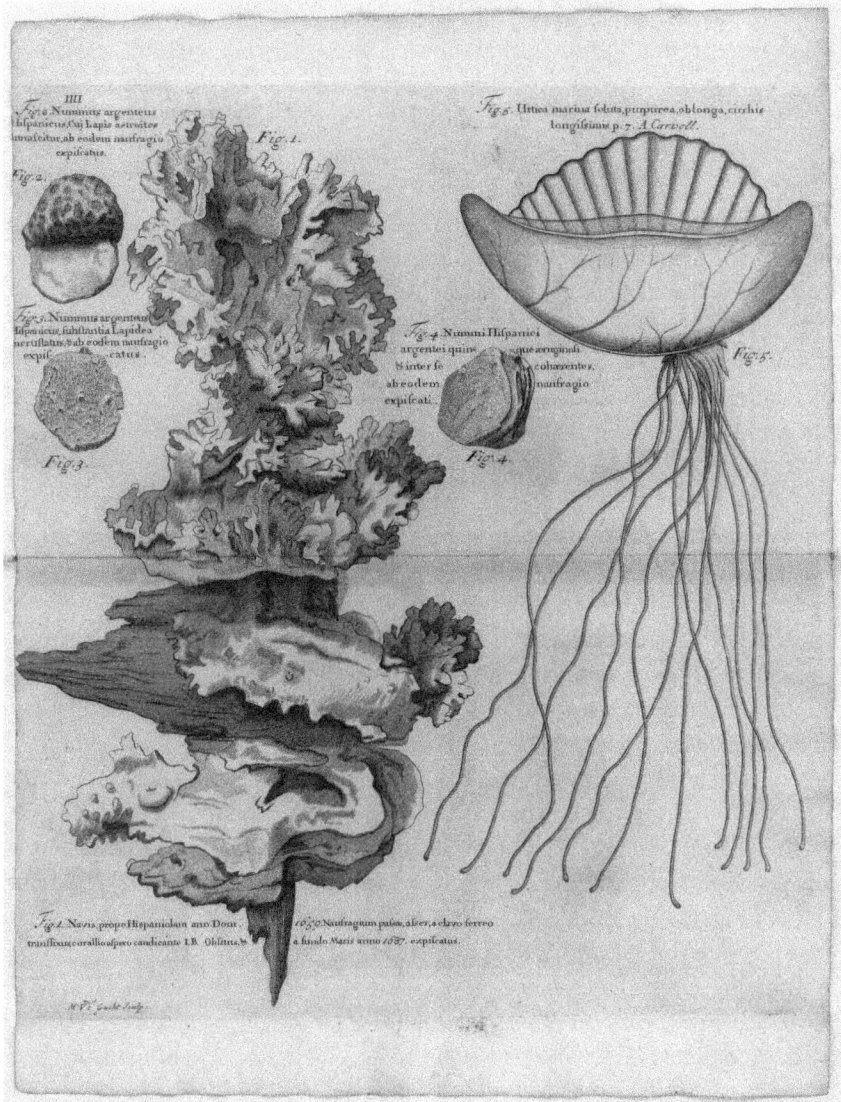

FIGURE 1.5 The establishment of the Royal Society in 1660 initiated a more systematic approach to the study of marine natural history. Sir Hans Sloane (1660–1753) was a particularly careful observer of oceanic nature, in this case depicting coral-encrusted ship planks and silver coins and the sailed jellyfish that evoked the Portuguese *caravela*, which in English came to be called the man o'war. "*Nummus Argenteus Hispanicus, Cuj Lapis Astroites Innascitur, ab Eodem Naufragio Expiscatus [...] [and] Urtica Marina Soluta, Purpurea, Oblonga, Cirrhis longissimis*," in Sir Hans Sloane, *A Voyage to the Islands Madera, Barbados, Nieves. S. Christophers and Jamaica: With the Natural History of the Herbs and Trees, Four-footed Beasts, Fishes, Birds, Insects, Reptiles, &c. of the Last of Those Islands* (London: Printed by B.M. for the author, 1707). © Courtesy of the John Carter Brown Library at Brown University.

Theologians also played a central role in advancing natural history as an important mode of scientific inquiry, so that religion and systematic investigation of the natural world went hand in hand (Rivett 2011). So called "physico-theology" endeavored to show that nature was a reflection of divine creation (Parish 2006: 53). In 1667 the naturalist-theologian John Ray—who later became a correspondent of Sir Hans Sloane—resumed production of the *Historia Piscium,* a work begun by naturalist Francis Willughby in 1663. The Royal Society supported his quest to create a natural history of fish rooted in accurate representations of fish morphology. Significantly, the book marked a departure from earlier works that tended to emphasize preternatural marine creatures. Whereas both Rondelet's and Gessner's books tended to emphasize the medicinal qualities of various forms of fish, Ray was keen to create a guide that would facilitate fish identification (Kusukawa 2000: 180–3). But so expensive was the *Historia Piscium* that it left the Royal Society on shaky financial footing, inhibiting its ability to print Isaac Newton's *Principia,* the publication of which required Edmund Halley to step in and foot the bill (192–3). Nevertheless, the *Historia Piscium* marked an important turning point in the development of oceanic knowledge. Although Ray had sought to recover a history of god's creation, he nevertheless managed to create one of the most accurate depictions of marine creatures of the time and set an important precedent for placing the creation and circulation of oceanic knowledge within a formally established (and government supported) scientific community.

Indeed, the establishment of the Royal Society in 1660 placed new attention on the science of the sea (Deacon 1971: 73–4; Rozwadowski 2001). Seeking sailor knowledge, in June of 1661 the society advanced a set of instructions to Edward Montagu, the Earl of Sandwich, proposing six topics to investigate during his upcoming naval voyage to the Mediterranean. In it, they urged him to observe the ocean depth, salinity, water pressure, tides and currents, and bioluminescence, and provided suggested methodologies on how those measurements would be carried out (Deacon 1971: 74). Writing on behalf of the Royal Society, in 1667 Lawrence Rook published a set of scientific instructions to "masters of ships, pilots, and other fit persons in their sea-voyages" (433–8; Deacon 1965: 32). In the following years, the Royal Society equipped sailors with instruments for taking measurements and provided directions on how to record their results. Vernacular knowledge about the sea underpinned new modes of systematic investigation.

The ocean, the Royal Society believed, provided a vast new area of inquiry. Robert Boyle, writing in the Society's *Philosophical Transactions*, expressed interest in the variations in salinity in different seas and "whether in the same Sea it be always the same?" "What is," he wondered, "the Gravity of Sea waters in reference to Fresh Waters and to one another?" Did seawater vary by season or climate? To what extent, he wanted to know, did it vary in "Odors, Colours, and

Tasts" [sic]? Was there a difference between the "Bottom of the sea, and … the Surface of the Earth"? Published in May 1667, Boyle's queries suggest that institutional knowledge of the sea was still suffused with a sense of mystery (1667: 315–16). He wanted to know why the sea shined at night and what produced ambergris. Could seawater cure rabies? Could sea plants manure the land? By the 1670s, Boyle had, on behalf of the Royal Society, advanced several tracts about the ocean's inner workings that drew heavily upon the "Authentick Informations from Sea Captains, Pilots, Planters, and other Travellers to remote parts" (Boyle 1674: "Advertisement," 15–16). Gleaned from those who frequented the seas, ocean knowledge held endless possibilities not only for aiding navigation but also for advancing an understanding of global geography and human health.

But knowledge of ocean life would also come to shape the patterns of imperial expansion. Over the course of the seventeenth century, numerous correspondents documented their travels, in some cases promoting colonial settlement by emphasizing the ocean's bounty. In 1634, for instance, William Wood's *New England's Prospect* provided a veritable catalog of the region's flora and fauna, both on land and at sea. Similarly, Thomas Morton's 1637 *New English Canaan* detailed the incredible abundance of fin and shellfish in coastal New England. In 1655 Adriaen van der Donck celebrated nature's abundance along the Hudson River Valley in his *A Description of New Netherland*. Similarly, Nicolas Denys's 1672 *The Description and Natural History of the Coasts of North America* provided a detailed account of coastal nature in New France. In describing what they saw, these chroniclers, among numerous other seventeenth-century observers, created a compendium of oceanic knowledge that underscored the promises of global expansion.

Print culture was central to the dissemination of their descriptions and the new ideas that they helped create. Moveable type privileged visual communication over oral transmission and aural reception, which, among other social transformations, altered the ways experimental knowledge was produced (McCluhan 1962: 18–19). As Elizabeth Eisenstein has shown, journals such as the Royal Society's *Philosophical Transactions* and the Académie des Inscriptions et Belles-Lettres's *Journal des Sçavans* "speeded up circulation of scientific news and enabled scattered virtuosi to keep abreast of each others' work" (Eisenstein 1979: 460). Print also allowed natural philosophers to amend earlier publications with fresh observations, making science an iterative process (487–8). And nowhere was this more evident than in the natural history of the seas. If early modern mariners had spilled considerable ink discussing shipboard navigation and instrumentation, by the seventeenth century natural philosophers began to study the substance of the sea and the things that lived in it in more systematic ways. By the eighteenth century natural historians had begun cataloguing sea creatures, adding them to cabinets of curiosity, and bestowing upon them new Latin names in keeping with Carl Linnaeus's standardized system of taxonomy. But the growing interest in oceanic knowledge was piqued by far more than the curiosity of polite society. As European empires vied for global dominance, knowledge of the world's oceans became integral to their abilities to erect jurisdiction in ways that asserted control over newly acquired lands and resources.

OCEAN LEGALITIES

If during the early modern period maritime print culture reshaped the ways ocean geography, navigability, and natural history was understood, it also ushered in radically new oceanic legal regimes. Long a lawless space that defied European conceptions of ownership, the ocean became a place capable of upholding positive law and susceptible to competing sovereignties. Based on common practice and precedent, the law of the sea emerged from "usage or custom" (Colombos 1967: 10). Yet, the indeterminate and ephemeral nature of the oceans made efforts to erect jurisdiction and enforce justice among them anything but complete.

Imperial competition effected legal partition of the oceans. Beginning in the 1450s, Spain and Portugal signed a series of treaties that assigned sovereignty to the Atlantic islands and access to trade along the coast of Africa. The 1479 Treaty of Alcaçovas gave Spain exclusive right to the Canaries, while Portugal secured the Azores, Madeira, Cape Verde Islands, and Guinea (Davenport 1917: 1, 33–48). When news of Columbus's voyage to America reached Spain, Ferdinand and Isabel promptly sent a dispatch to Pope Alexander VI, who summarily issued several papal bulls that recognized Spain's claim to the newly discovered lands and extended Castile's sovereignty to 100 leagues west of the Azores or Cape Verde Islands. The bulls also made it clear that no ship could approach the newly found lands without express permission from Castile, effectively extending Spanish sovereignty across the waters surrounding Spanish lands (71). In an effort to appease Portugal, which felt aggrieved by the decision, the 1494 Treaty of Tordesilla pushed that north–south line to 370 leagues west of the Cape Verde Islands, extending Portuguese sovereignty from Brazil east to Asia. Spain retained the lands west of the line extending across the Americas and into the Pacific (Gould 2003). The treaty also mandated that Spanish ships had to traverse Portuguese seas by sailing only the most direct route (Gould 2003: 84–5). Naturally, this clumsy partitioning of the globe would break down, as competing European empires vied with Iberia for control of lands in America and Asia, and particularly after the Protestant Reformation in 1517, which led much of northern Europe to challenge papal authority.

As European empires consolidated control of far-flung territories, their claims to sovereignty often overlapped. To mediate contention over ownership

Europeans developed a system of international law based on Roman legal practices (Churchill and Lowe 1999: 4). But as legal historian Lauren Benton has shown, on the periphery their claims were tenuous at best. "Empires," Benton explained, "did not cover space evenly but composed a fabric that was full of holes, stitched together out of pieces, a tangle of strings" (2010: 2). As European empires built this patchwork of sovereignty on land, they also erected new legal regimes at sea.

But few could agree on how to erect jurisdiction across oceanic space. Widely considered the father of international law, the Dutch jurist Hugo de Groot, or Grotius, advocated for the absolute freedom of the seas in his 1608 *Mare Liberum*. During the medieval period, Venice had claimed the Adriatic, and Genoa the Ligurian Sea. Denmark had claimed the Baltic, and in the fifteenth century England had claimed the seas surrounding Britain. Grotius rejected Pope Alexander VI's fifteenth-century bulls that divided the world's oceans between Portugal and Spain. He was particularly motivated to uphold the Dutch East India Company's right to trade in Portuguese controlled areas of Asia (Muldoon 2002: 16–20). He also believed that the freedom of the seas was fundamental to natural law because humans did not permanently inhabit the oceans and because in terms of navigation and fisheries it was "limitless" (Grotius [1608] 1916: 28).

Grotius's ideas sparked rejoinders from legal scholars who believed that the oceans could indeed be owned. Portuguese lawyer Serafim de Freitas argued that Portugal had the right to claim jurisdiction over the Indian Ocean. Scotsman William Welwood argued in his *Abridgement of all Sea Lawes* (1613) that the seas surrounding Britain could be owned but that the high seas were still free, thereby closing territorial waters to outsiders but allowing the British fleet to extend its reach farther afield (Muldoon 2002: 21). In 1616 or 1617 John Selden penned what was probably the most cogent response to Grotius. Although left unpublished until 1635, his *Mare Clausum* argued that the English crown could not only claim coastal waters near its possessions but could extend jurisdiction to its North American colonies, effectively claiming ownership of the North Atlantic (Muldoon 2002: 22). Indeed, Selden concluded that England's global empire "(crossing in a manner the whole Ocean) must of necessitie ... come within compass of his [the king's] power and jurisdiction" ([1635] 1652: 499).

If little agreement could be had in theory, the English admiralty courts played one of the most important roles in shaping the law of the seas in practice. Admiralty courts had first convened in the fourteenth century and over the years expanded their jurisdiction. Since they did not provide a jury trial and seemed to concentrate crown authority, this roused opposition from England's common law courts and parliament. Admiralty courts expanded their power and range during the reign of James I, who on at least one occasion took a seat on the admiralty court bench (Harrington 1995: 588; Colombos 1967:

11–17). In an effort to regulate overseas fishing, James I established a vice-admiralty court in Newfoundland in 1615, but once his son Charles I was overthrown in 1649, efforts to police American commerce were brushed aside. With passage of a series of navigation acts to control trade in 1651 and the restoration of the crown in 1660 it soon became evident that dedicated courts were needed to regulate the empire's increasingly complex maritime enterprise. Recognizing that many colonies were avoiding the navigation acts, the Crown and Parliament established vice-admiralty courts in Rhode Island, the Bahamas, South Carolina, Pennsylvania, and West Jersey in 1697 (Harrington 1995: 594). Although the colonies protested the increased oversight, the admiralty courts had, by the beginning of the eighteenth century, become one, if not the, most important arbiter of maritime law.

But legal authority was often limited by the practicalities of policing the seas. States might claim control over a stretch of ocean and the resources within it, while nevertheless recognizing that the sea was vast and uncontrollable. As England implemented a mercantilist economic system that sought to funnel trade through its own ports and on its own ships, it was forced to accept that the ocean was "a space that resisted civil authority (and hence, possession)" (Steinberg 2001: 101). Following the Treaty of Utrecht in 1713, English authorities began to prosecute piracy with new vigor and on a global scale, although the naval patrols were far more prevalent in American and Caribbean waters than they were in the Indian Ocean and along the Atlantic coast of Africa. While piracy was curtailed during the early eighteenth century, Spanish *guardacostas* began seizing British, Dutch, and French ships. French and Dutch privateers seized ships from rival traders as well. As lawyers and diplomats wrangled in prize courts, they developed new legal systems for regulating privateering and trade (Benton 2010: 148–56).

If the agents of empire believed that European legal authority extended to all corners of the globe, they nevertheless recognized that legality grew diffuse the farther one traveled from metropolitan centers. Treaties might promote peace in European waters, but when ships passed "beyond the line," pirating, privateering, and smuggling became commonplace (see Figure 1.6). "Europe was a zone of law," explained Eliga Gould, "the world beyond a place of competing jurisdictions and perpetual war" (2003: 481). As the English fell into conflict with Spain and then France during the first half of the eighteenth century, the Dutch were particularly well positioned to take advantage of the conflicts by both supplying Britain with arms and trading with its enemies. In keeping with the Anglo-Dutch Treaty of 1674, Dutch actions were largely countenanced in European waters, but English naval vessels and privateers seized Dutch traders in the West Indies with little compunction (487). Like the ever-shifting colors of the Caribbean Sea, early modern ocean legalities were deeply variegated and highly ephemeral.

FIGURE 1.6 During the early modern period the contest for empire encouraged the creation of new oceanic legal regimes. If at least a modicum of law and order reigned in metropolitan waters, violence often held sway "beyond the line." Here, the notorious New England pirate Edward Low executes an adversary while his crew watches. [*Edward Low Shoots a Man*], in Daniel Defoe, *Historie der Engelsche Zee-Roovers* (Amsterdam: Hermanus Uytwerf, 1725), plate following p. 590. © Courtesy of the John Carter Brown Library at Brown University.

But over the course of the eighteenth century those same European powers reached some agreement over how to regulate coastal spaces. In 1702 Cornelius van Bynkershoek argued that the high seas should be free but that sovereignty along a nation's coasts could be extended as far as a cannon could fire, roughly 5 kilometers. The Scandinavian states, conversely, had extended sovereignty from shore at a fixed distance of one Scandinavian league, or 6.5 kilometers (Pastore 2014: 170). By the middle of the eighteenth century, explained Lauren Benton, "a global maritime culture had produced a diversification of ocean regulatory spheres and had laid the groundwork for a new (but not peaceful) legal regime of the sea" (2010: 158). That new legal system provided the foundation for international law, which ultimately played an important role in creating conditions for the rise of the nation-state.

CONCLUSION

The Renaissance saw a flowering of oceanic knowledge that fundamentally changed the way the world was understood. Early modern savants reimagined global geography by melding Christian and humanist conceptions of space. As explorers probed the far reaches of the globe, they dismantled the earth island, creating a constellation of continents and smaller islands that were connected by oceans. Over time, those oceans were given place names that often corresponded with adjacent lands and the people who inhabited them. Once imagined as endless wastes, the oceans gained new identities.

The process of exploration was aided by new technologies that were crafted to solve practical problems. Breakthroughs in ship design and navigational tools helped sailors voyage over greater distances. They relayed their methods and discoveries via letters, information from which was included in a growing body of maritime literature that circulated across Europe. Maps and narrative accounts of the New World spurred still more voyages. The things they learned informed subsequent journeys, so that by the sixteenth century European sailors were circling the globe. This helped advance the idea that human know-how could dominate the earth. The pursuit of oceanic knowledge, in other words, had ushered in the age of globalization.

As exploration of the world's oceans continued, natural historians sought to unlock the mysteries of the sea. They wanted to know where the oceans came from, what they were made of, and how sea creatures came to be. In some cases, they saw similarities in marine life across ocean basins. In other cases, they marveled at the differences. On almost all accounts, they reveled in the sheer abundance of sea life along the European periphery. They committed much of what they witnessed to print, ushering in the age of ocean literacy. The establishment of formal scientific societies in the mid-seventeenth century provided a new institutional basis for the study of the sea and the publication of findings. Their efforts were driven not only by philosophical curiosity but also by the contest for empire. Oceanic knowledge provided a means to national wealth, prestige, and ultimately global power.

But there were competing claims to the ocean's endowments. In response, rival empires began erecting lines of jurisdiction across the sea. Through canon law, imperial treaties, by drawing on precedent, and appealing to convention, they divided the ocean into separate spheres of sovereignty. Legal scholars advanced their national interests through competing treatises. While some argued for the freedom of the seas, others contended that the oceans could be owned. Over time, they came to legal compromises. But in its vast and ever-shifting nature, the sea often subverted assertions of sovereignty and blurred notions of legality. As a result, control over distant shores was continually shifting, and the far reaches of empire were often plagued with violence. The collective effort to reach legal accord provided the basis for a new system of international law that would continue to develop throughout the early modern period. In sum, the creation of a new body of legal knowledge about the sea was a foundational element in the development of the modern nation-state.

The ocean has been long imagined as something boundless, eternal, and somehow beyond human comprehension, but the practical and scholarly pursuit of oceanic knowledge fundamentally shaped human history during the early modern period and beyond. As Elizabeth Mancke has shown, control of the sea was more important to the process of colonial expansion than control of the land, for it was the process of "mastering oceanic space" (1999: 225) that allowed for the construction of the nineteenth century's land-based empires. Oceanic inquiry also ushered in modern modes of scientific production. During the second half of the eighteenth century, for instance, Captain James Cook's voyages melded geographic exploration and marine science in ways that that made the acquisition of oceanic natural knowledge a priority for both the British and American navies (Rozwadowski 2005: 39, 46–7). As the law of the sea evolved, it shaped the contours of coastal development. Nowhere was this more evident than in Boston, where a 1641 law and subsequent interpretations of it led to such extensive filling of the foreshore that it fundamentally transformed the city's geography (Pastore 2015). In an age of industrial growth and seaport expansion, when plenty of money was at play, oceanic jurisdiction was a constant bone of contention (Bowditch 1832). Ultimately, the acquisition of oceanic knowledge was about renegotiating the human relationship with the natural world, about melding hand- and head-knowledge, and about connecting the local with the global. It was a process that began in the early modern period and continues to this day.

CHAPTER TWO

Practices

Translating Oral Traditions and Practical Experiences into Print

JOHN B. HATTENDORF

During the years between 1500 and 1680, maritime practices that had previously been communicated primarily orally and through practical experience began to be written down and communicated through printed books. This development created the beginnings of a professional literature of maritime practices. This development appears in a variety of maritime topics, including language, seamanship, navigation, ship design and shipbuilding, harvesting the sea, guns and gunnery, conflict at sea, religion, and regulation of maritime activities. Many of these practices were not new, though this period presents many of our earliest printed records. By surveying the print archive of early modern seafaring practices, this chapter provides a guide to scholarly resources and materials for further study. The chapter divides its materials into eleven categories: language, seamanship, practical navigation, navigation by scientific methods, flags and communication at sea, ship design and shipbuilding, harvesting the sea, guns and gunnery, violence at sea, personal life and religion, and regulation of

> This article is based on revised and reorganized selections from the text of John B. Hattendorf, *"The Boundless Deep ..." The European Conquest of the Oceans, 1450–1840: Catalogue of an Exhibition of Rare Books, Maps. Charts, prints and manuscripts relating to Maritime History from the John Carter Brown Library* (Providence, RI: John Carter Brown Library, 2003).

maritime activities. Based on materials gathered from the collections of the John Carter Brown Library in Providence, Rhode Island, these materials provide a comprehensive survey of European practices during the early modern age of global maritime expansion.

LANGUAGE

The distinctive terminology of seafaring arises from the combination of the professional maritime environment in which seamen live and the specialized nature of building, outfitting, and handling ships. Seamen from all of the major European maritime countries have developed a specialized vocabulary that had its origins as work-a-day jargon, but which has become embedded and preserved in a traditional form through instruction and training. It is, also, of course, embodied in much literature and poetry and has even found its way into many common expressions that landsmen use today. Sea words in English were already clearly established in the Elizabethan period. In the last decades of the sixteenth century and the first decades of the seventeenth century, scholars were just beginning to prepare dictionaries of European vernacular languages and to find equivalent meanings between vernacular languages rather than resorting to Latin. At the same time, practical seamen traveled around the world and visited ports where many different languages were spoken. This fact, along with the international character of the maritime labor market, in which sailors of various nationalities might join a ship's crew, were among the practical reasons why multilingual glossaries and dictionaries of sea words were often in demand.

Captain Sir Henry Mainwaring (1587–1653), who had "developed an insatiable love for adventure on the high seas," compiled the first book in English on nautical terms: *The Sea-man's Dictionary* (1644). He became Lieutenant of Dover Castle and Deputy Warden of the Cinque Ports on his return from a voyage in 1619 that was closer to piracy than to privateering. Between 1620 and 1623 he wrote this manual for the personal use of the Duke of Buckingham, the Lord High Admiral, an office of state that was typically held by courtiers, not experienced seamen. Mainwaring commented: "to understand the art of navigation is far easier learned than to know the practique of mechanical working of ships and the proper terms belonging to them." His book, which explains the latter, was first printed in 1644, when Parliament ordered it "imprinted for the good of the Republic."

From this beginning, the maritime dictionary in English developed further with William Falconer's *An Universal Dictionary of the Marine* (1769), which went through seven editions between 1769 and 1789. The English genre of maritime dictionaries reached its apogee in the age of sail with the publication in March 1815 of Dr. William Burney's *Universal Dictionary of the Marine*. Begun as a revision of Falconer's work and using the same title, Burney's work extended the dictionary format from an unembellished vocabulary list to an alphabetically arranged, highly illustrated, and comprehensive description of British maritime affairs at the end of the Napoleonic Wars.

John Smith (1580–1631) published his book, *A Sea Grammar* in London in 1627. The material had been previously published in 1626 under the title *An Accidence or Pathway to Experience: Necessary for all Young Seaman,* and John Smith revised, rearranged, and enlarged the volume in 1627 under the title *A Sea Grammar* using a thematic approach. The first printed work on ships and seamanship written in the English language, it was reprinted several times under this title until 1705 and the publisher continued to advertise it for sale until 1724. Although Smith's work appeared long before Mainwaring's *Seaman's Dictionary* was published, Smith had used Mainwaring's earlier manuscript as a source for his own work.

SEAMANSHIP

The essence of an accomplished sailor is found in seamanship. As a skill, seamanship demands a wide range of knowledge of how a ship at sea will react to changing natural conditions. It is the art of handling a ship or boat in all conditions of wind, weather, and tide. It involves steering, handling sails and lines, anchors, capstans, and other equipment involved in moving, mooring, and loading a vessel.

Six Dialogues (1685) by Nathaniel Butler (fl.1640) was titled in its original manuscript form as "A dialogical discourse concerning maritime affairs between the high admiral and a captain at sea." Laid out in the form or a question and answer dialogue, the book includes explanations of many aspects of contemporary seamanship.

A prominent member of the Virginia Company that sponsored the Jamestown colony and a member of the Council for Virginia, Butler served a three-year term as Governor of Bermuda from 1619 to 1622 and wrote a history of the island. In 1638 to 1640, he was "governor and admiral" of the beleaguered Puritan settlement on Providence Island off the coast of Nicaragua, where he supervised privateering operations. Butler began writing this volume in 1634 and revised it while at Providence Island, mixing information from Mainwaring's *Sea Dictionary* with his own original observations. He probably wrote the book mostly for his own amusement, but he may also have intended to give it to his friend Lord Treasurer Weston, who headed the Admiralty Board in 1634. It was first printed in 1685 and again in 1688. In the process, the printer Moses Pitt used a medieval form of Butler's surname, Boteler, which the author never used himself.

Henry Bond was a well-known teacher of navigation, but like many others skilled in navigation, he also taught the associated skills of seamanship as he did in his book, *The Boate Swaines Art* (1664). From about 1633, Bond held the title Reader of Navigation to the Mariners in Chatham Dockyard, a position that was established before 1631 and lapsed during the English Civil War. From the time it first appeared in 1642, his book became one of the standard texts, and it was regularly reprinted under the same title until 1787. From 1726 onward, it was usually issued with Andrew Wakely's *Mariner's Compass Rectified* (1704), a book that dated from about the 1660s.

PRACTICAL NAVIGATION

While Europe's leading intellectuals and scientists were working to understand the globe and sky and gaining a scientific understanding of the nature of the sea, ordinary seamen needed to acquire some part of this knowledge and to convert it to practical use. In many cases, the mathematical skills and scientific understanding that this required were far beyond the comprehension of an ordinary sailor, but the information on procedures and the necessary instruments became increasingly available and were initially brought into practice on an occasional basis to compare to dead-reckoning navigation. Sailors continued to share their traditional information and experience of navigation with one another by word of mouth, but this practice began to be supplemented by a specialized form of printed work that became widely used. Designed to communicate basic practices at sea, sailing directions and textbooks on navigation deteriorated quickly from regular use and exposure to the harsh conditions onboard ship. In many cases, these "how to" books have not survived or have become extremely rare.

One source of practical guidance were books that reported on voyages. Theodor de Bry (1528–98) in his *Petit Voyages* (1601; see Figure 2.1) pointed out that for the navigator, the sea itself provides a variety of indicators that help to point the way from place to place. Close to land, the color of the water can often suggest the depth. Out at sea, the presence of birds and schools of fish may offer important information to the experienced seaman. In the journal of his 1492 voyage, Columbus took particular note of the appearance of birds and fish as signs that he was approaching land. As he knew from experience in the Cape Verde islands, the frigate bird or man o'war bird rarely ventures more than 320 kilometers from land in the tropical Atlantic.

The earliest printed book of sailing directions was *Questa e vna opera necessari a tutti li naviga[n]ti chi vano in diverse parte del mondo* (1490) and as such it is the ancestor of all modern coast pilots. Printed in Venice in 1490 by Bernardino Rizo, it is an anonymous compilation from the voyages of many seamen and from a variety of sources "by a Venetian gentleman who had seen all this region." The book became a great commercial success and was reprinted a number of times. Most of the volume is devoted to

FIGURE 2.1 Theodor de Bry, *Petits Voyages* (Frankfurt, 1601). © Courtesy of the John Carter Brown Library at Brown University.

describing sea routes within the Mediterranean, such as the route from Venice to the Levant; however, about one-fifth of the book is devoted to areas outside the Mediterranean. In the eighteenth century, the volume was attributed to the Venetian trader, Alvise da Cà da Mosto (1433–77), but there is little convincing evidence that he was the author. The oldest

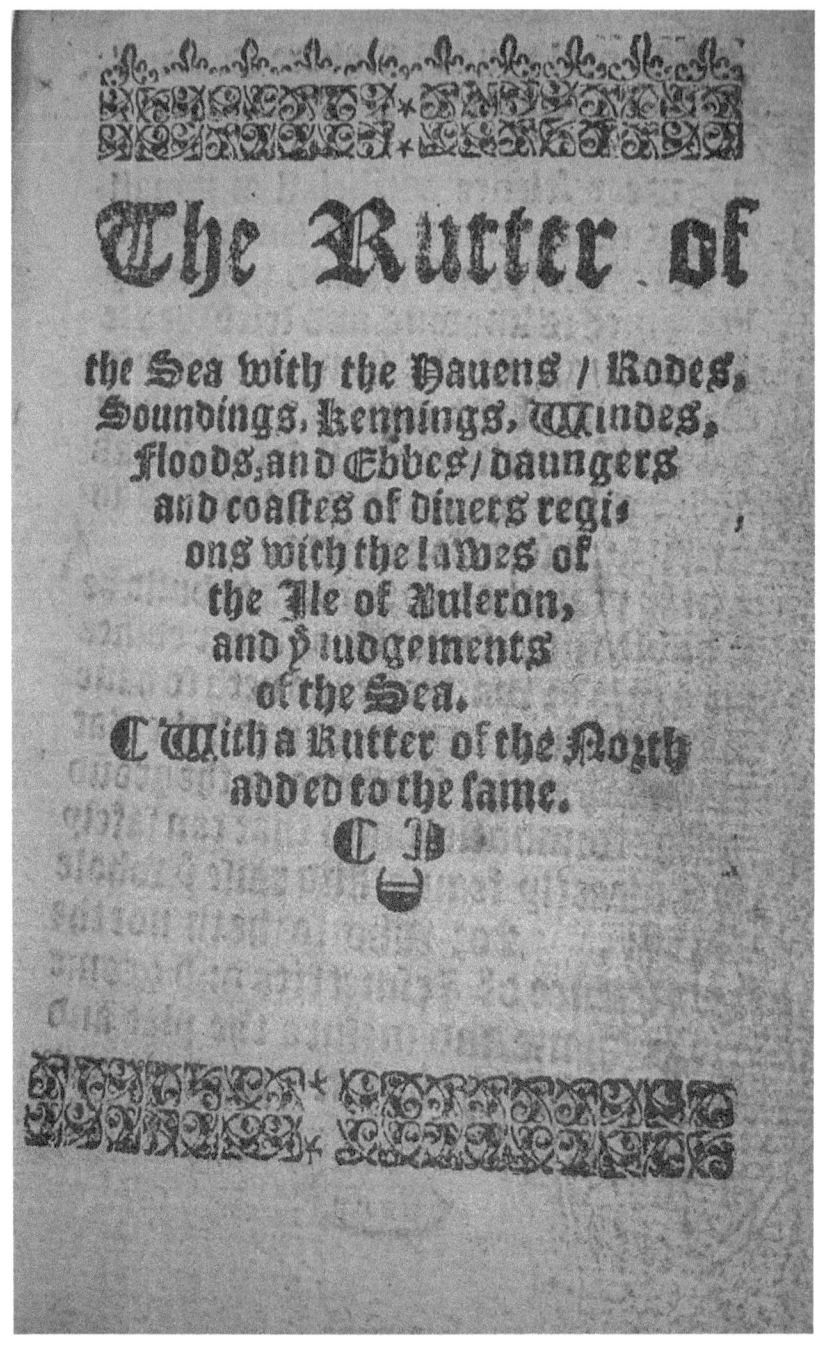

FIGURE 2.2 Pierre Garcie, called Ferrande, *The rutters of the sea: with the hauens, rodes, soundings, kenning, windes, floods and ebbes …* (London, 1567). © Courtesy of the John Carter Brown Library at Brown University.

surviving work of this genre is an anonymous Greek manuscript, *The Periplus of the Erythraenean Sea,* from *c.* 95–130 CE, which was not printed until modern times (Casson 1989).

Descriptive guides or sailing directions for finding one's way between ports at sea were called "Seebuch" in German, "portolani" in Italian, "derroteros" in Spanish, "roteiros" in Portuguese, "routiers" in French, and "rutters" in English and Dutch. The first printed book of sailing directions for the French and English coasts was by Pierre Garcie, called Ferrande (*c.* 1435–*c.* 1520), *The rutters of the sea: with the hauens, rodes, soundings, kennings, windes, floods and ebbes, daungers and coastes of divers regions with the lawes of the Ile of Auleron* (1567) (see Figure 2.2). Garcie's *Le Routier de la mer* was originally written in 1484 to 1485 and published at Rouen in 1520. Robert Copeland (fl.1508–47) translated Garcie's work into English, which first appeared in 1528. Editions published after 1555 also included Richard Proude's "A Rutter of the North."

Thomas Blundeville (fl.1561–1602) first published his fat volume of exercises in 1594: *M. Blundeville his exercises, containing eight treatises, the titles whereof are set downe in the next printed page.* It became so popular that it eventually went on to eight known printings through 1634. The book is important in that it encapsulates the way a novice Elizabethan seaman came to understand practical navigation. Blundeville was the first Englishman to describe the earlier work of Peuerbach and Regiomontanus on the use of trigonometric tables for astronomical calculations. His final section, "Navigation, what it is, and in

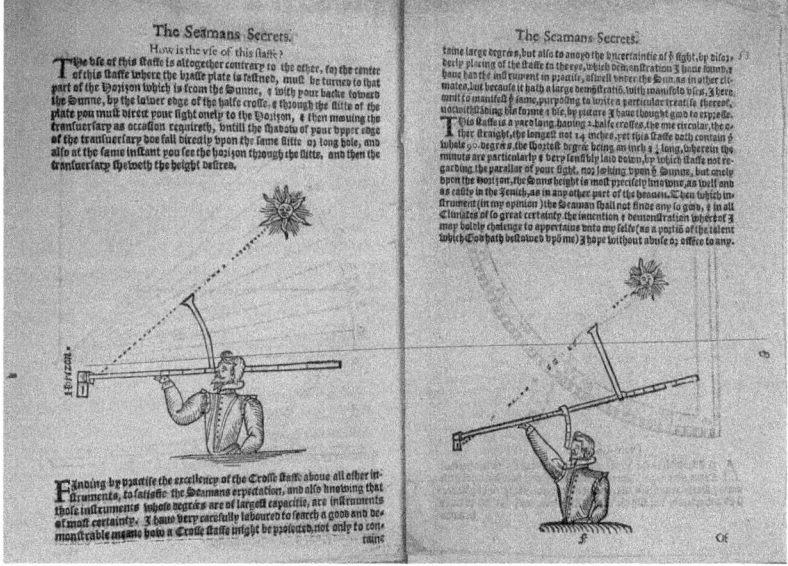

FIGURE 2.3 John Davis, *The Seaman's Secrets* (London, 1595). © The Folger Shakespeare Library.

what order the principles there of are," provided some of his own insights while drawing on all the key continental writers on navigation. Among his suggestions, he hinted that a new way of drawing charts was in progress, and he presaged the use of tide tables, an idea that did not come to realization until the nineteenth century.

John Davis (1550[?]–1605) was one of the most experienced seamen in Elizabethan England. Associated with such well-known figures as Sir Humphrey Gilbert and Sir Walter Raleigh, Davis is most well known as having been captain and chief pilot on voyages to find the Northwest passage in 1585 to 1586, exploring the coasts of Greenland, Baffin Island, Cumberland Sound, and the Davis Strait that bears his name. In 1591, he joined Thomas Cavendish's enterprise in the hope of finding the Pacific end of the Northwest Passage, but failed to get past the Strait of Magellan. Informed by his extensive practical experience on these voyages, Davis book, *The Seaman's Secrets ... wherein is taught the three kinds of sayling*, first appeared in 1595 (see Figure 2.3).

Portuguese navigators were the first to find a sea route to India by circumnavigating the southern tip of Africa at the end of the fifteenth century. For the next hundred years the Portuguese monopolized trade with India by sea. The passage between Lisbon and Goa, known as the "Carreira da Índia," typically required a passage of five to seven months.

Antonio de Maris Carneiro's *Roteiro da India Oriental* (1666) is a revised version of an earlier work by him first published in Lisbon in 1642, *Regimento de pilots e roteiro das navegações da India Oriental*. His writing reflected many years of Portuguese navigational experience. By the seventeenth century, however, competition from the Dutch and English greatly weakened Portuguese commerce with Asia. The number of vessels arriving in Lisbon from the East Indies fell from an average of 3.2 a year during the first decade of the seventeenth century to 1.8 a year in the 1630s.

Père Georges Fournier (1595–1652) was among a group of Jesuits in the seventeenth century who were interested in navigation and the education of naval officers. At the Jesuit house in Dieppe, Fournier had become a naval chaplain and first served at sea under Cardinal Sourdis in 1633 to 1641 and became professor of mathematics at Hesdin in 1640 to 1642. His book, *Hydrographie contenant la théorie et la pratique de toutes les parties de la navigation* (1643), which was dedicated to Louis XIII, is recognized as the first attempt to create an encyclopedia of contemporary maritime practice. In it, Fournier summarized information on matters ranging from naval architecture to ports, including principles of navigation, tides, charts, winds, naval organization and operations, and prayers for seamen. After publishing the first edition in 1643, the author revised and expanded the work for a second edition, which eventually appeared posthumously in two printings in 1667 and 1669. Fournier's book was widely used by mariners. The privateer Nicolas Gargot reported in a 1668 pamphlet that seventeen years earlier, when the crew of his privateer *Léopard* mutinied and attacked him at sea, he skillfully used a copy of Fournier's folio as a shield to protect himself.

Benjamin Hubbard's (1608–60) book *Orthodoxal navigation* (1656) is the earliest published contribution to navigation by someone who had been a resident of England's American colonies. Describing himself as a "late student of the Mathematiks in Charls Towne in New-England," Hubbard wrote this book to advance the method of using a Mercator chart for great circle sailing. While he did not claim to be original in this, it was an important practical matter for seamen that had been omitted in the usual textbooks of the time. Little is known about Hubbard, who is believed to have arrived in Massachusetts in 1633 and lived for a time in Charlestown, where he owned property. He apparently returned to England by 1644, where he was a nonconformist minister.

John Seller (fl.1658–98) became one of the most prominent teachers and writers on practical navigation in late-seventeenth-century England. Originally apprenticed in the Merchant Taylor's Company, he was freed in 1654 and eventually, as an instrument maker, became a brother in the Clock-Maker's company in 1667. In 1671, Charles II appointed him hydrographer to the king, and in 1686 the Navy Board appointed him to supply ships' compasses. In addition, he taught mathematics at Christ's Hospital, London. From his house and shop at the Hermitage Stairs, Wapping, London, Sellers pursued an active business selling both new and used navigational instruments, maps, and globes. His *Practical navigation; or an introduction to the whole art,* first appeared in 1669 (see Figure 2.4).

Nathaniel Colson's *The Mariner's new Calendar* was first published in 1676 and remained a standard work of reference for working seaman until the end of the eighteenth century. Typically, the hard use given these books has taken its toll, leaving few surviving copies. Following many reprintings and revisions, the last edition appeared in 1785. The famous maritime publishing firm Mount & Page produced the volume. Richard Mount purchased the established printing shop owned by William Fisher on Tower Hill, the north side of the Tower of London, in 1676, where he had been apprenticed in 1669. Marrying Fisher's daughter, he continued his father-in-law's work, which included publication of such key maritime authors as Colson, Norwood, Mainwaring, and many others. The firm had a long life and was successively known as Richard Mount, Mount & Page, Page and Mount, and Mount & Davidson, before becoming Smith & Ebbs in the nineteenth century.

The seaman's practice by Richard Norwood (1590[?]–1675) was another of the standard references consulted by working seamen. First published in 1637, it was regularly reprinted until 1732 and was still advertised for sale as late as 1776. An interesting feature of this work is the author's discussion of the length of the nautical mile. In 1633 to 1635, Norwood had calculated the length of a degree along the meridian between London and York at 6,120 feet (1.86 kilometers). The accepted value today is 6,080 feet (1.85 kilometers).

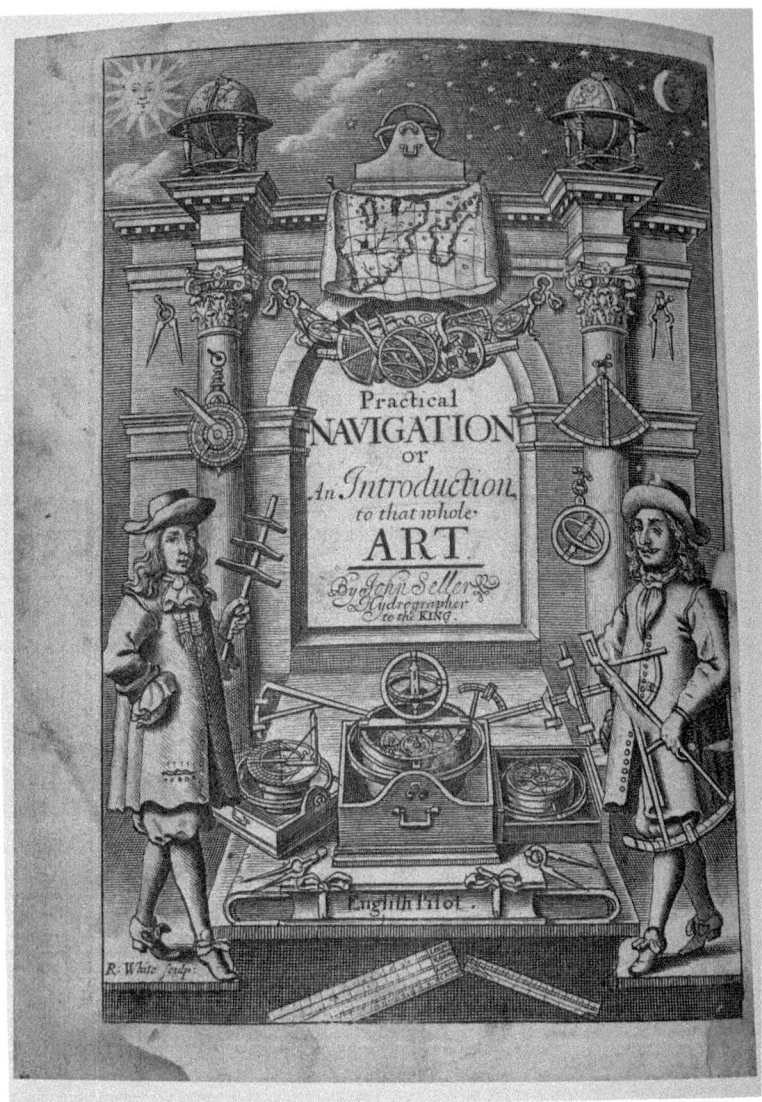

FIGURE 2.4 John Seller, *Practical navigation; or an introduction to that whole art* (London, 1680). © Courtesy of the John Carter Brown Library at Brown University.

NAVIGATION BY SCIENTIFIC METHODS

As the science of navigation was put to practical use, it slowly began to develop a technology to go along with it. The oldest instrument for gathering information at sea was the lead line, by which seamen were able to determine the depth of water and that brought up samples of the bottom as an additional aid to determining location. Next came the magnetic compass, which became the fundamental tool in deepwater navigation along with the nautical chart. Over centuries of practice, Mediterranean navigators had developed the art of sailing by compass into an accurate skill. As shown on the *Carta Pisana* made about 1275, the basics for dead reckoning, charts, compass directions, and a scale of distance, were clearly in use at the outset of the period when sailors from Amalfi, Genoa, Pisa, and Venice were moving outward in the western Mediterranean and beyond to the eastern Atlantic islands.

Dead reckoning remained a basic approach up to the eighteenth century and beyond. As practices in navigation slowly became more sophisticated, the chart, lead line, and the compass were joined by the parallel rule, the protractor, the mechanical compass used to measure a distance on sea charts; the ship's log and line to estimate speed; and the variety of instruments, from astrolabe and cross-staff to octant and sextant, to measure the angles between celestial bodies or between the horizon.

Most famous for his *Cosmography* (1524), Peter Apian (1495–1552) was also a pioneer in astronomical and geographical instrumentation. His *Instrument Buch* (1553) is profusely illustrated with woodcuts; he examined the range of instruments available to astronomers and navigators, including quadrants and dials. His investigation starts with a discussion of the ways that the human body can be used as a measuring device, with an illustration of a hand. More importantly, this book also contains Apian's calculation of sines for every minute of arc, with the radius decimally divided. These were the first such tables ever published.

Lucas Janszoon Waghenaer (1533/4–1606) first published *Spieghel der Zeevaerdt* in Leiden in 1584; some twenty-four different editions were eventually published in Dutch, French, German, Latin, and English. The original Dutch edition brought together for the first time a treatise on navigation, a description of instruments, and a collection of detailed sailing directions keyed to a set of accompanying charts. So influential was this book that the name of the Dutch compiler became widely used in English, from the late sixteenth to the late eighteenth century, as a generic term for such manuals: "waggoners." The English translation, *Mariners mirror* (London, 1588), is often considered one of the most beautiful books of the sixteenth century. The title page illustrates the variety of instruments and tools of navigation available to a seaman, including the lead line, the cross-staff, and dividers. The Lord High Admiral, Lord Charles Howard of Effingham, encouraged this translation into English, which appeared in print in October 1588, just after English forces fought the battle with the Spanish Armada. Theodore de Bry, then working in England, engraved its title page. Only two years before, he had been working in Frankfurt, where he began to publish his famous illustrated series of voyage narratives. Since January 1911, an adaptation of this title page has served as the front cover of a leading British academic journal, *The mariner's mirror: the journal of the society for nautical research*.

Thomas Blundeville (fl.1561–1602) was a country gentleman from Newton Flotman, Norfolk, who became fascinated with astronomy, navigation, and mathematics. In his first work, *A briefe description of universal mappes and cardes, and of their use: and also of Ptolemy his tables* (1589), he described an instrument that seems to have been his own original invention: the nautical protractor. Reporting its usefulness, Blundeville wrote, "I would use none other instrument of direction then halfe a Circle divided with lines like a Mariner's Flie. Truly I do thinke the use of this flie a more easie and speedy way of direction, than the manifold tracing of the Maps or Mariners' Cards, with such a number of crosse lines, as commonly are drawn therein."

Until the invention of reliable mechanical watches in the late eighteenth century, sundials were regularly used to determine time. Popular among scientists as well as wealthy estate owners, fine examples may still be seen in the quadrangles at Oxford and Cambridge colleges and at country houses in England. Instrument makers repeatedly tried to make sundials that were practical for use at sea. Despite their efforts, the various designs remained inaccurate at sea, due to the need to align a dial accurately on a North–South axis, adjust it for latitude, and hold it steady while reading it.

The cross-staff, originally called the "Baculus Jacob" or "Jacob's staff," was in regular use from the beginning of the sixteenth century to the end of the eighteenth century. It was the basic instrument by which sailors of all countries determined their latitude by measuring the altitude of the sun above the horizon, of the sun at noon, or of the North Star at night. Despite improvements in instruments during the eighteenth century, the simplicity and low cost of the cross-staff encouraged its continued use.

One of the key disadvantages of the cross-staff was that it required the observer to look directly at the sun while taking measurements. In the fifteenth century, a Portuguese Jew, Levi Ben Gerson, invented a prototype back-staff, but it was not adopted for general use. In England at the end of the sixteenth century, a number of experts began to work on the problem of developing an improved instrument. They included Edward Wright of Cambridge and Thomas Hariot from Oxford. However, it was John Davis who hit upon the most successful solution to the problem in about 1594, with an instrument for measuring the sun's altitude by the angle of the shadow that it cast. Known alternatively as the "Back Staff," "Davis's Staff," or the "English Quadrant," it quickly came into widespread use and remained popular, particularly with American seamen, through the end of the eighteenth century.

Manuel Pimentel (1650–1719) wrote the textbook that many consider the culmination of the classic books in Portuguese on the practical use of nautical instruments and on navigation: *Arte de navegar, emque se ensinam as regras practices* (1699). Pimentel's father, Luis Serrão Pimentel (1613–79) had been royal cosmographer in Portugal and, sometime before his death, had completed writing the text of a navigation manual, *Arte pratica de navegar e regimento de pilots*. Manuel Pimentel, who also became royal cosmographer, edited this text and published it in 1681 under his father's name. Eighteen years later in 1699, Manuel Pimentel published another book, this time under his own name and with the new title, *Arte de navegar*, but he based it on his father's earlier 1681 work. Manuel Pimentel revised this work and published a new version in 1712. Although he died in 1719, the work was reprinted in 1746 and in 1762.

FLAGS AND COMMUNICATION AT SEA

Flags play a role in seafaring that is often different from their use on land. In some languages, the difference is reflected in the distinctive terminology for sea flags: *pavillon*s in contrast to *drapeau* in French and *flaggen* in contrast to *fahnen* in German. In English, as in other languages, there are a variety of additional words used to describe maritime flags when they have particular uses or shapes, such as "ensign," "jack," "pennant," or "burgee." At sea and in a maritime context, flags served as identification, a means of communication, and even decoration. Throughout most of the sailing ship period, when seamen moved beyond shouting distance of one another, flags were the most practical and versatile means of communicating from one ship to another at sea or between ship and shore. The process of developing a language through the use of flags was slow and difficult, however. Eventually, single flags came to have specialized meanings that explained at a glance a vessel's national identity, function, and role. In attempting to communicate information or orders for action, an early method was found in the placement of particular flags at specific points in a ship's rigging. It was not until the late eighteenth and early nineteenth centuries that a standard code developed.

Nieuwe Hollandse scheeps bouw (1695) by Carel Allard (*c.* 1648–1709) is one of the earliest books that deals with sea flags. Allard's first work on sea flags originally appeared as an appendix to *Nieuwe Hollandse scheeps bouw*, a book on shipbuilding, and he later published it separately. Among its illustrations is the flag that William III flew from the mainmast of *Den Briel*, which carried him and a large force westward on a fair "Protestant Wind" from Holland to Torbay, England, to take the English throne in November 1688. Under the motto "For the Protestant Religion and the Liberties of England," the flag showed the arms of the Prince of Orange impaled with those of his English wife, Mary II.

SHIP DESIGN AND SHIPBUILDING

The design and building of ships is a traditional craft that has deep roots in a variety of local traditions that were closely tied to the particular practical uses for which a vessel was intended. In the southern European tradition of shipbuilding, one can trace aspects of fifteenth-century ship design and construction back to their origins at the time of the Roman Empire. In northern Europe, the traditions had both Celtic and Viking origins. The ships headed for oceanic exploration had to be built to withstand the conditions of the open sea and with a capacity for carrying provisions for a crew during a long voyage away from a base of supply. Ideas about design and shipbuilding, and the required skills in this traditional craft were passed by word of mouth and by example and were rarely put in written form. Much is currently being learned about this subject through the research that underwater archaeologists are doing on newly discovered shipwrecks.

There are few records of fifteenth-century shipbuilding in Europe, but some valuable information on the subject can be found in contemporary illustrations that focus on the biblical story of Noah's Ark. In composing such scenes, artists sometimes enriched their biblical images with observations of current practice. This practice can be seen in *Registrum huius operis libri cronicarum cu[m] figuris et ijmagibus ab inicio mu[n]di* (1493), compiled by Hartmann Schedel (1440–1514). More commonly known as the *Nuremberg Chronicle*, the volume is a general work of world history that may be the earliest instance of close cooperation between author, printer, and illustrator in the making of a book. The illustrators, Michael Wolgemut and Wilhelm Pleydenwurff, initiated the project, found funding for it, and commissioned Hartmann Schedel, a local scholar, to write the text, and Anton Koberger to print the work, adapting everything to their 1,700 woodcut illustrations. A few of the woodcuts can be traced to the young Albrecht Dürer, who worked as an apprentice in Wolgemut's studio around this time.

In *Grand Voyages* (1594), Theodor de Bry (1528–98) included an engraving of shipbuilding by members of the Diego de Nicuesa expedition to Panama in 1509. Under their commander Olando, they had run aground and were forced to build a new vessel, making use of the timbers of their wrecked ship, to return home. The details of sixteenth-century shipbuilding, however, probably derive from a Flemish shipyard that the artist had seen close at hand. Half a century later this same image was modified and republished elsewhere to show Noah building the Ark.

Tomé Cano's *Arte para fabricar* (1611) substantially completed about 1608 and printed three years later, provides valuable insight into Spanish ship construction for the early part of the seventeenth century. An experienced ship owner and mariner with decades of experience in transatlantic sailing,

Tomé Cano (fl.1580–1611) wrote this treatise in the context of government-sponsored debate regarding ideal ship sizes and configurations for Spain's American trade.

Galleys were a characteristic vessel in the days of classical Greece and Rome and even continued to be used up as warships up through the end of the eighteenth century in the Baltic. In France, Louis XIV began to create a large galley fleet in the Mediterranean in the 1660s. Huge sums were spent on constructing galleys, mobilizing the manpower to operate them, and maintaining the Galley Corps as a force that could fight for limited objectives and serve as a symbol of French power. Among its range of uses, the galleys were most notoriously used as prison ships until the Corps was dissolved in 1748. F. Dassié's, *L'architecture navale* (1677) provides a detailed illustration of a seventeenth-century galley (see Figure 2.5).

In Britain, *Marine Architecture* (1739) responded to the eighteenth-century demand for works on shipbuilding, but it copied without acknowledgment from three much earlier works.[1] Its contents were outdated by 1715, but it was reprinted in 1749, continuing to be advertised for sale as late as 1776. Its

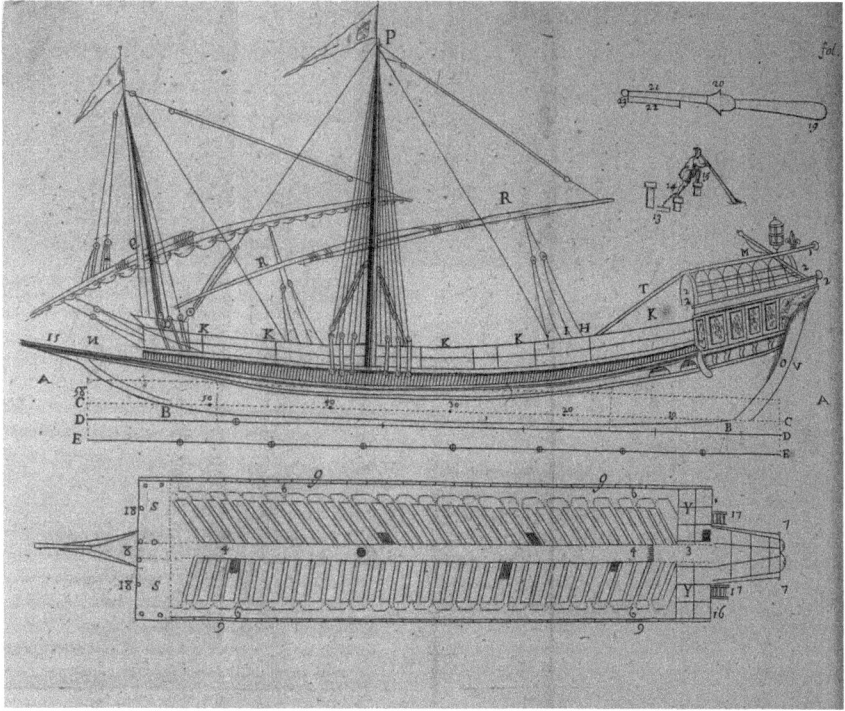

FIGURE 2.5 F. Dassié, *L'Architecture navale* (Paris, 1677). © Courtesy of the John Carter Brown Library at Brown University.

continued popularity may tell us something about the state of shipbuilding in small, local shipyards in contrast to the major yards that were leading the industry.

Edward Hayward's volume, *The sizes and lengths of rigging,* first appeared in 1656 and contains tables showing the amount of spar timber and rigging needed to equip a ship in this period.

HARVESTING THE SEA

Fishing and whaling are among the oldest and most fundamental maritime activities of human societies. Specialized types of vessels as well as distinctive patterns in social organization and trade developed from fishing. Even before Columbus reached the Americas, the rich fishing off the North American coast may have attracted Europeans to sail in that direction. In the sixteenth century, fleets made annual trips to North American waters to exploit the natural supply of fish as cheap food for Europe's growing population. Later, North American fish provided a major food source for the slave population in the West Indies. As competition between European empires grew, nations began to regulate and control fishing as a resource. These trends also brought fishing within the sphere of war and imperial competition.

In creating the first printed map focused on the area of New England and the Canadian Maritime Provinces, Giacomo Gastaldi in his *La Nuova Francia, Terzo voulume della navigationi et viaggi* (1556), decorated the sea areas with interesting vignettes that illustrate contemporary fishing practices. The cartography derives from the maps and reports that Giovanni de Verrazanno made during the first European exploration on these coasts in 1524.

Tobias Gentleman's book, *England's way to win wealth, and to employ ships and marriners* (1614) set out the argument that the best way for England to become prosperous was not to seek gold and silver, in emulation of the Spanish, but to follow the Dutch example by gaining wealth through trade, in particular to promote the English herring fishing industry. Little is known of Tobias other than the fact that he spent most of his life in the North Sea fishing area off Great Yarmouth, Norfolk. This is his only known writing. The pamphlet's publication in 1614 created a public debate on issues surrounding the herring industry and the accumulation of national wealth.

Taking up Gentleman's argument, the anonymously authored work *The trades increase* (1615), supported Gentleman's view on expanding the herring industry and argued that English merchants should promote a pattern of free trade as opposed to chartered monopolies. In the course of his argument, the author attacked the East India Company and ridiculed it for the loss of the 1,100-ton company ship, *Trade's Increase,* using the ship's name in the title as a pun. This criticism led the government to discover the identity of the author, Robert Kayll, and to imprison him.

Sir Dudley Digges (1583–1639) was a powerful and influential supporter of the English East India Company, who rebutted Kayll's attack in *The defence of trade* (1615) by using detailed information from the East India Company's records to argue that the Company's trade resulted in a substantial net gain.

Edward Sharp's *Britaines Busse: Or, A computation as well of the charge of a Busse or herring-fishing ship. As also of the gaine and profit thereby. With the States proclamation annexed unto the same, as concerning herring fishing* (1615) appeared only six weeks after Dudley Digges's defence of the East India Company, and it also directly referred to the earlier pamphlets by Gentleman and Kayll. Little is known about the author, but in his arguments to support Gentleman's defense of the herring fishery, Sharp shows extensive knowledge about it and underscores Anglo-Dutch rivalry in this area.

Newfoundland was the part of America that Englishmen knew first. Its fabulously wealthy offshore fisheries may have been known and exploited even before Columbus and Cabot, while the trade to Newfoundland certainly became the first regular trade between America and Europe. The Newfoundland trade flourished independently from the settlements in Newfoundland that first appeared in 1610. While the settlements were closely tied to exploitation of the fisheries, they were also involved in other activities, including attempts to find iron, grow food, and manufacture glass and soap, as shown in King Charles I's *A commission for the well governing of our people ... in Newfoundland* (1633).

The seas magazine opened: or, the Holander dispossest of his usurped trade of fishing upon the English seas (1653) was an anti-Dutch tract, written in the context of the events leading to the outbreak of the First Anglo-Dutch War, and contains much information on English maritime affairs and interests, including matters in Newfoundland and the West Indies, and timber in North America. The three Anglo-Dutch wars of 1652–1654, 1665–1667, and 1672–1674 give rise to a wide range of literature on both sides of the North Sea, which criticized, explained, or celebrated many of the maritime aspects of these conflicts. Some works, such as *The seas magazine opened*, were anonymous political tracts, others ranged from satire to poetry and even involved the major literary figures of the day.

GUNS AND GUNNERY

The development of efficient guns placed on maneuverable and multipurpose sailing ships was one of the major innovations in European history during the period 1450–1840. In this period, guns and gunnery were matters of high technology that involved an advanced understanding of metallurgy, ballistics, and the use of explosives. Gunners first appeared as specialists in English warships during the 1470s and became common within twenty years. The earliest guns fired stone shot and were built from wrought iron staves formed into a tube and fastened with iron rings. Gradually more guns were cast in bronze. With the transition to bronze, guns became heavier and more expensive.

An extreme example of this was the "cannon-royal" that weighed 8,000 pounds (3,629 kilograms) and fired a 66-pound (30-kilogram) shot. Such large guns were initially used ashore for siege operations and were gradually transferred to sea use, but more often they were used for attacking shore positions than other ships. During the sixteenth century iron shot gradually replaced stone shot, while at the same time guns cast of iron replaced the wrought iron and expensive bronze guns. Simultaneously, the methods of mounting guns onboard ships changed typically to a low wooden carriage on wheels. The innovation of cast iron guns in the 1540s revolutionized gunnery at sea by making them cheaper and more readily available onboard merchant ships. While many navies continued to prefer bronze guns because of their safety, the proliferation of iron weapons at sea required the greater circulation of information and training in their use. Along with improvement in the quality of gunpowder, gun barrels could be shorted and larger shot fired.

In the late sixteenth century, the sides of ships were opened with gun ports, increasing the number of large guns that could be used in an engagement. By the 1650s, iron guns had become the dominant weapons in battles between naval fleets. From this time until the Industrial Revolution, guns used at sea changed little and were generally classified by the weight of the shot fired. The only major innovation in the later period came about 1779 with the carronade, a relatively light gun that used a small charge to fire a large projectile a short distance. Many merchant ships were armed in wartime for their self-protection, some only minimally, while others, depending on their destinations, might be heavily armed. Some merchant ships might carry a letter of marque authorizing a more offensive defense, even if they did not fully take up privateering as an occupation. William Mountaine was an instructor in mathematics. His manual for shipboard gunnery was an expansion on two earlier works, one by Captain Thomas Binney, *A Light to the Art of Gunnery* (1676) and the other by Captain Francis Povey, *The Sea Gunner's Companion* (1702), both of which expanded on the information from the early seventeenth century in Boetler's *Six Dialogues* (1685).

VIOLENCE AT SEA

The nature of war at sea changed dramatically in the period between the mid-fifteenth and the mid-nineteenth centuries. Until about 1650, the nature of war at sea was highly varied, often governed by local and particular issues rather than by national circumstances and national fleets. Small groups, warlords, and local and regional authorities were the protagonists of warlike activities at sea. Their activities ranged from individual plundering raids and robberies at sea to the ongoing rivalries of small groups or warlords, who were independent of larger governmental authority. By and large, armed vessels that were not part of "national" navies undertook most of such activities. This reflected the fact that it was not until the nineteenth century that navies were able to acquire a nearly complete monopoly on the use of violence at sea. Piracy and privateering are two such closely related activities where the distinction between them can be blurred, sometimes purposely to put the face of legitimate privateering on illegal piracy. The word "privateering" only appeared in English during the seventeenth century, so historians' application of the term to earlier periods have tended to be misleading and inaccurate. During the seventeenth and eighteenth century, an admiralty court issued a license during wartime to a privateer—that is, to a privately armed and outfitted vessel—authorizing the vessel and its crew to attack and to capture the merchant vessels of specific enemies with whom the country was then engaged in a declared war. The privateer was then required to bring the captured vessel into specific ports, where an admiralty court examined the vessel with her papers and cargo. If legal requirements were met, the court condemned the ship and cargo as enemy property and they were sold at public auction with the proceeds divided by an established formula between the government, the capturing officers, and the crew. Privateering was eventually abolished in 1856 by international treaty.

In its strict legal definition, piracy is nothing more than theft at sea. Yet, the word has gained widespread romantic associations, and a huge popular literature has grown up around the topic, much of it purely fictional and with a very doubtful historical basis. Nevertheless, piracy is a serious theme in maritime history. From the mid-sixteenth century, seamen were involved in wartime privateering. In the periods of peace that followed, some seamen continued their wartime habits. In some cases, they established their own small communities in the Caribbean or the Indian Ocean, far from authority, where they became a threat to all merchant vessels. By the end of the seventeenth century, such piracy had become a serious problem that required organized efforts to control.

By the mid-seventeenth century following the formation of states in early modern Europe, permanent navies began to come into existence. These were bureaucratic organizations that were fully financed and maintained by a national government, using vessels that were designed to fight other similar vessels. These developments paralleled technological advances in ship construction and in weaponry that led to the employment of large guns at sea, which in turn led to the development of formalized tactics designed to maximize the effectiveness of the large guns in battle.

The first national naval history in English did not appear until Josiah Burchett's 1720 *A Complete History of the Most Remarkable Transactions at Sea*, but reports, diagrams, and maps illustrating naval events and battles were more commonly published. A typical example may be found in Don Álvaro de

Bazán (1526–88), marquis of Santa Cruz, was captain-general of Spain's Atlantic fleet from 1584 until his death in 1588, when the duke of Medina Sidonia succeeded him. Before serving as King Philip II of Spain's captain-general, Bazán had commanded galley squadrons in many Mediterranean naval campaigns, including the Battle of Lepanto in 1571. He organized the naval operations of the conquest of Portugal in 1580 and commanded the combined operations in the Azores in 1582—the subject of his pamphlet *Il succeso de l'armada del Re Filippo*, which was printed in Florence in 1582—and at Terceira in 1583.

Sir Francis Drake was the most famous seaman in Elizabethan England. Adventurer, privateer, naval commander, circumnavigator, and explorer. Baptista Boazio (fl.1589–1603) issued an engraved map, *The famouse West Indian voyadge made by the Englishe fleet* (1589), to illustrate Drake's voyage across the Atlantic that probably preceded the narrative accounts that participants published. It shows the track of Drake's fleet from its departure at Plymouth in September 1585 until its return to Portsmouth in July 1586. Elizabeth I ordered Drake to undertake an attack on Spain's American colonies as a preemptive strike to divert Spanish plans to invade England. During the voyage, Drake attacked Santiago in the Cape Verde Islands and Santo Domingo, Cartagena, and St. Augustine in the Americas. On his return voyage, he called at Roanoke, Virginia, where the mathematician Thomas Harriot and the artist John White embarked for the return passage, carrying with them their unique views and descriptions on America. Another uncolored version of the map has six printed columns of text pasted along the bottom edge of the map. Boazio drew the map from firsthand knowledge. Accompanying Captain Carleill, commanding the *Tiger* and the expedition's lieutenant-general and chief military officer, Boazio is mentioned in several accounts as a page or messenger sent to the Governor of Santo Domingo during Drake's attack. This map is Boazio's first-known work.

Another example of Baptista Boazio's work is his *Civitas Carthegena in Indiae occidentalis contiente sit, portu commodissimo ad mercaturam inter Hispaniam et Peru exercendam*, published in Walter Bigges (d.1586) *A summarie and true discourse of Sir Francis Drakes West Indian voyage* (London, 1589). Sir Francis Drake's attack on the Spanish colonial port of Cartagena in 1585 was a dramatic example of the type of raiding activity that was common in sixteenth-century sea warfare. Baptista Boazio drew a set of four illustrations of Sir Francis Drake's 1585 to 1586 voyage. The others were similar views of Santiago, Santo Domingo, and St. Augustine and all were specifically designed to illustrate the account written by participants in *A summarie and true discourse*. Captain Walter Bigges, the commander of the land forces under Carleill, began writing the work during the voyage. Following the attack on Cartagena, he died of illness and his lieutenant, Master Crofts, probably completed the work. Having completed the separate map and the four book illustrations, Boazio went on to gain a reputation for his work on regional maps, producing one for the Isle of Wight in 1591, and others for Ireland in 1599 and 1602 to 1603. The latter maps may have possibly been done through Boazio's connections with Captain Christopher Carleill made during the expedition and the publication of this book.

A Dutch example may be found in *Beschrreibung von Eroberung der spanischen Silberflotta wie solche von dem General Peter Peters Heyn, in Nova Hispania, in der Insul Cuba im Baia Matanzas ist erobert worden* (1628). In September 1628, an officer in the Dutch West India Company's fleet, Piet Pieterszoon Hein, with Admiral Hendrick Corneliszoon Lonq, captured the Spanish Mexican silver fleet at Matanzas Bay, Cuba. This was the first and only time that any enemy of Spain succeeded in capturing this entire fleet and its valuable cargo. This great success, along with an earlier successful looting expedition in Brazil in 1627, when he had captured thirty-eight Spanish and Portuguese ships, made Hein the most celebrated Dutch seaman of his era. On his return home in January 1629, Hein became lieutenant-admiral of Holland, the leading naval post in the Dutch Republic. In accepting this appointment, Hein became the first to have been selected for the post entirely on the basis of professional ability. His naval career was short lived: five months later, in May 1629, Hein was killed while pursuing a squadron of privateers near Oostend.

Very little was published in this period on concepts of naval tactics and strategy, although a number of manuscript works were circulating in limited circles. *L'Art des Armées Navales* (1697) by the Jesuit father, Père Paul Hoste (1652–1700), was the first serious professional study of naval tactics and naval warfare since Flavius Vegetius Renatus wrote his brief essay on the topic in the fourth century CE.[45] Hoste was the first to attempt to analyze in a major book the new naval tactics that involved large sailing ships carrying heavy guns. A Jesuit at the age of seventeen, Hoste soon became a specialist in mathematics and hydrography and was well versed in the methods of naval construction. Through the patronage of the Duke of Mortemarte, Hoste became chaplain successively to two leading admirals in the French Navy, d'Estrées and Tourville. Over a twelve-year period, Hoste accompanied them at sea and was able to observe the practice of naval operations and obtain insight directly from the officers with whom he served. Following the marquis de Seignelay's 1685 decision as minister of the navy to employ the Jesuits to teach the higher sciences to naval cadets, Hoste became professor of mathematics at the Royal Naval College in Toulon. During his career, Hoste published a number of important works relating to naval science and began to write on naval tactics as early as 1691. *L'Art des Armées Navales* was first published in 1697 and a second edition appeared posthumously in 1727.

PERSONAL LIFE AND RELIGION

Finding detailed and specific information on the personal lives of seamen is one of the most challenging tasks for modern scholars. Few ordinary seamen wrote down their impressions, and their contemporaries tended to dismiss the day-to-day routine of life at sea as uninteresting. In the past half-century, modern underwater archaeologists have contributed many new insights through the examination of artifacts that they have recovered from shipwreck sites. When such items of material culture are linked to the surviving contemporary documents a better understanding may be gained of the nature and character of a seaman's personal life onboard ship.

Life at sea inescapably confronts the overpowering elements of nature. The vastness of the ocean, along with both its remarkable beauty and its terrifying power, has always been part of the consciousness of sailors. These very elements have naturally placed elements of religious faith among the prominent features of a sailor's mentality. At the same time, while sailors are often acutely conscious of their dependence upon a supernatural or divine power, this facet of a sailor's life contrasts starkly with the rough and tumble, often amoral, character of maritime society.

The cover of Hans Staden's very popular book *Warhaftige Historia* (1557) shows two seamen on deck, one using a cross-staff and the other an astrolabe, while the caption asks the central question: "What use is the watchman to the city and the navigator to the safety of the mighty ship in its voyage at sea, if God does not protect them both" (see Figure 2.6). Staden was a German who had been shipwrecked off the coast of Brazil early in the sixteenth century, captured by Indians, and held for nine and a half months in captivity before being ransomed and returning home to write his narrative. The deeply religious element of life at sea is also reflected in Psalm 107: "They that go down to the sea in ships and occupy their business in great waters; these men see the works of the Lord and his wonders in the deep."

The Church of England's *Book of Common Prayer* first appeared in 1549 and has long been celebrated for the beautiful quality of its English prose. During the Commonwealth period, Parliament replaced it with *A Directory of Prayer* in 1641. Not entirely satisfied, Parliament then ordered a supplement to it published in 1645, *A Supply of Prayer for the Ships of this Kingdom*, which was the first set of English prayers designed specifically for use at sea. Following the Restoration, a similar set of supplemental devotions was included in the 1662 *Book of Common Prayer* and has been in use since that time.

REGULATION OF MARITIME ACTIVITIES

One of the principal features of European political development in the period of the conquest of the oceans was the rise of states with extensive bureaucracies,

FIGURE 2.6 Hans Staden, *Warhaftige Historia* (Marburg, 1567). © Courtesy of the John Carter Brown Library at Brown University.

centralized control, and permanent armed forces on land and at sea. This process resulted in each country creating specific offices and numerous national regulations for conducting maritime affairs. At the same time, long-standing practice among the ships of European nations laid the basis for an international understanding that became part of treaties and eventually evolved into international maritime law.

Every maritime nation established laws regulating the conduct of the ships and seamen that carried their own national flags. The laws touched the entire range of activities from commerce and fishing to navies and privateering. The process of creating such law in each country also created specific offices to enforce the laws. Those new officials typically issued reports and compiled information for the use of higher officials and such documents have benefited later historical research.

The origins of European maritime law may be traced to the island of Rhodes, whose laws formed the basis of the Eastern Roman Empire's maritime code. These laws dated from the seventh or eighth centuries and came to be known as the "Rhodian Sea Law," although some elements of them derive from the laws of Hammurabi, *The Babylonian Index*, of the eighteenth century BCE. Since the barbarian invaders who moved into the Roman Empire were not seamen, Mediterranean port cities continued to use the laws that had developed in earlier times. Some Italian cities, such as Trani, Amalfi, and Venice began to form their own laws in the medieval period, while others were drawn in Spain. The earliest maritime legal code to emerge outside of the Mediterranean was the twelfth century "Roll of Oléron," of French or Anglo-Norman origin, which was compiled on the island of Oléron in the Bay of Biscay and later promulgated in the thirteenth century by King Louis IX of France. The English *Black Book of the Admiralty* also dates from this period. "Roll of Oléron," later formed the basis for the maritime laws in northern Europe, including the Laws of Visby, the *Watterecht,* used by the Hanseatic League and established in a conference of league members in 1407. In addition to the development of international law, other types of laws emerged that were dealt with in specialized courts. Among these were admiralty and vice-admiralty courts that dealt with prize matters and naval courts-martial that dealt with discipline onboard warships.

One of the underlying issues in the early development of maritime law was the practice that arose during the Middle Ages of claiming sovereignty over areas of the sea. Venice claimed sovereignty over the Adriatic; Denmark and Sweden vied for the *dominium maris Baltici* until the agreed upon a portioned sovereignty of the Baltic in 1622. England claimed the sovereignty of the "British Seas," extending from Norway to Spain. Some of the claims to maritime sovereignty involved the enforcement of ceremonial rituals, such as firing a gun salute, dipping an ensign, or striking topsails to acknowledge another power's sovereignty. The issue was more serious when claims to the sovereignty of the seas were extended beyond the ceremonial to exerting exclusive fishing rights, levying tolls, and denying the passage of ships over broad areas of the world's oceans.

The germ of the broader legal dispute was planted when, following the discovery of America, Spain and Portugal attempted to apportion the world's oceans between themselves. At first, the seafaring explorers and traders from England, France, and the Netherlands merely ignored these claims. In 1580, the Spanish ambassador to England formally lodged a diplomatic complaint with Elizabeth I over Drake's incursion into Spanish sovereignty over the Pacific. The Queen's reply was based on the authority of Ancient writers, Ulpian and Celsus. Her views also anticipated the scholarly legal argument that arose in the seventeenth century, when she retorted that the use of the sea and air is common to all.

The most elaborate and widely accepted new body of maritime law in the Mediterranean in the Middle Ages came from Barcelona, where it was built up from the decisions of the city's magistrates on shipping matters. It was compiled in the thirteenth century, and called the *Consolat de Mar*, or Consulate of the Sea. In this form it became widely used in Spain, Provence, and Italy. The code was first printed in Catalan at Barcelona in July 1494 and was reprinted four times in Catalan. It was first translated and printed in Italian in 1519 under the title *Librio di Consolato* (see Figure 2.7).

The Dutch humanist and jurist, Hugh de Groot (1583–1645), known more commonly by the Latin form of his name, Hugo Grotius, had begun to consider the subject of maritime law early in his career. In 1604, he wrote a piece on prize law entitled *De Jure Predea* (1604), which put the subject in the broad context of international and natural law, rather than relying on the traditional basis for law in the Bible and the laws of the church. Continuing with his studies, Grotius dealt with the legal issues surrounding the Dutch capture of a Portuguese ship in the Strait of Malacca in light of the 1493 papal grant of joint ownership of the sea to Portugal and Spain. Beginning a large study on the broad subject, Grotius argued that the seas were free for all to use and not the property of any country. In 1609, one chapter of this work was published under the title *Mare Liberum*. Before he completed his full studies in this area, Grotius was sentenced to life imprisonment in 1618 for his political opposition to Prince Maurice of Nassau. In 1621, he escaped from Loevenstein castle, reputedly hidden in a chest of books, and fled to Antwerp and then to Paris. There, in 1625, he wrote his famous book on the law of war and peace, *De Jure Belli ac Pacis* (1625), which incorporated a revised version of his earlier work. In 1633, the *Mare Liberum*, originally published in 1609, appeared again in a booklet with a work by Paulus Merula (1558–1607), a legal scholar and historian from Dordrecht and later, Leiden (see Figure 2.8). In the context of international affairs of the 1630s, this particular edition of Grotius's work raised widespread interest and discussion. In 1634, Grotius became the Swedish Ambassador to Paris. While returning

FIGURE 2.7 *Librio di Consolato* (Venice, 1539). © Courtesy of the John Carter Brown Library at Brown University.

to France after a visit to Stockholm, Grotius was shipwrecked in the Baltic and died near Rostock. This fatal accident relieved the Dutch from taking any action to respond to England's demand in 1635 that the Dutch Republic punish Grotius for this book.

FIGURE 2.8 Hugo Grotius, *De Mari Liberio* (Leiden, 1633). © Courtesy of the John Carter Brown Library at Brown University.

Mare clausum seu de dominus Maris (1635), written by John Selden (1584–1654) was the most famous direct rebuttal to Grotius on the issue of freedom of the seas. He argued quite differently than Queen Elizabeth I had done in 1580 and, following English policy in the reigns of James I and Charles I, held that a nation had the right to limit others from using the sea. Selden wrote this treatise in 1618, but it was not published until 1635 at the command of King Charles I. Trained in the law, Selden wrote a history of government in England before the Norman Conquest, *Analecton Britannicon* (1615), and became a leading figure in the Antiquarian Society, a focus for historical research in early seventeenth-century London. He was twice imprisoned for supporting the House of Commons against royal authority, but later became a monarchist and dedicated his book to Charles I. In 1654, Selden bequeathed his large collection of books and manuscripts to the Bodleian Library at the University of Oxford, where his name is remembered in the extension of the library built to house them, "Selden End."

The debate in which Selden and Grotius engaged did not end with their most famous books. Although Selden's work is the most famous argument in support of a national claim to exclude foreign commerce and navigation, it was neither the first not the only one. Gentilis defended Spanish and English claims in his *Advocato hispanica* (1613); William Welford wrote on English claims in *De domino maris* (1613). In 1633, Sir John Boroughs wrote *The sovereignty of the British seas proved by records,* but it was not published until 1651. Echoing the similar views of Venice in regard to the Adriatic, Paolo Sarpi published his *Del dominio del mare Adriatico* (1676). Representing the opposing side, Johanus Isacius Pontanus (1571–c. 1639)—a Dane named Hans Isaksen—was one who took Grotius's side and argued for the freedom of the seas in his book, *Discussionum historicarum libri duo* (1637). Pontanus was professor at the Latin School in Harderwijk, one of the old Hanse port towns on the Ijseelmeer in the eastern Netherlands. In a tangential maritime connection, he is also known to have contributed to R. Hues, *Tractatus de Globis*, published by Judocus Hondius in Amsterdam in 1617 and also wrote a history of the Danish kings, *Rerum Danicarum Historia,* also published by Hondius in 1631.

Charles Molloy's (1646–90) book on maritime and naval law, *De jure maritimo et navali: or a treatise of affairs maritime and of commerce* (1676), became a standard authority on international law in England. First published in 1676, it was regularly reprinted during the eighteenth century. Earlier, during the Second Anglo-Dutch War, Molloy had written an anti-Dutch tract, *Holland's Ingratitude, or a serious expostulation of the Dutch* (1666). In *De Jure Maritimo,* Molloy made one of the most extreme legal arguments for England's sovereignty of the sea, which he claimed extended from Cape Finisterre to Van Staten in Norway.

The volumes described in this chapter comprise a representative, if not quite complete, survey of primary materials available in European languages regarding seamanship and maritime matters in the early modern period. A more comparative global perspective would include numerous works in Arabic, Chinese, Malay, and other Asian, African, and Native American languages. As scholarship expands in early modern global maritime culture, it is hoped that these comparative tasks will expand and clarify our understanding of maritime practices and cultures during this period.

CHAPTER THREE

Networks

Transoceanic Sea Routes and Early Modern Media Studies

DAN BRAYTON

The first two decades of the twenty-first century have witnessed the increasing prominence of social networks connecting individuals and organizations on a vast scale, disseminating information, memes, ideologies, and red herrings. So what, then, is a network? At the most basic level, a network is a system that links disparate elements through structures of circulation and exchange. The internet makes possible countless social networks, from friend groups to chat groups and book groups and online news outfits and political organizations composed of affiliated individuals and their personal computers. Networks of elective affinity (of varying coherence) proliferate within an electronic infrastructure that is at once a network in its own right and a medium. Social networks are thus, in a sense, meta-networks, and as such require differentiation from the Web itself as the platform that enables the creation of countless formal and informal organizations. An electronic network functions—and exists—by means of a coordinated set of sub-media—hardware and software—enabling the modalities of circulation. The differences between these two orders of network, the one an infrastructure enabling the exchange of ideas, memes, jpegs, pdfs; the other a particular social group that only exists by means of this digital infrastructure, is a question of media theory.

The notion of a hyper-mediated biosphere in which the nonhuman and the anthropogenic are profoundly intertwined surely characterizes the planetary environment in the twenty-first century. As John Durham Peters notes in a recent book retheorizing media (2015: 2), ours is a world in which "the ozone layer, the Arctic ice, and whale populations are all now what they are not only because of how they are covered by reporters, but because of how their being is altered by media, understood as infrastructures of data and control." Yet the media that enable—indeed constitute—modern social networks are not the first to create new transnational networks of exchange and thereby shrink the space-time experience of the global. In Peters's theorization, "media, understood as the means by which meaning is communicated, sit atop layers of even more fundamental media that have meaning but do not speak"; thus, "the idea that media are message-bearing institutions such as newspapers, radio, television, and the Internet is relatively recent in intellectual history" (2, 4). What might we gain by employing an older and less anthropocentric notion of the media that encompasses what Peters terms "the elemental legacy of the media concept" (4), turning instead to histories of earth, air, fire, and water? A theory of media attuned to the historical complexities of the human-environment interface returns us to fundamental and perennial problems of communication and civilization, opening up new horizons for media studies. For "digital devices," Peters argues, "invite us to think of media as environmental, as part of the habitat, and not just as semiotic inputs into people's heads" (4). While this characterization of the interplay between the material substrate and anthropogenic circuitry of global networks would seem to belong to a post-internet world, it is an interplay with an early modern history ripe for reconsideration.

For surely the elements—earth, air, fire, and water—represent an older theory of media that those of us who partake of the hyperreal digital world forget at our peril. Just as surely, the early modern expansion of human activity into pelagic space—a mid-ocean realm previously inaccessible to all but a few cultures—relied upon the conceptual mastery of fluid media on a global scale. "To understand media," Peters suggests, "we should start not on land but at sea" (53). And so we do. The media that interest me here are the liquid flows that enabled the early modern sea routes. Air and water, as every physicist, aviator, and sailor knows, are fluid media that enable myriad forms of human enterprise and exchange. Governed by the same laws of fluid dynamics and planetary forces (e.g., the Coriolis effect), the movement of air and water distributes massive quantities of energy in consistent, if not entirely predictable, patterns on the surface of the world's oceans.

A history of the networks created by early modern world-making requires a history of winds, currents, and of the conceptual mastery of these phenomena, as revealed in visual and literary texts ranging from world maps and pilot charts to plays and poems. For the transoceanic sea routes established by early modern navigators were the first truly global social network, an internet of seasonal circuits built upon the fluid media of wind and water, that in turn proved generative in the arena of cultural production. Beginning in the early fifteenth century, the establishment of these networks began connecting continents in hitherto unimaginable—or perhaps only imaginable—ways, as new aquatic pathways proliferated to form a network of seaports and sea routes spawning new polities, contact zones, empires, and narratives. Winds and currents became, for early moderns, a vast system of energy that would enable the creation of equally vast networks of human exchange. This history has only been partially told.

In this chapter I excavate the genealogy of early modern transoceanic sea routes in terms of *media studies*, arguing that the conceptual mastery of the subtropical ocean gyres by early modern navigators transformed the fluid media of winds and waters into qualitatively new global networks of exchange. Early modern sea routes formed a global network built upon geophysical energy flows that were media networks in their own right and formed the basis for new modalities of intercontinental communication and interaction. These routes, which were both real patterns of wind and water as well as abstracts circuits laid out on charts and world maps, as well as in the minds of navigators, were the "fundamental media" upon which a vastly ambitious new system of circulation and exchange would be built. Instead of pursuing the global trajectories of mariners such as Diaz, Columbus, Da Gama, Cabral, and Magellan, I shall explore the representation of *fluid media* and sea routes as overlapping global networks in a handful of sixteenth- and seventeenth-century literary and cartographic texts.

FLUID MEDIA

Photos of the earth taken from space reveal a singular feature of our planet, the atmosphere, which is visible to the naked eye in the form of vast cloud formations shaped by weather patterns on an enormous scale. In *Earthrise at Christmas*, a photo shot in 1968 by the astronauts of Apollo 8, the earth appears as a demi-orb, covered in white-and-blue streaks, emerging from a shroud of darkness.[1] Moisture covers most of the visible portion of the planet's surface like a mottled white blanket with bright patches of the blue ocean discernible in the gaps between the clouds. The atmosphere, the planet's enveloping layer of gases, densest at sea level, carries an immense amount of water in its lower depths, then gradually thins to nothingness within approximately 485 kilometers of the surface of the earth—after which is space. The viewer of this astonishing new vista beholds a world whose surface is dominated by fluid dynamics. As the great oceanographer Sylvia A. Earle puts it in the title of her book, "the world is blue" (2010). Yet even *Earthrise* fails to represent the dynamic nature of the fluids that cover this planet, for the atmosphere is a constantly moving sheath of moisture in dynamic interaction with the denser moisture of the ocean beneath. A photo is a synchronic image, a static moment fossilized in time; to capture the intimately interconnected dynamics of oceanic and atmospheric phenomena a video clip would be far more effective by allowing the viewer to take follow the complex movements of the fluid media that cover this planet. *Earthrise* challenges us to reconceive what we mean by *the world*.

The world is made, not given, a concept that depends upon models of planetary totality. In early modern Europe, conceptions of the world were highly contested and continually subject to revision. As Ayesha Ramachandran has recently argued, "it would be no exaggeration to identify the central intellectual task of the late Renaissance, which affected all aspects of early modern life and thought, as the problem of 'the world' itself" (2015: 6). New discoveries of all kinds—geographic, anatomical, cultural—cast doubt on traditional cosmology, throwing early modern European intellectual life into crisis. Traditional understandings of heaven and earth no longer seemed sufficient. World-making, as Ramachandran describes it, was a form of "planetary imagining," or more specifically, "the methods by which early modern thinkers sought to imagine, shape, revise, control, and articulate the dimensions of the world" (6). What interests me about the early modern world-making project is the ways in which cartographers, playwrights, and poets attempted to incorporate such ephemeral planetary features as wind, waves, and clouds into their work in new ways. The ability to apprehend the world as a visual object and to imagine it as a totality was a key part of early modern cultural processes engaged in reimagining the earth as a finite globe.

In his history of European cartography Lloyd A. Brown (1949: 150) argues that, between the middle of the fifteenth century and the end of the sixteenth, "three of the most important events in modern history occurred": the development of the printing press, the voyages of Columbus, and the dissemination of Ptolemy's *Geographia* by means of the new print technology. Print culture, pre-Christian geography, and transoceanic voyages combined to expand the world of a sudden; soon they would combine to shrink it by connecting peoples across oceans by means of mutually constitutive media—biophysical and cultural. All three of these developments contributed to the project of world-making that Ramachandran describes. If globalization can be defined as the establishment of a series of planetary networks enabling material and symbolic exchange beyond traditional geographic barriers, then these three developments were its conditions of possibility.

Oceanography and meteorology have played a minor role in the historiography of early modern world-making. Until the advent of environmental history as a subfield, few scholars acknowledged the central significance of winds and currents in the establishment of global sea routes. One exception to this trend, historian Felipe Fernandez-Armesto, tellingly argues for the significance of biophysical limitations on human endeavors: "To master an oceanic environment, you have to penetrate the secrets of its winds and currents. Throughout the age of sail—that is, for almost the whole of human history—geography had absolute power

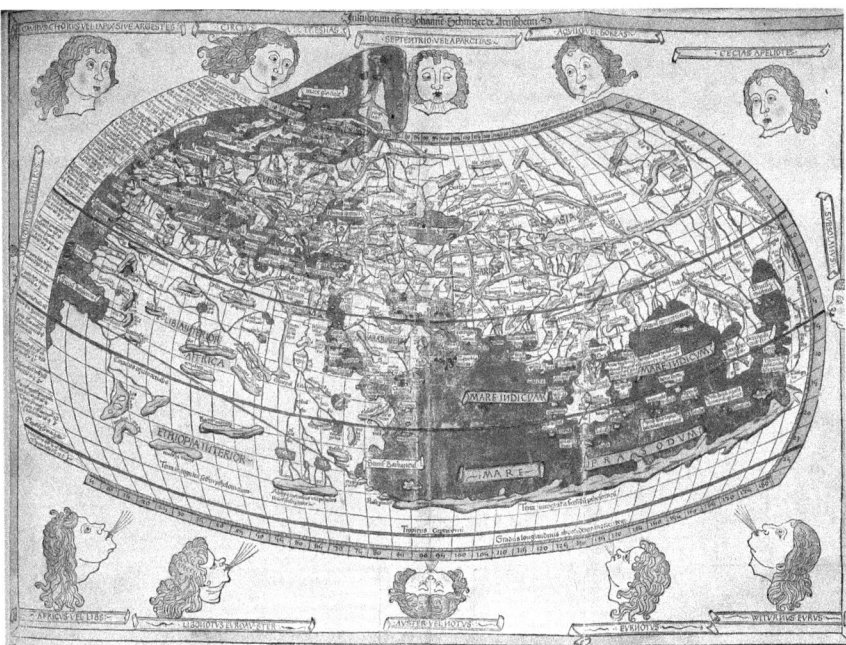

FIGURE 3.1 *Ptolemaic World Map*, 1482. © Bible Land Pictures / Alamy Stock Photo.

to limit what man could do at sea" (2006: 149). By "geography" Fernandez-Armesto means oceanography and meteorology as well as the size and contours of continents and oceans; thus, he concludes, "in most of our explanations of what has happened in history, there is too much hot air and not enough wind" (149). A history of the elemental media of early modern world-making, then, requires a history of wind, not merely in terms of the rise of meteorology, well chronicled by meteorologist Marc Monmonier (1999), but an account of the representation of fluid media over the *longue durée* of European maritime expansion. In his mappa mundi, Ptolemy depicts a world *blown into being* by a host of surrounding wind-blowers whose breath metonymically evokes the atmosphere (Figure 3.1). Historians have only occasionally contributed to the history of wind; next to no attention has been paid to the surface effects of the winds, waves, and currents, which have a profound impact on navigation, on limiting the paths that mariners could choose for ocean transit.

The pioneering of sea routes by early modern navigators was never merely a matter of going in the right direction, for pathways at sea are defined by prevailing winds and currents. No sailing vessel can sail directly into the wind; early modern sailing vessels, whether *nao* or *caravela* (later, galleon and *fluyt*), made very little headway against an adverse wind. Sailing off the wind, by contrast, any of these ship models could average five to eight knots in favorable conditions. Discovering a watery path to the Indies involved a centuries-long effort to understand the physical dynamics of the ocean. As the historian J.H. Parry noted, "the Great Age of Discovery was essentially the age of the discovery of the sea" (1974: xii) by which he meant the open ocean. For Parry, "the discovery of the sea, in the sense of the discovery of continuous sea passages from ocean to ocean, was a European, specifically an Iberian achievement" (xii). Indeed, the immensely long transoceanic passages of Diaz, Columbus, Da Gama, and Magellan were in large part determined by shifting winds and moving waters. What truly distinguishes the astonishing voyages of these (mostly Portuguese) mariners, according to Parry, was not the discovery of "the uninhabited and the unknown" so much as the "linking, by usable maritime routes, [of] separate areas of the inhabited and the known" (xii–xiii). The term "linking" is key here, for the sea routes pioneered by these navigators and their crews formed, by the early sixteenth century, a new, growing, and genuinely global network that enabled the propagation of myriad new commercial networks. Sea routes themselves were composed of a congeries of prior existing networks both anthropogenic and natural.

This structure of overlapping networks, a mix of cultural practices overlaid upon complex geophysical systems, emerged rapidly in the fifteenth century, which Parry describes as "The Age of Reconaissance":

> In a hundred years or so of maritime reconnaissance European seamen linked together nearly all the major existing areas of seaborne communication. They did so not by chance discovery, by blundering and drifting where winds and currents took them, but by systematic navigation—crude navigation, certainly, but accurate enough to enable them to return on their tracks, and their successors to follow them in regular voyages; so that eventually the existing networks were embraced in a super-network, so to speak, of known ocean routes encircling the world. (xiv)

The "super-network" developed by early modern navigators denotes the sum total of sea routes by which ocean going vessels would traverse the globe under sail for some four centuries after the celebrated voyages of Da Gama and Columbus. These routes could only be established as optimal courses for ocean transit through particular latitudes by the slow accumulation of knowledge gleaned from hard experience and deposited in the cartographic archive.

Crossing the Atlantic is fundamentally unlike sailing in the Mediterranean, which has almost no discernible tides (with some local exceptions with tidal ranges of a foot or two). To leave the Mediterranean for the far vaster and more tumultuous waters of the Atlantic was to enter a zone of fluid dynamics on a vast scale. Although recent historical studies of the Mediterranean, such as *The Corrupting Sea* by Horden and Purcell (2000), emphasize its regional and cultural heterogeneity, to a sailor the region presents a finite and familiar set of features. As Ernle Bradford notes in his encompassing *Mediterranean: Portrait of a Sea*, "Two factors in particular distinguish the Mediterranean from the oceans of the world. The first and most important of these is the comparative absence of tides throughout the area" (1971: 33) (the second is its high salinity). Tides, scarcely a presence in Mediterranean waters, have an immense effect on Atlantic navigation. The comparatively vast tidal ranges of the Atlantic make exiting and entering seaports such as Lisbon, Brest, and Le Havre a more challenging proposition than, say, docking at Valencia or Dubrovnik. Similarly, the winds, waves, and currents of the Atlantic follow completely different patterns—on a vaster scale—than they do in the Mediterranean, where the winds are quite local. To a sailor, the Mediterranean is a very large and very salty lake; the Atlantic, by contrast, names but one part of the far vaster world ocean.

For millennia Mediterranean sailors relied on seasonal winds with markedly regional characteristics. The *Meltemi*, for example, a strong northerly wind both powerful and fickle, dominates the Aegean, rendering the Cyclades a difficult archipelago for sailors. In the western Mediterranean, the *Mistral* howls southwards from the Alps, dictating when mariners can safely ply the waters of the Balearic and Ligurian Seas. Likewise, the *Scirocco*, a hot, strong wind off the Sahara, determines a sailor's experience of the North African coast. And so it goes with any number of local, periodic winds that are so distinctive as to bear proper names throughout the region. These periodic winds are often brief and violent, and in most regions they are punctuated by calms of long duration that make long passages difficult for sail-powered vessels. Hence the need for galley slaves and other rowers throughout Mediterranean history—at least, until the advent of steam and diesel engines. To leave the Mediterranean and enter the Atlantic was to cross into a fundamentally different world dominated by hitherto-unimagined forces and patterns of flow. The novel achievement of the early modern navigators who ventured beyond the Gulf of Cadiz and the so-called "Mediterranean Atlantic" between Cape St. Vincent and the Pillars of Hercules in the course of the long fifteenth century was an act of practical world-making. Early modern mariners learned to exploit vastly different circulatory patterns than those of the Mediterranean, eventually employing those patterns to bypass the African continent. The challenge was both physical and conceptual, requiring feats of endurance and the accumulation of nautical data over centuries.[2]

Early encounters with the Atlantic often proved fatal. When the Genoese brothers Vadino and Ugolino Vivaldi put the Pillars of Hercules behind them in search of a sea route around Africa after the fall of Acre in 1291, they ushered in a new era for European navigators. They set themselves an impossible task, for without knowing the patterns of prevailing ocean winds they had to rely on coastwise navigation, and coasting around the African continent under sail was wildly perilous for vessels powered by medieval technology. The Brothers Vivaldi never returned, but less than half a century later, in 1336, Lanzarote

Malocello followed suit and happened upon the Canary Islands (one island in that group is named for him) (Crosby 2006: 71). Thereafter the nautical peoples of western Europe, Italians, Catalans, Castilians, Portuguese, and French, embarked on a vast oceanic quest that necessitated a certain set of navigational skills, not least among them understanding the dynamics of winds and tides in a distinctively new marine environment. No civilization before the Portuguese in the fifteenth century had ever harnessed the vast forces of the subtropical gyres to circumnavigate a continent—and, more importantly, returned to home port.

Traditional European navigation was resolutely coastal and based on "the harbor-finding art." Diaz, Cabral, and Da Gama overthrew this paradigm by mastering the North and South Atlantic gyres, successfully doubling the Cape of Storms (later relabeled *Bona Speranza*). When Da Gama clawed his way through the squally variables off the southeast African coast and entered the monsoonal system of the northern Indian Ocean, navigation became a global phenomenon for the first time. The types of sailing vessel employed by the likes of Columbus and Da Gama, the *caravela* and the *nau*, or carrack, traveled at approximately five nautical miles per hour.[3] Even the most favorable breeze cannot push a caravel faster than about seven or eight knots, and conditions at sea are rarely ideal. Because of this limitation, a favorable ocean current could nearly double a ship's speed, while and adverse one could stop it in the water, as Ponce de Leon observed while bucking the Gulf Stream off Cape Coral in 1516 (Crosby 2006: 127–8). To transit an ocean or circumnavigate a continent, early modern mariners had to learn how to keep the winds and currents at their backs.

Until the series of voyages associated with the Portuguese Duke Henrique, later dubbed "the Navigator," nautical knowledge lay concentrated among mariners of diverse cultures in regions with long-standing cabotage and extremely rare transoceanic routes, such as those of the Arabian Sea, the mastery of which differed substantially from the knowledge required to cross the Atlantic or the Pacific. The merchant-navigators of the Arabian sea employed the monsoon, which in summer blows from the south toward the Indian subcontinent and in winter blows from the north; the east–west passage from the Arabian Peninsula, Mombasa, or Zanzibar to the Malabar Coast or to Java thus required a knowledge of seasonal winds. Arab traders in their *dhows* and *baghlahs* were monsoonal sailors who nearly always sailed on a beam reach, perpendicular to the wind, capturing it in their lateen sails on a long and steady port or starboard tack, depending on season and direction. North African and Arabic traders did not develop the squaresail for the simple reason that they rarely sailed directly downwind. By contrast, the European (specifically Iberian) caravel evolved, in the long fifteenth century, from a small lateen-rigged vessel, the *caravela latina*, to a larger vessel carrying a mixed rig of lateen and squaresails, the *caravela redonda*, to maximize efficiency on long downwind passages.[4]

To this local knowledge the Portuguese *marinheiros* added a crucial new navigational tool, the *Volta do Mar* ("turn to the sea") that allowed them to take advantage of the spiraling patterns of the gyre to sail downwind and, whenever possible, in the same direction as the prevailing surface currents. Environmental historian Alfred Crosby characterizes the *Volta do Mar* as the signal achievement of the Portuguese *marinheiros* during the long fifteenth century: "When the sailors of the Mediterranean and Iberia first into the pelagic waters beyond Gibraltar, they were familiar with only the winds of their home waters" (2006: 107–8). Quite simply, the Volta was a matter of turning a ship westward, out to sea, and sailing away from Portugal to find westerly breezes that prevail above about the thirty-fifth parallel. This was how the Madeiras and the Azores were discovered by *marinheiros,* steering west to escape the southward flow of wind and current off the northwest shoulder of the African continent. Once past the southward pull of the Canaries Current and Portuguese Trades one encounters the light and fluky variables of the North Atlantic High and, with patience, the westerlies that will waft any craft back toward the Iberian coast. The Volta was, in a nutshell, a means of exploiting the clockwise pattern of prevailing winds and currents in the North Atlantic Subtropical Gyre, an immense system of prevailing winds and currents flowing in a clockwise direction that dominates the prevailing conditions in the Atlantic from the variable and fluky Equinoctial Zone to the south, to the distinct Arctic system to the north.

At the center of this vast fluid swirl sits the Bermuda-Azores High, the high-pressure center that acts as the axis around which the Gyre spins. The High moves seasonally between Bermuda on the west and the Azores on the east; within the High, prevailing winds are light and variable. On the northern curve of the High, westerlies prevail; on the eastern shoulder, off Portugal, northerly winds prevail; to the south, the easterly Trade Winds offer a downwind run to the Antilles. Off the North American East Coast the prevailing summer winds are southwesterlies; the entire circuit holds steady as a permanent clockwise flow of winds and surface waters. Ocean current follows the same pattern as the winds. On the east side of the Gyre the Canary Current transports surface water southwards along the Iberian coast toward the Canary Islands and thence the Cape Verdes, in whose vicinity the vast surface river bends westward. Between the Cape Verdes and the Caribbean the surface waters flow west at approximately two miles per hour, propelled by the Trade Winds and what remains of the Canary Current. At the Lesser Antilles this path divides, with the Antilles Current flowing due west toward Central America, where it then hangs a right, northwards to the Yucatan and rushes almost to the Louisiana Coast and finally turns sharply east and south in a formation known as the Loop Current. After that it joins the Gulf Stream off Cape Coral. This relatively compact, intense pattern flow turns east between Cuba and the Florida Keys, where the

Gulf Stream races east then north into the Atlantic, from there gradually bearing right between Cape Hatteras and Nantucket Island to form the Azores Current and the North Atlantic Drift. After transiting the Atlantic the Azores Current makes its way toward Portugal and is then pulled southward into the Canaries Current, where it repeats the cycle.

Mariners planning to cross the North Atlantic study these patterns closely, seeking favorable conditions for sailing, which for traditional sailing vessels universally meant winds and currents from behind, but until the fifteenth century no human knew how to exploit these oceanic media or anything about them beyond a subset of local features of this system. Early modern navigators had no systemic, totalizing knowledge of the North Atlantic Subtropical Gyre, governed as it is by solar energy, the Coriolis Effect, and coastal boundaries on its eastern and western peripheries. But mariners had enough knowledge of certain parts of this system to exploit its major features; the great early modern navigators were those who divined enough of this system to use it to their own advantage. Columbus would have been hard pressed to cross the Atlantic at latitude 40° north, yet at the Tropic of Cancer he was wafted to the Antilles with relative ease. Finding the westerlies off what is now the East Coast of North America was critical to his return to Europe. Similarly, Diaz and Da Gama could not have found the southern end of the African continent without having realized that a gyre inverse to the one they knew from their home waters dominated the South Atlantic.[5]

The prevailing winds and currents of the great Atlantic gyres were the media by which the agents of early modern nation-states—navigators, planters, colonists, slavers—developed the constitutive networks of the modern world system. On the literal level, the physical oceanography of the great oceanic gyres constitutes a matrix of forces enabling voyages under sail. On the conceptual level, early modern mariners, cartographers, and patrons built a piecemeal understanding of how to harness these vast systems of moving fluids (air and water) in the centuries following the loss of the Crusades. This developing conceptual mastery of the massive systems known today as ocean gyres, evidenced by world maps, nautical charts, and imaginative literature, enabled the establishment of transoceanic sea routes. The story of this centuries-long piecemeal process of network-formation has rarely been told with physical oceanography taking center stage. The networks associated with globalization, whether economic, political, ecological, or cultural, have their origins in the long fifteenth century, when western European nation-states established new economic and political systems of transport, trade, and domination on a global scale. This set of networks originated as a series of separate but loosely linked networks of navigation, trade, and political negotiation. Yet these networks rest on physical structures pertaining to physical geography, meteorology, and oceanography, that form a basic geophysical infrastructure of energy to those capable of exploiting it—a bedrock matrix the conceptual mastery of which, in early modern Europe, made transoceanic voyages possible and increasingly frequent.

ROARERS AND SWEET AIRS

Early modern cartographers, playwrights, and poets often depicted fluid media in anthropomorphic fashion as *elements that speak*. Late medieval and early modern maps and charts were often illustrated with wind-blowers—cartoons of old men's or young children's faces—that personified the four (or eight, ten, or twelve) winds surrounding the world. As one cartographic historian notes, "on a tenth century map of the world in the Royal Library of Turin the four wind-blowers are human figures seated on Aeolus bags that bear a striking resemblance to nineteenth-century cannon" (Brown 1949: 99–100). Harkening to Homer's story of the wind-bag of Aeolus in *The Odyssey*, the wind-blowers that populate the margins of many a sixteenth-century world map mediate the human relationship to the cosmos; they reveal an environmental conception of the elements, for they surround the world. In one of the most vividly illustrated examples of this tradition, the 1515 world map by Johannes Stabius (see Figure 3.2), wind-blowers hover around the margins of the globe, blowing through—and perhaps speaking to—the spherical world. This anthropomorphization of the atmosphere recalls Peters's notion of the "elemental legacy of the media concept," for the winds are cosmic media.

FIGURE 3.2 Johannes Stabius, *World Map*, 1515. © Print Collector / Getty Images.

These wind-blowers are not merely fanciful illustrations that allude to the Homeric tradition but elemental figures of orientation, for the winds also denoted direction. A compass rose and a wind rose are one and the same (Brown 1949: 120–35). This model of the world as a globe surrounded by anthropomorphic forces transmitting supernatural messages by means of the elements can readily be found in early modern imaginative literature as well as cartography.

William Shakespeare's works evince a model of elemental interconnectedness between the human and the nonhuman—a man in the moon, a sky that has a human face, winds with cheeks, and waves that roar like beasts or angry men. In *Hamlet*, for example, the proverbial calm before a storm is described in terms of an unnatural quiet, a moment when the winds stop speaking: "we often see, against some storm / A silence in the heavens, the rack stand still, / The bold winds speechless, and the orb below / As hush as death, anon the dreadful thunder / Doth rend the region" (2.2.507).[6] How is it possible to see "a silence in the heavens?" Only if the winds are imagined as living and breathing. The winds here are in the plural as is often the case in Shakespeare's writings, personified as "bold" and "speechless," implying that their temporary silence is uncharacteristic. The notion of the winds as supernatural forces capable of speech animates a similar passage in *Pericles, Prince of Tyre* when the eponymous prince prays during a storm: "The god of this great vast, rebuke these surges / Which was both heaven and hell; and thou that hast / Upon the winds command, bind them in brass, / Having called them from the deep!" (3.1.1–4). Here the sea itself is "this great vast," while the waves, "these surges," are subject to "rebuke." Natural phenomena are again personified (a surge can only be rebuked if it is personified). If the winds can be commanded then they must be capable of sentience. Shakespeare's anthropomorphic winds have a thoroughly classical and cartographic basis in Homer and in mapmaking.

Shakespeare's awareness of air and water as fluid media is apparent throughout his writings. In *Troilus and Cressida*, the character Nestor compares the courage of soldiers and sailors in battling the elements as a trial by fluids: "But let the ruffian Boreas once enrage / The gentle Thetis, and anon behold / The strong-ribb'd bark through liquid mountains cut, / Bounding between the two moist elements / Like Perseus' horse: where's then the saucy boat / Whose weak untimber'd sides but even now / Co-rivall'd greatness?" (1.4.488–93). Boreas is the classical name for the north wind, while Thetis was a sea goddess (and the mother of the Greek hero Achilles). Here Thetis personifies the sea. Thus, Nestor describes a sudden squall or tempest as an argument between two supernatural beings arguing, inviting his audience to imagine a boat ("the strong-ribb'd bark") as a horse "bounding between the two moist elements" of air and water. This description reveals the extent to which Shakespeare understood air and water as fluid media that interact in the marine environment.

In similar fashion, in *The Tempest*, a play in which the action takes place during an interrupted sea voyage, we behold an animated cosmos populated by elemental characters and a fluid dynamics of confusion. Etymologically, confusion refers to the flowing together of waters: in *The Tempest* air and sea are signifying media through which occult forces operate through acoustic confusion, for human and nonhuman actors flow through one another (*OED Online*, s.v. "confusion"). The opening and closing scenes depict wind and breath as synonymous. The first stage direction in the play indicates "a tempestuous noise of thunder and lightning heard." Right away the visual and acoustic are muddled, as are the human and the nonhuman. The closing lines of the play, delivered by Prospero as The Prologue, offer a plea for the breath of the audience to act as a favorable breeze: "Gentle breath of yours my sails / Must fill, or else my project fails" (5.1.329–30). Again, one aspect of human (and animal) life, is indistinguishable from a feature of the biophysical environment—the winds.

Scene 1 opens with a ship at sea suddenly beset by the eponymous storm. When a defiant Boatswain shouts to the storm, "Blow till thou burst thy wind, if room enough," he apostrophizes the elements, a confusion of winds and waves, inviting the audience to imagine the wind-blowers that often surrounded sixteenth-century world maps (Brayton 2012: esp. ch. 7, pp. 166–95). As the professional mariners try everything in their power to avoid shipwreck on a lee shore, a group of meddling Neapolitan aristocrats interrupts their work, and the Boatswain shouts at them: "What cares these roarers for the name of king?" (1.1.16). The breaking seas and shrieking winds of the eponymous storm are "roarers." "If you can command these elements to silence," the Boatswain tells Gonzalo, "we will not hand a rope more—use your authority" (1.1.21–3). The Boatswain, who shouts commands at his crew and yells at the passenger, is an elemental character who resembles the storm; he, too, is a roarer. The physical description of the Boatswain paints his puffed visage in graphic terms. The villain Antonio accuses the Boatswain of drunkenness by calling the latter a "wide-chopped rascal," suggesting that his full cheeks and big mouth are as dangerous as the storm (1.1.56). To this charge the Neapolitan courtier Gonzalo replies "He'll be hanged yet / Though every drop of water swear against it / And gape at wid'st to glut him" (1.1.57–9). In this bizarre image we are invited to imagine drops of water as voiced beings capable of swearing and glutting (swallowing) a human form.

Later, when Prospero vows to punish the rebellious Caliban, Stefano, and Trinculo, he exclaims, "I will plague them all, / Even to roaring," and when he subsequently makes good on his threat the sprite Ariel observes, "Hark, they roar" (4.1.192–3; 4.1.262). In these scenes, roaring is a kind of elemental self-expression born of a confusion of voices and purposes. The sky of *The Tempest* is an animated one; Miranda exclaims that the sea "mount[s] to th' welkin's cheek," further developing the imagistic connection between the "wide-chopped" Boatswain and elements that roar (1.2.4). An eerie mirroring effect links the sailor with the storm, for here too the sky has cheeks and the atmosphere speaks, sings, and roars. Like the argumentative Boatswain, the winds converse with characters. Miranda recalls being set adrift with her father aboard "a rotten carcase of a butt" (a derelict small boat) twelve years before as a conversation with the winds: "There they hoist us / To cry to the sea that roared to us, to sigh / To th' winds, whose pity, sighing back again, did us but loving wrong" (1.1.158–61). Here again the fluid media communicate, not in fully articulate language but as breath.

Characters in *The Tempest* are ontologically connected to the elements (the Boatswain as wind-blower), and the elements can speak. The fluid media take human form in the character of Ariel, an "airy sprite" whose invisibility only highlights the ebb and flow of fluid dynamics. Auden described Ariel as being "neither a singer, that is to say a human being whose vocal gifts provide him with a social function, nor a nonmusical person who in certain moods feels like singing. Ariel is song; when he is truly himself, he sings" (Auden 1950: 64). Ariel is equally compounded of air and water; Prospero commands, "Go, make thyself like a nymph o'th'sea" (1.2.301). Ariel groans, murmers, howls, and "flame[s] amazement" (1.2.287, 294, 296, 198). Because Ariel is invisible to all save Prospero, the stranded characters with whom "he" interacts struggle to locate the source of the "strange airs" that surround them. The Neapolitan Prince Ferdinand wonders aloud, "Where should this music be?—I'th'air or th'earth?" (1.2.288). Later, Prospro asks Ariel, "Has thou, which art but air, a touch, a feeling / Of their afflictions?" (5.1.21–2). Sound and breath enact magic throughout *The Tempest*, allaying the illusory storm, confusing Prospero's adversaries, enabling the royal marriage of Miranda and Ferdinand (hence of Milan and Naples), and eventually wafting the Neapolitan fleet back to home port.

The Tempest is an elemental play. It is easy to identify the Boatswain with water, Ariel with Air, Caliban with earth (Prospero addresses him as "Thou earth, thou"), and Prospero with fire (1.2.314). Yet we can also see Ariel and the Boatswain as dramatizations of cartographic wind-blowers reconceived as theatrical characters; the one roars, the other sings, and both play a key role in Prospero's machinations to get his dukedom back. These are not the only forms taken by the fluid media, for the island is enveloped in fluid dynamics over which Prospero exercises control. "I have bedimmed / The noontide sun," boasts Prospero in a famously borrowed passage, "called forth the mutinous winds, / And twixt the green sea and the azured vault / Set roaring war" (5.1.41–2). Yet we might well ask if this is a passage borrowed from Golding's translation of *Medea* or a passage describing the elemental *media*. For Prospero's "rough magic" is explicitly figured as the mastery of the elements, particularly air and water, an art that derives from an understanding of the *elements as fluid media*

(5.1.50). At play's end Prospero, who can "command these elements to silence," prefigures the power of Enlightenment rationalism to banish the winds from the wings of the theater of the world (1.1.21).

NAUTICAL MEDIA

It is not only in early modern imaginative literature that representations of oceanic space evince an awareness of sea routes as world-making media networks. I now turn to a chart of the Pacific drawn by the great Dutch cartographer Hessel Gerritsz in 1622, just six years after the death of Shakespeare. Gerritsz was a brilliant artist and cartographer now largely overlooked. Appointed cartographer to the Verenigde Oost Indische Compagnie (VOC), the Dutch East India Company, and also head of the VOC's Hydrographical Office, Gerritsz produced a series of cartographic masterpieces at a moment when Dutch navigation in the Eastern Hemisphere was outstripping that of the Iberians as well as the English and French. For a decade he charted overseas regions of particular interest to Dutch merchants and mariners—the Indonesian Archipelago, Sumatra, and the Baltic.[7] Most noteworthy about his work, for my purposes, is his innovative use of illustrations to convey key oceanographic and meteorological information to those who knew how to look. To my knowledge this aspect of his *oeuvre* has never been discussed.

Gerritsz's 1622 *Chart of the Pacific* celebrates the 1615 to 1617 circumnavigation by Jacob Le Maire and Joost Schouten, whose busts look down benignantly from the top of the tableau (see Figure 3.3). Gerritsz depicts the coastlines of the Pacific rim, from North and South America to Japan and parts of New Guinea, as well as the major island groups of Oceania. Three Dutch fleets sail through distinct regions of the Pacific, north, east, and south. Not only are the sailing vessels depicted with extraordinary accuracy, their sail configurations perfectly matched to the prevailing conditions in the waters where they are located, but the cartographer has expended an enormous amount of talent and energy into representing the texture and movement of the ocean's surface in a lovely indigo. By scrutinizing the sea state and the ships themselves we can learn a good deal about the conditions experienced by the Dutch (Schouten, Le Maire, Van Diemen) whose observations made the chart possible. The *Chart of the Pacific* offers a ship-in-a-bottle display of technical information of great value to mariners. The apparently decorative illustrations also offer an object lesson in early modern media studies.

Moving from north to south, we first encounter a fleet plying the waters between Japan and Baja California (inaccurately located on roughly the same latitude). Four ships head east, while a fifth, having lost its mizzenmast, points in the opposite direction, clearly in distress. The confused sea state and disabled vessel suggest that a squall has just past, suggesting that sailors should proceed with caution in this region. Indeed, that the waters between about latitude 25–30° north, known as the Horse Latitudes, are notorious for their variable, fluky winds, sudden squalls, and long calms. For sail-powered vessels these were inauspicious waters, tempestuous and variable, to be avoided. Next we see a proud group of three *fluyts* sailing due west near the Galapagos, with their main trucks just scraping the Equator, quaintly labeled in Latin and Dutch as "*Linea Equinoctialis dat is de Middelijn*." Standing forth under all plain sail, the ships bowl along through the easterly Trade Winds that predominate in those waters, renowned among sailors for their propitious combination of strength and steadiness (Crosby 2006: 104–44).

While these painstakingly detailed drawings might, at first glance, appear to be mere illustrations or embellishments of the sort that was common on *mappae mundi* and portolan charts throughout the sixteenth and seventeenth centuries (particularly on so-called "princely charts"), they are in fact technically precise illustrations of the prevailing conditions in the precise regions of the Pacific where they are placed. The point is worth emphasizing: Gerritsz drew ships not as illustrations but as a graphic means of describing the prevailing winds and currents of the North and South Pacific. Moreover, the colorful illustrations of the sea's surface in varying weather conditions, from the moderate Trades of the three-ship fleet near the Galapagos to the gale-force westerlies in the South Pacific, are a rigorous attempt to convey crucial information about the characteristic wind strength and sea state in those regions. The precise details of Gerritsz's drawings provide exceptionally accurate information about the prevailing physical oceanography and meteorology of the North and South Pacific Subtropical Gyres. They are in fact illustrations of the fluid media that the agents of the VOC needed to master in order to ply the spice trade in the Indies.

But it is the flotilla of five ships on the bottom of the chart that has the most to teach us about the waters through which they sail. These ships carry only main and fore course (the lowest squaresails), a clear indication of heavy winds. The cartographer has given his viewer a precise image of a heavy-weather tactic used by tall ships—a tactic that Shakespeare describes in the first scene of *The Tempest*. As the Neapolitan ship struggles to stay off a lee shore, the Boatswain commands the sailors to lower the main topmast: "Down with the topmast," he roars, "Yare! Lower, lower!" Then he shouts, "Bring her to try with main course" (1.1.33–4). Gerritsz has drawn one ship with a mizzen topmast that has been lowered (or blown off), the one farthest to the west. To bring a ship to try meant steering an upwind course with just the lowest sail or sails; this is exactly what the three easternmost ships are doing in Gerritsz's chart, as they strive to "make westing" off the dangerous coast of Patagonia (their topmasts are still rigged).[8] The dangerous sea state that surrounds the ships illustrates the powerful winds and enormous waves that prevail in the notorious Great Southern Ocean, a region known among mariners in terms of the winds at specific latitudes: the Roaring Forties, Howling Fifties, and Screaming Sixties. In this part of the world, known only to the occasional Polynesian navigator before Magellan, the winds blow for thousands of miles without impediment and waves build along the planet's longest fetch.[9]

Gerritsz provides technical information about prevailing winds and characteristic sea states in specific regions of the Pacific using a metonymic strategy, by drawing ships that have adjusted their sails and rigging to the size of the waves and the force of the winds. Yet he also devotes painstaking attention to empirical description, most spectacularly in his drawings of the ocean's surface. The waves, eddies, wakes, ripples, spray, and spume of the *Chart of the Pacific* are faithfully rendered with extraordinary verisimilitude—to such an extent that any scientific illustrator would be proud to claim them. The ships just north of the Tropic of Cancer sail through pods of whales, as the various spouts, ripples, and wakes suggest, with a light wind of perhaps Beaufort Force 2 or 3. To the south and east, the three-ship flotilla going westward has just picked up the Trades south of the equatorial variables; they run free, wafted by a lovely breeze of approximately Beaufort Force 3 or 4. In the Great Southern Ocean, by contrast, the sea state indicates a Fresh Gale, or even a Strong Gale, of Beaufort Force 8 or 9. The fact that any sailor could recognize these conditions at a glance testifies to Gerritsz's extraordinarily empirical artistry.

FIGURE 3.3 Hessel Gerritsz, *Chart of the Pacific*, 1622. © Wikimedia Commons (public domain).

The most striking ocean feature of the *Chart of the Pacific* is the steep wall of water off southern Chile. What matters here is the precise location of this steep and narrow wave, which is markedly different from other waves in the tableau. The captures the effects of a strong wind coming up against a surface current. This is exactly what happens off the southwest coast of Chile, where a powerful ocean current flows north from Antarctic waters, while the westerlies blow unabated. Gerritsz has depicted the Humboldt Current two hundred years before its "discovery" by the Prussian polymath Alexander Von Humboldt in 1846. Did Dutch mariners know of the Humboldt/Peru Current in 1622? Gerritsz certainly did. In all likelihood a mariner from the voyage of Schouten and Le Maire described for him the steep waves to the west of Cape Horn (named by Schouten for a headland in Holland). Gerritsz's systematic attempt to represent the dynamics of fluid media in the marine environment make the chart nothing less than a brilliant multimedia study of the complex dynamics of the winds and waves of the Pacific Ocean.

ART'S ELEMENTS

During the half-century between the first performance of *The Tempest* in 1609 to 1610 and the publication of Dryden's lengthy poem *Annus Mirabilis* in 1666, as the Dutch build their maritime empire in the East, a nascent empiricism begins to displace traditional notions of winds and waters as speaking elements—and with this semiotic regime shift the representation of fluid media also transforms. During the seventeenth century the oceans became a vast arena of geopolitical contention between rival maritime powers, especially the Netherlands and Britain, and the fluid media become inert, losing their Renaissance animation. In imaginative literature the elements become gradually less anthropomorphic, the roaring, singing winds and waves of *The Tempest* a thing of the Renaissance past. John Dryden's *Annus Mirabilis* recalls the events of the year 1666 in jingoistic fashion, offering a vision of England's bright future as a mercantilist imperial nation. A panegyric in heroic couplets, the poem celebrates England's apparently miraculous recovery from an outbreak of the plague, which was followed by the Great Fire of London and the outbreak of the Second Anglo-Dutch War. Dryden's aspirational verse account of recent history proclaims England's mastery of the high seas, offering victory at sea as an anodyne of sorts for the recent disasters and global expansion as the bright future that awaits the nation as compensation for its sufferings.

A crucial context for the mercantilist agenda Dryden describes is the rivalry between the English and the Dutch for control of the spice trade, particularly in eastern Indonesia. *Annus Mirabilis* is not just about events in London, or even England, but is instead a poetic commentary on a geopolitical struggle of global proportions. For in the first half of the seventeenth century, when the

Dutch muscled the Iberian powers (which were unified at the time) out of their nautical monopoly over the Spice Islands, establishing a lasting presence based in Batavia, the English sought a way into the spice trade. The national rivalry was often violent, as when the Dutch tortured and executed twenty rival trading agents at Ambon Island, in the Moluccas, in 1623, ten of whom were employees of the English East India Company. In 1665 the Dutch captured an English fort in the Banda Islands of South Sulawesi (modern Indonesia) (Ng 2012). The wars between the English and the Dutch in Europe and the Indies, argues Su Fan Ng, "were not regional but world events in the 1660s; they were connected contests over maritime dominance fought in many parts of the world" (356). Dryden's panegyric of English maritime ascendancy, Ng notes, was "written as propaganda for the Second Anglo-Dutch War" (356). Not surprisingly, then, *Annus Mirabilis* "has been read as both a poem of Nation and a poem of Empire" (356). International competition over control of transoceanic routes are thus a crucial context of the poem.

Dryden's poetic claims of English preeminence among those who "have used the open sea," while hardly supported by the historical record, are delivered in tripping iambs and full rhyme: "Of all who since have used the open Sea, / Than the bold English none more Fame have won; / Beyond the Year, 49 and out of Heav'n's high-way, / They make discoveries where they see no Sun" (lines 637–40). Although Drake's circumnavigation of 1577 to 1580 was only the second one undertaken, by the seventeenth century Dutch mariners ranged much further afield than the English. After Le Maire and Schouten discovered and named Cape Horn and explored the South Pacific, Abel Tasman, sailing for the VOC, left Batavia, coasted along northern and western Australia, discovered Tasmania, and came upon New Zealand, Fiji, the Melanesian Islands, and New Guinea between 1642 and 1644. Dryden adds a verse chapter to the ongoing debate about the freedom of the seas, then raging between Dutch adherents, such as Hugo Grotius, whose *Mare Liberum* ("The Free Sea") was published in 1609, and English claims to national control over territorial waters, as articulated by John Selden, who published *Mare Clausum* ("The Closed Sea") in 1635.

What interests me is Dryden's portrayal of English naval achievement in terms of a tactical understanding of the elements; the poet offers a sort of alternative cartography that situates English mariners on new nautical pathways enabled by the conceptual conquest of the ocean. Thus, Dryden proclaims, "The Ebbs of Tides and their mysterious Flow, / We, as Arts Elements shall understand, / And as by Line upon the Ocean go, / Whose Paths shall be familiar as the Land" (lines 646–9). Dryden depicts the "mysterious flow" of ocean currents as a purely tidal phenomenon, which is only largely incorrect, framing tidal currents as "Arts Elements," the understanding of which will enable ships to sail straight across the ocean sea. By "Art" Dryden means something more like "craft" or *tekne* than purely expressive art.[10] With this newfound understanding, the poet asserts, ships will transit the oceans on pathways "familiar as the Land": "Instructed ships shall sail to quick Commerce, / By which remotest Regions are alli'd; / Which makes one City of the Universe; / Where some may gain, and all may be suppli'd" (lines 650–4). Here Dryden presents the Enlightenment conceit of the world as a global commons, a perspective more in line with Grotius than with Selden.

The world, as Dryden realized, effectively shrank with the establishment of transoceanic sea routes between Europe and the colonies. Understanding the flows of oceanic "tides," Dryden understood, meant that global shipping would tighten the networks of commerce, command, and communication ocean voyaging. Dryden's triumphalist poem gestures, then, to the role of the fluid media on which the modern colonialist nation-state was built. By Ng's reading, "the globalized world closes distances to bring separate nations together in trade networks. Consequently, such a model of circulation or networks imagines cross-cultural ties built laterally" (2012: 376). *Annus Mirabilis* can, then, be read as an English riposte to the claims of Gerritsz' *Chart of the Pacific*, which clearly depicts the maritime ascendancy of the United Provinces as a function of such "lateral" learning.

SUBMARINE MEDIA AND THE MESSAGE IN A BOTTLE

If we learn nothing else from the media history of ocean transit I have been tracing, we should at least understand that what Dryden calls "Art's Elements" are historically contingent. The fluid media of winds and waters play a different role in cultural production today than they did before the development of self-propelled ocean going vessels powered by steam in the nineteenth century, and by diesel, gas, turbine, diesel-electric, and nuclear propulsion in the twentieth. The first successful transoceanic telegraph communication took place in 1858, made possible by the transatlantic cable. From that moment onward a new medium of international communication begins to displace the ship and, thus, the fluid sub-media on which the ship depends to reach its destination. What Peters calls "the elemental legacy of the media concept" moves into the wings of the theater of history. The tides no longer determine the fate of navies and nations; access to digital technology does. And yet such access remains oceanic, for the internet itself is made possible by a vast infrastructure of transoceanic cables. Hundreds of fiber-optic cables, spanning hundreds of thousands of kilometers, cross the ocean floor to make internet connectivity possible, yet even while data is transmitted through these cables by lasers at the speed of light, a nostalgia for older media haunts cultural production. Artists continue to imagine the significance of winds and waves in the transmission of meaning across oceanic space through the message-in-a-bottle leitmotif.

This nostalgia is itself nothing new. The message-in-a-bottle leitmotif recurs frequently in modern cultural production, from Poe's "MS Found in a Bottle" to the 1979 smash-hit song "Message in a Bottle," sung by the popstar Sting of The Police. More recently, Ruth Ozeki's novel *A Tale for the Time Being* (2013) coalesces around the conceit of a bottle thrown into the sea from Japan that finds its way to the coast of the Pacific Northwest, there to be opened and decoded by a future reader who pieces together the world of the letter's writer. On one level, the media at play in this scenario, "understood as the means by which meaning is communicated," to use Peters's phrase, consist of a brittle bottle made of glass (itself a fluid substance) and the ink-scratched paper or parchment contained inside. The enduring appeal of the motif, from Poe to Ozeki, surely derives from its association with shipwreck and other nautical contingencies from the age of sail. The medium is again the message, as the vessels of meaning transmission, bottle, paper, and ink "sit atop layers of even more fundamental media that have meaning but do not speak"—the sea and its fluid vectors. In the age of instant (and constant) electronic communication, the message-in-a-bottle motif enables an alternative history of modernity based on decoding messages delivered by means of slow haphazard long-distance communication in what remains of the world outside digital media. Set into perpetual motion by the winds, the surface of the sea transports objects—coconuts, castaways, bottles, and boats—across vast differences at a rate of speed that is utterly inimical to the instantaneity of the internet. The message-in-a-bottle speaks of divine providence, yet it just as surely acts as a symbol for the sea's historic role as the medium of global communication.

A nostalgia for the adventure of sea travel haunts cultural production even as the world shrinks and the networks by which humanity transcends its physical limitations grow ever-more sophisticated. One variant of the message-in-a-bottle is the *ship-in-a-bottle*, a pastime for old sailors and antiquarians; in this version of bottled seaborne transmission a nostalgic art form evokes a world before ocean transit by self-propelled vessels. In this instance the medium, a vessel in a brittle liquid vessel floating at the interface of two fluid media, is the meta-message, gesturing as it does to a human history of transoceanic voyages and exchanges. Longing for a bygone world in which crossing the ocean involved untold risk and adventure—when navigation entailed in Shakespeare's words, "A wild dedication of yourselves / To unpathed waters, undreamed shores" (*The Winter's Tale*, 4.4. 554–5)—we move deeper into the Anthropocene, where atmospheric carbon, ocean plastics, and multimedia conglomerates deploying satellites and submarine cables proliferate, shrinking the world still further. The deafening tumult of a world overrun with technology mutes but cannot silence the voices of winds and waters, those fundamental media that enable various forms of exchange between humans and the nonhuman world.

CHAPTER FOUR

Conflicts

Naval Wars, Violent Migrations, and Silent/Silenced Archives

DYANI JOHNS TAFF

Naval warfare, shipwreck, and piracy: these are the primary reasons for conflict on the early modern sea, and they are all bound intimately to slave labor and the rise of global capitalism.[1] In addition to increased naval fighting to secure fishing grounds, to protect or capture shipping lanes, or to make a show of national or monarchical strength, people, plants, and animals began to move more rapidly and to cover greater distances in the period 1500–1680. This increased movement and violence was made possible by improvements in sailing technologies. Steve Mentz has described this era as characterized by "catastrophic clashes of cultures, peoples, viruses, and ecosystems" (2015: xxvii). We are still grappling with the consequences of these conflicts in our own moment; current movements for environmental, social, racial, and indigenous justice address systemic wrongs with roots in early modern sea conflicts.

Well-studied naval conflicts on the early modern sea include the Battle of Diu (1509) in the Indian Ocean, the Mediterranean Battle of Lepanto (1571), the Spanish Armada's defeat by the British Navy (1588), the Anglo-Dutch wars (1652–74), and pirate and merchant raids on the increasingly global and maritime trade routes. These newsworthy conflicts made their way into epic and lyric poems and onto stages across the world, celebrating naval captains such as Zheng He, Vasco da Gama, or Francis Drake, and probing the implications of sea power for rulers, regions, and people. But naval war was not the only kind of conflict that mattered for early modern maritime cultures; coastal and island geography as well as currents, winds, and sea conditions shaped violent encounters between Ottomans, Africans, Inuit, Caribs, Inca, Indians, Chinese, Japanese, Europeans, and many others, and enabled Puritans, Jesuits, and Franciscans to bring their beliefs and their books into conflict with people and ideas around the world. The sea's violence and mystery served as a vehicle for writers who explored religious, political, and social conflict: poets and political theorists from Erasmus to Mary Wroth to John Milton wrote and rewrote Plato's metaphor of the ship of state. Writers used the antagonism between a ship and rocks, waves, or storms to figure clashes between Protestants and Catholics as well as between humans and God, ruler and subject, husband and wife, Spaniard and Englishman. The sea was a metaphor but it also materially shaped human conflicts via storms, calms, currents, hidden rocks, and so on. Humans cannot live on the sea forever. As one historian has remarked, waging war at sea is rarely about seizing and controlling territory; rather, naval conflict aims to control "economic lifelines, nodal points, and networks" (Wade 2005: 51). To write a cultural history of sea conflicts is also to excavate human representations of the maritime world that reveal bids to define a firm boundary between human and nonhuman but that also provide evidence that such a boundary was not a given.

The English word "conflict" had capacious cultural and symbolic meanings in the early modern period that add texture to my investigation of sea conflicts. The word comes into English from the Latin noun *conflictus* and the related verb *confligere* meaning to strike (*fligere*) together or with (*con-*), possibly via Old French (*OED Online*, s.v. "conflict," noun, def. 1–2 and verb, def. 1). From its earliest uses in English in the 1430s to 1440s, it could denote both physical struggle—"an encounter with arms; a fight, a battle" ("conflict, n." def. 1a)—as well as "a mental or spiritual struggle within a man" (def. 2b), and could be used as a verb to denote fighting, contending, or doing battle ("conflict, v." def. 1a; first citation *c.* 1475). Early science writers, such as Francis Bacon and Margaret Cavendish, drew on the connotations of "conflict" as aptly representing the struggles between hot and cold and between bodies and environments that they observed in their experiments in natural philosophy. Considering why water does not quench "Wild-fire," Bacon cites the example of volcanic activity in the coastal Italian city of Puzzuoli where "you shall heare, vnder the *Earth*, a Horrible Thundring of *Fire*, and *Water*, conflicting together" (1626: Dd1r). Bacon's point is that *"bitumen"* is made of forever-conflicting water and fire, making water ineffective in putting out the fire, whereas *"Sulphur"* is just fire, and hence quenchable by dousing. Cavendish is concerned not with the conflict of one element with another but rather with internal conflict that creates a change from water vapor to liquid to ice. In answer to a philosophical question from her fictitious, female interlocutor about why water breaks its vessels when it freezes, Cavendish asserts that "water being naturally dilative, when as cold attractions do assault it, the moist dilations of water in the conflict use more then their ordinary strength to resist those cold contracting motions, by which the body of water dilates it self into a larger compass, according as it hath liberty or freedom, or quantity of parts" (1664: Dddddd2r). Water, assaulted by cold, expands and bursts its holder, violently asserting its expansive nature.

Both Bacon and Cavendish were likely aware of Richard Eden's popular 1555 translation of Peter Martyr de Anghiera's *De orbe novo decades*, a collection of reports about Spanish exploration and conquest in central and south America in the post-Columbus period. Eden uses "conflict" to translate Martyr's Latin *certamen* and *bellum*, words for the clashes between indigenous Americans and Europeans, but he also uses this word to translate Martyr's *conflictatio,* a word that Martyr does not generally use to describe interpersonal violence. In recounting the wonders of Hispaniola, Martyr writes, "sed quia sint montesardui, tantam esse puto vim declinantium aquarum, vt impulse stagnantium ea fiat conflictatio, & ne falsae aquae ingrediantur in finum resistant" (1530: Fol. xxxv. r.). Eden renders this sentence: "And for as muche as the mountaynes are excedynge highe and stiepe, I think the violence of the faule of the waters to be of such force, that this conflicte between the waters, is caused by thimpulsion of the poole that the salte water can not enter into the goulfe" (1555: X.iv.v). With his translation choice, Eden connects human–human conflicts to elemental conflicts, centering the violence of fresh water slamming into the sea. Of Eden's approximately twenty-four uses of "conflict" in the whole of the *Decades*, half describe violence between Europeans and indigenous people, and the other half describe "conflictes of water" in one way or another, with occasional uses that blur the line between the two. For instance, after narrating Vasco Núñez de Balboa's "discovery" of the Pacific Ocean, seen from a Panamanian mountaintop, Martyr describes their dangerous winter sea voyage with the indigenous king Chiapes and his followers, with whom the Europeans had fought and made peace. Eden translates:

> Therfore as soone as they were nowe entered into the maine sea, such *sourges and conflictes of water* arose ageynst them that they were at theyr wyttes endes whither to turne them or where to reste. Thus beinge tossed and amased with feare, the one loked on the other with pale and vncherefull countenaunces. But especially Chiapes and his coompany, who had before tyme with theyr eyes seetle thexperience of those jeoperdies, were greatly discomforted. Yet (as god woolde) they escaped all, and landed at the nexte I|lande: Where makynge faste theyr boates, they rested there that nyght. (Z.iv.r–v, my emphasis)

Eden annotates this episode as indicating "The manly corage and godly zeale of Vaschus [Balboa]" as well as "The faithfulnes of kynge Chiapes" (1555: marginal notes, Z.iv.r). Despite Chiapes's and his peoples' warnings about the unnavigable winter sea, Balboa charges ahead, straining his alliance with Chiapes and endangering all of their lives. It seems a pigheaded move. Yet for Eden and perhaps for his European contemporaries, Balboa's decision bespeaks a divine mandate: his denial of "thexperience" of the indigenous people as well as his conflict with the violent environment are evidence of his "godly zeale." Miraculously, "as god woolde," all survive to continue the Spanish project of exploration and conquest. The "conflicte of waters" instigates "feare," discomfort, and I surmise, thoughts of mutiny among the humans "tossed" on the waves. Human emotions and bodies are depicted as microcosm of or in a porous relationship with the violent surroundings.[2] But Martyr also, contrastingly, positions the sea as an adversary, and Eden underscores this point with his marginal glosses. The sea is an obstacle that Balboa meets with heroic and religious "zeale" and which, when he survives the encounter, confirms his divinely sanctioned voyage. This episode indicates the complex relation of human to environment that underpins many representations of conflict at sea.

A catalog of the many conflicts that took place on or that were enabled by the early modern sea between 1500 and 1680 far exceeds my scope. Instead, I have gathered an eclectic set of examples—historical events, images, literary texts—with which to sketch a cultural history of maritime conflict. I focus in my first three sections on naval warfare and its representations, particularly in paintings and epic poetry, and then I turn to global violent encounters. In each section, I examine social conflicts that writers imagine or theorize by means of maritime metaphors. I have aimed for a global cultural history rather than a Eurocentric one, but I have been limited by my training in early modern English literature; as a result, my literary examples are primarily English and European. Though they are beyond my scholarly ambit, I have included African, American, and Asian texts, relying on and directing readers to other cultural historians' work. Because the early modern sea so often constitutes a violent cultural contact zone, gathering evidence from historically underrepresented sources, such as texts by women or oral histories or archeological records from cultures that either left no texts or whose texts were destroyed by Europeans, is vitally important to gaining a textured and decolonized understanding of the sea in early modern culture. Truly interdisciplinary work may be beyond my grasp here, but my examples will ideally prompt readers to pursue transcultural scholarship and to continue the work of making visible and audible previously invisible, inaudible records and voices.

THE BATTLE OF DIU

The Battle of Diu (1509), a conflict between Portuguese and allied Mamluk and Gujarati forces, was fought near Fort Diu on the northwest coast of India. Although it is a less well-known battle than the others listed in my introduction, popular historians refer to it as a battle that "changed the course of world history" (Chavan 2018) because it enabled the Portuguese to take their first imperialist steps into the Indian Ocean. But such accounts at best over-simplify the historical record and at worst reinscribe a Eurocentric view of the past (see Figures 4.1 and 4.2). Historian Sanjay Subrahmanyam demonstrates the value of resisting this view: taking as his focus letters and state papers of the Mamluk Empire and the Delhi Sultanate alongside records from Venice and Portugal, Subrahmanyam sees the Battle of Diu as one in a series of conflicts between the Portuguese and the Mamluks, who had allied with Malik Ayaz, a "semi-independent" ruler of the port of Diu and the region surrounding it (2007: 277). The Portuguese victory in 1509 was due not to any great strength or innovation of the Europeans but rather to the breakdown of the alliance and Ayaz's decision not to fight (272–3). Historians examining only Venetian and other European accounts of the Battle of Diu have recreated a Venetian worry about the Portuguese aim to blockade the Red Sea spice trade route. As Subrahmanyam argues, though, examining Mamluk and Gujarati sources shows that conflict about succession in Egypt created the interruption in trade that historians have seen, not the Portuguese (278). Giancarlo Casale further reveals an abiding but misleading tendency of modern historians to meld "Mamluk naval campaigns" and later "Ottoman operations" into a "single, continuous, and undifferentiated historical process" (2010: 32). Such a melding obscures that this battle was not a Portuguese victory against undifferentiated Muslim forces but rather a Portuguese victory as a result of Malik Ayas's shift in allegiance away from the Mamluks and toward the Ottomans (31). Casale sees this shift as one step toward the "Ottoman Age of Exploration" and global conflict: a war between the Ottomans and the Portuguese, staged in the Indian Ocean, where each country's proto-imperial desires had staked a political claim (27).

The story of Diu takes another turn when we consider Geoff Wade's discussion of the Zheng He voyages and other Chinese expeditions to the Indian Ocean in the late 1400s. Wade resists popular historians' classification of the Zheng He ventures as "voyages of friendship," showing that the Chinese had proto-colonial motives for these voyages and often used violent tactics in their encounters with new people (2005: 37, 78).[3] Indeed, violence from newcomers in ships might have prompted Gujarati rulers to build Fort Diu: Wade examines sources that assert "that the city of Diu was built by a king of Gujarat in memory of victory in a sea fight with the Chinese who had frequented

FIGURE 4.1 Plate, from Jerónimo Corte-Real, *Sucesso do Segundo Cerco de Diu* (Lisbon, 1574), p. 35r. © Courtesy of the Arquivo Nacional Torre do Tombo.

Indian shores …. These are … very likely references to the Zheng He fleets" (78). The Battle of Diu represents not a single, decisive moment of conflict and the confirmation of new Portuguese sea power, but rather a deadly fight in a series of global conflicts enabled by the early modern sea, with combatants from east, west, north, and south who sought to construct the Indian Ocean as a political space within their control. Diu represents one node in a network of early modern conflicts over sea power, but cannot be pointed to as the site of a battle that changed the world.

Luís de Camões and his European contemporaries might have disagreed.[4] In *Os Lusiadas* (1572), Camões celebrates Portuguese history, focusing what he sees as their manifest destiny as conquerors of "the degenerate / Lands of Africa and Asia" (*as terras viciosas / De Affrica, & de Asia*) ([1572] 1997: 1.2; 1572: A1r). In Canto 10, Camões lands his hero Vasco Da Gama and his men on a paradisal isle prepared for them by Venus and peopled with nymphs who become the men's "lovers" (*amantes*) (10.3; X1r). He allegorically genders female the lands that they have conquered. With their lovers, the men listen to Tethys "prophesy" Portuguese maritime pursuits up to Camões's own time. Tethys gives an account of the Portuguese captain Francisco de Almeida's actions in the Battle of Diu:

> Then sailing into the bay of Diu,
> Scene of famous battles and sieges,
> He will scatter the vast but feeble fleet
> Of Calicut that is powered by oars;
> While the ships of wary Melik-el-Hissa,
> Caught in a hail of cannon-fire,
> Will be relegated to their cold, dread
> Burial places on the ocean bed.
>
> (10.35)

> (*E logo entrando fero na enseada*
> *De Dio, illustre em cercos & batalhas,*
> *Farâ espalhar a fraca & grande armada,*
> *De Calecu, que remos tem por malhas:*
> *A de Melique Yaz acautelada,*
> *Cos pelouros que tu Vulcano espalhas,*
> *Farâ yr ver o frio & fundo assento,*
> *Secreto leito do humido elemento*)
>
> (X6v)

Camões has studied accounts of the battle but presents a version of it in which Malik Ayas does not withhold his ships, ensuring a Mamluk defeat. Rather, Malik engages in the sea battle with Almeida, and loses his ships to the "cold, dread" of the ocean floor.

Camões subsumes Indians and Mamluks under an undifferentiated rubric of religious and racial others. The narrator maintains that the Portuguese will easily conquer all of these others, for "Africa's land, ... and Oriental seas / [are]

FIGURE 4.2 Plate, from Jerónimo Corte-Real, *Sucesso do Segundo Cerco de Diu* (Lisbon, 1574), p. 165v. © Courtesy of the Arquivo Nacional Torre do Tombo.

The promised theatre of your victories" (*Comecem a sentir o peso grosso, ... De exercitos, & feitos singulars, / De Affrica as terras, & do Oriente os mares*) (1.15; A3v). In the "theatre" of the world, the Portuguese play the heroes: "On you the fearful Moor has his eyes, / Fixed, knowing his fate prefigured" and "At a glimpse of you, the unbroken / Indian offers his neck to the yoke" (*Em vos os olhos tem o Mouro frio, / Em quem ve seu exicio afigurado, / So com vos ver o barbao Gentio, / Mostra o pescoço ao jugo ja inclinado*) (1.16; A3v). The narrator distracts us from the bloody deaths of Africans and Asians by focusing on the great deeds of the Portuguese heroes, using religion to justify the violence of these encounters. The winds obey the prayers of the Portuguese sailors. In Canto 5 they "bellowed / 'God speed!' and the north winds as usual / Heard and responded, shifting the great hull" (*ceo ferimos, / Dizendo Boa biagem, logo o vento / Nos troncos fez or usado movimento*) (5.1; K7v). For Camões, telling a story about Portuguese national heroism requires both a description of divinely sanctioned control of the sea and also repeated disdain for Muslims and Indians to contrast with his assertions about the deeds of Lusitanian heroes.[5]

Camões's mythmaking in *Os Lusiades* participates in a nationalist project to control maritime lines of communication. Other cultures also forged myths connecting the human relationship to the sea with state formation or maintenance. Robert Wessing describes Cambodian, Sumatran, and Javanese traditions in which "the land or the state often originates from the waters of the underworld or needs the cooperation of its denizens" (2006: 211). One version of this tradition from the Kingdom of Mataram in Java details how its "founder, Panembahan Senopati, forged an alliance with Nyai Roro Kidul, the crowned *naga*-goddess [*naga* = snake in Indian myth, or half-snake, half-human] of the Southern Ocean .... Senopati reemerged from the waters of the Indian Ocean after a three-night tryst with the Goddess ... [and] his reemergence implies the coming into being of the state" (211). In Southeast Asia, an anonymous Malay writer recorded oral stories about the Melakan sultanate in a text called the *Sejarah Melayu* (see Figure 4.3), mythologizing the origins of their state's power with reference to some of these myths, as when the Indian Raja Chulan descends into the sea in a "glass case .... from within which he could see all that was outside," discovers living under the sea "a race of men, the Barsam, so numerous that no man, but only Almighty God could know how many they were," and marries the Raja's daughter (Brown 1970: 11).[6] Similarly, Sri Tri Buana, the eleventh-century founder of Singapore, survives a storm during his journey from Palembang by throwing his crown into the sea: "the boatswain said to Sri Tri Buana, 'It seems to me, your Highness, that it is because of the crown of kingship that the ship is foundering.' ... And Sri Tri Buana replied, 'Overboard with it then!' And the crown was thrown overboard. Therupon the storm abated, and the ship regained her buoyancy and was rowed to land" (20). In one sense, Raja Chulan's story differs from the others because he and

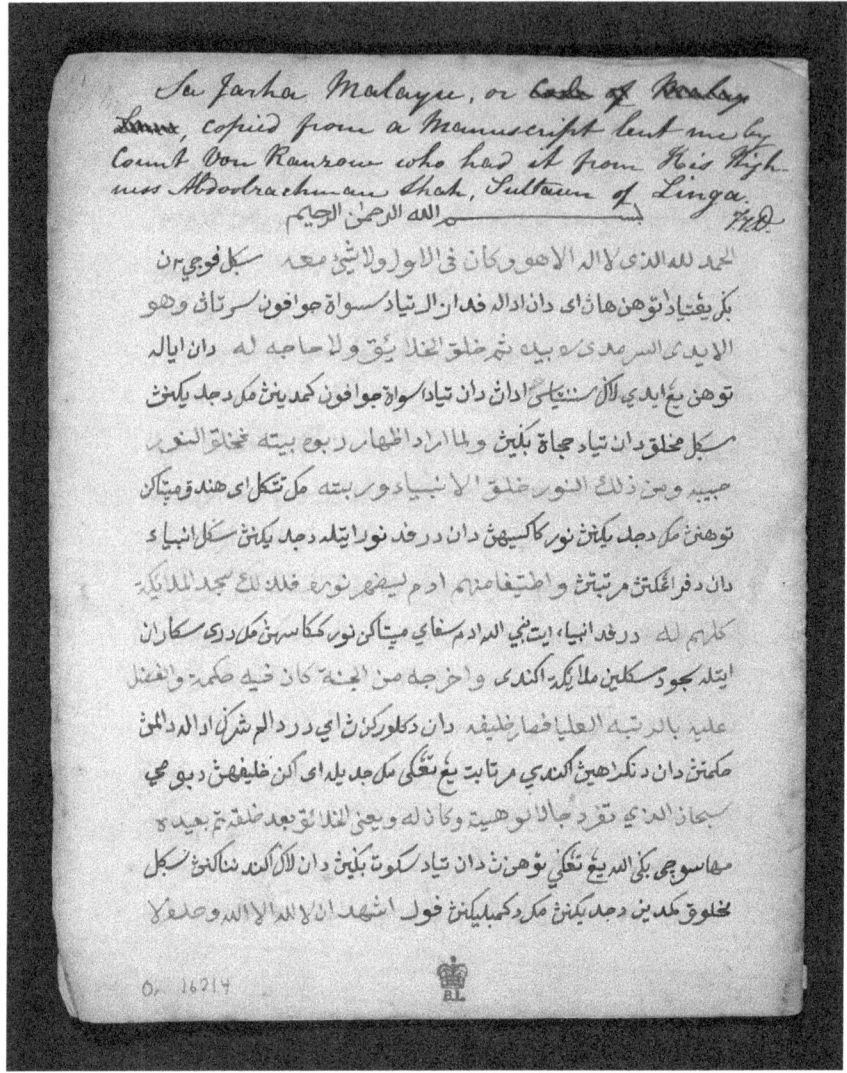

FIGURE 4.3 First page of the *Sejarah Melayu* manuscript. British Library, Or.16214, f.1r. © The British Library.

his subjects use technology to explore the ocean and to make a political alliance with another human community. Raja Chulan is instantly beloved and revered by the community under the sea, leaves three sons, and is mourned for his departure when he leaves. But all three Asian stories speak more broadly to a need, if not for partnership with then for reverence to the strength of the sea in human affairs. Senopati's power results from a marriage with a nonhuman force and Sri Tri Buana must give up his crown—symbolic of his claims as a sovereign over land and sea—to pass safely from place to place. These humans give up much to avoid conflict with the sea.

The writer of the *Sejarah Melayu* details the arrival of five Portuguese ships in Melaka, a cosmopolitan trading city in Malaysia, in the same year as the Battle if Diu.[7] The narrator records the surprise and fear of the encounter with new foreigners, but as translator C.C. Brown notes, the text tells how "time after time the 'men of Malacca' are too clever for the foreigner"—Chinese, European, or other (1970: x–xi). The translations of this episode by John Leyden in 1821 and by Brown in 1952 vary in some significant details, but both describe the Bendahara Sri Maharaja adopting a "Frengi"—a Portuguese captain, perhaps Diogo Lopes de Sequeira who arrived in Malacca in 1508—as his "son" (Brown 1970: 151; Leyden 1821: 324). When this captain reports to Alfonso d'Albuquerque about how prosperous and friendly he found Melaka to be, "the Viceroy was seized with desire to possess it, and he ordered a fleet to be made ready consisting of seven carracks, ten long galleys and thirteen foists" (Brown 1970: 151–2). The foreigners' desire to possess Malayan wealth and land drives the conflict, and in the first description of violence, the Malayans prevail: the "men of Malaka under the leadership of Tun Hasan Temenggong went out to repel [the Portuguese]" despite the "two thousand men armed with matchlocks" and the "vast horde of sailors and sepoys" (152).[8] Weapons from both sides were "falling like rain" and by "charg[ing]," the men of Melaka drive out the foreigners (152). On hearing the news, "The Viceroy [i.e., Albuquerque] was very angry and was for ordering a fresh fleet to be made ready there and then for another attack on Malaka. But the commander of the Moors dissuaded him, saying, 'As long as Bendahara Sri Maharaja is alive, Malaka will never fall'" (152). Albuquerque vows to go himself, and eventually does so, leading a force that defeats the Sultan Ahmad (grandson of Bendahara Sri Maharaja) at Melaka and drives him into exile in Bentan. The Portuguese feature prominently in the final episodes of the *Sejarah Melayu*, but they are not central. Interspersed before, between, and after the descriptions of the war are stories of court intrigues, the movements of Rajas and Sultans, stories of love, adultery, abortion, and succession that undermine the sense that the Portuguese were the final cause of the decline of the Melakan sultanate. Yes, the Portuguese slaughtered soldiers, gained land, and built forts, but more compelling for the writer of the *Sejarah Melayu* in 1511 and for the seventeenth-century revisers of the text were stories about Malay royalty and governors.

THE BATTLE OF LEPANTO

The battles of Diu and Melaka likely did not happen in the way that either the Portuguese or the Malays described. These accounts and textual representations, though, do engage in shoring up ideological rhetorics of sovereignty, and in disseminating those rhetorics. These moves to promote sovereignty were an essential part of early modern nation and empire building. Giancarlo Casale describes the Ottoman Sokollu Mehmed as having mastered such moves during the "Ottoman Age of Exploration" in the period 1512–89. Casale writes of Sokollu's "intellect and ... insatiable curiosity of the world" during the 1570s when he was Pasha to Sultan Selim II and remarks that "Sokollu's genus was to combine an appreciation of the vast rhetorical potential of Ottoman claims to universal sovereignty with an understanding of the technical prerequisites of building and maintaining a global network of communications—the principal vehicle through which these claims could be expressed" (2010: 120). That network, Casale claims, was maritime, and the Ottoman strategy for empire building in the Indian Ocean relied more on "maritime links" than on the possession of territories (120). Historians focused on territories have argued at length about the Battle of Lepanto (1571) and the effects of the Ottoman loss on global politics and trade. European paintings and narratives represented the battle as a decisive victory for the Holy League—Venice, Spain, and Rome—against the Ottomans. Although Ottoman sources described the battle, according to Casale, as a "crushing naval defeat," the Ottoman Empire did not end because of the Holy League's victory, and in fact Sokollu dismantled the Holy League through a series of engagements in the following year (138). According to Guilmartin, the Ottoman and Holy League fleets were remarkably well matched: "Lepanto is a rarity in military history: a battle in which both sides fought skillfully and well, where the random strokes of chance which infest the battlefield were largely neutralized by the skill of the commanders against whom they fell, and where the stronger side won—though by a narrow margin and not in the expected way" (1974: 240). Christian observers, having feared invasion from the east for several centuries, wanted to see in this victory a decisive beatdown of Islam and of the Ottomans. As a result, they represented the conflict in ways that contradict sources that describe the balanced, narrowly won battle and its place in a complicated series of conflicts between the Ottomans and Europeans. Giorgio Vasari painted two scenes from the battle in the Sala Regia of the Vatican, commissioned by Pope Pius V in 1572.[9] He depicted the *Fleets Approaching Each Other* and the *Fleets Engaging* in two enormous canvases on either side of a doorway.

Vasari had a moral and religious agenda in his paintings; although he sought eyewitness accounts to paint the numbers and kinds of ships and combatants accurately, he also "insert[ed] Christ, saints, angels, and the personification of Faith, as well as juxtapose[ed] the Turks with hovering demons, ... suggest[ing] that this is not just a fight between men, but between opposing principles; a battle of Good against Evil" (Strunck 2011: 223–4).[10] The ships in the first painting float in strict formation, the Ottoman fleet facing the ships of the Holy League (see Figure 4.4). Without the bottom third, Vasari's painting

FIGURE 4.4 Giorgio Vasari, *Battle of Lepanto: Fleets Approaching Each Other* (Sala Regia, Vatican Palace, 1572). © Niday Picture Library / Alamy Stock Photo.

supports Guilmartin's historical assessment: these fleets were not identical but were evenly matched. Vasari's patron and a welter of other culture pressures compelled him to add the allegorical figures below the ships, instructing viewers on how to read the impending battle. In the second painting, Vasari accurately paints the chaos and devastation of a naval battle, with drowning figures and a mass of galleys that are difficult to distinguish from one another (see Figure 4.5). Yet as Christina Strunck notes, Vasari once again paints the Turks as "ethically inferior: in the foreground are three instances in which soldiers of the Holy

FIGURE 4.5 Giorgio Vasari, *Battle of Lepanto: Fleets Engaging* (Sala Regia, Vatican Palace, 1572). © Photo SCALA, Florence.

League rescue fallen comrades from the water. The Turks, meanwhile, leave their own compatriots to drown" (2011: 222). The confusion of the scene is genuine, though; were it possible to excise the angels, demons, and allegorical figures, an observer might have difficulty distinguishing between Turkish and Holy League soldiers and ships. To make the Holy League commander Don Juan de Austria visible, Vasari puts an angel above his boat, signaling a widespread cultural idea about the God-given victory at Lepanto for Christian forces over Islamic ones. The legacy of this cultural idea is long; in 2019, the Christchurch mosque shooter had inscribed "Lepanto 1571" onto his gun along with other historical events and figures claimed by white supremacists in their violent misreadings of history (*Daily Sabah Asia Pacific* 2019). But Vasari's need to spell out the Holy League's divine blessing in their victory can also open a space to question the Christian view of the battle, inviting us to critique the painting's single vantage point and imagine the view from other sets of eyes.

Miguel de Cervantes experienced the Battle of Lepanto from the level of the deck, a far different vantage than the distant view of Vasari's paintings. He fought as a harquebusier and was injured; he was later taken captive by Barbary corsairs and lived for five years in captivity in Algiers (Fuchs and Ilika 2010: xvi–xviii). Cervantes crafts repeated references to the Battle of Lepanto in his texts and invites readers to consider different questions about sea power and religious identity than did Vasari. In "Historia del Cautivo" (The Captive's Tale), chapters 37–42 of *Don Quixote* (1605), the titular captive—a naval officer named Ruy Pérez de Viedma—refers to the battle with all of the Christian patriotism we might expect.[11] He tells Don Quixote his life story, saying "I became part of that most glorious of all campaigns" (*yo me hallé en aquella felicísima jornada*), detailing that "on that very same day, so blissful for all of Christianity, ... Ottoman pride and arrogance were shattered" (*aquel día, que fue para la cristiandad tan dichoso, ... quedó el orgullo y soberbia otomana quebrantada*) (Cervantes [1612] 1999: 266; [1612] 2004: 402). Viedma separates himself from all of this Christian glory, though:

> among the many, many overflowing with joy ... only I was miserable, because instead of the naval crown I might have hoped for, in the days of old Rome, on the night that followed that celebrated day I found myself with chains on my legs and shackles around my wrists. (266)
>
> (*entre tantos venturosos como allí hubo ... yo solo fui el desdichado; pues, en cambio de que pudiera esperar, si fuera en los romanos siglos, alguna naval corona, me vi aquella noche que siguió a tan famoso día con cadenas a los pies y esposas a las manos.*) (402)

While Viedma views the Holy League as gaining a righteous victory for Christianity at Lepanto, his own story punctures the heroism of the account, creating space for readers to remember the many people who died, and the many people—of various colors and religions—who became galley slaves or suffered in other ways during this naval war.[12] Cervantes's fiction suggests that is not easy to discern when God—a Christian or a Muslim one—has designated a campaign "glorious." The cultures that clash in a naval battle are rarely so discernable as "Christian" and "heretic" as painters and writers and sovereigns—and modern terrorists—might wish.[13]

THE ARMADA VICTORY

Methods of representation change when the monarch is a woman. The largely male naval spaces that I have so far examined show how stories about good men, honorable soldiers, and loyal servants were integral to the ways that conflict at sea was made to underwrite national sovereignty projects. Elizabeth I strategically deployed these rhetorics of masculinity in her portraiture, prayers, poems, and speeches. For example, in her much-discussed 1588 Armada Speech to the troops at Tilbury before the English fleet engaged the arriving Spanish Army, she refers to herself as a "weak and feeble woman" who yet possesses the "heart and stomach of a king" ([1588] 2000a: 326). In her prayer on the defeat of the Armada from September 1588, she describes her gratitude that "the weakest sex hath been so fortified by Thy strongest help" ([1588] 2000b: 424). On these and other representations of Elizabeth's sovereignty, Louis Montrose writes, "from Elizabeth's accession until her death, the circumstantial fact that the body politic of English kingship was incarnated in the natural body of an unmarried woman ensured that gender and sexuality were foregrounded in representing the Elizabethan state and in articulating its relations with other states and with its own subjects" (2006: 116). The "Armada Victory" of 1588 was one engagement in the Anglo-Spanish war, a conflict spanning the years from 1585 to 1604. As N.A.M Roger argues, "So much does the 1588 Armada dominate the general view of the Spanish War that it is hard to remember that it was only the first major campaign in a war which still had fifteen years to run" (1997: 272). According to Roger, neither Elizabeth I nor Philip II wanted to go to war. Despite their religious differences, Philip saw England as an ally and Elizabeth recognized the "enormous maritime and military resources"—not to mention new world silver—that Philip had at his disposal (254–5). Familiar factors, such as the English sailors' heavier and longer-range cannons, their fire-ships, and the weather, played a role in England's 1588 victory. The English were indeed able to shoot the Spanish ships at a faster rate and from farther away than in previous naval battles, they did send fire-ships toward the Spanish fleet, and the wind did ultimately aid the English (256–69). But disorganization in the Spanish fleet was an equally if not more important factor: by mandate from Philip—who "never excused failure to carry out his orders, even when they were impossible" (255)—the Spanish captains Santa Cruz and then Medina Sidonia had to follow orders from Pope Sixtus V's chosen commander, the Duke of Parma, and were not free to react to illness in their fleets, weather, or the rapidly changing circumstances of this war in the difficult waters around southern England (256–9; 263).[14] Like Lepanto and Diu, this battle's outcome was the sum of complicated actions and counteractions. These battles only bolster nationalistic or religious zeal when represented with strategic omissions or emphases.

Renderings of the 1588 Armada battle in England perform this strategic occlusion in the service of shoring up narratives about English religious, racial, and political authority. Medals commemorating the battle read "'Flavit [Jehovah]. ET. Dissipati. Sunt 1588' ('He blew and they were scattered')", pointing to "the hand of God supporting the Protestant Cause" (Wells-Cole 2012: 836). Elizabeth makes a similar claim about divine sanction in her poem and prayer on the occasion. In "Song on the Armada Victory, December 1588," calling herself the lord's "handmaid," Elizabeth praises God's "wonders": "He made the winds and water rise / To scatter all mine enemies" ([1588] 2000c: lines 3, 10–12). In her prayer "On the Defeat of the Spanish Armada, September 1588," Elizabeth gives thanks for the creation of the four elements—that is, air, earth, fire, water—which keep the world in "orderly government," and which God has "this year made serve for instruments both to daunt our foes and to

FIGURE 4.6 Marcus Gheeraerts, Portrait of Queen Elizabeth I (Armada Portrait), c. 1588. Oil on panel. © Photo 12 / Getty Images.

confound their malice" ([1588] 2000b: 424). The anonymous painter of the *Armada Portrait* engages in the same attribution of the victory to environmental manifest destiny: because the English fight for a protestant cause, the narrative goes, God has intervened to protect them and destroy the Spanish fleet.

According to Anthony Wells-Cole, though, the winds filling the English ships' sails in the foreground of the portrait's left-hand window blow the English fleet in more than one direction; the painter worked from a Bruegel engraving of ships contending with squall-winds, ignoring the westerly and channel winds that affected the actual battle (2012: 836–7). If viewers read the painting from left to right, we move from the English fleet—sun-lit, with full sails, its fire-ships meeting the approaching Armada—to the Spanish fleet—in the shadow of a storm with its ships sinking after having been dashed on the rocks. The composition echoes the movement from the lining up of the fleets to their engagement in Vasari's two portraits of the Battle of Lepanto. Many elements of the *Armada Portrait* underscore a similar triumphalist narrative: the light defeats the dark; calm movement on the sea is opposed to the storm. Such a narrative implies both that the fire-ships in the left-hand window were effective and that the English benefited from a divinely driven environmental counter force.[15] But none of the ships in the right-hand window are on fire; the fire-ships did not succeed in burning the Spanish ships, and along with the confused winds, they indicate the lack of control that the painter, the English, and the Queen have over the sea and the winds, and over the messy, complex world of naval warfare. We can see bids to control the story vying with the ruptures that history, environments, and humans make in those propagandistic efforts.

Complicating this portrait's narrative further is the body of the Queen. She rests her hand on a globe and turns slightly toward the English fleet and a crown.[16] Her elaborate dress is decorated with—as critics including Montrose, Valerie Traub, and several others have noticed—a very strategically placed bow and pearl at the bottom of her stomacher, representing the queen's virgin knot and her sexuality at the same time (Traub 2002: 126; Montrose 2006: 146–7). Montrose sees an "iconic connection between the English sovereign's virtuous chastity and the English nation's emerging power and influence across the globe" (146). The image links the chastity of the monarch's body to the security of her realm. Yet, in drawing attention also to the queen's sexuality and to her emerging power "across the globe," the portrait links biological reproduction to exploration and proto-empire building. The right kind of going in or out of geographical space, like the right kind of bodily penetration, is integral to the future of the state.

Three years after the Armada Portrait, the Earl of Hereford made another bid to represent the naval conflict with Spain as a narrative confirming English control of the sea. He ordered his servants to create a lake on his Elvetham estate on which to stage an elaborate *naumachia*—or sea battle—as entertainment for

Elizabeth I on her progress of 1591 (Wilson 1980: 96–118). With music and poetry presented by water nymphs and punctuated with cannon fire, Hereford's entertainments transferred the Anglo-Spanish naval conflict from the terrifying sea to an inviting, tame, man-made lake. The violence is displaced: cannons and fireships are no longer killing sailors and winds are no longer destroying Spanish galleons. Rather, excavation and river redirection radically reshape the land into a microcosm of the globe in celebration of what John Dee had referred to in 1577 as Elizabeth I's (potential) sea "Souereignty" and rulership over the "Brytish Impire" (Biiv; Aiir). Dee anticipates the political and economic power that Elizabeth and later English monarchs will win when they bet on sea sovereignty despite the massive risks involved. Hereford and the workers at his estate transform his land into a miniature ocean to entertain Elizabeth, but also to reimagine the sea as a controllable, transformable element, subject to the English monarch's will.[17]

VIOLENT ENCOUNTERS: NORTH, SOUTH, EAST, AND WEST

How long does conflict take? I have focused on naval battles, each of which was fought on a specific day even though the temporal boundaries of the wars were blurry. What kinds of conflicts—on the sea or facilitated by it—might we see if we look not for a day of conflict but for a longer temporal span and for kinds of conflict that weaponize ideas or beliefs or changing social structures instead of guns and fire-ships? As Hillary Eklund argues, "the ongoing 'discovery' of the New World and the inexhaustible resources it was imagined to contain put new pressures on the question of what it meant to have enough […]. Standards of economic sufficiency moved from strict regulations against excess toward the increasing pursuit of plenty through plunder, trade, and plantation" (2015: xiii). Trade in slaves and sugar and the use of those imagined "inexhaustible resources" of the New World drove European economies in this period. It also, according to one analysis, initiated human-driven geological change on a global scale; geographers Simon L. Lewis and Mark A. Maslin have proposed the "Orbis hypothesis," which places the beginning of the Anthropocene in 1610 (plus or minus fifteen years) (2015: 171). Their hypothesis seeks to explain the dramatic dip in atmospheric carbon levels that created the Little Ice Age and which was followed by a period of steady warming that continues to the present; according to the hypothesis, that dip was caused by the purposeful as well as accidental movement of biota—animals, crops, and so on—with more speed and broader reach than previously recorded, and by the massive enforced migrations and equally massive decline in New World populations caused by "exposure to diseases carried by Europeans, plus war, enslavement and famine" (175). Dagomar Degroot cautions that the Orbis hypothesis does not confirm that European colonialism caused the Little Ice Age, but reminds us that "the so-called 'Age of Exploration' linked not only the Americas but many previously isolated lands to the Old World, in complex ways that nevertheless reshaped entire continents to look more like Europe. We are still reckoning with and contributing to the resulting, massive decline in plant and animal biomass and diversity" (2019).[18] The "slow violence"—to employ Rob Nixon's (2011) term—made possible by early modern sea travel was invisible at the time because of the distances involved and because of the existing media landscape. It remains invisible now because of the persistent habit of some writers to refer to the heroism of figures such as Sir Francis Drake or Vasco da Gama or to the lucrative sugar, tobacco, and spice trades without reference to the people killed over the centuries to make European expansion possible.[19] Furthermore, as Susan Sleeper-Smith argues, writing of North Atlantic multiethnic fishing communities in 1500, "encounter was an extended process during which Indians and Europeans lived and traded together for well over a hundred years, before Jamestown was founded, and well before Pocahontas met John Smith" (2015: 41). Describing early modern sea conflicts involves not only revising our timescales and our definition of conflict but also reevaluating the entrenched narratives about what early modern conflicts in contact zones entailed.

Despite the high costs of sea travel, English gentlemen in the 1500s were eager to join other Europeans traveling to the Indies. They hoped to find a route north to avoid competition in the Mediterranean and around the Cape of Good Hope. Robert Thorne advocated in 1527 for a northeast route, asserting that "the coste heerin will bee nothing, in comparison to the great profite" (quoted in McDermott 2001: 96). Willem Barents's 1596 to 1597 Arctic expedition and Martin Frobisher's attempts from 1574 to 1579 to find a northwest passage failed so spectacularly and expensively that to sail north became a byword for failure, as when in William Shakespeare's *Twelfth Night*, Fabian figures Sir Andrew Aguecheek as a ship or a sailor who has missed his opportunity to come into the harbor of Olivia's favor, and has instead "sailed … north" ([*c.* 1610–11] 2008: 3.2.20–4).[20] From this perspective, as well as from some modern ones, the north is cold, deadly, and barren. But early European fishermen and later explorers who sailed northwest met not only ice but also people who had lived on Baffin Island and in other northern regions for centuries. As Lowell Duckert shows, Europeans fit Inuit and other groups into their existing narratives about the world: for Frobisher and his men, "the natives were meant to be signposts on the way to Cathay, their dark skins corroborating the closeness of tropical climes …. the natives at first [were] mistaken for seals and, once on board, [ate] raw fish. Since they were sometimes animals, cannibals, and eaters of uncooked flesh, Frobisher could kidnap and discriminate with a clear conscience" (2017: 127–8). The stories that the Europeans told themselves about the sea, about where they were sailing to, and about the lines distinguishing human from nonhuman enabled men like Frobisher to inflict violence that they deemed necessary either for survival or to put a rival group in their place.

Margaret Cavendish makes a similar move but with a difference in her prose fiction *The Blazing World* (1666). Cavendish's protagonist, a Lady who later becomes an Empress, makes the journey that Frobisher and the other explorers only dreamed about: after being abducted by a merchant, she survives a northern voyage into a new world—the Blazing World—during which her companions die. She arrives in a paradise which "was very pleasant, and of mild temper" (Cavendish [1660] 2000: 160), described in terms that echo contemporary travel narratives such as those gathered by Peter Martyr and Richard Hakluyt. The people in this new world "were of several complexions, but none like any of our World," yet the narrator insists on the peacefulness of this encounter (160). When she meets the Emperor, he at first mistakes her for a goddess, but then "rejoicing [that she is mortal], made her his Wife, and gave her an absolute power to rule and govern all that World as she pleased" (132). In parallel to the awed inhabitants of the undersea world who instantly revere Raja Chulan in the *Sejarah Melayu*, the Emperor's subjects "tender'd her all the veneration and worship due to a Deity" (162). The Lady becomes the Empress by marriage, and lives out a fantasy version of the European voyage of discovery, wherein the inhabitants of the new world immediately recognize her natural superiority and wherein the ice, the sea, the land, and the people are instrumental to her creation of a perfect, nonviolent government.[21] Although she refers to them as "fly-men," "bear-men," and so on, the Empress' subjects are not simply animals; they challenge the boundary between human and nonhuman and are valuable advisers who she depicts as wiser than the men of her own world. In the end, she chooses to undo many of her own mandated changes, returning the people and the world to the way they lived before her arrival. Her northern journey opens, at least for some readers, a challenge to the familiar European narratives of discovery and invites reflection on the ethics of monarchy exercised across—and also, spectacularly, on—the sea.

One decision that the Empress does not reverse is her choice to convert the inhabitants of the Blazing World to Christianity. Her first attempt seems easy: calling their religion "defective," she considers "whether it was possible to convert them all" (191). By building churches and preaching with charisma, she makes a "Congregation of Women …. and by that means, she converted them not onely soon, but gained an extraordinary love of all her subjects throughout the world" (191). Cavendish radically suggests not only that women should be allowed to speak in church—contra Paul's prohibition in 1 Corinthians 14—but also that women are naturally more devout Christians than her male subjects. Yet the Empress immediately worries about the "inconstant nature of Mankind," and so builds two new chapels, one decorated with "Fire-stone," which "appear[ed] all in a flame," and one with a "splendorous and comfortable light" (192). Of this project the narrator declares, "that Chappel was an emblem of *Hell*, ... this was an emblem of *Heaven*. And thus the Empress, by Art, and her own ingenuity, did not onely convert the Blazing-world to her own religion, but kept them in a constant belief, without inforcement or bloodshed" (193). The Empress does not kill her subjects, but the question of "inforcement" is murkier. One can imagine a Blazing-worlder deciding to convert out of fear of the Empresses' stories about hell, underscored by the real flames in the chapel. Her governance of the Blazing World is not as easy as the narrator would like us to believe.

The story of traveling to a new land by boat with the goal of converting the indigenous population to Christianity was a familiar and violent one in the period 1500–1680. Less told are the stories about how and when people resisted European evangelism, and about the role that women played in that resistance. Writing about Portuguese efforts to convert or reform Ethiopian Christians from their inherited faith traditions—present in the region since the fourth century—Wendy Belcher fills in an essential silence in Eurocentric histories of evangelism. Working with texts in Latin, Portuguese, and Gəʻəz from the 1600s, Belcher details the actions of royal "Ethiopian women who led their people in resisting early Portuguese proto-colonialism" by speaking out against their husbands, sons, and fathers who had converted, and by resisting that conversion themselves to the point of death or banishment (2013: 122, 126–7, 141). Comparing Portuguese travel accounts—in which these women appear as "'diabólica' (diabolical women)"—and Habesha hagiographies—in which they are "'qəddusat' (female saints)"—Belcher asserts that the "bloody conflict" between the Portuguese and the Habesha, which ended in a decisive Habesha victory in 1600, came about not only because of Portuguese "cultural insensitivity" and "rebellions among the Habesha military" but also, crucially, because "Habesha royal women were partly, and perhaps largely, responsible for evicting the Portuguese and Roman Catholicism from Ethiopia" (126). Drawing on Anjali Arondekar's warnings about what we seek in the archive, Belcher cautions that while her research provides exciting insights about early modern women in Africa, "our reading practices must be attentive to how the archive both declares and fills absence [...]. In the case of seventeenth-century Ethiopia, both the European and the Habesha texts have biases and blind spots. Both traditions absent women. And yet, both also retain traces of women's extraordinary actions" (149).[22]

Learning to ethically read absences and traces, is, as Belcher's work demonstrates, an essential tool for decentering Europe in cultural histories of the early modern period. Jennifer L. Morgan's work on the slave trade provides another example of what we can read in archival silences. The desire for slave trade records to show historical reality, Morgan argues, leads modern historians to recreate "the lacuna between what the records of the slave trade both say and refuse to say," especially with regard to "the lives of Western African women and children" (2016: 186, 191). As Morgan asserts, "the narrative histories of female captives aboard the slave ships plying the early modern and modern Atlantic come to us in a pastiche of demographic records, distant witnesses, polemic images and autobiographies" (201). Nonetheless, reading the silences in the archive can prompt new questions and new ways to understand the consequences of the trade for women:

> Europeans simultaneously knew and refused to know that African captives were embedded in families and communities [...]. By failing to record the sex and age of captives, merchants constructed those spaces of sociality as outside of the market. And thus, when biological sex, parenthood or other familial relations do make their way into the records, they need to be understood as marking a particular type of eruption. (191)

One understanding of such "eruptions" can revise the idea that slave traders—captains, merchants, sailors, owners, and so many other people involved—participated in the atrocities of the Middle Passage because they had dehumanized their captives. On the contrary, by looking, with pain but continuing to look, at accounts of rape, of naming and taking "favorite" slaves to quarters, of torture, and of other violence that took place on the ships, Morgan shows that "the absence of gender or age designations on a slave trader's manifest was an act of disregard not uniformly applied: slave traders articulated a deeply vexed recognition of captives' personhood through repetitive acts of sexual violence" (196).[23] We can look, too, for what we have missed in the less painful silences if we seek to know, with John Thornton, how Africans navigated rivers and coasts and how oceanic currents and winds as well as riverine geography shaped the stories of African sailors (Thornton 1998) or if we seek to know, with Gwyn Campbell, how Africans contributed—via trades in plants, architecture, textiles, and many other ways, not just with bodies and labor—to the development of the Indian Ocean World global economy throughout precolonial history (Campbell 2010).

Travel, commerce, and war at sea required dangerous, difficult labor. As a result, forced labor is an unavoidable part of the culture of the early modern sea all over the globe, not just in the Atlantic world. We can make visible those who worked or were forced to work at sea by reading laws and manifests governing who was allowed to sail and how many slaves of what kind could be brought aboard; these laws differ by nation and by route. As Sarah E. Owens notes, Manila galleons transported not just spices and silver but also "chinos as slaves from Asia to Mexico," a transpacific slave trade that was smaller than the transatlantic trade in terms of the number of people who were displaced, but that was no less brutal in the violence of the journey or in the enslaved life that awaited in New Spain (2017: 81). Drawing on Tatiana Seija's work, Owens points out that about one-quarter of people transported across the Pacific were women, despite a Spanish "royal decree in 1608 banning female slaves on galleons" (82).[24] The galleons and port cities in this era were racially and religiously complex spaces; as Owens reminds us, people of non-European descent were not only slaves but also occupied other social and cultural positions. The severity and duration of the institution of slavery itself also varied: "some black slaves worked on ships as common sailors, while even a few freed mulattos served as pilots. These sailors of African descent had come via the Iberian Peninsula and were Christians by acculturation—as opposed to those 'converted' by the ineffectual mass baptisms inflicted on enslaved Africans in trading ports before sending them to the New World" (81–2). Owens traces the journey of a group of Spanish nuns from Toledo through Mexico to Manila—following the *Carrera de Indias*—and details their work founding a convent in Manila. The nuns, as female travelers, represent yet another group in the mix on the galleon, and the account of one of the nuns—Sor Ana—provides a perspective on female travel and slavery that is otherwise missing from contemporary accounts. While en route from Acapulco to Manila, "Sor Ana describes how a negra, or black woman, named María tried to commit suicide by throwing herself overboard" (80). Despite the ban on female slaves and despite rules forbidding sexual activity for male sailors, Sor Ana's account of María's fear and possession of money suggests that "sailors used her for sex" and that Spanish laws and promises of punishment "did little to deter this behavior" (80). The nun's account of Maria's words and actions are filtered through her own racist and classist lenses; she and the other nuns do not denounce the whipping that María receives as punishment for attempted suicide. But Sor Ana does tell María's story and relates the nuns' concern with "her spiritual wellbeing" and their desire to comfort her; as Owens argues,

> perhaps without knowing it, [Sor Ana's] portrayal of the scene speaks to slaves' resistance to bondage and cruelty [...]. When María's drastic attempt to throw herself overboard fails, she resigns herself to her fate by exhibiting a remorseful and submissive attitude; in other words, she turns to another coping mechanism as opposed to suicide. [Ginés de] Quesada, on the other hand, silences María's plight by omitting any reference to her situation. (89–90)

Owens, like Morgan, has adeptly read the silences in the archive, but also demonstrates powerfully how seeking out women's writing provides us with a fuller picture of the many conflicts onboard a seventeenth-century galleon.

Oceanic travel in the Atlantic, the Pacific, or the Indian Ocean involved terrors such as typhoons, pirate raids, dysentery, mutiny, and rape or enforced labor. Travel and warfare in the Mediterranean as well as on the many rivers

FIGURE 4.7 "A Pyigyimon boat, which consists of two conjoined gilded boats, with a seven-tired roof (pyatthat). There are two separate dragon-headed hulls, while on the bow are figures of a garuda (mythical bird) and a naga (mythical dragon), with Sakka (a celestial king and the ruler of Tavatimsa heaven) standing between them." Caption by Annabel Gallop, British Library blog post November 21, 2018, https://blogs.bl.uk/asian-and-african/2018/11/beautiful-burmese-barges-and-boats.html. British Library, Or. 14005, f. 1. © The British Library.

that form important connections in the networks of global trade, culture, and conflict could be just as punishing. Rowing a boat is hard work, work often done in the Mediterranean by captives of war, slaves, or criminals—as Cervantes's narrative illustrates—and work that was not conducive to long careers. Some early modern evidence suggests that conditions in Southeast Asia for rowers were at least slightly better than elsewhere (see Figure 4.7). There, too, oarsmen were often "captives," and at least on the rivers, "it was easier to procure men for river fleets through warfare" than by other means (Charney 2004: 118). But as Michael Charney observes, "because oarsmen were supposed to fight as well as to row, unlike some of their European counterparts, Southeast Asian kingdoms had to have a reliable force at the oars" and this need for reliability produced at least marginally better conditions for the oarsmen (118). Charney quotes the Jesuit Christoforo Berri, who remarked in 1633 that although the Nguyen King's men

> doe seise and presse all such as they find fit to handle an Oare, and bestow them in the Gallies, … that course must not be thought so hard and difficult, as at first it may seemse, because, they are as well intreated in the Gallies as anywhere else: and better payd: and besides, their Wives, their Children, and all their Familie, is maintained at the Kings charge, with whatsoever is needfull according to their rancke and condition, during all the time that their Husbands are thus absent. (quoted in Charney 2004: 119)

This compensation was perhaps poor comfort to the men who were "presse[d]" into rowing, but some attention to the families of the oarsmen—to whom the men could hope to return if they survived war—was at least marginally preferable to the lot of many rowers in Mediterranean galleys.

Positive views voiced by Europeans such as Berri about East and Southeast Asian cultures were fairly common in the early modern period. Ricardo Padrón describes Iberia's "decidedly sinophilic" discourses about China in the mid- to late 1500s, which praise their government, agriculture, well-planned cities, and straight streets, asserting that for many Iberian writers, "Only in matters of religion could the Middle Kingdom be found at fault […] While its false religion was worthy of censure, everything else elicited praise and admiration" (2014: 96). Sinophilic discourses in Iberia coexisted with sinophobic ones generated by travelers who were taken prisoner and others. They focused on Chinese "tyranny" and their "draconian brand of justice," symbolized for some Portuguese and Spanish writers by the *bastinado*, a punishment for criminals involving beating a person on the backs of the thighs with a cane, and which could be fatal (96, 100). A Castilian Jesuit named Alonso Sánchez traveled the same route as Sor Ana from Spain to Mexico to Manila, though he made his two journeys in 1583 and 1588, about forty years earlier. After his travels, Sánchez wrote a treatise designed to spur Phillip II to attempt a conquest of China like his conquest of Mexico. Blending sinophobic and sinophilic discourses, Sanchez voices proto-orientalist attraction to and denigration of the people and culture he has encountered. As Padrón observes,

> Sanchez marvels at the large number of sizable vessels that make up the Chinese coast guard, and praises the ships for their astonishing cleanliness. But he also notes that the Chinese junks are "delicate and slender," suggesting that they are all effeminate show, rather than indications of manly prowess […]. He does something similar with the army and the cities. (104–5)

Sánchez blends envy and fear to create a portrait of Chinese culture that draws on previous accounts' admiration to encourage deep-seated distrust and to justify war.

Padrón remarks that Sánchez did not get what he wanted: Phillip II was preoccupied in the 1580s with his war with Elizabeth I, and he was not inclined to start another one with China (2014: 105). Although Sánchez's treatise did not spark immediate violence, his writings speak to both the rapid violence of conquest—massacres and enslavement and forced labor—and the slower violence that enabled Spaniards and other Europeans first to admire, then denigrate, and then destroy the cultures they encountered. Spaniards were impressed, for example, that Filipino men and women wrote fluently; a priest in 1604 wrote, "There are few who do not write [their language] excellently and correctly" and yet, as Craig Lockard concludes, "Spanish priests considered the writing to be heretical [...] and destroyed most of the bamboos" (2009: 80). Steve Russell describes similar admiration for and then destruction of Mayan codices by the Spanish, who burned Mayan books for at least 150 years, from 1562 to 1697, acts of violence justified by one Spanish priest this way: "We found a large number of books in these characters and, as they contained nothing in which were not to be seen as superstition and lies of the devil, we burned them all, which they regretted to an amazing degree, and which caused them much affliction" (2017). Russell effectively counters claims that indigenous Americans had no written language. On the contrary, he shows that records of those languages were systematically destroyed for their supposed heresy.

These acts of destruction—of texts, of people—because they are so often related by colonizers and their descendants, often consume our vision to the point that survival or acts of resistance seem impossible. But of course, indigenous people did survive and did resist, at every turn. Tony Castanha, writing about the Jíbaro people in Borikén (Puerto Rico), puts the matter succinctly: "One of the greatest myths ever told in Caribbean history is that the indigenous inhabitants of mainly the northern Antilles were extinguished by the Spaniards around the mid-sixteenth century" (2011: 3). Castanha and other scholars of indigenous history and anthropology have found ample contrary evidence when they search available archives for instructive silences and when they ask people who live in Borikén to tell their oral histories. Indeed, "Indian descendants have in fact known who they are and have maintained and continued to practice their culture [...]. [Castanha in his book] provide[s] a political history and ethnological account of five centuries of Carib or Jíbaro Indian resistance and cultural survival" (3). Castanha works to dispel several iterations of the myth of indigenous extinction, generated from the sixteenth to the twenty-first century and perpetuated in academic scholarship. Mythmaking was integral to European imperial pursuits in all sorts of ways, but had a direct impact on Castanha's ancestors because the

> early Spaniards often exaggerated the effects of colonization and impacts of the spread of disease to secure favors from the Crown. Population

counts were routinely downplayed in order to booster the importation of African labor. Spanish chroniclers like Fray Bartolomé de Las Casas, for all the important work he did do, also deflated the post-contact numbers to promote the argument for the "peaceful conversion" of native persons. (16)[25]

Given the violent relations between the Spanish and the Caribs in the sixteenth century, it is not surprising that the Carib's response to the escalating conflict was to revolt—as they did in 1511 and after—or to flee to safer communities in the mountains, where the Spaniards did not reach until the nineteenth century (55–7). When the Spanish governor Francisco Manuel de Lando conducted a census in Puerto Rico (San Juan) and San German in 1530 to 1531, he left out "the large number of Indian people in villages, valleys, caves, and other places in the mountainous interior" (64). Which of these people was likely to come forward for the census?[26]

CONCLUSION

How should we tell the cultural history of sea conflict in the early modern period, and what are the consequences of how we tell it for our own moment? In their introduction to a 2018 special issue of the journal *Decolonization*, titled "Indigenous peoples and the politics of water," Melanie K. Yazzie and Cutcha Risling Baldy define *"radical relationality"* as a term useful in decolonization efforts and in the "reclaiming of our accountability to water" (2018: 2). According to Yazzie and Baldy, radical relationality is "radical in the sense of roots or origins, as in a relationality from which all life and history derives meaning and shape, [...] and also in the sense of a dramatic and revolutionary change from our current epoch of power" (2). They assert that:

> Within [a] framework of relationality, water is not seen as a resource to be weaponized for the interests of capital by corporations that harness, obstruct, pollute, and discipline water through infrastructure projects like dams and pipelines to boost the capitalist economies of settler nation-states. No, within an Indigenous feminist framework, water is a relative with whom we engage in social (and political) relations premised on interdependency and respect. (2–3)

Contributors to their special issue encourage us not only to change the present but also to decolonize historiography. Rosemary Georgeson and Jessica Hallenbeck remind us that talking to indigenous people can reveal "the ways that Indigenous women's relationships have transformed and persisted, despite generations of erasure" down to the very names that these women retained despite colonial mandates about "proper names" (2018: 21). Eleanor Hayman,

Colleen James/Gooch Tláa, and Mark Wedge/Aan Gooshú challenge definitions of the Anthropocene that reinscribe antagonistic, firm boundaries between nature and culture, bringing to bear indigenous stories about glaciers:

> Tlingit and Tagish narratives describe glaciers as sentient beings; glaciers that listen, glaciers that can smell, glaciers with attitude [...]. Tlingit oral traditions hold within them precise ecological knowledge about glaciers, flows, circulations, water, and water bodies, as well as protocol for valuing and respecting glaciers. When combined with empirical science, these oral traditions provide the core elements of glacial narratives that create a complex, sensory glacial imaginary. (2018: 80, 86)

The combination of oral tradition and ecological knowledge has promise both for how we understand the past and for what we do in the present; Hayman, Tláa, and Gooshú "suggest that slow activism is one counter-story to Rob Nixon's (2011) slow violence [...]. At a time when many First Nations are struggling to retain identity and coherence in a rapidly changing world, it is the power of strong stories that offers a unique combination of knowledges for conflict resolution and survival" (85). The cultural history of the sea, as I have attempted to sketch it, is a history of radical relationality that has involved struggle and conflict; we should engage with stories of struggle as well as with the struggle of decolonizing our own periodization, methods, and commitments as scholars.

CHAPTER FIVE

Islands and Shores

Early Modern Islomania

DEBAPRIYA SARKAR

No man is an *Iland,* intire of it selfe; every man is a peece of the *Continent*, a part of the *maine*.
— John Donne, *Devotions upon Emergent Occasions,* No. 17 (1624)

This sceptered isle,
This earth of majesty, this seat of Mars,
This other Eden, demi-paradise,
This fortress built by nature for herself
Against infection and the hand of war,
This happy breed of men, this little world,
This precious stone set in the silver sea,
Which serves it in the office of a wall,
Or as a moat defensive to a house
Against the envy of less happier lands;
This blessèd plot, this earth, this realm, this England.
— William Shakespeare, *Richard II* (1597), 2.1.40–50

I would like to thank Steve Mentz, Hillary Eklund, Brian Pietras, Caralyn Bialo, David Hershinow, Laura Kolb, Vin Nardizzi, Lauren Robertson, and Katherine Schaap Williams for their insight and thoughtful suggestions on earlier versions of this chapter.

> This happy island where we now stood was known to few, and yet knew most of the nations of the world; which we found to be true, considering they had the languages of Europe, and knew much of our state and business; and yet we in Europe (notwithstanding all the remote discoveries and navigations of this last age), never heard any of the least inkling or glimpse of this island.
> — Francis Bacon, *New Atlantis* (1627), 466

An isolated entity that serves as a contrast to sociable human life. A symbol of national identity, of mythical strength, and even of ideality—both natural and theological. An undiscovered location whose state of perfection simultaneously exposes the limited knowledge of maritime travelers and invites them to venture into chaotic seas to map a seemingly expandable globe. The excerpts with which I begin my chapter offer a glimpse into the varied ways that islands animated the early modern imaginary. They signal how these landmasses, defined by their physical proximity to water, could conjure up distinct notions: of precise location and universal desire, of ambitions of conquest and promises of retreat, of epistemological lack and political success, and of home and alternate world. These brief examples only begin to gesture to the "islomania" that gripped early modern writers, as they grappled with profound uncertainties of religious controversy, political turmoil, scientific innovation, and environmental disaster.

I borrow the term "islomania" from Lawrence Durrell, who defines it as an "affliction of spirit" that is characteristic of people "who find islands somehow irresistible" (1953: 15). Expanding on Durrell's formulation, John R. Gillis documents the poly-temporal "fascination with islands" that both sparks the imagination and instigates action:

> Islomania in its many different guises is a central feature of Western culture, a core idea that has been a driving force from ancient times to the present. "The island seems to have a tenacious hold on the human imagination," notes Yi-Fu Tuan, "but it is in the imagination of the Western world that the island has taken the strongest hold." The island of the mind is not just an object of passive contemplation. It has been an incentive to action, an agent of history. (2004: 1)

Drawing on Gillis's theorization of islomania, I explore how various forms of island thinking mobilized early moderns, from philosophers to artists, from writers to sailors, and from merchants to monarchs. The islands that clutter the literary worlds of John Donne, William Shakespeare, and Francis Bacon exist alongside narratives of actual voyages to isles documented by Christopher Columbus, Samuel Purchas, Walter Raleigh, and Richard Hakluyt, among many others. Together, their works exemplify the diverse ways in which the perceived "insularity" of islands "provided space to imagine new worlds and to rethink the social order" (Gillis 2004: 4). Accounts of islands thereby spanned the imaginative and historical divide. As scholars including Mary C. Fuller (1995) and Mary Baine Campbell (1988) have shown, writers habitually blurred distinctions between actual and fabricated travels, suggesting that the boundaries between creating fictional worlds and rethinking extant social structures were more porous than can be captured by categories such as imaginative writing or voyage narrative.

Fictive accounts and descriptions of actual travels worked in symbiosis with each other. On the one hand, maritime expansion brought islands—both as mapped places and as cultural symbols—to the center of early modern European culture. As Columbus's narratives of his voyages (1492–1504) highlight, expansion, conquest, and colonization often occurred by island-hopping. Imaginative works such as Lady Mary Wroth's *Urania* (1621), to which I will return later in this chapter, dramatized similar forms of island-hopping—its characters traverse islands in the Mediterranean in ways that are comparable to the movements of voyagers who navigated the Atlantic, Pacific, and Indian Oceans. On the other hand, claims that fictional locations were discoverable enabled literary writers to use islands not only as exemplars of alternate worlds but also as sites of public engagement and provocations for political action. For instance, Thomas More's *Utopia* (1516), whose titular island I study in more detail in the next section, was instrumental in shaping what Campbell identifies as the "rhetorical situation of the travel writer" in the sixteenth and seventeenth centuries (1988: 212). Renaissance literature repeatedly incites the desire to locate fictional islands in the actual world, functioning alongside epistemological and representational forms such as the *isolario*, the atlas, and the portolan chart to reshape understanding of physical and metaphysical worlds.[1] "For many, the sea was the ultimate source of investment in this era of exploration, colonization, and emergent imperialism," claims Julie Sanders, documenting how "water-based operatives such as smugglers and pirates [...] pace the stages of commercial Caroline theatre" (2011: 55, 53). Pirates, shipwrecks, and nautical voyages were not only the stuff of drama but also crucial features of poetry and prose narratives.[2] As I explore below, genres such as utopia and epic-romance in particular embrace the structuring logics of maritime and archipelagic environments. Islands—discovered, constructed, imagined, and mundane—became ubiquitous features of early modern thought. This place "betwixt and between" inland and ocean, between calm and chaos, and even between self and world, afforded opportunities to reflect on facets of the natural realm, to explore questions of identity and alterity, and to test how immaterial notions could shape physical reality (Gillis 2004: 4).[3]

To illustrate how islomania governs early modern thought, I turn to imaginative works of the period that deploy the island concept to varied ends. After all, islomania is, at its core, an imaginative, even visionary, force. While it is impossible to survey the myriad accounts of actual and fictitious islands in early modern media, the literary examples I study serve as symbolic touchstones that allow us to unpack the cultural logic of this terraqueous entity. This focus underscores how imaginative writings distill and crystallize the island thinking prevalent in early modern culture into specific episodes, events, and acts. My particular attention to English literary texts further highlights how islands kindled the social, political, and philosophical yearnings of a culture on the cusp of becoming a maritime global power. Shakespeare's positioning of England as an island-nation, in addition to the country's expanding seafaring ventures, offers varied indications of how "the nation at large, responded to and thought about the rivers, waterways, and oceans that surrounded them" in innovative ways (Sanders 2011: 22). Literary works, across a variety of genres, demonstrate how the country perceives it extending dominion and anticipates its colonial reach. Early modern islomaniacs channel the nation's aquatic sensibility to mediate relations between nature and culture, between the local and the global, and between fiction and reality.

In studying the island as an imaginative force, I do not intend to suggest that they are only—or even predominantly—ideational. A variety of imaginative works, ranging from Edmund Spenser's allegorical epic-romance, *The Faerie Queene* (whose first six books were published in 1590 and 1596) to John Fletcher's tragicomedy, *The Island Princess* (1647), explicitly link literary isles to the ostensibly insular locations that fueled imperial ambitions. This intertwining reveals the dark side of early modern islomania: as poets and dramatists reframe the connectivity of travel as the isolation of cultures, they erase, mythologize, or exoticize particularities of distant realms. This paradoxical exoticization and erasure occurs on one of the most famous islands in English literature. In *The Tempest*, the European traveler Gonzalo describes the "islanders" in antithetical terms:; they possess a "monstrous shape" but display "manners [that] are more gentle-kind" (Shakespeare [1610–11] 2008: 3.3.29–32). These "islanders" concurrently represent the physical other and the socially assimilable. I will examine the play's islandic spirit in more detail below. For now, we might hypothesize that as early moderns navigate a "sea of islands," to borrow Epeli Hau'ofa's phrase, they must reconcile expansive ideas about creation, navigation, and natural abundance with sociopolitical realities of power, conquest, and a nascent imperialism (1993).[4] To do so, they approach the island as a "master metaphor" of foundational aspects of early modern culture (Gillis 2004: 3). The terraqueous entity serves as an experimental concept-place where established facts mingle with imagined futures, where precarity and shelter coexist, and where humans, in attempting to control their surroundings, are instead themselves altered by their environs.

UTOPIA: LITERARY BEGINNINGS, PROJECTING FUTURES

Thomas More's *Utopia*, published in Latin in 1516, and first translated in English in 1551 by Ralph Robinson, becomes a seminal work for early modern writers on how to approach the island as an engine of creation, innovation, and boundary crossing between fabrication and existence. The titular island's name, which means no place (from the Greek word *ou-topos*) foregrounds semantic and ontological absence. Yet, both characters within the fiction and the paratextual materials, which consist primarily of letters by well-known European humanists, continually animate readers to discover this ideal place; the name of the island, readers will recall, also puns on *eu-topos* (good place). *Utopia* thus offers a powerful example—and template—of the fictional island that is vehemently defended as real even as its fabrication is highlighted by its characters and its first readers. This geographical conceptual feature becomes a recurring trope of early modern imaginative writing. For instance, Bacon's *New Atlantis* teases readers by beginning with a detailed description of the narrator's maritime route—they "sailed from Peru, (where we had continued by the space of one whole year), for China and Japan, by the South Sea"—only to withhold

FIGURE 5.1 Abraham Ortelius, *Map of Utopia*. © The Picture Art Collection / Alamy Stock Photo.

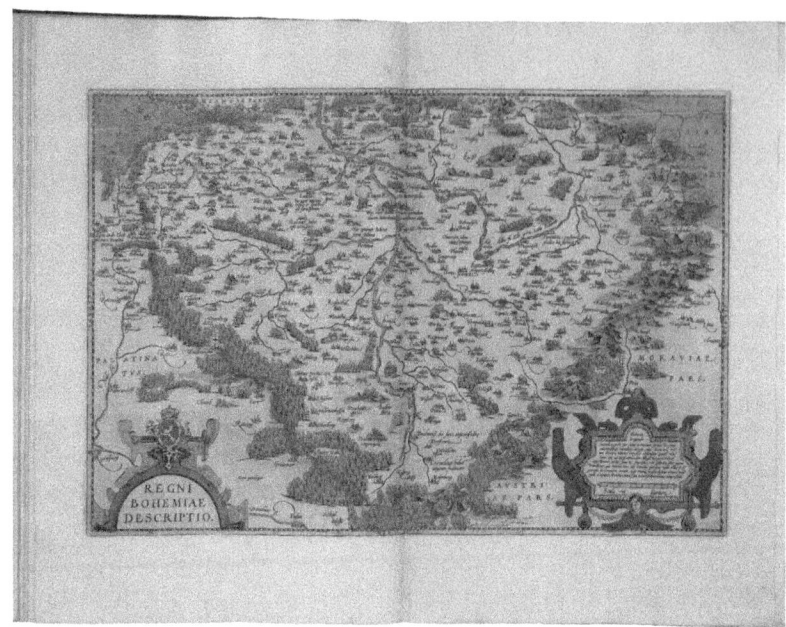

FIGURE 5.2 Abraham Ortelius, *Map of Bohemia,* from *Theatrum Orbis Terrarum.*
© The Folger Shakespeare Library.

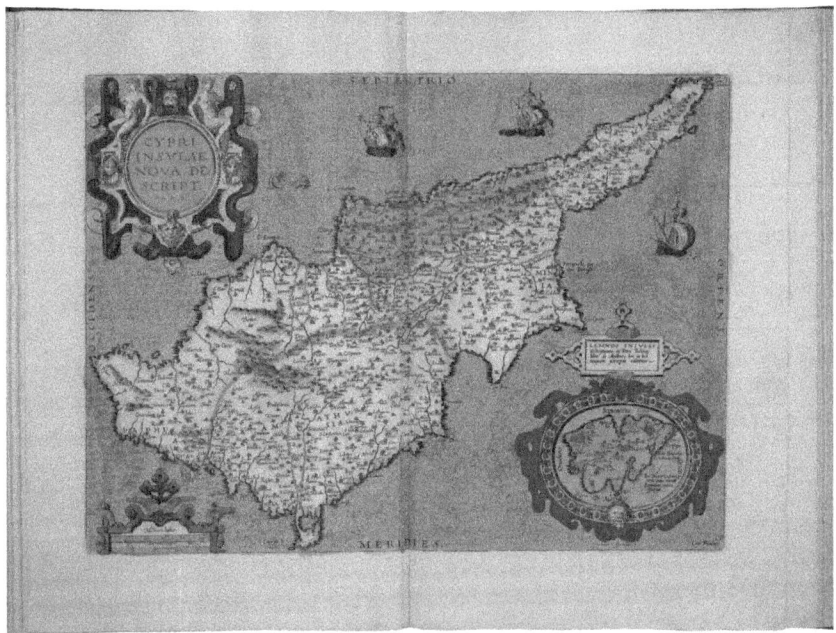

FIGURE 5.3 Abraham Ortelius, *Map of Cyprus and Inset Map of Lemnos,* from *Theatrum Orbis Terrarum.* © The Folger Shakespeare Library.

the information about the location of Bensalem, the island on which they find reprieve from the "greatest wilderness of waters" (1627: 457). The fascination with *Utopia*'s existence extended well beyond textual adaptations. The artist Ambrosius Holbein and the cartographer Abraham Ortelius would produce pictorial depictions of the island "all by itself, untouched by a mainland and strategically fortified against neighboring countries" (Pearl 2014: 25).[5]

By the end of the sixteenth century, travel writers including Humphrey Gilbert and Lawrence Keymis would distance their navigated realms from *Utopia*'s fictionality (see Campbell 1988: 211–13). Given this trend, Ortelius's rendering, usually dated to 1595–6, is particularly intriguing. This depiction (Figure 5.1) mirrors the maps he compiled in *Theatrum Orbis Terrarum* (1570), considered to be the first modern atlas. Utopia's cartographic representation echoes the strategies and topographical features of the charted locales depicted in the atlas. It is hard not to see similarities, for instance, between the portrayals of Utopia and Bohemia (Figure 5.2)—the comparable shapes of the landmasses, their detailed terrains, the textual addendums, and the decorative cartouches collectively obscure the fact that one place exists and one is invented. We could also compare Utopia's islandic status to the plate depicting the island of Cyprus (Figure 5.3). While nautical vessels and sea-creatures flank both isles, the increased number of ships surrounding Utopia hints that it is, perhaps, more reachable than the Mediterranean island. This illusion of accessibility exemplifies the prevailing fantasy that any unknown region will be eventually mapped. The varied linguistic and visual representational techniques propagate the myth that Utopia exists but is perennially barely out of sight, its condition both motivating and frustrating voyagers who cannot quite arrive at its perfect shores.

Utopia thus creates and invites its own mythologizing, an act that readers were eager to perform. The wish to reimagine utopia arises partially because the prose work foregrounds several elements that imply its aesthetic, intellectual, and cultural mores are adaptable—indeed, the text's invitation to seek the island and emulate its norms and practices suggest they are *meant* to be adapted. *Utopia* unabashedly revels in the insularity and potential unreachability of the island. Yet, as Ortelius's maps indicate, the notion of isolation is both a delusion and a catalyst for action. "The geographic and cultural histories of islands insist that these remote places cannot remain isolated," Steve Mentz reminds us (2015: 51).[6] *Utopia* uses this aura of seclusion to engage in the dual pulls that, according to Gillis, govern islomania: a "space to imagine new worlds" and "to rethink the social order." *Utopia*'s descriptions of the island's features, both natural and sociopolitical, offer a model to imagine "new" realms. It does so by introducing a new genre that literary writers can adopt and revise, and by propelling seventeenth-century reformers and projectors to develop projects in the Americas.[7] At the same time, Utopia's ideality serves as a call to "rethink"

England's current "social order," as More's characters deploy its state of perfection to critique practices such as enclosure and lament bad counsel to kings.[8] *Utopia's* idealized status stands in stark contrast to the inadequacies of English society and institutions.

Ultimately, *Utopia* becomes a prototype for modeling boundary crossings between fiction and actuality by establishing that its titular island is not only a physical edge but also an epistemological one.[9] As an intellectual project, *Utopia* traffics in the connections between literary making and practical knowledge, that is, between *poiesis* and *techne*. These linkages would be instrumental in reshaping the parameters of literature and science in the next century.[10] In *Utopia*, this interplay is most vivid in the instance when the poetically created island is presented as a place that is constructed through physical labor and skill: "Utopus, who conquered the country and gave it his name … had a channel cut fifteen miles wide where the land joined the continent, and thus caused the sea to flow around the country" (More [1516] 2002: 42). By sequestering the island, Utopus designs an artificial setting where social norms, domestic practices, and political systems can be tested and refined unadulterated by transcultural influences. We might posit, then, that the island of Utopia becomes a laboratory. As Elizabeth Spiller argues, "the construction of such a controlled environment [for experiment] is inherently artificial and is not only an exception to the ordinary workings of nature but even produces (creates) phenomena that had never occurred and presumably would never have occurred without human intervention" (2004: 31). She could be describing the creation of the *island* of Utopia. Its physical and epistemological isolation makes possible, indeed, is essential to, the idyllic conditions of its purported existence. Like the text to which it gives its name, this place would not have existed without "human intervention." Its "inherently artificial" setting—segregated from the rest of the world and its social, political, and environmental concerns—allows utopians to perfect their society.[11] Reflecting on contemporary conditions and envisioning an ideal future, *Utopia* is a blueprint that galvanizes generations of writers, artists, and philosophers.

NAVIGATING EDGES: THE ISLAND'S SHORE IN *THE TEMPEST*

The Tempest, which traffics in similar utopian longings,[12] is even more deliberate in obfuscating the location of its island setting: it lacks both "local habitation" and "name" (Shakespeare [1594–6] 2008: 5.1.17). The unnamed isle in Shakespeare's last individually written play continues to captivate audiences and readers; the majority of scholarship associates the significance of this landmass to the question of *where* it is located. Such a response is unsurprising, because the play both recalls the experiences of contemporary travelers to the New

World, and its geographical particulars harken back to the "Old World" of the Mediterranean and to "the North African coast" (Brotton 1998: 24, 33).[13] On the one hand, *The Tempest's* European characters hail from Naples and Milan, Claribel (the daughter of the King of Naples) marries the King of Tunis, and Caliban's mother, Sycorax, was an inhabitant of "Algiers" (Shakespeare [1610–11] 2008: 1.2.263); these places of origins and alliances underscore the characters' situatedness in the Mediterranean world.[14] On the other hand, it is commonly accepted that William Strachey's *A True Reportory of the Wracke* (1610) and Sylvester Jordain's *A Discovery of The Barmudas* (1610) are important intertexts for *The Tempest,* a play without a singular source-text. The play's opening sea-storm channels the rhetoric and pathos of the experiences represented in Strachey's and Jordain's writings. Both works provide eyewitness accounts of the 1609 shipwreck of the *Sea Venture* on Bermuda, a locale that loomed large in the English imagination because of its perceived physical isolation, its extreme storms, and its "function as symbol of the untamed ocean" (Mentz 2015: 63). Mentz's description of Bermuda as "sea-land" underscores its paradoxical status: it "was the land-sea on which England's

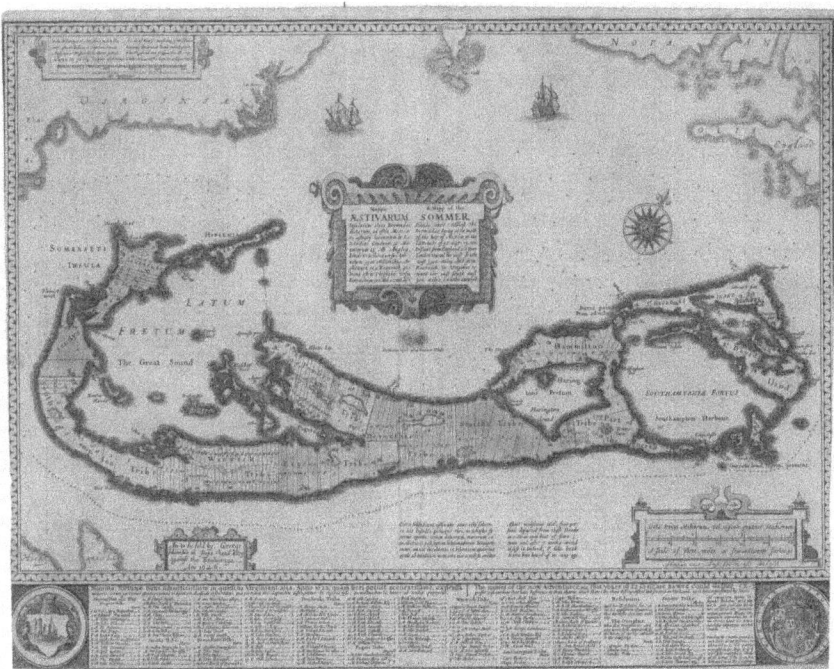

FIGURE 5.4 Richard Norwood, *Map of Bermuda*, made after his survey of the island in 1616, published in 1626. © Courtesy of the John Carter Brown Library at Brown University.

North American ventures first wrecked and the strand on which they salvaged themselves" (52). Cartographic representations of the island also wrestled with this ambiguity. Richard Norwood's map (Figure 5.4, 1626 version), D.K. Smith argues, exemplifies that while Bermuda's "economic development was slow and difficult," the location's "imaginative domestication took almost no time at all" (2008: 160). The map's "mixture of specificity and arbitrariness suggests both a desire to impose imaginative order on the land, and a lingering anxiety about the uncertainty still implicit in an island so recently settled" (161). Bermuda's ability to accommodate multiple meanings made it the ideal ecosystem on which early moderns could project their fluctuating concerns about nature and culture.

Given the numerous echoes of contemporary events and geographical locations in *The Tempest*, the anonymity of the island is even more striking. This namelessness suggests that the play is less interested in locating this "liminal" site within mapped or mappable places than in deploying this threshold, "partaking of both earth and water, something betwixt and between," to explore an array of conceptual, social, political, and environmental issues (Gillis 2004: 4). Denise Albanese's description of the play's setting "as *utopian* space, a space for the readier configuration of new social and ideological relations," affords one possible reason for the refusal to name the isle (1996: 69, my emphasis). *The Tempest*, I propose, *enacts* More's theoretical depiction of the island as laboratory.[15] The island's functioning in a manner analogous to a controlled laboratory setting is most apparent in Prospero's plotted manipulation of characters—from his daughter Miranda to the island's original inhabitant Caliban, from the spirit Ariel to the marooned Europeans—and of events including the storm, the masque, and the final reunion.[16] Prospero creates an artifactual environment to test intersections of power and knowledge, and the stage becomes a physical manifestation of the insular concept-place. It thus offers a perfect example of Jonathan Bate's description of the island as a "special enclosed place," an "experimental place where opposing forces are brought together in dramatic confrontation" (2004: 290). In fact, *The Tempest* dramatizes how distinct terrains of the island can offer heightened understanding of its status as an "experimental place": while the entire landmass operates as a theoretical and physical threshold "betwixt and between" things, the shore of the island—its boundary or edge, we might say, or a threshold of the threshold—serves as the imagined site where some of the play's central issues find their first "dramatic" instantiations.

Audiences enter Shakespeare's late romance through its opening sea-storm; the first reprieve they get from this event is when they witness a character lament its effects:

The sky, it seems, would pour down stinking pitch,
But that the sea, mounting to th' welkin's cheek,

> Dashes the fire out. O, I have sufferèd
> With those that I saw suffer! A brave vessel,
> Who had, no doubt, some noble creature in her,
> Dashed all to pieces! O, the cry did knock
> Against my very heart! Poor souls, they perished.
> Had I been any god of power, I would
> Have sunk the sea within the earth, or ere
> It should the good ship so have swallowed and
> The fraughting souls within her.
>
> (Shakespeare [1610–11] 2008: 1.2.3–13)

The stage directions do not indicate where on the island this speaker is, but she inhabits the persona of the shoreline observer, claiming to recount an event at sea that she has just witnessed. This character grapples with her conflicted relation to the figures she perceives to be lost at sea: her physical distance is at odds with her emotional proximity to "those that [she] saw suffer." The sea-storm not only enthralls the speaker but also continues to fascinate audiences and readers. Scholars repeatedly attempt to situate the play's titular tempest alongside the numerous maritime disasters littered across early modern writing.[17] This focus is to be expected. Catastrophes at sea are, after all, among the most mundane of wonders in literary history—these spectacular occurrences condense crises that characters experience into a singular event, amplifying their dramatic effect.

The viewpoint of this figure (who we soon learn is Miranda) is crucial in setting up key concerns of *The Tempest*. Her words establish the terraqueous space's symbiotic relationship to the sea: the island's shore is a site of witnessing, a symbol of safety for maritime travelers, and a vantage from which to reinterpret catastrophes. This scene also presents Miranda as the latest manifestation of the motif of "shipwreck with spectator."[18] Book II of Lucretius's *De Rerum Natura* begins with the words "How sweet it is to watch from dry land when the storm-winds roil / A mighty ocean's waters, and see another's bitter toil –/ Not because you relish someone else's misery – / Rather, it's sweet to know from what misfortunes you are free" (2007: 1–4). This trope is also adopted by Renaissance natural philosophers such as Francis Bacon.[19] Miranda, however, revises Lucretius's sense of spectatorial distance and contentment, suggesting that her perspective from the island's shore, full of suspense, apprehension, and identification with the travelers, will chart a different path in maritime literary history.

Miranda becomes an active participant in shaping audiences' perception of the relation between land and sea. She presents a totalizing view of past events as an immersive experience. Recalling her observation of the tempest, she recasts the disaster in terms of its effects on her. It triggers her suffering and her desires to identify with "those that [she] saw suffer." More importantly, in this play obsessed with authorial and creative power—Prospero has long been identified as the figure for the author-dramatist, and even as a representation of Shakespeare taking a bow from the stage—the first pronunciation of creative desire comes from Miranda, when she declares "Had I been any god of power, I would / Have sunk the sea within the earth."[20] She longs for the "power" to actualize what she imagines and projects an alternate world by mentally transporting herself to the shore, a location Gillis identifies as a "precarious but seductive plac[e], freighted with dread as well as invested with great expectations" (2012: 60). Miranda's desire that she could have subsumed the waters into the land envisages an act of geographic reorientation at par with Utopus's artificial construction of an island. It also aspires to the level of control that her father demonstrates over their environment throughout the play. Her ambitions, then, foreshadow the kinds of dramatic actions that Prospero undertakes—actions that demarcate the formal parameters of what can be staged in the island theater. Remembering herself on the island's edge, Miranda mimics the possibilities and dangers that characterize the shore itself.[21]

THE PARADOX OF THE SHORE: SAFETY AND PRECARITY IN *NEW ARCADIA*

Miranda presents the island's shore as a refuge from the storm, but this feeling is soon revealed to be a fantasy. Once they arrive on land, the marooned voyagers have to navigate the mysteries, dangers, and unnatural events orchestrated by Prospero. In fact, the shore, as the "archetypal ecotone, where marine and terrestrial ecosystems meet," is definitionally a place of instability, unpredictability, and precarity (Gillis 2014: 155). The tussle between danger and security at this site is visible in many early modern works, where an initial escape from oceanic travails promises comfort on land, only for unfolding events to undermine this assumption. From the perspective of shore-dwellers, the formlessness of sea gives way to the relatively contained form of land—an island is surely more bounded than the vast oceans. But as survivors begin to explore the ground they occupy, they are exposed to new dangers. These issues of disaster and rescue, and of precarity and shelter are acutely rendered in one of the period's most iconic works.

Philip Sidney's *New Arcadia* (1593), which precedes *The Tempest* by approximately two decades, opens with two characters conversing at the shore.[22] The romance begins by situating readers "in the time that the earth begins to put on her new apparel against the approach of her lover, and that the sun, running a most even course, becomes an indifferent arbiter between the night and the day" ([1593] 1977: 61). In this moment "*between* the night and the day" (my emphasis) the shepherds Strephon and Claius recall past events on "the sands which lie against the island of Cithera" (61). These opening lines hint that the liminal nature of the shore is inextricable from the ways in which characters relate to their nonhuman environs. These shepherds represent the terrestrial domain of the pastoral, but they also share affinities with the maritime environment. United in their "remembrance" of Urania, the "friendly rival[s]" refuse to "leave that shore unsaluted from whence [they] may see to the island where she dwelleth" (61–2). For the speakers, "this place" (62) is the site of celebrating the past and of lamenting loss. It also provides manifold perspectives, allowing them to look from land to water and then beyond to "the island where she dwelleth."

Strephon's description of Urania's departure also mirrors the liminality of their environs: "yonder, did she put her foot into the boat, at that instant, as it were, dividing her heavenly beauty between the earth and the sea. But when she was embarked, did you not mark how the winds whistled and the seas danced for joy, how the sails did swell with pride, and all because they had Urania?" (62). Urania exists in symbiosis with her natural habitat—she is intimately tied to the "winds," "seas," and "sails." Moreover, she can activate, and thereby change, the environment. This description makes her seem almost-terraqueous, a figure whose act of "put[ting] her foot into the boat" enables her to "divid[e] her heavenly beauty between the earth and the sea." Urania's pluralistic ontology reflects the multivalent state of the physical space.

This "call to memory" (63) presents the shepherds as passive observers on land, but it also enacts *their* environmental fantasy. Strephon anthropomorphizes the "winds," "seas," and "sails" but presents Urania as precious cargo—the elements of nature "had" her. The shepherds describe the inaccessible Urania in terms of a familiar surrounding they can navigate. Indeed, they soon take on an active role in this setting when "they both perceived a thing which floated, drawing nearer and nearer to the bank, but rather by the favourable working of the sea than by any self-industry" (64). Witnessing this floating "thing" being brought to the shore by the "favourable working of the sea," the "friendly rival[s]" become collaborators, we might say, with the aquatic environment. They transform "this place" of reminiscence into one of action. In his compelling reading of this scene, Julian Yates focuses on the prolonged moments of narrative suspension between the instant when the shepherds realize that there is "some 'thing'" "*already* in the water" and "the arrival of the 'thing'" on shore, at which point it is revealed to be a man (2003: 11). Yates claims that the emergence of the man, Musidorus, "punctuates [the shepherds'] nostalgia" (11). This is a "moment of shipwreck, of an environmental catastrophe that assumes the power of a beginning, of a foundation" (9). As the "thing" "leaves the natural economy of tides and flows [it] enters an economy of fixed, human agents. As it crosses this threshold, the 'thing' is instantiated within an ethical, cultural, and social system; it becomes a man" (15). This analysis focalizes the shift from "thing" to "man," and the movement from the "natural economy of tides" to the "economy of fixed, human agents"—implicitly terrestrial—as the conditions propelling the narrative forward. It thus contrasts the flexibilities of nature to the fixity of human networks. But we can extend this argument to note that the location facilitates the *simultaneous* suspension and propulsion of action: the shore functions as the "threshold" that blurs the borders between rumination and activity, thing and man, tableau and narrative—it is the physical-environmental equivalent of the fluctuating roles of the romance's actors and events.

Having barely stepped into the world of the *New Arcadia*, readers are unaware of the significance of this rescue, although for those familiar with romance conventions, the subsequent descriptions of the "young man" would surely signal his importance. The shepherds aid his deliverance:

> drew they up a young man of so goodly shape and well-pleasing favour that one would think death had in him a lovely countenance, and that, though he were naked, nakedness was to him an apparel. That sight increased their compassion, and their compassion called up their care; so that lifting his feet above his head, making a great deal of salt water come out of his mouth, they laid him upon some of their garments and fell to rub and chafe him till they brought him to recover both breath, the servant, and warmth, the companion, of living. (Sidney [1593] 1977: 64)

In rescuing the "young man," the shepherds, it seems, cede the plot to the new character. Yet, the text remains ambiguous about a swift severance of the narrative from the shore or from these minor actors. The "threshold" is not so easily escapable—"this place" extends its pull a little longer. The new figure's transition from "thing" to "young man" does not occur as a linear progression from water to inland that drives the narrative forward. Instead, he is defined through his alignment with both shore and sea. He brings "a great deal of salt water" with him, this description highlighting his polyvalent state of being. By dispelling this water, he comes back to the "living." He concurrently makes the ground on which he spills the "salt water" terraqueous. The character's pluralistic state and the multiplicity of the environment mirror each other.

Musidorus cannot dissociate himself from the dangerous waters he had apparently left behind: "Therewithal he offered wilfully to cast himself again into the sea: a strange sight to the shepherds, to whom it seemed that before, being in appearance dead had yet saved his life, and now, coming to his life should be a cause to procure his death" (64). Musidorus responds to the crisis of his separation from Pyrocles, who is still at sea, by desiring to return to his erstwhile precarious condition. While the shepherds consider their shore a safe haven, Musidorus's emotional response implies otherwise. What they consider a "strange sight," he sees as the source of salvation. At first glance, the shore offers physical safety from the perilous waters that threaten maritime travelers. But from the perspective of the character who has left behind his companion at sea, the land at its edge is a space of anguish. Musidorus's sense of loss and "strange" desire suggest that the shore, at best, provides, temporary and partial shelter. He is safe, but his willful offer to "cast himself again into the sea" is also an expression of obligation to another—Pyrocles—who might have no such recourse to safety. The offer to renegotiate this zone between land and water hints at a form of communal responsibility that overrides, even as it is a product of, his physical safety.

Musidorus's response exemplifies the ethos of the opening scene: just when the narrative is on the brink of moving on from the maritime events, characters continue to remain in or at the edge of the treacherous waters. In Patricia Parker's influential formulation, the early modern romance is "a form which simultaneously quests for and postpones a particular end" (1979: 4). Following her argument, we could classify the *New Arcadia's* initial deferral as another example of romance dilation, where promised security—if security is indeed synonymous with escaping oceanic storms, pirates, and shipwrecks—is delayed. I would propose, however, that this scene is not merely an *instance* of romance dilation. Instead, the shore's status as an "edge" is an essential *vehicle* for the construction of the romance's dilatory form. The characters' treatment of the shore as the physical-conceptual element through which they revise their relation to their environs is constitutive to expanding the temporal fabric of the narrative.

The shore's function as a transitional space that defines the parameters of literary form becomes clearer when we witness characters unable to escape their maritime origins. Musidorus lingers at the edge of water, his initial role as a unique figure who punctures the shepherds' rumination receding from view as he adopts their observational stance. He too becomes a witness to nautical events. When the "fisherman" takes him, along with the shepherds, out to the waters, he watches events unfolding on the sea from afar:

> the young man no sooner saw [a stain of the water's color, and by times some sparks and smoke mounting thereout] but that beating his breast he cried that there was the beginning of his ruin, entreating them to bend their course as near unto it as they could; telling how that smoke was but a small relique of a great fire which had driven both him and his friend rather to commit themselves to the cold mercy of the sea than to abide the hot cruelty of the fire. (Sidney [1593] 1977: 65)

As Musidorus laments his friend's loss by recollecting their past experience, he comes to occupy a vantage analogous to the shepherds'—he too indulges in "remembrance." In fact, all of the pathos that the shepherds initially invested in Musidorus, he now transfers to Pyrocles. Musidorus's singularity, as one of "so goodly shape and well-pleasing favour," fades from view as Pyrocles replaces him as strange, inaccessible, even majestic.

The text cements these shifts by establishing Pyrocles as a truer maritime figure:

> But a little way off they saw the mast, whose proud height now lay along, like a widow having lost her mate of whom she held her honour: but upon the mast they saw a young man—at least if he were a man—bearing show of about eighteen years of age, who sat as on horse back, having nothing upon him but his shirt which, being wrought with blue silk and gold, had a kind of resemblance to the sea on which the sun (then near his western home) did shoot some of his beams. His hair … was stirred up and down with the wind, which seemed to have a sport to play with it as the sea had to kiss his feet. (66)

Pyrocles's description—his hair "stirred up and down with the wind"—confirms his dynamic presence. This depiction also aligns him with Urania, in that both are intimately connected to their environment: he "had a kind of resemblance to the sea" and his hair "which seemed to have a sport to play with it as the sea had to kiss his feet," makes him one with his immediate location.

Pyrocles's maritime identity—and his role and function in the seas—continues to haunt him. As Claire Jowitt has shown, Pyrocles is repeatedly associated with pirates. Even after he comes to Arcadia, he and other characters recall his adventures at sea (2010: 100–8). Musidorus will even criticize him by saying, "thyself is the pirate" (Sidney [1593] 1977: 117).[23] These instances adumbrate how Pyrocles cannot escape his nautical past. Musidorus, on the other hand, disguises himself as a shepherd to gain closer access to Pamela. I would argue that he too has embraced his association with the figure of the shepherd, whose perspective he mimicked when he stepped on the shore—the shepherd has become both agent and product of the location. The events at the shore leave an indelible mark on both characters and influence their subsequent stories. The shore's unstable positionality invites the coexistence of various roles and affective states of being, and Pyrocles's and Musidorus's polymorphous identities find their genesis in—or in proximity to—this terraqueous region.

URANIA'S ARCHIPELAGIC SUBJECTIVITY

Oceanic travel and maritime disasters are not unique to the *New Arcadia*. These destabilizing forces are the staple of early modern romance. If seventeenth-century readers were in search of a work whose ambitious scope simultaneously revels in and wrestles with the instabilities constitutive to the genre, they would need to look no further than *The Countess of Montgomery's Urania*. In the remaining space of my chapter, I explore how Wroth's massive corpus—deeply invested in exploring questions of authority and authorship, in inquiring about forms of female subjectivity, and in charting domestic, social, and political networks—invokes a capacious nautical ecology to represent the dynamism of human actions and to accentuate the indeterminacies of literary form.

Wroth was the first Englishwoman to publish an original prose romance.[24] It is commonly accepted that she models her work on her uncle Sidney's work—even echoing its assigned title, *The Countess of Pembroke's Arcadia*— and names her eponymous heroine after the *New Arcadia's* absent Urania, whose departure Strephon and Claius mourn at the seashore. But Wroth is even more deliberate in using islands and shores to structure her narrative. Situating characters and their adventures across isles in the Mediterranean, she constructs an international, geopolitical network that is inseparable from the text's explorations of individual crises and interpersonal relationships. Here, islands are not isolated entities that make them ideal for social or intellectual experiments. Instead, they are the material form of the *Urania's* archipelagic world, in which island-hopping structures not only human and nonhuman relations, but is also instrumental to the evolution of the narrative.

Scholars have variously demonstrated that the *Urania's* expansive transcultural imagination must occupy a central place in critical conversations on the "Global Renaissance."[25] Josephine A. Roberts suggests in her critical "Introduction" (1995) that Wroth might have studied various cartographic representations, including

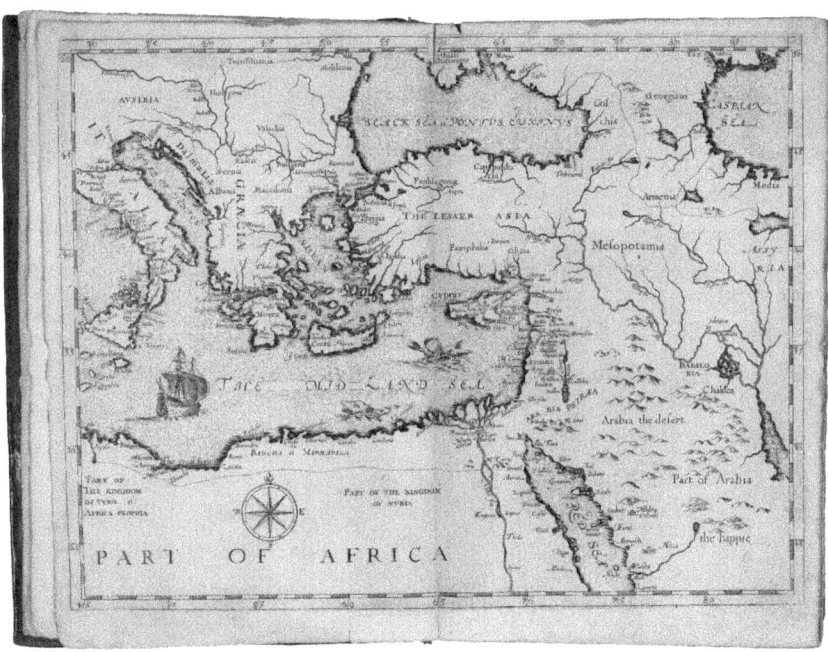

FIGURE 5.5 George Sandys, *A Relation of a Journey Begun an: Dom*, 1610. © The Folger Shakespeare Library.

the maps of Gerhard Mercator and Ortelius. George Sandys's *A Relation of a Journey* (1615) "contains a frontispiece map that conveniently includes nearly all of the key countries mentioned in the *Urania*" (Roberts 1995: xliv; see Figure 5.5). In her groundbreaking study on the intersections of gender and race, Kim F. Hall argues that in an era of maritime expansion, when misogynist discourses often framed travel as an escape from women, "Wroth demystifies a tradition of European male refusal to acknowledge that the seduction of conquest and exploration and the seductiveness of native women are often the same. European women thus are always in subtle competition with the glory of travel and adventure that is the essence of male romance" (1996b: 189). Recent scholars have shown the particular forms such competition can take. Bernadette Andrea's recent study of the romance's "gendered and racialized negotiations of authorship" reveals how "early modern Englishwomen aligned themselves with their countrymen's imperial ambitions" (2016: 61, 62). Rachel Orgis further elaborates how the text's "narrative strands" form "distinct travel patterns on the early modern maps that underpin the universe of the *Urania*" (2017: 10). Focusing on the *Urania's* maritime tropes, Sheila T. Cavanagh uncovers how "the sea operates metaphorically, metonymically, and literally" to provide "emotional release by offering escape" and "also enabl[e] externalized manifestations of strong emotions" (2001: 103). In this nautical environment, romance world-building is contingent on the materialization of an archipelagic vision.

Islands are omnipresent in the world of the *Urania*. The text notes almost in passing that "they [knights] entred many Islands, seeking and finding adventures"; it is a commonplace that islands are among the principal sites of romance quests (Wroth [1621] 1995: 132). As travel by sea keeps the plot moving, the text invokes isles of all kinds—small and large, central to the action or marginal to the plot—that characters must navigate. Readers read about "Ciprus," with its barbarous people (46) and "Cerigo, Dragonero" (97), and they learn about exploits in Sicily, "Cephalonia" (41) and "Stalamine, anciently Lemnos" (192). Perissus, who offers one of the first digressive narratives that is a key formal feature of the *Urania*, situates himself in reference to island-states: he is "Nephew ... to the King of Sicilie, a place fruitfull and plentifull of all things" (5). In much of the romance, Antissia's isolated and somewhat ostracized status is reflected in the diverse aquatic and terraqueous locations where she finds herself. The daughter of the King of Romania, Antissia exemplifies Wroth's negative model of the woman writer.[26] By perusing only a few early episodes, readers learn that she has been captured by pirates and left on "some Island," and that she is seized by rovers at a coast, is soon taken to another coast before a storm and shipwreck drive her to Morea (30; see also 29, 31, 38, 40). Antissia's relationship to islands might be even more elemental; as Roberts notes, her name may derive partially from the town of "Antissa" on Sappho's home, the island of Lesbos (1995: xxxiv). Furthermore, some of the *Urania's* most significant events take place on islands. For example, the Throne of Love, the culminating adventure of the first book, occurs on Cyprus. Various characters get imprisoned in this structure until Amphilanthus and Pamphilia—Wroth's positive model of the woman writer—travel to the island to successfully undergo the trial that sets everyone free. And in a work that constantly documents political liaisons, the boundedness of islands is used to define and demarcate specific alliances: Philarchos and Orilena inherit islands, when her father confers to them the isle of "Metelin, and some other neighbouring Ilands which lye in the Archepelago" (Wroth [1621] 1995: 201).

Even this small selection highlights the abundance of evidence one can accumulate when studying islands in the *Urania*. I would posit that this profusion is an essential formal feature of the romance, which requires an archipelagic land-seascape to construct its intricate networks of relationships among characters, localized communities, or nation-states. In a fictive universe where diverse figures recall past events, participate in trials, and navigate affective and geographical distances, the "sea of islands" affords both physical and symbolic opportunities to gather, ruminate, and act. It is not only *Urania's* characters who engage in island-hopping. The romance unfolds as a series of motions across islands, its formal structure a terraqueous assemblage. The *Urania* offers a strong case that the island is, to draw on Helen Cooper's work, a "meme" of romance.[27]

Mobility, whether physical or conceptual, is the governing ethos of the romance, where isolation (as in Antissia's case) and imprisonment (in the Throne of Love, for instance) are cast as unnatural, and ideally temporary, states of existence. In this environment, islands serve as discrete settings that characters traverse to actualize an array of chivalric quests, geopolitical events, and interpersonal encounters. But as edges or liminal spaces, Wroth's islands also emerge as thresholds of emotional transformation. To foreground their function as sites of transition, even metamorphosis, I examine two moments in which Wroth conjoins her eponymous character's evolving understanding of selfhood to the particularities of this threshold. Urania is part of the romance's international aristocratic network but has been severed from it at infancy. She has grown up as a shepherdess and only recently discovered her origins. In the narrative's opening sections, she grapples with this newfound knowledge by linking her memories to aquatic and terraqueous realms.

Urania recalls being "found hard by the sea-side, not farre from these rocks" sixteen years ago (22). The infant's perilous position is reflected in the island's rocky terrain. Being abandoned "by the sea-side," she has been disconnected from courtly cultures. In the narrative present, however, she is on the brink of reclaiming her original identity; meeting Parselius on the island sets in motion her physical and social transition to court. On the verge of this change, she relates differently to the island, declaring it to be a "sweet Iland" that is called Pantalaria, govern'd by an ancient worthie Lord called Pantalerius, who having receiv'd some discontent in his owne Countrie, with his family, and some others that lov'd and serv'd him, came hither, finding this place unpossesst, and so nam'd it after his owne name, having ever since in great quiet and pleasure remained here. (21–2)

The island has become a refugium (instead of a dangerous place) for the adult Urania, much as it did for its ruler. Through his act of naming, Pantalerius binds himself to his environs. And while their associations with the island follow different trajectories—Pantalerius moves from court to "this place unpossesst," and Urania will undertake the opposite journey—both participate in the fantasy of coexistence with an isolated natural refuge. When she relives her abandonment, Urania's language parallels her sense of herself as a blank slate— she did not know who she was—with her original perception of the island as an unknown territory. But her current conditions also reverse the island's significations: the closer she comes to regaining self-knowledge, the more familiar—and knowable—the place becomes. Such intimacies between human and environment also recall Sidney's Urania. As Wroth's Urania reclaims an identity that had been foreclosed to her, the rocky terrain morphs into an idyllic landscape.

Urania also experiences a profound transformation that alters her memory, and by extension, her fundamental understanding of self, on an island's edge. She is heartbroken after Parselius goes missing (she does not yet know that he has deserted her). To cure her of her anguish, her brother Amphilanthus takes her "straight unto the sea," and they travel to St. Maura, an island in the Mediterranean (212). The waters at the edge of the isle have curative powers, and he believes her immersion in them will release her of this love.[28] The question of what constitutes a stable self is at the heart of Wroth's romance, which explores the varied ways in which (especially) female characters negotiate issues of subject-hood, desire, and authority. It thus seems fitting that to reorient Urania's self-knowledge—by terminating one of her foundational relationships—the text, once again, marshals the instabilities of the maritime environment.

At yet another precarious juncture, Urania must again navigate nature's threatening forces. Taking her to the "Rocke" at the perimeter of the island, Amphilanthus declares,

Fortune (never favourable to us) hath ordain'd, a strange adventure for us, and the more cruell it is, since not to be avoyded, nor to be executed but by my hands, who best love you; yet blame me not, since I have assured hope of good success, yet apparent death in the action … I must throw thee into the Sea. (230)

Urania's fate is unknown. Despite the "assured hope of good successe," Amphilanthus remains suspicious of the "apparent death" she will face when he throws her "into the Sea." In his ambivalence about the "cruell" nature of their "strange adventure," Amphilanthus takes the extreme step of "resolving, if she perish'd to ende with her," and

> he took her in his armes, and gently let her slide, shewing it rather to be her slipping from him, then his letting her fall, and as shee fell, so fell his heart in woe, drowned in as deepe an Ocean of despaire; but soone was he call'd to wonder, and all joy; for no sooner had she suncke into the water, but the waves did beare her up againe, to shewe the glory they had in bearing such perfections; but then the Deepes, ambitious of such a prize, sought to obtaine her, opening their hearts to let her sincke into them. (230)

As Urania "slip[s]" into the water, Amphilanthus is "drowned in as deepe an Ocean of despaire." This scene equates physical and psychological perils, stating that "as shee fell, so fell his heart in woe." Such sympathy between the characters flattens their different levels of precarity. Amphilanthus's emotional fall is founded on a much lower degree of risk than Urania's physical plunge. But this flattening also transfers responsibility from him to her, intimating that *she* controls her fall: even though "he took her in his armes, and gently let her slide," it appeared "rather to be her slipping from him, then his letting her fall." This transference raises the possibility that in her surrender, Urania exercises a form of agency.

This shift is even more striking when we notice how the romance transfers her physical experience and her emotional turmoil to an anthropomorphized ocean. The sea's will and volition echo her unsettled state. The aquatic environment's force makes her oscillate between a promise of release ("the waves did beare her up") and the danger that she will be consumed by nature ("the Deepes, ambitious of such a prize, sought to obtaine her"). Ultimately, the "operation of that water" functions as Amphilanthus hopes, freeing Urania of her memories of loving Parselius (230). Stepping back on land, "Urania's desires were no other, then to goe into Italy to see her father" (231). Here, the sea is a being with conflicted desires, wishing both to "beare" Urania up and to swallow her. One desire ultimately wins out, and this resolution parallels the ways in which Urania's unstable self, riven with wild desires, gets unified by a single, new wish: to go "see her father." The sea enacts, and then resolves, Urania's emotional chaos. The dynamism of the nautical environs accommodates the fluctuating fortunes of the human actor when she surrenders control, and her return to land signals the emergence of an altered, stable self. This scene at the "edge" of land and water functions both as an affective and a *narrational* "threshold," revealing how the shore both shields and exposes. Urania's acknowledgement of vulnerability to natural (and supernatural) forces ensures shelter from physical and affective danger. Releasing the character from past passions, this encounter opens up the formal space to forge new connections and to design new plots.

ISLOMANIA AND THE BLUE HUMANITIES

Early modern islomaniacs celebrate the island's multiplicity: by exposing the fantasy of insularity while also indulging in it; by suggesting that a self can be rediscovered, even re-formed, here; by shadowing new worlds of the imagination and colonizing uncharted lands in the actual world; by inciting experimentation; by dramatizing loss and survival; by empowering marginalized voices to rewrite literary history. Islomania is striking both in its scope and in its ambitions, and it enables its acolytes to transform a bounded physical place into a capacious vehicle of inquiry on critical questions of epistemology, ontology, and *poesy*. This "fascination with islands" gave form to the chaotic and brought the unthinkable within one's cognitive grasp. Even as the island serves as the raw material on which artists and writers fashion their notions about the nonhuman environment, their ideas are transformed by their encounters with this terraqueous entity.

By approaching the island as an imaginative force whose effects are traceable in realms including aesthetics, politics, and philosophy, we are better able to uncover its vital function as an object as well as an instrument of knowledge production. The island, I would suggest, is uniquely positioned—as physical space, as intellectual concept, as imagined ideal—to bring together different strands of questions being raised in the "blue humanities." This cross-disciplinary field of study has demonstrated how attention to maritime themes, metaphors, and habitats are indispensable to gaining a fuller picture of social, political, and environmental issues. This work has also foregrounded the conflicting pulls that exist in the study of marine environments. On the one hand, research on the ocean aims to counter the "terrestrial bias" that is prevalent in a lot of ecocritical work (Brayton 2012: 18). At the same time, studies of terraqueous spaces must pose a "challenge not only to the conventions of *terracentric* history, but also to the *deep-sea* preoccupations of conventional maritime studies" (Gillis 2012: 5, my emphasis). As an ecotone, the island spans these divisions, indeed, thrives on muddying the distinctions between the earthbound and the aquatic. By focusing on what exists "betwixt and between," rather than privileging either land or water, we rediscover in this "this little world" a microcosm of our pluralistic environs.

CHAPTER SIX

Travelers

Voyages to Known and Unknown Worlds

JOSIAH BLACKMORE

The sixteenth and first half of the seventeenth centuries witnessed a wide-ranging practice of transoceanic travel by navigators, explorers, merchants, and religious figures who sailed from southern Europe into the Atlantic, the Indian Ocean, the Red Sea, and the Pacific. From the late fourteenth century with the Iberian voyages to the Canaries, followed (beginning in the fifteenth century) by voyages around Africa, to the New World, and to Asia, a large number of travelers left records of their voyages in the form of rutters, ships' diaries, chronicles, maps, portolan charts, eyewitness accounts, and poetry. These documents, collectively, register a multifaceted interest in topics such as language, religion, culture, politics, trade, nautical science, geography, and cosmography. The early modern culture of sea travelers who breached the confines of the Mediterranean has its initial focus on Africa, with Portuguese expeditions to north Africa that eventually advanced along the west African coast and into east Africa and then the Indian Ocean. By the time Columbus reached the New World in 1492, and Vasco da Gama arrived in India in 1498, Portugal had already been sending travelers to Africa for eight decades.[1] The well-known voyages of Columbus and Gama were part of an existing culture of seafaring and encounters with non-European peoples, so we cannot read Columbus's famous voyage and resulting diaries as events that emerged *ex nihilo*. The fifteenth-century Luso-African contact is the first arena of early modern maritime empire. Portuguese expeditions along the west coast of

Africa through the fifteenth century resulted in the creation of *feitorias* (trading factories) and the capturing of native inhabitants, especially those living south of Cape Bojador beginning in 1441, who were then shipped to Portugal for sale in the incipient Atlantic slave trade. This trade brought slaves to Europe on ships as opposed to the Islamic caravans of the trans-Sahara. It was Portuguese court chronicler Gomes Eanes de Zurara (1410[?]–74) who recounted the Portuguese voyages to Africa that were pursued during the lifetime of Prince Henry, "the Navigator" (d.1460), in such texts as the *Crónica da tomada de Ceuta* (Chronicle of the Capture of Ceuta) on the Portuguese invasion of the Moroccan city in 1415 or the *Crónica dos feitos notáveis que se passaram na conquista de Guiné por mandado do infante D. Henrique* (Chronicle of the Remarkable Deeds relating to the Conquest of Guinea by Order of Prince Henry), which includes the first Portuguese voyages beyond Cape Bojador and into sub-Saharan Africa.[2] Also important is the eyewitness account (*Navigazioni*, written 1464–5) of the Venetian merchant Alvise da Cadamosto (d.1488) who made two journeys to Africa in 1455 and 1456 under the orders of Prince Henry. Zurara's and Cadamosto's narratives are important moments in the culture of writing that was part of Iberian imperial encounter and seafaring.

1500 was the year of the voyage of Pedro Álvares Cabral, whose fleet sailed from Lisbon in March and arrived at the coast of what is now Brazil the following month. Cabral remains the first-documented European to visit these shores, although his status as the first European ever to see Brazil is open to question as is the extent to which Cabral's landing in Brazil, occurring on a voyage to India ordered by King Manuel I as a follow-up to Vasco da Gama's 1497 to 1499 expedition to the subcontinent, was accidental or deliberate (Disney 2009: 204–5). The three eyewitness accounts that survive of Cabral's presence in the New World are: the *Carta* (Letter) of Pero Vaz de Caminha (the onboard secretary of Cabral's expedition), dated May 1, 1500, in Porto Seguro and addressed to Manuel I, which is the most well known of the accounts, and describes only the experiences in the "Terra da Vera Cruz" (Land of the True Cross); another letter by the onboard astronomer Master John; and the Narrative of the Anonymous Pilot, which includes only a a brief mention of the Brazilian landing as the result of a storm, and then describes the continued journey of Cabral on to Africa and India.[3] The narrative of Euro-Amerindian contact recounted in Caminha's *Letter* (written eight years after the first voyage of Christopher Columbus) continues the tradition of writings about meetings and exchanges between Old World navigators and non-European peoples initiated in travels to Africa.

Caminha's *Letter* rehearses a number of conceits and tropes that are characteristic of the rhetoric of (initial) encounters between Europeans and non-Europeans under the aegis of maritime imperialism. These conceits include the view of indigenes as largely uncivilized (albeit amenable, in the present case) with a disposition that would make conversion to Christianity relatively easy; an interest in the physical traits of native peoples; the appropriation of newly discovered geographical places and natural resources through acts of naming; and the search for precious metals for the financial benefit of the Crown. The nautical origin of the contact brings ships and the sea into the authoritative historical and ideological story being told, in that texts such as Caminha's that were created within the networks of imperial power were always to some degree ideological. Caminha begins his epistolary report by stating:

> Although the chief captain of this your fleet, and also the other captains, are writing to Your Highness the news of the finding of this your new land which was now found in this navigation, I shall not refrain from also giving my account of this to Your Highness, as best I can, although I know less than all of the others how to relate and tell it well. (Greenlee 1995: 5)[4]

Three concepts here create a frame of authority and the putative veracity of the letter's content. First, the *capitão-mor* or royally appointed commander of the fleet, is the seafaring proxy of the monarch. The newly encountered land is already part of Manuel I's dominion with the adjective *vossa* (your). Second is Caminha's use of *navegação* (navigation). In the first instance the term refers to the specific voyage of Cabral's fleet, but it also designates the entire, interconnected imperial and commercial enterprise of seafaring exercised by the monarch, or the geographic domain circumscribed by such enterprise. *Navegação* therefore designates the maritime dominion of the monarch, and this meaning of the word continues to be used throughout the sixteenth century. Here, the "navigation" in question is the *carreira da Índia*, or the oceanic trading route between Portugal and India inaugurated by Vasco da Gama's 1497 to 1499 voyage; in the closing paragraphs of his letter, Caminha identifies Cabral's journey as part of "esta nauegaçam de calecut" (the voyage to Calicut). Calicut was one of the standard ports of call of Portuguese Indiamen of the *carreira*. So it is that the sovereign's imperial, mercantile interests subtend Caminha's act of New World witnessing and confer authority to the narrative. This act of witnessing brings us to the third concept present in the opening sentence of the *Letter*, which is Caminha's labeling of his own discursive activity as "contar e falar" (to narrate and to speak). If *contar* designates the author's narrative activity, the amplification of this activity with *falar* is of note. Such textual "speaking" may simply be a holdover of the humanistic understanding of letters in the *ars dictaminis* as speeches (Witt 1982: 9–10). However, it is more likely that "to speak" here emphasizes Caminha's eyewitness status in the face of the novelties found in the "Land of the True Cross." Epistolary speaking is decidedly a discursivity of the first-person presence.

Caminha goes on to note that, of the technical details of the voyage west he will not write, since such details are the proper concern of the pilots. Caminha records the day and date of the departure from Belém, and notes other dates and incidents (such as the passage of the ships by the Canary Islands, or the loss of the ships of Vasco de Ataíde) prior to the sighting of signs of land. Although brief, these daily notations of the voyage situate the *Letter* within the textual genre of the *roteiro* (rutter), records of sea voyages exhibiting varying degrees of technical (e.g., sea routes, compass bearings, distances, or descriptions of shorelines), meteorological, ethnographic, and historical information related to a voyage between two identifiable locales. *Roteiros*, in their differing registration of the realities of any one itinerary, are a mix of navigational guide, ship's diary, scientific record, historical chronicle, and even cosmographic treatise. Álvaro Velho's eyewitness account of Vasco da Gama's first voyage to India is one of the best-known early examples of this nautical genre, and the ship and seafaring in it and Caminha's letter perform the same (symbolic) functions.

Consider, for example, oceanic space. Margaret Cohen's idea of the chronotope of the sea (specifically the blue-water chronotope) is of interest. Cohen's argument builds on Bakhtin's chronotope of the road, the "poetic dimension to the literary representation of space" in which "the representation of space always entails the representation of time […] time and space are intrinsically connected" (Cohen 2006: 647). Although Cohen's discussion of the "chronotope of the sea" focuses on eighteenth- and nineteenth-century novels, it is possible to relate this idea to *roteiros* since they invest movement through maritime space with a pronounced temporal dimension. In recording the movements of ships, *roteiro* authors characteristically parse those movements into diurnal units as the entries in a ship's log. Daily, chronological time is the temporal building block of the rutter. This unit of time is especially pronounced when there is no progress in the voyage per se, such as those days on which ships are buffeted by storms or bad weather, and no log of movement is made. In such cases, the habit of daily entries is nonetheless maintained. A ship's movements, therefore, are not only defined by daily, chronological time but the ship also becomes a bearer of that time. In their plotted, repeated, and continuous movements ships temporalize the sea. The ship becomes a kind of stylus, writing history onto maritime space and onto the land- and seascapes that the ship reaches.[5] Ships are seaborne clepsydras, clocking oceanic vastness and concatenating it into familiar, temporal units. Thus, with the arrival of Cabral's fleet to the shores of Brazil, history and chronological time itself arrive.

The sea—or, more specifically, the sound of the sea—figures in the description of the initial meeting on the beach between members of Cabral's crew and the indigenes. Caminha writes, "there, [Nicolau Coelho] was unable to have any conversation or useful understanding with them because of the sea breaking on the shore."[6] Caminha's reference to the sea as an impediment to communication between Europeans and New World natives is an important dimension of the beach as a primordial space of encounter between worlds. In the *Letter*, the most common space of interaction between Portuguese and Tupi is the beach or riverbank near the natural port where Cabral's ships are anchored. The littoral, an archetypally liminal space where water metamorphoses into land and land into water, is also, in Greg Dening's arguments, a cultural space of meeting where categories are made including definitions of "we" and "they" (Dening 1980: 3). The failed attempt at communication on the beach, due to the sound of breakers, suggests that Nicolau Coelho (the head of the landing party)—and by extension, the entire Portuguese company—could have understood the natives had it not been for the sound of the waves crashing on the beach. The comment provides a sort of first sound recording of Brazil, an initial instance of the sonic as a dimension of imperial encounter. To Caminha's (or Coelho's) Portuguese ear, native speech and oceanic sound mix indistinguishably. This aural equivalence seems all the more significant because, apparently, the Portuguese had no problems understanding each other on the same beach. In Caminha's *Letter* the beach instantiates an acoustemology or a "world view centered on sound" (Smith 1999: 289) in which the sounds of the New World come into contact with, and contest the sound of, Portuguese as the implicit standard that casts native speech as "berberia" (gibberish). Acoustics are therefore instrumental in cementing a Lusocentric realm over the newly encountered world along the shore, one in which the sounds of the Portuguese language were a world of power and culture unto themselves. The unintelligible sounds of Tupi, like a raw force in nature, invite an acoustic/linguistic act of possession of the Land of the True Cross, a conquest of human sound that is analogous to the conquest of the sea that aurally reverberates along the beach.[7]

Caminha describes Luso-Tupi interaction throughout the *Letter* as a harmonious interaction, however precarious that harmony is felt to be by the Portuguese travelers. The narrative of sociability is expedient to the purposes of colonialism since it suggests that the natives are disposed favorably to Portuguese presence, so it foresees a peaceful conquest. The ship is an important locus for building and demonstrating this intercultural dynamic. During one meeting onboard, the Tupi fall asleep on the ship, a notable moment that testifies to an evolving indigenous trust in the Portuguese. The ship, in addition to the beach, is a privileged meeting place for Euro-Tupi diplomatic exchange, a temporary "hybrid shipboard community" (as Bernhard Klein describes the onboard community of Columbus's *Santa María* in the Caribbean [Klein 2004: 92]) that presages the transcultural dynamic of colonialism.

On the other side of the Atlantic, the first years of the sixteenth century saw the creation of a Portuguese imperial state called the *Estado da Índia* (State of India). The *Estado* was a vast, geographical domain of empire that stretched from the Cape of Good Hope to China. "India" is a toponym that includes, but is not exclusive to, the subcontinent itself, and the State of India had the ocean "as its sovereign territory" (Newitt 2009: 69), and "created a template for subsequent European maritime empires" (74).⁸ The *Estado* was established in 1505, shortly after Vasco da Gama's 1497 to 1499 voyage. It was in the context of the newly formed State of India that three notable travelers wrote influential books based on their experiences. Duarte Pacheco Pereira, Tomé Pires, and Duarte Barbosa all served the State and made long-ranging oceanic voyages. Pereira had extensive experience in Africa and Asia that informed his *Esmeraldo de Situ Orbis* (written 1505–8), a book that combines geography, cosmography, and the science of navigation and describes the world as it had become known through Portuguese seafaring. Although Pereira announces in the prologue that the treatise will include sections on Asia, the *Esmeraldo* remains incomplete and only contains information on western and southern Africa. Pereira begins his historico-scientific narrative by commenting on ancient understandings of the location of the ocean in the center of the earth in authors such as Pliny the Elder, but with special attention granted to the account of the separation of the waters from land in Genesis. This discussion, in essence, rehearses the theory of the *congregatio aquae* (congregation of waters), which sought "to explain the existence of emerged land in harmony with Aristotelian physics" (Relaño 2002: 9). This point is worth mentioning because it demonstrate how Pereira's book is a moment in the transition from received, a priori knowledge of antiquity and the Middle Ages to empirically based knowledge, an epistemological shift that previous and forthcoming travels through the territories of the *Estado da Índia* made inevitable. Tomé Pires and Duarte Barbosa are other outstanding, early sixteenth-century examples of travelers through the State of India, the authors of the *Suma Oriental* (*c.* 1512) and the *Livro de Duarte Barbosa* (*c.* 1516–18), respectively. These books, in Joan-Pau Rubiés's assessment, constitute "the two most comprehensive early Portuguese accounts of the East" (2000: 2). Barbosa made two voyages to India: the first one in 1500 to 1501, and the second—which was his definitive relocation to the subcontinent—in 1511. He served as an official in Cochin (Kochi) and Cannanore, learned Malayalam, and practiced as an interpreter.⁹ Tomé Pires, an apothecary by profession, traveled to India in 1511 and was head of Manuel I's first (unsuccessful) diplomatic mission to China.¹⁰ In both Pires's and Barbosa's books, seafaring and knowledge are inextricable. In his prefatory dedication to King Manuel, Pires begins by noting that "naturally men desire to know."¹¹ He then ascribes this desire superlatively to the monarch, who possesses it to a degree "like no other prince in the world."¹² The reason, Pires explains, is the geographical reach of Manuel's domain, which extends from the head of Africa to China and contains "all of Africa, Asia, and part of Europe along the shore of the Ocean Sea, with an infinity of islands that are great, wealthy, and populous."¹³ In acknowledging the king's military might in the form of *armadas* (fleets), Pires observes that the conquest of foreign political states becomes synonymous with a worldwide project of knowledge gathering that is oceanic in expanse and in the manner of its pursuit. Imperial fleets both conquer Middle Eastern and Indian states and serve as the means by which knowledge is encountered and accrued. Duarte Barbosa, for his part, underscores the genesis of his narrative as the result of years of extensive maritime travels during his youth, the results of which he now records. The *Book*, Barbosa notes in the preface, recounts marvels difficult to believe but that the author personally witnessed. This eyewitness record exists alongside other information on the kingdoms and countries of the Moors and "gentile" peoples and their customs.

Experienced sea travelers such as Pires and Barbosa produced one kind of encyclopedic book with their interests in geography, navigation, mercantile routes, and the political and military dimensions of overseas empire. The writings of the polymath João de Castro (1500–1548), fourth viceroy of India, are similar compendia of knowledge acquired by personal experience. Castro penned a cosmographic treatise, and he also—and more significantly for our purposes—authored three rutters: the *Rutter from Lisbon to Goa* (1538), the *Rutter from Goa to Diu* (1538–9), and the *Rutter of the Red Sea* (1540). These texts are a result of the viceroy's own travels. Castro's *roteiros* differ from previous examples of the genre. While previously rutters were basically an accumulation of details related to the specific voyage described, the viceroy expanded the content of this genre to include systematic reflections on, and criticisms of, scholarly traditions bearing on nautical travel and science, such as cosmography and (historical) geography. As J.C. da Silva Dias observes, the viceroy's rutters supercede an exclusively empirical utilitarianism, since Castro's scholarly method is characterized by a combination of continuous observation and experience, which includes reflections on the differences between theory and practice and often pits Castro against the observations and claims of earlier pilots and scholars (Dias 1982: 83, 84). In the viceroy's hands, the rutter became an important moment in sixteenth-century maritime culture and intellectual history.

This expanded remit of the content of *roteiros* is part of a larger culture of books on navigational science in sixteenth-century Iberia that can be traced to the first years of this relentlessly expansionist and travel-oriented century.[14] Another Renaissance traveler, scholar, pilot, priest, and prisoner of the Portuguese Inquisition who contributed to this nautically inflected intellectual culture was Fernando Oliveira. Oliveira is perhaps best known as the author of the first grammar of the Portuguese language, the *Gramática da linguagem portuguesa* (1536), which was followed four years later by another grammar by the noted historian of Portuguese empire (and friend of Oliveira) João de Barros. Like Castro, Oliveira was also a scholar and scientist dedicated to navigational science, who penned the *Arte da guerra do mar* (The Art of War at Sea, 1555) and the *Ars nautica* (Nautical Art, *c.* 1570) which he later revised and left incomplete as the *Livro da fábrica das naus* (The Book of Shipbuilding,

FIGURE 6.1 Panoramic view of Lisbon in 1622; the shipyard is at the far left, from João Baptista Lavanha, *Viagem da Catholica Real Magestade del Rey D. Filipe II. N.S. ao Reyno de Portvgal e rellação do solene recebimento que nelle se lhe fez*. © Courtesy of Houghton Library, Harvard University.

c. 1580). While this treatise on the science of shipbuilding is not the first of its kind in western Europe (Domingues and Barker 1991: 15), it brings this genre of scholarly writing to Portugal and includes observations on practices current in the Lisbon shipyards or *estaleiros* (Figure 6.1).[15] Oliveira's *Livro* spans many disciplines including history, dendrology, the theory and practice of navigation, and of course details on the architecture and construction of ships.

It is no surprise, given the historical context of maritime empire in which the book was written, that Oliveira acknowledges the primacy of the "art of navigation" in maintaining control and governance of Portuguese overseas territories and colonies. The importance of seafaring in the imperial, oceanic enterprise in Oliveira's discussion, however, implicitly claims a Portuguese superiority in the science since Portugal is a nation historically steeped in nautical voyaging, both in terms of the common people whose lives depend on the sea and in terms of the nation-state. Moreover, for the author of the *Livro*, nautical travel is a phenomenon of the natural world in addition to technological artifice. Oliveira defines "ship" (*navio*) as anything "that moves or carries something over the water" (1991: 153), citing two basic types of vessels: sail, and craft that are propelled by oars. Ships are examples of art imitating nature, and Oliveira cites Aristotle's description of the shape of fish as being a model for a ship's overall form; for Oliveira, fish are even examples of *navios*. The various components necessary for movement and steerage (rudder, mast, and oars) are comparable to the members of organic, animated bodies, like the tails of fish and birds. If, on the one hand, Oliveira's naturalizing rhetoric counters ancient injunctions against sailing as an unnatural human transgression

(Horace's *Ode* 1.3 is perhaps one of the more well-known examples),[16] on the other it subtly casts imperial seafaring as part of the natural world and, by extension, naturalizes imperialism.

In comparison, it is interesting to note two Spanish books of navigation and nautical science that are roughly contemporaneous with Oliveira's *Livro* but which center on Spanish voyages to the New World. Juan de Escalante de Mendoza's *Itinerario de navegación de los mares y tierras occidentales* (Navigational Itinerary of Western Lands and Seas, 1575), dedicated to King Felipe II, is a high point in the tradition of Spanish nautical and cosmographical writings, which includes such books as Martín Fernández de Enciso's *Suma de Geografía* (Compendium of Geography, 1519), Alonso de Chaves's *Quatri Partitu en cosmographia pratica i por otro nombre llamado Espejo de Navegantes* (Four Parts of Practical Cosmography, also called the Mariners' Mirror, 1518–38), Francisco Falero's *Tratado del Esphera y del Arte de Navegar* (Treatise on the Sphere and the Art of Navigation, 1535), or Pedro de Medina's *Arte de navegar* (Art of Navigation, 1545) and *Regimiento de Navegación* (Rules of Navigation, 1563) (Barreiro-Meiro 1985: 11). Like the other books that we have been considering so far, Escalante appeals to his own experience as a sea traveler as the authoritative basis of his treatise, and declares that his book is meant to aid seafarers in avoiding maritime dangers in the service of imperial Christianity, a tradition of navigation that Escalante traces back to Noah and the flood. In 1587, Diego García de Palacio's *Instrucción náutica para navegar* was published in Mexico, in which the author argues that navigation, although condemned by classical thinkers, is necessary for civilization and that the uses to which navigation is put can be beneficial and good. In the introductory comments, García de Palacio elaborates a long history of Spanish nautical travel and of ships that dates to antiquity, an exposition that we might read as imputing a Spanish preeminence in the science and practice of seafaring as opposed, say, to the Portuguese. Collectively, the books of navigation—from Castro's rutters onward—are a response not only to the ever-increasing frequency of nautical voyaging but also demonstrate how navigation was a major dimension of Iberian intellectual culture since it was a preferred basis for scientific and scholarly tours-de-force.

The figure of Portuguese poet Luís Vaz de Camões (*c.* 1524–80) necessarily looms large in any study of the culture of the sea in early modern Europe. Author of the epic poem *Os Lusíadas* (The Lusiads, 1572) which takes as its historical basis the voyage of Vasco da Gama in 1497 to 1499 and which was the first entirely maritime journey between Portugal and India that established the Luso-Indic trading route. Camões also authored lyric poems collected under the title of *Rhythmas* (published posthumously in 1595 and 1598), and a handful of plays. Camões is the sea traveler and writer par excellence of the Iberian sixteenth century. Although biographical documentation of his life is scant, we do know that Camões traveled to Africa, India (Goa), and most likely, Macau.[17] The sea and seafaring suffuse all ten cantos of Os Lusíadas and many of the lyric poems, so the sea informs Camonian poetics in many of its imaginative, historical, metaphorical, symbolic, cosmic, cartographic, and mythological dimensions. While it is reasonable to propose that Camões's own experience as an oceanic traveler provides a vividness and immediacy to his poetry, it is the poetic engagement with the long-standing Portuguese culture of the sea that distinguishes Camões's epic and lyric voices.[18]

Os Lusíadas is a hallmark in the European engagement with the sea. Ever since its publication in 1572, the poem has garnered a long line of critical appreciation as one of the remarkable epics of the sixteenth century and has resided at the center of the Portuguese literary canon. Recently, scholars have studied the poem in terms of its underlying tenets of "worldmaking" or its "emergent understanding of the world's structure," which "celebrates the birth of the post-Columbian world and the vistas for imagination, travel, conquest, and contemplation that it invited" (Ramachandran 2015: 113), or have placed it within the history of "cartographic humanism" (Piechocki 2019). In a 2010 study, Bernhard Klein notes that "few other sixteenth-century instances of

FIGURE 6.2 The gods ordain Vasco da Gama's journey to India, from Manuel de Faria e Sousa, *Lvsiadas de Lvis de Camones / Principe de los poetas de España*, vol. 1 (1639). © Courtesy of Houghton Library, Harvard University.

epic poetry are so heavily invested in the culture of seafaring" (2010: 232), and it is this literary representation of seafaring that makes the poem so urgent for the study of the culture of the sea.[19] Camões invests the ocean with a wide-ranging polysemy, the raw matter of worldspace, historical realities, and mythological creation. It is the lens through which Portuguese travelers perceive and read the new worlds that unfold before the prows of Gama's ships. Gama's fleet, under the orders of Manuel I, seeks nothing less than the *"governo do mar"* (control of the seas), the expansionist ambition that coalesces in the sovereignty of the world's oceans and seas (Figure 6.2).

The motif that encapsulates expansionist desire in the form of oceanic sovereignty is the piloted ship. The command of a high-seas vessel is the realization of expansionist designs, for the controlled errancy of a *nau* manifests human and divine will. While, as Helder Macedo argues, it is possible to read Gama's pathfinding voyage as a voyage that "gathers in history" (2009: 37), it also, importantly, enacts history. The piloted vessel tacks a course that creates history. In this, the figure of Vasco da Gama as a navigator is crucial: for if, as Fernando Gil posits, *Os Lusíadas* is in part characterized by a "first-person effect" (2009: 97), that effect depends on Gama's position as the admiral-viewer of the seas and of new realities.[20] The eyewitness presence that is part of the narrative perspective of Camões's poem and which lends the poem its immediacy as history in the making and as a witness to worlds is inextricably linked to seeing the world from the deck of a ship (we also saw this in Caminha's *Letter*). In other words, the ship is an eyewitness presence, a concept we also find in rutters, which "place the figure of the pilot at the forefront of the nautical narrative" (Safier and Santos 2007: 462).[21] The first-person gaze as that which structures the sea journey also carries with it an epistemological function since, as Klein contends, the sea voyage "is a kind of modern epistemology of uncertainty; it encodes knowledge as always preliminary or partial, and engages, by necessity, with the other and the unfamiliar" (2013: 171).

We find corroboration of the correlation between sea voyaging, the first-person perspective, and the enactment of history in another genre of maritime text as well. The ship at full sail on the high seas, propelled auspiciously by currents of wind, is Camões's favored image of the plenitude of expansionist designs, repeated throughout the ten cantos of the poem. In Fernando Gil's words, expansionist ships are "creatures of the wind" (2009: 98), and the conjoining of nautical vessel and wind is perhaps nowhere more apparent than in the enumerations of the India fleets in the *memória das armadas* (memorial of the fleets) books. Around thirty manuscripts of this genre are extant. They list the ships, captains, and captains-major that departed for India in a designated chronological period, beginning with Gama's fleet in 1497. Some of these manuscripts contain illuminations of individual ships.

FIGURE 6.3 Illuminations of ships of the fleet of Francisco de Almeida, first Portuguese viceroy of India, from *Livro de Lisuarte de Abreu*. © Courtesy of the John Carter Brown Library at Brown University.

Arguably the most well-known book of this genre, and certainly the most lavishly illustrated, is the *Livro de Lisuarte de Abreu* (Book of Lisuarte de Abreu), compiled around 1563 (see Figure 6.3). This codex contains hundreds of images, in vibrant colors, of every Portuguese vessel that made the India voyage between 1497 and 1555, as well as full-page portraits of the more preeminent

FIGURE 6.4 Portrait of Vasco da Gama, from *Livro de Lisuarte de Abreu*. © Courtesy of the John Carter Brown Library at Brown University.

captains-major and imperial administrators of Portuguese India (see Figure 6.4). The ships are typically depicted at full sail. Wind suffuses the nautical iconography of the *Livro de Lisuarte de Abreu* even more so than water and invests the miniatures with a sense of swift movement and directionality. The coexistence, in the same codex, of portraits of noteworthy sea travelers and the portraits of individual vessels establishes that ships and humans are co-protagonists of oceanic exploration and history. These illuminations grant vessels the same exercise of imperial agency and subjectivity as the noted mariners and administrators who are typically depicted in attitudes of confidence. It bears noting that the iconographic depictions of hundreds of often identical ships, however visually repetitive, is significant. This visual reiteration reflects and consolidates a multifaceted and unified seafaring community, across time, whose numeric abundance is testimony of a successful and concerted maritime enterprise. The iconographic proliferation of ships asserts a seamless, expansionist protagonism that supercedes, even erases, the occasional and regular loss of ships due to shipwreck or other dangers. In the *Livro*'s folios, as in the *memórias das armadas* in general, Gama's vessels are the progenitors of this seafaring effort.

In the poetic logic of *The Lusiads*, Camões allows Gama the prerogative of narrating the entirety of Portuguese (and European) history in an episode in which Gama visits the sheikh of Melindi. Throughout the long, historical peroration, Gama frequently aligns *narração* (narrative) and the nautical voyage. It is possible to understand historical narrative as a form of seafaring and vice versa. If Gama is the heroic figure of the poem who exemplifies the collective, Portuguese epic achievement of global seafaring that Camões sings, then there exists a tight alliance between navigation and poetico-historical narrative. When the sheikh of Melindi asks Gama to recite to him the long story of how he arrived in Africa (and implicitly the history of Portugal as a seafaring nation), the scene happens aboard Gama's longboat. The historiographic account that is a discursive centerpiece of the poem thus has its origin *in loco maritimo*. This locale fortifies the relationship between Portuguese/Western historical agency and oceanic space in that not only is the sea the primary medium of history but it is also the condition and genesis of its telling. Gama tells of the distant past as much as he recounts the immediate past of his ongoing expedition, a move that elides past and present into a vivid moment of historical eyewitnessing. Gama narrates and sees history unfolding, a continuous consciousness of historical agency.

If Camões construes oceanic travel as the structural and imaginative center and presiding metaphor and empirical motor of *Os Lusíadas*, he also does so in many of his lyric compositions. A few brief comments will illustrate this. In the sonnet "Como quando do mar tempestuoso," Camões compares the shipwreck survivor (who escapes danger by swimming) to the danger and anguish of love.[22] The maritime and the sentimental realms are mutually constitutive. While there is a Petrarchan precedent to maritime and seafaring motifs, Camões's invocation of the shipwreck swimmer and seafarer occurs within a culture actively engaged in oceanic enterprise, a facet of quotidian, Portuguese life. Oceanic travel and peril are historical realities as much as metaphoric conceits on which Camões builds poetic ipseity. In another sonnet, "Seguia aquele fogo, que o guiava," the poet rehearses the legend of Hero and Leander, a common theme of Iberian poets of the sixteenth century. Camões's version centers on Leander's final moments as he begins to drown as he swims across the Hellespont. As Jason McCloskey (2013) observes in a study of the poem *Leandro* (1543) by Catalan poet Juan Boscán, there are a number of parallels between love and navigation that we also find in other (Spanish) poets of the time.[23] One of those parallels is the metaphor of the body as a nautical vessel, an idea present in Ovid's *Heroides*, a source of many Renaissance versions of the legend. In the Portuguese sonnet, Leander's crossing of the water and the imminent peril of drowning causes a shift in nautical agency: the poem begins with Leander in control of his body like the pilot of a ship who then loses that control and begins to suffer shipwreck. In swimming toward Hero, Leander as a pilot is as determined and bold as any navigator, and controlled steerage is an expression of amorous purpose and resolve. But the shift from steered to shipwrecked body-ship, borrowed from Ovid, is also a shift from agency to passivity, a mark of the transitivity of the amorous relationship. Leander is both lover and the beloved, the agent of love as well as its object in the waiting eyes and heart of Hero.

If the Leander story borrows on a long tradition of rewritings of the story that would have had a special resonance for readers steeped in the everyday realities of seafaring, other poems in the Camonian lyric corpus draw on the poet's own travels and experiences for their subject matter. More specifically, oceanic travel is usually cast as an experience of exile, and this stands in marked contrast to sea travel in *Os Lusíadas* as an expression of destiny, history, and the revelation of new worlds. For example, Elegy I begins with a conversation between the Greek poet Simonides of Ceos and his friend the preeminent Athenian statesman and naval commander Themosticles. Simonides promises to create for his friend an art of memory, but Themosticles rejects the offer, saying he would rather have an art of forgetfulness in order to cast into oblivion his unhappy life as an exile from his home country. The central portion of the poem details Themosticles's voyage to India, a lyric rendering of sorts of the voyage of Vasco da Gama as told in *Os Lusíadas*. Themosticles's journey triggers an overwhelming sense of *saudade* (nostalgia, or nostalgic longing). This acute consciousness of the past also characterizes the hero's relationship to the sea in Camões's pen, in which the sea voyage enacts a separation from home and a loss of sense of community. Themosticles's exilic ship bears witness to a potentially endless voyage of personal wandering through the spaces of the world. The Greek mariner asks the sea nymphs who accompany the vessel to return to Portugal and write verses in the sand about his fate and his life, in essence petitioning them to become poetic, melancholic messengers of the existential crisis of being lost in the world. Interestingly, the nymphs or Nereids

FIGURE 6.5 Sea nereids supporting and steering Gama's ship, from *Os Lusíadas*, ed. of Miguel Rodrigues (1772). © Courtesy of Houghton Library, Harvard University.

that accompany Gama's ships in *The Lusiads* are part of a worldwide maritime harmony, who reinforce destiny and the achievement of a global, seafaring order (Figure 6.5).

If Camões and Vasco da Gama represent two notable transoceanic travelers of the sixteenth century, Ferdinand Magellan (Fernão de Magalhães) represents another. Portuguese by birth, Magellan began his seafaring career on an expedition to India with Francisco de Almeida, the first Portuguese viceroy of India. After a falling out with the Portuguese monarch Manuel I, Magellan traveled in the service of the Spanish Crown and his fleet of five ships left Spain under the orders of Charles V, the Holy Roman emperor, in 1519. When the expedition returned in 1522 (without Magellan himself, who had been killed in the Philippines [Cebu] in 1521), it had completed its circumnavigation, the first global, oceanic voyage in Western history. Magellan discovered the link in South America between the Atlantic and Pacific Oceans in what he first called the "*strecho de todos santos*" (All Saints Strait) and that now bears his name, the Strait of Magellan. Magellan's name is generally associated with the discovery of the Pacific for Europeans, although Vasco Núñez de Balboa had already sighted it in Panama in 1513 and Martin Waldseemüller included it in his 1507 world map.[24] The narrative of Magellan's voyage was written by an Italian, Antonio Pigafetta, who was part of the expedition. The text was completed *c*. 1525; the original is lost. The consequential editor of early modern travel narratives, Giovanni Ramusio, prepared an edition of Pigafetta's story that was first published in 1536 and later included it in a volume of his influential *Delle navigationi et viaggi* in 1550.[25] Pigafetta was translated into numerous languages. The first full translation into English was published by Samuel Purchas in *Hakluytus Posthumus or his Pilgrimes* (1625), and an earlier translation was known to Shakespeare.

Arguably no other genre of sea traveler's tale at the time was more dramatic than the shipwreck narrative. Often dangerously overburdened with cargo, and tacking through the perilous waters near southern Africa where Atlantic and Indian Ocean currents meet, Portuguese vessels making the return trip to Portugal from India frequently wrecked and left passengers of all stripes stranded in the African wilderness. Those who managed to return home would tell their tales of terror, hardship, and woe. These gripping stories were usually printed as pamphlets and sold on the streets, or sometimes were part of more extensive, learned works; many of them read like scripts of a modern action film. In the eighteenth century, a Portuguese bibliographer by the name of Bernardo Gomes de Brito collected as many of these stories as he could find and published them as an anthology called *História trágico-marítima* (Tragic History of the Sea) in 1735–6.[26] The narratives themselves date from the sixteenth and seventeenth centuries, with the earliest extant example being the account of the wreck of the S. João, which occurred in east Africa in 1552.

We can read the story of the S. João as a model of the genre of sorts, in part because it was the most widely known, translated, and circulated outside of Portugal.[27] These gripping tales of maritime disaster and survival, collectively, are remarkable for the details of protracted hardship and of the contingencies of sea travel that were prevalent in the culture of

FIGURE 6.6 Woodcut of shipwreck, from *Naufragio e lastimoso sucesso da perdiçam de Manoel de Sousa de Sepulueda, & Dona Lianor de Sá sua molher & filhos* ... (1594). © Courtesy of the John Carter Brown Library at Brown University.

transoceanic enterprise, including but not limited to imperial expeditions. They present another dimension of Western/non-Western ethnographic encounter that characteristically saw European travelers at a decided disadvantage. In documenting the increasingly frequent presence of Portuguese castaways in southern Africa, it is possible to think of some of these stories as proto-diasporic. There is a certain irony in the fact that much of the useful information (geographical, ethnographic, botanical, or zoological) gathered on account of these violently interrupted sea voyages would have been unavailable otherwise. And although Portuguese travelers and writers established the genre of the shipwreck narrative per se in early modern Europe, travelers, writers, and anthologizers of other nations (e.g., France, England, the Netherlands) soon followed suit (Figure 6.6).[28]

The crisis of maritime disaster and peril at the heart of the shipwreck narrative, and the unforeseeable conditions of survival and of further dangers once the remaining passengers of a wrecked or disabled ship are on land, create a crisis at the narrative level as well as storytellers' attempts to impose meaning and order on what is, prima facie, meaningless and disordered. Such attempts include detailed considerations of the cause(s) of the shipwreck itself, but also touch on "classical literary forms, Christian Providence, maritime enterprise, empiricist critique, and attacks on human folly" (Mentz 2015: 10).[29] Interpretation, often times pushing at the edges of rationalization, is one of the crisis categories of shipwreck tales. Such hermeneutic struggles, in addition to the scenarios of extreme tribulation, lend these accounts a compelling humanity.

In the early years of the seventeenth century, a book appeared that is one of the most wide ranging in the Iberian tradition in terms of oceanic errancy and of the drama of its adventures. Fernão Mendes Pinto's *Peregrinação* (Pilgrimage) was published in 1614 (but written 1569–78), some thirty years after its author-protagonist's death. Mendes Pinto was a merchant who traveled across the world's oceans in the mid-sixteenth century and led a life of adventure, misery, and derring-do. His travels, which began with a voyage to India in 1537, took him into the Atlantic, the Indian Ocean, the Red Sea, the South China Sea, the East China Sea, and eventually to Japan. Throughout his world sojourn, Mendes Pinto, at different times, was a pirate, was a slavery, a diplomat, a trader, a captive of the Tartars and the Burmese, was sentenced to one year's hard labor on the Great Wall of China, suffered shipwreck, practiced cannibalism, and befriended the noted Jesuit Francis Xavier, all before retiring to a house in Almada across the Tagus River from Lisbon. He was something of a Portuguese Indiana Jones. The story of his travels, which remained in manuscript during his lifetime, saw the light of print one year before the publication of the Second Part of *Don Quijote*.

The lengthy and engaging *Peregrinação*, in the assessment of Rebecca D. Catz, is a "maverick" book and an enigma since, at a basic level, it is hard to classify in terms of genre (Pinto [1614] 1989: xxiii). It is a proto-novelistic eyewitness travel narrative and historical chronicle. But, for Catz, the real issue is that Mendes Pinto openly critiques the morality of Portuguese overseas conquests, and his book is essentially satiric in intent. Mendes Pinto is not alone in terms of criticisms of

Portuguese empire, since such criticisms are also part of Camões's *Os Lusíadas* and other works such as historian Diogo do Couto's *O soldado prático* (1980). The sui generis nature of Mendes Pinto's book might best be understood not in terms of a particular, overarching genre but in terms of a multiplicity of genres. By turns, the *Peregrinação* is historical chronicle, eyewitness travel account, captivity narrative, shipwreck narrative, epic poem, moral contemplation, and satiric narrative. Mendes Pinto's variegated experiences over a vast geographical arena during the course of decades defy the contours of any one textual genre. This should come as no surprise, since Mendes Pinto himself occupies a number of subject positions throughout his book that were typical of oceanic travelers operating in the sphere of empire: merchant, slave (or captive), pirate, shipwreck survivor, diplomat, seafarer, and warrior.

The transoceanic travel epitomized so dramatically by Mendes Pinto continued throughout the seventeenth century. As representative of these traveler-writers we will focus on Jerónimo Lobo, the Portuguese Jesuit who spent eighteen years abroad and recorded his adventures in his *Itinerário* (Itinerary) after being first dispatched to India in 1621. Lobo spent nine years in Ethiopia as part of the Ethiopian mission, and later resided in India. His oceanic voyages saw him shipwrecked in Africa in 1635, and he visited Havana soon after. He visited Spain, Italy, and Africa, and presumably worked on his book while back in Lisbon in 1639 to 1640 before embarking once again for India. When he died, according to C.F. Beckingham, he was the "greatest living authority on Ethiopia" (Lobo 1984: xxiv). The *Itinerary* encompasses Lobo's travels and adventures in Ethiopia, India, and Africa which include descriptions of the Red Sea and the Nile.

The *Itinerary* was first published in French in 1692, in an edition prepared by Joachim Le Grand.[30] This French edition was then translated into English by Samuel Johnson as *A Voyage to Abyssinia* and published in 1735. As with virtually all of the texts we have been considering here, Lobo's account records travels both over sea and over land. The Jesuit frequently emphasizes this by noting that his journeys are "parte por mar, parte por terra" (part by sea, and part by land), so that the *Itinerário* is what we might call an "amphibious narrative" in terms of the manner of errancy contained in its pages. The amphibious narrative is one that tells of repeated movements from sea to land to sea, movements between the ship and land, or movements between vesseled and seaborne communities and terrestrial or "land" communities. Lobo spends a considerable amount of narrative space in describing life onboard ship. Paul Gilroy argues that ships are "a living, micro-cultural, micro-political system in motion" (1993: 4); on Lobo's ships, the aquatic community of culture and politics recedes from view in favor of stark and unsettling descriptions of nautical vessels as places of bodily suffering, disease, and putrefaction. When narrating life onboard, Lobo frequently acts as an amateur epidemiologist by speculating on the causes of disease and the possible origins and mechanisms of their contagion throughout the shipboard community. The amphibious logic at work in the *Itinerary* is that, with an emphasis on bodies, suffering, and survival in descriptions of the seaborne portions of his travels, the story is intensely and acutely presentist when the physical confines of the ship are at stake. Hardships are markers of a seaborne temporality in that the ship is a relational device that creates a contrast between ocean time—a time with no evident or discernible historical dimension—and terrestrial time in which inheres historiographic, geographic, and ethnographic dimensions. Lobo's amphibious narrative thus shuttles from temporality to temporality, between temporal boundedness and an open-ended present. However, within the culture of maritime travel and expansion itself, it would be wrong to conclude that the ocean is therefore ahistorical. Gama's journey in *The Lusiads* effectively temporalizes and historicizes the sea by inscribing it into the worldly domain of the monarch. Expansionist ships carry culture and time across the oceans of the world.

CHAPTER SEVEN

Representations

The Maritime Visual Arts in the Global Early Modern Period

JAMES SETH

For centuries, artists have asked a question about the sea often posed about art: is it a true mirror? Is the image we see in front of us, even in the most placid pools, our own? Or is it altered, corrupt, or illusory? Caravaggio's *Narcissus* (1597–9; see Figure 7.1) engages this question by representing water as a mirror, as well as a means of infinite obsession. As Narcissus gazes, he forms a circle in his transfixed pose. The painting presents water as a kind of artwork to admire and long to enter into. In the early modern period (1450–1650), the ocean became increasingly populated with traders, explorers, and seafarers. Oceanic art, from paintings and maps to poetry and drama, reflect a desire to explore and uncover the sea's mysteries.

Visual representations of the ocean and oceanic subjects often convey the feeling of longing, capturing an event that is temporal, sublime, or mythic. Renaissance artwork of Venus often depicts her birth from the foamy sea, the womb from which her beauty and sexual power emerges. One of the most famous of these, Sandro Botticelli's *The Birth of Venus* (*c.* 1482/5), portrays the goddess as Ovid describes her in *Metamorphoses*—emerging from the foam naked and fully grown, standing on a shell on the seashore.[1] Botticelli's rendering of the Venus Pudica ("modest Venus") depicts the goddess covering herself while the wind blows roses toward her. Nature's energetic force surrounds Venus; waves surge in the background, and the ocean wind blows her hair away from her body, forcing her to cover her genitals to prevent exposure. Her stillness and calm expression contrast the wild movement of the wind and water. Artists during this time period often depict the sea as a space of the ideal or unfathomable.

In early modern oceanic art, seafarers and human subjects engage in struggles that mirror the jagged voyages of life. A series of dominant themes and subjects emerge in early modern oceanic art including shipwrecks, shorelines, turbulent weather, dangerous or mythical creatures, allegorical figures, historical events,

FIGURE 7.1 Caravaggio, *Narcissus*, c. 1597–9. © Wikimedia Commons (public domain).

and biblical events. In biblical paintings, the sea often displays the profound limits of divine power. Subjects like Jonah experience this power through the deadly force of the sea and its menacing creatures. Realistic portrayals of the sea also capture its vastness and strength in relation to the ships and naval fleets occupying it. The color palettes for the sea are often represented in dark or muted hues of blue and gray, often emphasizing the sense of melancholy and toil of seafarers, as well as to recreate the sense of tension and unease when navigating fickle waters. Sea paintings frequently capture the disruptions to a voyage, those moments where the seafarer is most vulnerable. The sea was also represented in maps, objects, sculptures, and on the stage. In all of these various representations, the artist renders the sea and its creatures as subjects of intrigue and terror. Oceanic art gives the sense of only acquiring a partial understanding, only a glimpse at what lies at the bottom on the ocean.

THE MYTHICAL SEA
The biblical sea

In early modern European culture, the history of the ocean begins with Genesis, as the sea was created after the heavens, separated with firmament, named "sea," and filled with creatures (Gen. 1:1–1:21).[2] Artists during this era interpreted the sea through biblical narrative to represent the intensity and "polarities" of God's power, Lawrence Otto Goedde notes (1989: 38–9). The biblical ocean is depicted in extremes, tranquil or turbulent, to portray God's dual nature as the deliverer of mercy and punishment. The biblical sea is not only a representation of divine power but also the means to test characters, usually through the sea storm: Psalm 107:23–30, the shipwreck of St. Paul in Acts 27:13–44, Noah's Ark in Genesis 7–8, and most notably, the book of Jonah. Jonah's story is one of the most popular interpretations of the biblical sea in early modern representations, as it is referenced in paintings, maps, literature, and travel narratives.

Paintings such as the *Prophet Jonah* by Michelangelo (*c.* 1542–5) and *Jonah Leaving the Whale* (*c.* 1600) by Jan Brueghel the Elder both depict Jonah with a large fish, and the viewer's attention is drawn to Jonah rather than the sea or the whale. Brueghel's expansive painting of the biblical sea presents the sea as a devastating force, with rows of choppy waves enveloping the scene. Yet, the diminutive figure of Jonah emerging from the whale in striking red clothing, hands clasped in prayer, is still the most prominent feature, and the violent sea seems to disappear in darkness behind him. A towering rock also looms behind Jonah, signifying that the potential dangers (bodily and spiritual) are now in the distance. The rock may also be a symbol of God's presence to represent the foundation of faith amid rough waters (Ps. 18:2).

The *Voyage of Jonah* (*c.* 1600) by Flemish painter Paul Bril portrays the sea as a particularly formidable force. Bril, who befriended Bruegel in Rome in the early 1590s, painted in a Mannerist style influenced by German painter Adam Elsheimer, and the way that Bril interprets the biblical sea shares notes with Bruegel's oceanic works (Paul Brill 2019 [note: the Encyclopædia Britannica lists Bril's name as "Brill," but his name was (and continues to be) spelled "Bril"]). Bril and Bruegel portray the sea in a manner that conveys the spiritual turmoil of the subject, and their paintings' dismal, desaturated color palettes emphasize the internal struggle of the spiritual test. Both artists juxtapose striking, bright subjects with the darkness of the ocean, suggesting the polarity of God's test; within the "belly of hell," the "waters compassed [Jonah] about, *even* to the soul" (Jon. 2:2–5). By surviving "hell," Jonah then follows God's directive. In Bril's work, the dark hues from the clouds and the sea portray nature itself as menacing and hellish, and the black ring of clouds allows Bril to contrast the object within the sun's rays, the bright white sails of Jonah's vessel, and the shadowy sea below. While the greatest source of light appears on the sails, the ship itself is in a state of near-collapse, vulnerable to attack by the nearby whale and the waves that threaten to tip it over.

The story of Jonah is also an integral part of early modern maps, as depictions of whales served to warn seafarers of potential dangers in particular regions. Sebastian Münster's *Cosmographia* (1540), for example, depicts a man being eaten by a sea monster in the Mediterranean, near the northern African coast. The man could possibly be Jonah, Chet Van Duzer (2013: 38, 17–19) suggests, as maps dating from the medieval era include Jonah figures. The figure of Leviathan is also a frequent presence on early modern maps and globes. Leviathan was often portrayed to represent the mysterious, deadly power of the sea; as it is described in Job 3:8: "Let them curse it that curse the day, who are ready to rouse up leviathan." Though Leviathan appears more frequently on medieval maps, it appears notably on Johann Schöner's 1515 globe, just off Africa's eastern coast.

A biblical sea narrative that attracted artistic interpretations in the early modern era was the storm on the Sea of Galilee, calmed by Christ in the fourth chapter of the Gospel of Mark (Mt. 8:23–7). Dutch painter Rembrandt van Rijn's *Christ in the Storm on the Sea of Galilee* (1633; see Figure 7.2) is one of the most well-known representations of this scene, not only because of its artistry but also because the painting was stolen in the theft of the Isabella Stewart Gardner Museum on March 18, 1990 (Zell 2003: 145). Though *Galilee* is Rembrandt's only seascape, it remains one of his most famous works and a masterpiece of the Dutch golden age. Like Bril's *Voyage of Jonah*, Rembrandt presents the sea as chaotic and darkly hued, with yellow light penetrating the sea-tossed vessel through a hopeful break in the clouds.

FIGURE 7.2 Rembrandt Van Rijn, *Christ in the Storm on the Sea of Galilee*, 1633. © Wikimedia Commons (public domain).

Another representation of Christ's calming of the Sea of Galilee appears on a book leaf from a Mughal Indian devotional text, *c.* 1650, acquired by the British Museum. The artwork shares striking similarities to Rembrandt's in its composition. While Rembrandt's image notably features a vessel with sails, the Mughal piece includes a streak of lightning positioned at the same angle as the mast in Rembrandt's. The break in the clouds in the Mughal artwork also resembles the outline of the sails in the Rembrandt piece. Whether the composition similarities are merely coincidental, the reimagining of Christ's narrative in the Mughal devotional seem to be in conversation with European interpretations of the event. Other famous representations of the biblical sea in Renaissance paintings include *The Crossing of the Red Sea* in the Sistine Chapel (*c.* 1481–2) and *The Miraculous Draught of the Fishes* by Raphael (*c.* 1515).

The classical sea

Ancient epics also inspired early modern English representations of the ocean. Translations of Homer's *Odyssey* by Arthur Hall (1581) and George Chapman (1616) describe an ancient sea that, on the surface, resembles the biblical ocean. However, beneath Homer's ocean lies sea creatures that prove fatal upon close contact: Scylla, Charybdis, the Sirens, and Poseidon are all formidable enemies of Odysseus and his men. Each sea creature signifies a test that Odysseus must overcome to demonstrate his fortitude on the ten-year return voyage after the Trojan War. Like Jonah, Odysseus can be restored if he can survive the perilous ocean. Ovid's *Metamorphoses* and Lucan's *Pharsalia* were often interpreted by Renaissance artists, emphasizing the bizarreness of the creatures found in the ocean's depths, or the tremendous power of the ocean to disrupt voyages and destroy fleets.

Poseidon is arguably one of the most popular classical figures in Renaissance art, as the god of the sea and earthquakes was depicted not only in paintings from 1450 to 1650, but in sculptures, vases, bowls, and other decorative art, which I discuss in the section devoted specifically to these objects. Poseidon's importance to art in this period is owed in part to his role in the Homeric epic, sending tempests to thwart the titular hero in the *Odyssey* (1870: V.291–332). However, Poseidon's importance is also owed to increased sea travel during the time of Europe's "discovery" voyages and the expansion of networks and sea routes during the spice trade. The ocean was being navigated more than ever, and its destructive power over the fate of ships was often attributed to fickle gods such as Poseidon and Fortuna in artistic representations. Odysseus's tortuous journey mirrors those of sea travelers whose experiences with fateful tempests seem like the work of capricious gods. A plate of painted enamel on copper (*c.* 1633) by François Limosin II, currently at the Louvre, depicts the mighty sea god riding the waves, pulling sea horses with one hand while holding his trident with the other. This is perhaps the most popular depiction of the sea god, merging with the sea while remaining in complete control.

Andromeda, the daughter of Cepheus and Cassiopeia, is also reimagined in oceanic art that reimagines her story in Ovid's *Metamorphoses* (2010: 4.669–901). After Cassiopeia claims that Andromeda's beauty surpasses the Nereids, Poseidon sends the sea monster Cetus to kill Andromeda. While chained naked to a rock (as a sacrifice), she is saved from Cetus's ravaging by Perseus.

A mid- to late-seventeenth-century German etching of the scene acquired by the British Museum depicts this scene just before Andromeda is saved. In the etching, she sits on the rock with her right profile facing the devastating sea monster, while Perseus is shown flying through the air behind them, preparing to attack Cetus (described as a "sea-dragon"). Oceanic representations of Andromeda were common in Renaissance painting and visual art, particularly by European artists. The scene depicting Perseus saving Andromeda was reimagined by Jacob Matham (*c.* 1597), Jan Pietersz (*c.* 1601), William Janson and Antonio Tempesta (*c.* 1606), Pieter Symonsz Potter (*c.* 1642), Stefano della Bella (*c.* 1644), and in a series of similar paintings, Peter Paul Rubens (*c.* 1634, 1638, 1640s).

Maritime writings often reference Fortuna to account for their circumstances, whether good or bad. Thus, she is often an emblem of the fate of voyagers, given the capriciousness of the weather and the seas. Frans Il Fracken's *Fortuna Marina* (*c.* 1615/20) portrays the goddess Fortuna in her "maritime guise," dispensing the good and bad fortune to a crowd on the sea coast. Fortuna is standing on a globe, with one hand giving her fortune and the other holding a large sail. Behind her is a dark, troubling ocean, and the capricious wind billows the sails to reiterate the inconstancy of Fortune. Sunlight shines on the landed left side, while the right side of the painting depicts frail ships under dark clouds. Fortuna herself stands in the middle, emphasizing her dual role to offer peace and discord—much like the polarization of God's roles in biblical sea paintings.

The story of Icarus was also reinterpreted in early modern oceanic art, most notably in *Landscape with the Fall of Icarus* (*c.* 1555), attributed to Pieter Bruegel the Elder. The painting portrays the narrative of Icarus as a singular event in an otherwise uneventful day. The focus is not centered on Icarus's fate, as his legs are barely visible in the lower right-hand corner of the crowded sea near Crete. Icarus's father, Daedalus, is nowhere to be found; instead, the landscape, as the title explains, is what the artist's eye privileges. W.H. Auden famously describes the work in "Musee des Beaux Arts," pointing out "how everything turns away / Quite leisurely from the disaster" (1940: 14–15). For the ploughman, Icarus' fall "was not an important failure" but just another splash in the ocean (17). As John Sutherland explains, the painting is "a parable on human aspiration ... Earth abides: the ploughman ploughs. Trading vessels go about their commercial business. Life goes on. The death of an unlucky aviator is of no more importance than the fall of a sparrow. Mankind deludes itself if it thinks otherwise" (2016). Bruegel's painting comments on the relative unimportance of the event in a world that continues to move at a clip, not hesitating when a man falls into the sea. The painter also highlights the fact that the sea and its bustling shores are complex, dynamic spaces—multiple ships move closer to their destinations, sheepherders raise their flock in anticipation of sheering, and the ploughman anticipates a full harvest. Human and nature continue their movements in the midst of rare accidents; everyone is their own protagonist in a complex narrative.

The sea in Eastern myth

Eastern mythology of the sea is often found in cross-cultural interpretations of other countries and religions. Paintings, scrolls, and decorative objects often allude to places that many Asian artists had never visited, people they likely had never interacted with, and events that they had not seen for themselves. Chinese art during the early modern period, for example, often reimagines India and Buddhist figures with exaggerated aspects and whimsical visual effects. As John Kieschnick and Meir Shahar explain, "the Buddhist influx of Indian philosophy and mythology, art and material culture led inquisitive Chinese minds to ponder their source" (2014: 1). An early Chinese representation of Indian culture, Liu Songnian's (c. 1155–1218) *Arhat* (defined in Sanskrit as "one who is worthy") reimagines its Buddhist subject surrounded by and living in total harmony with nature; the arhat gazes serenely upon a family of deer while monkeys play in a tree above. In the Chinese artistic imagination, Indian Buddhist arhats lived peacefully with nature and engaged with it in fanciful ways. This is especially prevalent in sea paintings and artwork with bodies of water. Chinese and also Japanese interpretations of Indian culture present mythical Buddhist figures interacting with the sea in ways that resemble the representations of biblical and classical figures in Western oceanic art, mainly in the supernatural bond that exists between the subject and the sea.

There are a number of artistic representations between the years 1450 and 1650 of Buddhist figures crossing various bodies of water. Often, these figures cross while sitting or standing on small objects that would be otherwise unfit or unstable for such a feat. The British Museum currently has a mid-seventeenth-century Japanese silk scroll painted by Mo An from 1640 to 1684 portraying the Buddhist monk Bodhidharma, who lived during the fifth or sixth century, crossing the Yangtze River on a single reed.[3] Though there are myths of Bodhidharma across Asia, the river-crossing myth is of Chinese origin (Bodhidharma 1989: ix). According to Chinese legend, Bodhidharma was a son of a Brahman king from southern India, who traveled to China to spread the teachings of his master, Prajñātāra (the twenty-seventh Indian Patriarch continuing from the Historical Buddha) (x). After a three-year voyage, Bodhidharma reached China and formally introduced himself to Emperor We of the Liang Dynasty in Nanking (Nanjing) (xi–xii). Once informed that his statues of Buddha, ordaining of monks, and copying of sutras had no karmic merit, the Emperor became distraught (xii). Following this, Bodhidharma went to the Shaolin Temple on Mount Song to meditate, crossing the Yangtze River on a small reed. Japanese legends of Bodhidharma, named *Daruma*, extend beyond the Chinese myths. In Japanese myth, Daruma was also linked to fertility and phallic imagery, presenting a connection to Bodhidharma's crossing on the phallic reed. The Japanese silk scroll illustrating Bodhidharma's crossing portrays the subject's adeptness in engaging with nature, recalling earlier portrayals of arhats in Chinese art.

A sixteenth-century Chinese handscroll acquired by the British Museum depicts a Buddhist arhat crossing the sea on a gourd. The features of the piece resemble earlier Chinese portrayals of Indian arhats, first by facial features that had long been associated with Western foreigners: "prominent nose, bushy eyebrows, bulging eyes, and a bearded chin" (Kieschnick and Shahar 2014: 1). Similar to Songnian's portrayal, the arhat has crossed arms and is surrounded by nature, but his facial expression is less serene and more pensive, much like the appearance of Bodhidharma on the Japanese scroll. The arhat on the Chinese handscroll could be inspired by the myth of Bodhidharma, but the figure's diminutive appearance and crouching stance do not correspond with other artworks of Bodhidharma, which portray him as a large, powerful figure.

Mythical sea creatures

Mythical sea creatures have been reimagined in Eurasian artwork and beyond, with many variants of each kind. They include sea dragons, sea dogs, Nereids, sirens, and mermaids, among many other hybridized sea animals. Sea dragons are prevalent in European and Asian artwork, possessing both monstrous and humanoid faces. An early fifteenth-century manuscript page from Muhammad al-Qazwini's *Aja'ib al-makhluqat* (Wonders of Creation), currently at the Smithsonian's Freer and Sackler Asian Art Galleries in Washington, DC, depicts the Sea-Serpent or Sea-Dragon (al-Tannin) in the center of a page. The artist gives the sea dragon a humanlike face and depicts it coiled in a knot. The sea serpent illustration disrupts the boundaries of the border that aligns the text, perhaps a nod to its power and slipperiness.

Interpretations of the sirens were also prevalent during this era, and many drawings and etchings accompanied translations and reprinted volumes of Ovid and Homer. Wilhelm Janson and Antonio Tempesta's drawing, *The Sirens* (1606), is part of a series of images depicting figures in *The Metamorphoses of Ovid*, published the same year. *Sirens* shows the titular creatures trying to the get the attention of seafarers, one with arms open and another pointing to a rocky island. Though seemingly helpful and inviting, the sirens use their charms to thwart the voyagers' expedition. Works such as Vasari's *Birth of Venus* portray various kinds of sea creatures living in harmony, or at the very least, coexisting in a shared habitat. Another example of this is Angelo Falconetto's etching *Sirens, Naiads, and Tritons* (c. 1555/67), which portrays the three types of creatures together in a crowded sea, surrounded by cherubs and dolphins. While many realist interpretations of the sea emphasize its vastness and expanse, classical interpretations often depict it as a busy space as energetic and crowded as the landed world. In fact, the sea in Falconetto's work is barely visible behind the sea creatures, merely a backdrop for the central action. Early modern maps, which I will discuss in a later section, also portray the sea as a bustling space full of creatures, including sirens, sea monsters, and hybrid sea creatures.

Whether illustrating oceanic scenes in the Bible, reimagining a narrative from Ovid, or depicting a Buddhist arhat crossing waters, artists depicting the mythical sea emphasize its transformative power. Jonah is a witness to the divine and frightening power of the sea, and thus maritime artists adapted Jonah's story to represent oceanic survival. During a period of increased oceanic navigation, artists used Jonah's story to convey the feelings of helplessness and vulnerability, both to the workings of nature and God. Artists also used classical figures such as Poseidon and Fortuna to show how external oceanic forces disrupt and control the destinies of seafarers. In these works, mythical oceanic subjects help illustrate the lack of (and desire for) control when at sea. Certain subjects, such as Venus and the sirens, also portray the sea as a birthplace and home, respectively, for sexual desire itself. Lastly, Renaissance artists capture the dualism of the sea in their reimagining of mythical narratives; it beckons, threatens, and devours, but it also purifies and inspires.

REALISM IN OCEANIC ART

Early realism and sea warfare

European marine art in the fifteenth century captured the sea in a fashion distinguished by realistic depictions of the sea, ships, and weather. In the Netherlands, marine art became increasingly popular and profitable by the end of the fifteenth century, and artists of different mediums were interested in visualizing maritime subjects with great detail. Critics often cite the beginning of the realist movements in the Netherlandish tradition to illuminations such as *The Prayer on the Shore*, included in the Turin-Milan Hours (*c.* 1420) by Jan van Eyck or his brother, Hubert van Eyck (Goedde 1989: 49). In the works that succeeded *Prayer*, maritime artists invoke a sense of danger and tumult by capturing their subjects' sea-tossed movement. Whether capturing a prototypical tempest scene or reimagining a historical moment, realist maritime art captures the tension and vulnerability of seafaring peril. An engraving on paper, *Ship with Sails Furled and Arrow Pointing to the Right* (*c.* 1475–85), foresees the preoccupation of Netherlandish artists with ships tossing in rough waters. The unidentified Netherlandish artist of *Ship with Sails Furled*, known as "Master W with the Key" for the unique signature (the letter W with an image of a key), produced a series of engravings with maritime subjects that were copied by printmakers, including Israhel van Meckenem.[4] *Ship with Sails Furled* draws the viewer's eye to the intricacies of the structure and the ship's movement, giving the scene a striking sense of realism. The ship is pointed upward like a ship's compass pointing north, yet the arrowed harpoon at the top of the mast points behind the ship, which could be true north. The Ottoman wars

FIGURE 7.3 Vittore Carpaccio, *The Legend of St Ursula*, 1497–8. © Wikimedia Commons (public domain).

in Europe inspired a series of paintings capturing the tumultuous encounters between Christians and Turks during the fifteenth and sixteenth centuries. Vittore Carpaccio's *Arrival of the Pilgrims in Cologne* (c. 1490) anticipated the detailed depictions of large ships in the sixteenth century. Carpaccio's *Arrival*, one of a series of paintings on the legend of Saint Ursula, *Storie di sant'Orsola* (see Figure 7.3), is currently held at Gallerie dell'Accademia in Venice. Carpaccio highlights the significance of the event in Cologne, then under siege by the Huns, as the fleet also carried the Pope to the Ottoman-controlled city. The composition of the image places the sea harbor almost squarely in the middle of the painting, dividing the pilgrims' ships and the bright red army awaiting them on the shore. Carpaccio emphasizes the sea's political function as a boundary and a thoroughfare during a tumultuous era. At the tops of the towers on the Ottoman shore, red and white banners with three gold crowns fly above to indicate the rule of Mehmed the Conqueror (1432–81), who controlled Asia, Greece, and Trabzon. Maritime art continued to depict the Ottoman invasions in western Europe in the mid-sixteenth century, as the sea remained a warzone for territorial control. The Ottoman's failed invasion of Malta in 1565 was reimagined in multiple works, including several late sixteenth-century paintings by Matteo Perez.

The Anglo-Spanish War (1585–1604) also inspired maritime art that captured the drama of the dueling fleets. A sixteenth-century painting in the National Maritime Museum, *English Ships and the Spanish Armada, August 1588*, credited to an artist from the English School, highlights the spectacle of the battle. The museum suggests that the painting captures what is most likely "the action of Gravelines, the only point at which large numbers of ships from both sides were engaged in sustained conflict" (National Maritime Museum n.d.). The artist emphasizes how the sea, in spite of its spaciousness, can become a crowded and volatile space for military exploit. The museum dates the painting closely following the event, and the painting exhibits subtly anti-Catholic elements. The Spanish galleass in the front center of the painting (flying the Papal banner and Spanish arms) is carrying a number of satirized characters, including a preaching monk with hands raised and a skeleton character wearing jester's attire. As the latter image clearly reveals, the English artist is portraying the galleass as a "ship of fools" (National Maritime Museum n.d.).

The National Maritime Museum also has a Flemish interpretation of the English launching of "fire-ships" (ships armed with flammables) against the Spanish on August 7, 1588. The painting, produced around 1590, differs significantly from that of the English School painting. The colors of the Flemish painting use a bluer color palette than the English School painting, which is warmer and redder. The Flemish artist also positions the English and Spanish fleets on opposite sides, rather than mixed together, as the Gravelines incident would have suggested. The polarization of English and Spanish fleets heightens the anticipation of sea battle following the launch of the "fire-ships," which are positioned in the middle of the painting, as they slowly approach the Spanish Armada.

Dutch realism

Modern maritime painting owes much to the Flemish and Dutch movements during the sixteenth and seventeenth centuries. The Netherlands experienced increasing wealth made up primarily of sea trading, fishing, and whaling, and as Dutch culture became "inextricably bound with water and boats" (Archibald 1980: 14), thus their artistic subjects followed suit. As E.H.H. Archibald explains:

The evolvement of paintings of marine subjects occurred quite suddenly in the middle years of the sixteenth century, owing its emergence directly to the Reformation and the release of men's minds and spirits from the restrictions of choice imposed by the mediaeval church. This artistic flowering was initially confined to those parts of the new Protestant nations which already had a flourishing school of painters using sophisticated techniques—in effect the Netherlands. (14)

Marine painting was especially prominent in Antwerp, Amsterdam, Rotterdam, Haarlem, Hoorn, and Utrecht. Painters such as Joos de Momper the Younger (1564–1635) beget the realist movement in the Netherlands with their focus on maritime activity, as depicted in *River Landscape with Hunt* in 1600 (see Figure 7.5) and works that depict the chaotic sea. De Momper's *The Storm at Sea* (c. 1569) is a prominent example of the way that early realist artists captured the movement and vulnerability of oceanic subjects. The ship in the lower center of the painting is dwarfed by the towering waves swooping against it. Sailing against the wind, the ship is at a serious disadvantage, and de Momper frames the painting in menacing black hues from clouds to sea. Though de Momper mainly painted landscapes, his marine paintings were inspired by Pieter Bruegel (1528–69), who was originally thought to have painted de Momper's *Storm at Sea*.

Haarlem is notable for being the birthplace of Hendrik Cornelisz Vroom (1566–1640), who is generally considered the father of marine painting (Archibald 1980: 158). The Haarlem Guild and the Netherlands marine painting school dramatically influenced the style and substance of marine painting. There were many marine painters who directly inspired Vroom, particularly Paul Bril (1554–1625). Early marine painters who anticipated Vroom's style include Pieter Cock (1502–50), Pieter Brueghel (1528–69), Cornelis Bol (b. c. 1580), and Jan Porcellis (1584–1632).

Porcellis claimed to have been the innovator of the new Dutch realist palette, based on the "pearl grey skies of Holland" that was almost monochrome (Archibald 1980). His marine paintings of turbulent waters, such as *Ships in Distress on a Stormy Sea* (c. 1616), epitomize the darker-hued palette of grays, blue grays (like glaucous), and dark grays that came to define Dutch realist painting. Porcellis's *Ships in Distress* also illustrates the dualism often presented in Renaissance maritime painting. From right to left, the painting gradually lightens, though the bright sky is nearly obscured. The darker-hued right half of the painting portrays a ship in a state of near-collapse amidst choppy waters, with black clouds billowed above. The ship on the right-hand size is on the verge of being capsized, and it is not as easily identified as the sister ship on the left side. Porcellis shows the ship blending in with the water, the two merging into the same force; there is the sense that the ship is becoming consumed by the sea, especially with the pointed teeth-like waves surrounding it.

FIGURE 7.4 Hendrick Cornelisz Vroom, *A Number of East Indiamen off the Coast*, c. 1600–1630. © Wikimedia Commons (public domain).

Paul Bril (1554–1625), whose *Voyage of Jonah* was mentioned above, is also an important painter of realist maritime works, particularly since his landscape and seascape paintings inspired the work of Hendrick Vroom. Born in Antwerp in 1554, Bril was brought up in a household of landscape painters, his father being Mattheus Bril (the elder) and brother to Mattheus the younger (Archibald 1980). Paul Bril was a student of Damien Oortelmans, a member of the Antwerp Guild, and he left Antwerp for Rome when he was twenty years old to join his older brother, who was already working as a landscape artist. Though Paul's time in Rome was spent working on commissioned paintings, miniatures, and engravings, he also produced marine paintings. Brill's connection to Vroom begins in Rome, where the two artists met.

Hendrick Vroom was a master of painting naval scenes and sea battles in a much more realistic fashion than his predecessors, evidencing his passion and knowledge of naval affairs and maritime history (see Figure 7.4). Contemporaries of Vroom in Haarlem, such as Pieter Savery (d.1638), may have imitated or inspired Vroom's technique. Born in Haarlem to a family of artists in 1566, Vroom paved his own career by leaving a life of pottery painting and boarding a ship for Spain, which led him to Livorno, Florence, and Rome, where he met Paul Bril (Archibald 1980: 195). Vroom pioneered the painting of naval scenes and battles in a manner never seen before. His approach to his work clearly shows a love and understanding of ships and a strong interest in naval history. This is evident in his large-scale paintings of naval battles, including *Return to Amsterdam of Cornelis de Houtman from Sumatra in 1599* (c. 1610–20). Vroom was also commissioned to produce maritime art for English patrons often depicting

English naval successes against the Spanish Armada. Vroom was hired by the Lord Admiral, the Earl of Nottingham to make drawings for a set of tapestries on the Spanish Armada campaign of 1588, which were of great value to the state until they were destroyed in the fire of 1854 in the British Houses of Parliament (195). Today, only a set of eighteenth-century engravings by W.H. Pyne reveals what they looked like (195). Vroom was also hired by a Dutch weaver, Francis Spiernicx, to depict the Battle of Gravelines (c. 1595) for the Armada campaign, commissioned by Howard of Effingham; some critics deem Vroom's painting the finest representation of the event (195).

Vroom was also commissioned for two large paintings presenting the English fleet arriving in the Solent led by the *Prince Royal*, which bore Prince Charles and the Duke of Buckingham on their return voyage from Spain in October 1623. Vroom also painted two similar works that were meant for the King and the Duke; the former is in the Royal Collection, and the latter is in the National Maritime Museum. Vroom's *Arrival of the Elector and the Electress Palatine at Flushing* depicts another English event. Archibald, who deems it the "finest of all his maritime paintings," notes Vroom's "care for the minutiae of naval detail" in comparison to other works (195). There are two different versions of "*Arrival*": one in Haalem, which shows the vessel rigged for summer sailings, and one in Greenwich, which shows the vessel with winter rig and most of the masts and yards down.

Another influential realist painter during this period was Bonaventura Peeters, the Elder (1614–52), who trained at the Flemish School and produced many marine paintings. He trained at the studio of Andries van Eertvelt, who frequently painted stormy seas, and some of Peeters's works reflect Eertvelt's influence. Peeters's *Sunlight on a Stormy Sea* (c. 1640s) depicts a ship surviving tempestuous waters, and the sun's rays illuminate the ship in a striking manner. Much like the work of Porcellis, Peeters's sea paintings are dominantly gray and highlight the sense of powerless and vulnerability to the elements. However, Peeters's color palette is even more striking and defined. *Sunlight* masterfully captures the power of light breaking through clouds, both as a relief to distressed sailors and also as evidence of nature's ability to give and take at a whim. Peeters's *Dutch Ferry Boats in a Fresh Breeze* (c. 1640s) and *A Dismasted Ship in a Rough Sea* (c. 1635) present similarly composed skies, full of dark clouds pierced by sunlight.

Maritime painters inspired by Peeters also included his younger sister, Catharina Peeters (1615–c. 1676), who was also his pupil. Born in Antwerp, Catharina was not only responsible for domestic duties for her older brother, with whom she lived with, but she also took care of her younger brother, Jan, while studying under her older brother, Bonaventura. Her work includes a naval battle scene, currently held in the Kunsthistorisches Museum in Vienna. She is notable for being one of the few recognized female maritime painters

FIGURE 7.5 Joos de Momper, *River Landscape with Hunt*, c. 1600. © Wikimedia Commons (public domain).

of this period. Notable artists also inspired by or working contemporarily with Bonaventura Peeters and Jan Porcellis until 1650 include Mathieu van Plannenbuerg (1608–60), who called himself "Plattemontagne" in Paris; Pieter Mulier, the Elder (1615–70); and Pieter van der Croos (1610–77).

SCULPTURES, OBJECTS, AND MAPS

Sculptures and objects

The oceanic sculptures and objects produced from 1450 to 1650 reflect a particular obsession with classical mythic figures such as Neptune, as well as the sea monsters who also appear in the works of Ovid and Homer. The Louvre features an assortment of bronze pieces and earthenware inspired by these figures. One such object, simply titled *Neptune*, is a bronze sculpture from Germany produced in the latter half of the sixteenth century. In this rendering, a bearded Neptune holds a two-pronged trident, looking slightly downward while reaching his hand out. This could be a gesture of oceanic manipulation, controlling the seas as he looks upon it with a sense of authority, as a character like Shakespeare's Prospero would imitate in the early seventeenth century. The sense of movement associated with Neptune, who conjures storms and earthquakes, is also felt in artists' reinterpretations of the sea god. Another piece contained at the Louvre and likely produced in Germany in the late sixteenth century is titled *Covered bowl surmounted with a statuette of Neptune*. The piece depicts Neptune in a state of action, much more so than the bronze statue. On the covered bowl, Neptune sits on a rock at the top, wielding his trident with ferocity. His arm movement and turned position on the rock suggests that he will imminently swing the trident, and his beard is depicted as blowing toward eastern winds. The bronze statue and the smaller statuette on the covered bowl both present the god as a figure of terrible forces but also as a figure separated from the natural forces he controls.

There are also European artifacts during this era depicting Neptune in states of movement with other mythological creatures. A vase on display at the Louvre, *Neptune and Amphitrite* (1570), features the sea god riding the creature with his feet planted on it and balanced very much like a surfboarder.[5] Neptune's stance, bending at knees as though sitting on chair, presents him as a kind of oceanic chariot racer. Behind him lies a Roman seascape with lively fish jumping energetically from the sea in the foreground. Also at the Louvre, *Neptune on a Sea-Horse* is an early-seventeenth-century glazed earthenware piece.[6] This piece presents Neptune as far less menacing; in one hand, he holds a small trident in his left hand, and a fish in his right while riding atop the sea horse. His eyes are looking upward contemplatively rather than downward in a state of authority. The scene itself is a comparatively serene depiction of bearded Neptune, and the horse is presented as a regal courtly creature rather than being ridden competitively in a chariot race. Holding the fish gently, Neptune is presented as a god of compassion for oceanic life.

Early modern Asian artists also depicted mythological figures in oceanic landscapes on bowls and other decorative objects. The British Museum holds a Chinese blue porcelain bowl depicting Shou Lao, god of longevity, dated between 1620 and 1635.[7] This piece has a decorate underglaze, and inside the bowl, a painted figure of the god appears flying on a crane over ocean waves. In addition to painted flower heads, there are two figures "on a background of 'shou' [longevity] characters, with a border of 'ruyi' heads below and a band of white flower heads in octagonal frames above" (Harrison-Hall 2001: 12:20). The museum curators also suggest that the figures could be any of the Eight Daoist Immortals (12:20). The ocean waves are only part of the background, but the blue porcelain glaze gives the waves a striking appearance.

Another porcelain glazed jar at the British Museum, also with blue painted underglaze decoration, depicts several carp leaping out of water in one panel, and a dragon with horns and whiskers rising out of clouds. Chinese porcelain art depicts idealized versions of nature, and the porcelain jar emphasizes this ideal beauty. There is even the symbol for "wan" or "all that is good" on the jar, perpetuating the idyllic nature of subject matter. The identical carp leap in perfect harmony out of the crested waves, looking up toward the sky. Interestingly, the museum explains that while "the shine of the glaze has been eroded by this jar's three-hundred-year sojourn on the ocean bed, its underglaze decoration is resplendent still" (12:70). Coincidentally, the oceanic artwork had been long submerged in water, as well, though it apparently did not significantly affect the shine or the painting.

In addition to the classical, mythological, and ideal representations, there are also objects from this era that portray the sea in Christian narratives. Christian iconography in oceanic objects and sculptures often depicts a significant spiritual trial, usually turbulent weather or terrifying creatures. These trials represent the outside influences which test Christians (represented as mariners or fishermen) and their loyalty to the Cross (Christ), often symbolically rendered as the mast of a ship. The British Museum includes one such object: an ivory carved plaque presenting the Christ child as "the Mariner on the Ship of Salvation," based on an Italian print of the same scene.[8] In this Portuguese Indian depiction, the size of the Christ child is disproportionately larger than the ship. Christ clings to a mainsail, which is decorated with hands, heart, and feet. The image of the Christ child on the Ship of Salvation recalls a number of oceanic biblical parables, reminding "voyagers" on the Christian journey of the power of prayer in times of distress, just as it worked for Jonah, St. Paul the Apostle, and the merchants in the Psalms. In Acts 27:27, for instance, St. Paul is shipwrecked on Malta, having been driven across the Adriatic Sea. The sailors feign lowering anchors while trying to escape the ship, but Paul tells them that unless they stay with the ship, they cannot be saved.

Maps

Early modern maps are some of the most illuminating representations of the sea, as they not only show how voyagers and traders interpreted the sea but also how they engaged with it. Chet Van Duzer's study of sea monsters in medieval and early modern maps reveals not only the functionality of such representations but also the artistry and creativity of the cartographers. Van Duzer argues that the "most important and influential sea monsters on a Renaissance map are those on a nine-sheet map of northwestern Europe by Olaus Magnus (1490–1557) … published in Venice in 1539" (2013: 81). Magnus's 1539 map, *Carta marina et description septemtrionalium terrarium ac mirabilium* (*Nautical Chart and Description of the Northern Lands and Wonders*), served as a visual encyclopedia for the various sea creatures across the northern Atlantic. Southwest of Iceland, a whale is mistaken for an island, as men are shown lighting a fire on its back. To the right of the "island" whale is a giant sea serpent attacking a ship. There are sea pigs, giant lobsters, seals, sea unicorns, ziphiuses, and various types of whales. Magnus's map depicts the sea as a space of inescapable danger and predation. Animals are depicted attacking ships, sailors, and other sea creatures. As Van Duzer explains, Magnus's map influenced Gerardus Mercator's famous globe of 1541, especially in Mercator's recreation of seven of Magnus's sea creatures (86–7). In many cases, illustrations of oceanic creatures had a

FIGURE 7.6 *Americae sive quartae orbis partis nova et exactissima descriptio*, 1562. © Wikimedia Commons (public domain).

pragmatic purpose in warning sailors and navigators of the possible dangers in certain waters. However, in other occasions, these drawings may also simply demonstrate the whimsy and imagination of the artist.

Cartographers depicted more than threatening sea creatures such as whales and sea dragons. Mermaids and sirens are also commonly found in early modern maps, eliciting both danger and delight. The *hortus sanitatis* (1491) features a siren in chapter 83 of "De piscibus" with long, blonde hair and two tailfins, and a siren is also depicted in Johann Schöner's 1515 globe. Diego Gutiérrez's *Map of the Americas* (1562) features several sirens holding mirrors and combs, tempting a passing ship (see Figure 7.6). As Van Duzer points out, the vain sirens in Gutierrez's map attempt to "practise their wiles" on a ship west of the Strait of Magellan (2013: 39). Mermaid sightings were prevalent during this time, as navigators such as Captain Richard Whitbourne (1561–1635), who sailed to Newfoundland to look for potential English settlements in 1620, claimed to have seen a mermaid with blue streaks instead of hair (Ellis 1994: 79). These sightings and myths emphasized not only beauty but the elusiveness of these figures. In the Madrid manuscript of Ptolemy's *Geography* (c. 1455–60), there are two different mermaid figures swimming near a sea dog, as other figures—sea rabbits, sea pigs, and other generic sea monsters—swim around them. Other significant cartographers of this period include Giacomo Gastaldi, Jean Mansel, Martin Behaim, Martin Waldseemüller, Casper Vapel, Sebastian Münster, Gonzalo Fernández de Oviedo, Cornelis de Jode, and Giuseppe Rosaccio.[9]

THE SEA ON THE STAGE

Just as Renaissance visual artists were captivated by the sea, playwrights such as Shakespeare explore the sea's unfathomable treasures in oceanic drama. Though these are not purely visual representations per se, the dramatic works of early modern playwrights capture both the mythical and realistic depictions of the sea. Among literary and mythological sources, oceanic plays were also inspired by published accounts of travel, trade, and scientific discovery. Richard Hakluyt's *Divers Voyages Touching the Discovery of America and the Islands Adjacent* (1582), and his compilation of histories, *The Principal Navigations, Voyages, Traffiques, and Discoveries of the English Nation* (1589/99–1600), gave early modern society the first glimpses of brave new worlds with such people they had never imagined.

Early modern accounts of voyages to the Americas contain material that may have inspired a number of maritime plays. The account of John Rolfe's shipwreck on Bermuda while traveling to Virginia in 1609, published in Sylvester Jordain's *A Discovery of the Barmudas* (1610), could have served as the basis for Shakespeare's *The Tempest* (1610). Having lost his wife and island-born daughter, Bermuda, Rolfe built a ship and sailed to the American mainland, where he later met and married Pocahontas (Games 2008: 133). Rolfe's daughter Bermuda, born out of the sea, shows affinities with Shakespeare's young sea-tossed heroines, Marina and Miranda. John Fletcher's *The Island Princess* (c. 1619–21) is another play inspired by the travels of European voyagers and their engagements with dignities and indigenous peoples. The sources for Fletcher's play include two navigation books: Le Seigneur de Bellan's, *L'histoire de Ruis Dias, et de Quixaire, Princess des Moloques* (1615), and the work from which Bellan's novella is based, Bartolemé Leonardo de Argensola's *Conquista de las Islas Molucas* (1609).

Fletcher's *The Sea Voyage* (1622), cowritten with Philip Massinger, is another notable travel play during this period of exploration. The play is known for its similarities to Shakespeare's *The Tempest* (1610), opening with a violent sea storm and detailing the survival of the shipwrecked crew on an unwelcoming island. The crew includes a group of French pirates, one of the crew's love interests, and several Portuguese castaways that the group meets upon arrival, who had viewed the sea storm from shore. The French and Portuguese voyagers discover that the island is inhabited by a community of Amazonian women who have sustained a life without men. On coming into contact with their new visitors, the Amazons realize they can continue to populate the island and sustain their race. This situation seems to be the direct inverse of Caliban's in *The Tempest*, as he is the last of whatever race he is, desperately attempting to "people" the island with "with Calibans" (1.2.353). Being a comedy, *The Sea Voyage* concludes with a reunion of families and the marriage of a string of couples, including the play's central romantic leads, Albert (a French pirate) and the woman he abducted and fell in love with, Aminta.

The Sea Voyage relies on many of the same technical features of *The Tempest*, including the recreation of a sea storm, as well as the appearance of multiple ships, an island environment, and a hoard of treasure. However, the play also relied on even more state-of-the-art stagecraft. Anthony Parr explains that "the use of different levels and sight lines to evoke [*The Sea Voyage*'s] archipelago setting" evidences that "the playhouses were quite capable of turning much of what they could find in Richard Hakluyt's *The Principal Navigations* into vivid theatre" (2018: 28). Yet, as Parr suggests, the "unflattering" comic portrayal of stranded colonists and sea voyagers would have made a sour impression on the Virginia Company investors who viewed the played at the Blackfriars in 1622 (31).

There are a number of plays that refer to the language of the sea, and water travel, more generally. The titles of Thomas Dekker and John Webster's *Westward Ho* (1604) and its response play, *Eastward Ho* (1605), by George Chapman, Ben Jonson, and John Marston, refer to the watermen's shouts on the Thames as they gave boat taxis in the respective directions. There are also plays portraying the daily lives of sea traders. Shakespeare's *The Merchant of Venice* (c. 1596) begins with Antonio's anxiety as he awaits for his cargo to arrive, though he protests that his grief is not related to his merchandise (1.1.45). In Thomas Middleton and William Rowley's *The Changeling* (1622), Alsemero ventures to Malta while his bride-to-be, Beatrice, devises a murder plot and becomes entangled in a blackmail plot with her father's servant De Flores.

Walter Mountfort's *The Launching of the Mary, or The Seaman's Honest Wife* (1632) has three plots involved in the effects of trade. In the first plot, the East India Company (which Mountfort served as clerk) justifies its aims of global trade to the Lord Admiral; in the second, a sailor's wife maintains her chastity in spite of a series of attempted suitors; in the third, a band of shipyard laborers finish working on the titular ship, the *Mary*, while engaging in antics and celebrations. In John Day, William Rowley, and George Wilkins's *The Travels of the Three English Brothers* (1607), the titular characters must engage the Great Turk while navigating Muslim Persia. The playwrights portray Persia as a country of intense violence and treachery, with beheadings and inhumane characters. The English brothers demonstrate courage against adversity, and in the end, they persuade the Sophy (Shah) to give Christians tolerance.

Spanish sea drama and epic poetry

One of the most influential Spanish playwrights of this era, Lope de Vega, produced several works chronicling the history of European colonial exploits across the sea. His epic poem, *La Dragontea* (1598), describes the last expedition and death of English privateer and sea captain, Sir Francis Drake. Notably one of early modern Spain's villainized figures, Drake earned the nickname "El Draque" (the dragon) after pirating a series of Spanish ships, most notably the *Cacafuego*, a treasure-laden transport ship, during his circumnavigation (1577–80). Lope's epic poem is, to quote one critic, "el poema épico más importante de las letras españolas del Renacimiento," or the most important epic poem of the Spanish letters of the Renaissance (Lerner 2012: 147). In Canto II, Lope describes the manic frenzy of shipboard activity before Drake's departure, with shouts of "lastra, carga, sube, pone y quita" (ballast, load, raise, lay and remove) echoing aboard (2.31). He infuses the epic with maritime terminology and technical knowledge, and often these terms are used in long lists, emphasizing the rhythm of labor and the perpetual continuation of maritime work. In Canto IV, when describing Drake's unsuccessful attempt to attack Puerto Rico, Lope lists a series of objects, beginning with "el bauprés, mesana, árbol, trinquetes" (bowsprit, mizzen, tree, ratchets). As the poem explains, these materials are all *cenizas* (ashes), emphasizing the ephemerality of ships and boards.

Lope's sea drama, *El Nuevo Mundo descubierto por Cristóbal Colón* (The World Discovered by Christopher Columbus) is one of the first plays explicitly about America, rather than representing it in a reimagined setting (i.e., Shakespeare's *The Tempest*). Written nearly a century after Columbus's journey, *El Nuevo Mundo* is full of historical inaccuracies, such as the notion that the navigator aimed to discover a new world rather than a new route to India. Columbus asks himself at the beginning of the play, "Where am I going? Where is the road?" (1.1.16–17) (Lope de Vega 1950). Lope portrays Columbus as a kind of "New Moses," as one of his sailors calls him, guiding his people to a new land in search of new possibilities, with the implication that his journey was also divinely inspired.

In addition to the "New Moses" myth, *El Nuevo Mundo* also preserves the "aquaman" myth, which tells of a man who turned into a fish after spending too much time in the water. The reference to the man-fish appears early in the play when Columbus's men are on the ship, hopelessly searching for their new world. Two sailors, Brother Buyl and Arana, argue over their Captain's worthiness as a navigator and seafarer:

ARANA
To the sea! There, if he likes he can change himself into a fish, like the man, who, it is said, swam around so much he finally transformed himself into one.
BROTHER BUYL
If God allowed Jonah to be thrown into the sea, it was because he had not conformed to His orders. But such is not the case with Columbus, no!
(2.1.27–32)

Lope depicts Columbus as a navigator following God's compass, "conform[ing] to His orders" in his search for a new land. But the playwright also includes the sailor's tale of the man who "can change himself into a fish" and "transformed himself into one." This story notably resembles the tale of Glaucus, whose legs and arms were transformed into a fish's tail and fins.[10] A variation on the man-turned-fish story also appears in Shakespeare's *The Winter's Tale*, when Autolycus tells a "true" ballad of a woman-turned-fish: "it was thought she was a woman and was turned into a cold fish for she would not exchange flesh with one that loved her" (4.4.281–3). While Arana characterizes Columbus as a man-fish who could leave at any time, the more spiritually minded Brother Buyl defends Columbus in comparing him to Jonah, emphasizing his role in God's plan.

Pirate plays

In addition to works about actual pirates, such as Lope's *La Dragontea*, playwrights also created their own versions of sea plunderers. Pirates generally appear in minor roles in much of the drama produced until 1650. William Shakespeare's *Hamlet* (1600) and his coauthored work *Pericles* (1609) both feature pirates in lesser roles, while Charles Johnson's *The Successful Pyrate* (1713) and John Gay's *Polly* (1729) elevate the pirate out of brief appearances and anecdotes. In Shakespeare's plays, pirates are tasked with transporting central characters, whereas Johnson and Gay's pirate-heroes are protagonists in their own right. Prior to 1650, piracy was a vital economic strategy for European nations, as it promised a large return on investment while laying the physical burden on ambitious seafarers. The years after 1650 begin what Marcus Rediker deems piracy's "golden age," as piracy became a popular livelihood in the eighteenth century for non-merchants and outcasts seeking individual gain (Egerton et al. 2007: 133). Though the draw of piracy was palpable, it came with a range of occupational hazards. With their fates threatened by storms, rough waters, sea warfare, sickness, and mutiny, carriers were all but impenetrable. To quote Shylock: "ships are but boards, sailors but men" (*Merchant* 1.3.21–2). The sea was always a space of vulnerability.

In Shakespeare's *Hamlet* and *Pericles*, pirates are portrayed as necessary transporters for the plays' protagonists. Their role is shaped by their setting; like the sea, they are violent and unpredictable. Steve Mentz argues that the pirates in these plays "serve as a narrative shorthand for radical disruption" (2009: 76). In this way, pirates seem to be a kind of embodiment of Fortune's wheel, which could land on wealth or disaster. As his letters to Horatio entail, Hamlet is abducted by pirates described as having a "warlike appointment," and yet they are also "thieves of mercy," bringing Hamlet safely to Denmark (4.6.16–20). Though likely a fictional account, Hamlet's pirate narrative allows him to ascribe his fate to his abductees and gives him an excuse for his whereabouts and a justification for his return. In *Pericles*, Marina grows up among "canvas-climber[s]," and like a sailor she is continually caught in the waves of fate and misfortune, as her life story is one of continual disorder (4.1.62). Marina is abducted by pirates and later sold to a brothel for a considerable price, turned into both captive and commodity. The pirates deem her a "prize" and intend to "have her aboard suddenly" (4.1.93–6). Once she crosses the threshold and becomes a "prize," she is then treated as sexual baggage for trade.

Unsurprisingly, eighteenth-century plays produced during the "golden age of piracy" often portray pirates in more significant roles—though many remain stock characters—and the pirate-hero emerges as a protagonist in several seafaring plays. Charles Johnson's *The Successful Pyrate* (1713) retells the adventures of Henry Avery, renamed Arviragus, and his exploits in St. Lawrence, or Madagascar. *The Successful Pyrate* was first performed at the Theatre Royal in Drury Lane in 1713. That same year, the War of the Spanish Succession ended, and many sailors "turned to piracy, swelling the ranks of Caribbean buccaneers to several thousand persons" (Wood 2004). One of these sailors, boarding a privateer during the Spanish conflict, was Edward Teach, who would eventually be known as "Blackbeard" (Wood 2004). In the drama of piracy's golden age, the pirate-hero mirrors the historical pirate rulers of the Caribbean, a group that included Avery, Blackbeard, and Benjamin Hornigold, whose seafaring skills and ruthlessness served as a direct model for Blackbeard.

In *The Successful Pyrate*, Johnson restyles Avery to Arviragus, emphasizing avarice and rage in the pirate-hero's dramatic persona and more overtly in his name. *A General History of the Robberies and Murders of the Most Notorious Pirates* (1724) briefly mentions the play but dismisses the various plots within it as "no more than false Rumours, improved by the Credulity of some, and the Humour of others who love to tell strange Things" (Johnson 1999: 33–4). While *A General History* focuses on Avery's exploits prior to settling in Madagascar, *The Successful Pyrate* centers on a romantic plot involving Zaida, daughter of the Great Mogul, and Aranes, an Omrah in her train who loves her and has been contracted to marry her. With its central romantic plot and its diverse cast of satirical characters, Johnson's play navigates between comedy and problem play, the problem perhaps being how much its title character contradicts himself. In this way, pirates' natures are symbolic of the turbulent environment they navigate.

Polly (1729), John Gay's much-maligned sequel to *The Beggar's Opera* (1728), takes place in the West Indies, which was a vortex of economic and sexual exchange. As the titular Polly traverses the West Indies and finds herself in the underbelly of piratical crime, she is taken in by the predatory culture and finds ingenious ways to outwit, deceive, and successfully navigate her new and unfamiliar terrain. Polly's former love, Macheath, has traveled to the West Indies to seek riches, reinventing himself as a pirate and, later, adopting the persona of a black man named Morano. Like Macheath, Polly also engages in subterfuge, disguising as a man and joining a pirate band to reunite with her former love, to whom she is still emotionally attached. Robert G. Dryden argues that "Gay is one of the first eighteenth-century writers to represent the English colonial merchant, not as a hero, but as a kind of pirate" (2001: 540). In doing so, Gay presents the merchant-pirate as one who uses cunning and quick wit, engages in risky business, and pursues fortune on their own terms.

CONCLUSION

As it was depicted in art, objects, and theatre, the early modern sea was a focal point of desire and possibility. It represented the struggles of life and the rewards of labor; sea paintings often capture these struggles at their most violent and difficult, whether in a sea storm or a deadly encounter with a whale. But oceanic art also acknowledges the brevity of these hardships and the continuation of new life. Paintings of grand portside entrances such as Carpaccio's *Arrival of the Pilgrims in Cologne* depict the hopefulness that comes after a long journey, while Bruegel's *Landscape with the Fall of Icarus* demonstrates that the sea is a vortex of activity that keeps going in spite of unusual happenings. Magnus's *Carta Marina* tells seafarers how to navigate dangerous waters, while Lope de Vega's *El Nuevo Mundo* tells how sailors survived them. There is an inescapable feeling of circularity and fluidity with each work that retells the sea's myths and histories. Whether calm or chaotic, the early modern sea was both a mirror of the flux and change of the world, as well as an unfathomable trove of everything the world desired.

CHAPTER EIGHT

IMAGINARY WORLDS

Imagining Early Modern Arctics

LOWELL DUCKERT

> It may seeme needlesse to make any mention of *Scandia*, which is that whole *peninsula* of huge circuit, which is almost incompassed with the waues of the sea, and abutteth northward and eastward vppon the *German* and *Sarmatian* coastes, because it is as it weere scituated in another world.
> — Giovanni Botero, *Relations of the Most Famous Kingdoms* (1608)

In their unflagging attempts to find the fabled Asiatic otherworld of Cathay in the late sixteenth and early seventeenth centuries, English navigators depended on a specific geographical point to help them travel north by northwest: Cape Farewell (now Nunap Isua), Greenland's southernmost tip. John Davis (c. 1550–1605) named the cape on the first (1585) of his three voyages because he was forced to follow the land's western coast after facing impassible ice on the opposite side. This spot, strangely enough, could be recognized hydrologically as well as terrestrially, as John Janes points out in his account of the voyage: "The water about this coast was very blacke and thicke, like to a filthy standing poole" (Markham 1880: 5). A similar sentiment is repeated by George Weymouth (c. 1587–1611) in 1602: "This day sometimes we came into blacke water as thicke as puddle … then we sounded, and could fetch no ground in one hundred and twenty fathomes" (Purchas [1625] 1906: 14:308). James Hall (d.1612), too, "came in blacke water, as thicke as though it had beene puddle water" in 1605 (Purchas [1625] 1906: 14:321). While the puzzling and puddly phenomena they witnessed is probably white summer ice melting and exposing the darker ocean water underneath, their swampy characterization of the Arctic Ocean reveals it to be a simultaneously frigid and fecund place: according to the Aristotelian tenets of spontaneous generation, "standing" water was insalubrious because it bred. Olaus Magnus (1490–1557), the Scandinavian Mandeville, lists "*Northern marvels*" such as the savvy drinkers who save pieces of ice to cool their drinks in the summer but carefully avoid the snow "for it has hidden worms innate in it" ([1555] 1996: 1:102). It should not be surprising, then, that Janes pictures the icebergs as bedeviling insects when he complains about the incessant "pester of yce" (1: 6). For him, "the yrksome noyse … seemed to be the true patterne of desolation," a phrase that came to define eastern Greenland as "The land of Desolation" (1: 3–4). But something pestilent escapes the "patterne": the small circles spotlighting stirring creatures who populate a sprawling Circle undersea, those weird pools passed over but not fully occluded.

Some explorers expected a lifeless void up north, it is true; Jacob Segersz van der Brugge (fl.1634), sailing to Spitsbergen on behalf of the Dutch Noordsche Company, cited classical authorities: the surrounding ocean deserves the appellation "Mare Cronium," he believed, "because Saturn, a cold planet, is said to rule in these places. For the same reason it is also called Concretum and Amalchim, which formerly meant frozen in the language of that people, and Morimarusa (signifying a dead sea), on account of the long darkness and the exiled aspect of milder constellations" (Conway 1904: 85). His peers, however, dreamt differently than he did: "Hyperboreans," shielded from the north wind ("Boreas"), sat atop the world in a supra-tropical Eden;[1] competing tales from mythology and folklore told of pygmies and giants warring in one place;[2] and the freshly printed narratives of Davis's immediate predecessor like Martin Frobisher (1535[?]–94) recounted increased contact with local Inuit communities. (Van der Brugge's journal, ironically, is wholly occupied with a slew of polar bear attacks that harassed his overwintering on the island.) Nothing in the northern ocean was, or had ever been, "concrete."[3] It was "sea-lung," after all, that ultimately thwarted Pytheas of Marseilles's (far) northern progress in the fourth century BCE; famous for discovering the land of "Thule" after six days' sail from Britain, this gelatinous (not gelid) mixture of elements stymied the Greek geographer. When they did see blank space on the map, this "heart of whiteness" (Hill 2008: 1–28)—not the "blacke"-ness of indigeneity nor the "thicke"-ness of ecological relations—helped perpetuate colonializing projects of erasure, supersession, or both, each constituting a brazen act of "cartographic silence" (Harley 1988). The cryosphere's given title of "desolation," as a hollow emptiness utterly devoid of worth and of life, is, in fact, inaccurate; in reality, it bespeaks an act of avoidance (from *desolare*, "to abandon")—a silencing of the cape's flourishing, even if "filthy," creatures.

Plumbing the opaque paths of the frozen sea was, and still is, an opportunity worth considering. Published approximately seventy-five years after Janes's account, the French theologian Isaac de la Peyrère's (1596–1676) compilation of contemporary visitors to the region, the "Relation du Groenland" (1663), depicts the cape and its inky waters as a traveler's trusty point of departure—a valuable, measurable, midway point between England and Newfoundland—but it also mentions it as a place that significantly points past known horizons: "Doubtless it is thus called because those who go beyond this cape seem to be going into another world, and to be taking a long leave of their friends" (White 1855: 238). The cape consequently takes on the power of otherworldly transportation; its impulse to embark offers the ability not only to traverse the boundaries of this world but also to exceed its perceivable limits, and as such, it escapes definition: "It would be difficult to represent its form, on account of the snow and ice, which vary, and on account of their whiteness, which dazzles the eyes" (238). All that dazzles is not white either; peering into ice's wondrously shifty "difference of colour" on a sled route from Elsinore to Copenhagen—from "very white" to "beautiful azure" (186)—reminds him of the phrase Virgil uses in the *Georgics* (first century BCE) to describe "the black and dark countries" that comprise the opposing poles: "*Cœrulea glacie*," or "blue ice" (186).[4] Seen with Peyrère's prismatic vision, the cape begins to look tri-colored: blue, black, and white all over. The changes in color shift to scale as well: in the seas off Spitzbergen "there are places ... where the water is frozen from the bottom to the top, and on the surface of this are blocks of ice as high above as the sea is deep below" (236). Parroting Weymouth's observation about the unfathomable ice-pool, Peyrère cites Virgil again, this time to underscore the "immense" size of ice: "Quæ tantum vertice ad auras Aerias, / Quantum radice ad Tartara tendunt" (236). As the oak tree extends equally above and below ground—"as far as it lifts its top to the airs of heaven, so far it strikes its roots down towards hell" (Virgil 1999: 452–3)—so do the icebergs. But to underscore does not necessarily mean to understand; these ice pillars, somehow arboreal in their vegetal metaphor but rhizomatic in their flight-lines capable of launching bodies past the Greenlandic "beyond," touch the depths of Tartarus ("Tartara") and act as vertical ("vertice") ice bridges that lead to an elsewhere, an "other" (under-)world. (Peyrère might be punning here on Greenland's unfortunate misnomer as a verdant country as well as the written resemblance between Tartary-Tartarus.[5]) In their multidimensional ability to usher in another world-within-world, Farewell's pools are also portals. What was a clearly delineated "frozen zone" according to classical and medieval science that split the globe latitudinally into five circular segments, is now, on the contrary, an entryway that impinges upon and propels forward. If it must keep a "pole," then, the far north encompasses the Greek *polos* (pivot, axis, sky) rather than the stolid *palus* (stake) of Latin: containing vectors instead of points, its environs slingshots ships; it causes turns. Peyrère's catapulting cape asks us to bid farewell to telos, to take a "leave" of current friendships by stretching our journeys and imaginations "long" in an effort to accrue new Arctic relations and fare *well* together.

It is important to note that Peyrère personally saw these portals as lethal: "dead bodies keep well," he warns the erstwhile Arctic explorer, "but the living always fare ill" (236). His is a motto fit for Dante's *Inferno* (1320), a poem that famously, of course, put the lowest circle of hell on ice. Although he did not dare "fare" forth himself, there are those who tried. To the German naturalist Frederick Martens (1635–99), for example, the Spitsbergen cold sea performs a kind of carpentry. Physically skimming these "places" in 1671, he espies "round and four square tables, with round and blew pillars underneath: the tables was very plain and smooth at the top, and white with the snow; at the sides hung down a great many icikles close to one another, like a fringed table cloth" (White 1855: 37). Martens, who speaks of ice's "taste" (37), including some "frozen quite curled, it look'd just like sugar-candy" (35), views the sweet matter around him as a potential "messmate" (Haraway 2008: 15–19). He then fantasizes further, placing himself (impossibly) under the variegated table: "you shall commonly see the water look blew or yellow, if you walk under water with your eyes open and look upwards" (37). The "if" is entirely speculative, of course, yet his beautiful ice banquet nevertheless allows him to visit the ocean floor in his imagination, inverting spatial orientations by rendering the sea below as the "blew"-yellow sky above. The communal "tables" represent a deep-water daydream of a habitable north for humans, but they are a vision, at the very least, of the waters' untold vivaciousness. A living sea creative and companionate because of, and not despite, its quickening "close"-ness: in Martens's mind, the sharpness of "icikles" can seem keenly inviting. It is interesting to think of Prospero's chilling lines to Ariel through this bluer lens of enchantment: "Thou … think'st it much … To run upon the sharp wind of the north, / To do me business in the veins o'th' earth / When it is baked with frost" (*The Tempest* [1611], 1.2.252–6).[6] (And remember, too, the "*several strange shapes, bringing a banquet*" to the beleaguered Italians at the end of 3.3.) Eschewing southern locales "baked" by the sun (images which the "New World" usually conjures and with which William Shakespeare's [1564–1616] play is commonly associated), Martens conceives of a friendlier world "fringed" with frost instead.

Contrary to Giovanni Botero's casual dismissal of historical material "scituated in another world," this chapter finds it necessary to "make … mention" of frigid feasts (and more) that led to otherworldly multispecies Arctic kinships. To rephrase what Peyrère already knew from his "poole"-side precursors: *the Arctic is a portal, not a pole*. Cool-water accompaniment, in fact, is the intended "business" of modern-day onlookers who share Martens's sapid fascination with delectable oceans. The Russian photographer Viktor Lyagushkin tellingly calls his pictures of the warming White Sea—its sea angels, caprellas ("skeleton shrimp"), and comb jellies—"otherworldly" (Stacke 2018) (Figure 8.1).

FIGURE 8.1 Other Worlds. Photograph by Viktor Lyagushkin. © Moment Open / Getty Images.

Going out of the blue and into the black (and back) of human–nonhuman creaturely interconnectivity entails suspending ontological differences, whether or not by aesthetic means.[7] The otherness I evoke is one of enfolded intimacy rather than outsourced distancing. In short, my overarching argument is that *the Arctic is of this world, not out of it*. In what follows, I introduce the early modern imaginations of "septentrionally excited" (Browne 1646:

62) thinkers who envisaged the Arctic less as a complete and single circle (Circle), and more as a series of swirling portals (circles) in overlay, of un/locking archipelagos of islands veering in and out of sequence, of passages orienting in their geographical and scalar specificity as well as dizzying in their collapses of distance. At the same time, their narratives demonstrate that to inhabit an "other" faraway world that oddly connects with, and is strangely similar to, your own is dependent on who the "your" is at the moment of speaking. As the perspectives of Inuit "others" will attest, the oceanic dynamics of encounter change when the European orbit unwillingly extends into yours. Peter Davidson remarks that "north" is a "shifting idea" because it always recedes from our attempts at encapsulation: it is better to speak of "a," not "the," north (2005: 8). My outlook might seem facile at first—affording an amusing kaleidoscope effect, perhaps, or supporting the conspiracy theories of a "Hollow Earth," or both—but the Danish, Dutch, and English multifaceted views of the "otherworldly" north as whirl/pool, archipelago, and passage (as we will see) usefully distort our perceptions about this supposedly remote marine world. Their Arctics, I maintain—purposefully plural and pluralizing—allow us to imagine the northscape in new ways. In keeping with Martens's companionate model and Peyrère's pivotal portrait, I will present the rest of this chapter as a map of portals, three (plus) routes limned with a motto of my own (I have already inscribed two) that serves to highlight the energetic qualities of the "yce"-y seas seen beyond.

THE ARCTIC IS A SPIRAL, NOT A CIRCLE

When the Flemish cartographer Gerhardus Mercator (1512–94) published his 1569 world map that boasts his famous "projection," he added a smaller window on the bottom left considered to be the first map of the Arctic Circle. Jodocus Hondius (1563–1612) updated his predecessor's depiction in 1606 as the *Septentrionalium Terrarum Descriptio* (see Figure 8.2). What immediately strikes the viewer is the black rock ("Rupus nigra et altissima") situated at the exact center of the "Polus Arcticus," or North Pole, surrounded by four islands cut by four channels. This tricky god's-eye view looking straight down on the spherical globe provides a geometric, somewhat becalmed symmetry; the fabled pygmies (perhaps Laplanders) reside in the land to the bottom left—"Here live pygmies, at most 4 feet tall, who are like those in Greenland called Scraelings"—while adjacent to them sits "the best and healthiest [island] of the whole north." Partitioned and preserved as if in crystal, its placid stillness is nevertheless betrayed by the other Latin inscriptions therein. Although the centrical black rock is a permanent fixture on the map, the waters around it are on the move. As written on the island slightly above the cliffs, the Arctic pulls the southern waters into its gluttonous orbit: "The

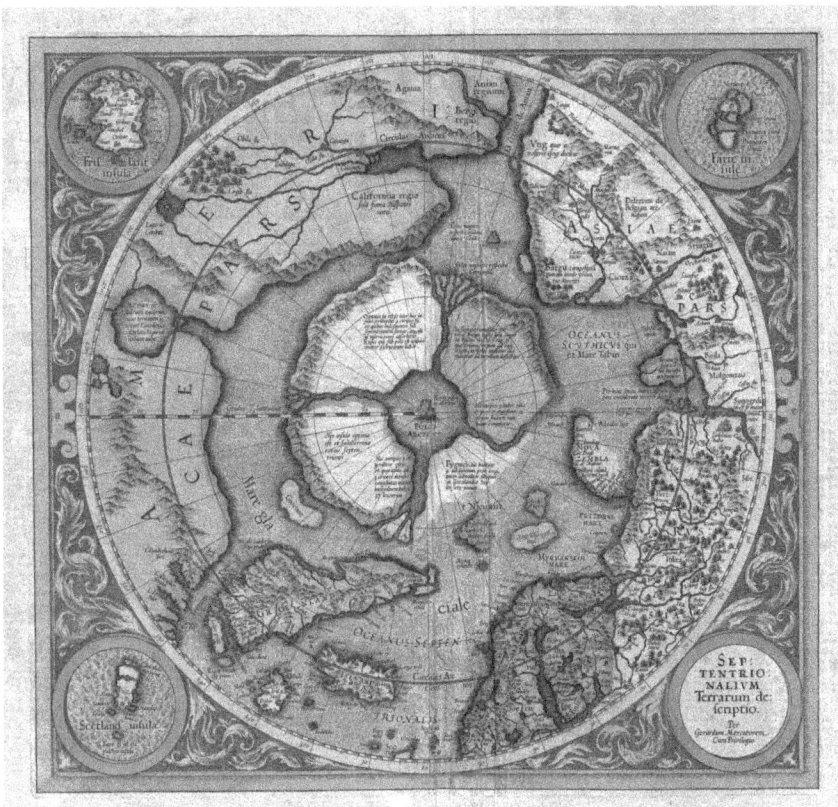

FIGURE 8.2 *Septentrionalium Terrarum Descriptio*, 1606. © Wikimedia Commons (public domain).

Ocean rushes in between these islands by 19 mouths and makes 4 channels by which it is incessantly carried northwards & there disappears into the bowels of the earth."[8] And as it sucks, the pole, incredibly, spins. In a personal letter sent to the English polymath John Dee on April 20, 1577, Mercator explains his rationale: "In the midst of the four countries is a Whirl-pool ... into which there empty these four Indrawing Seas which divide the North. And the water rushes round and descends into the earth just as if one were pouring it through a filter funnel" (Taylor 1956: 60). Mercator's four-part display repeats, he insists, the reports of one Jacob Cnoyen, a traveler who referenced the lost *Inventio Fortunata* (Fortunate Discoveries) from the fourteenth century, a fabulous work whose anonymous author's testimony lent the map its peculiar structure: "in the yeere 1360, a certaine English Frier, a Franciscan, and a Mathematician of Oxford, came into those Islands, who leaving them, & passing further by his magical Arte, described all those places that he sawe"

(64). But the whirled waters at world's top break this tidy system; in fact, so does the element of earth. Unlike his contemporaries, Mercator did not believe this black mountain attracted the compass needle: the magnetic pole, "polus magnetis," is up and to the right. What we now know to be the changeable geomagnetic pole as opposed to the plottable geographic one was anticipated by this maneuver. The "pole," according to his projection, is a moveable marker ("magnetis") as well as a place ("Arcticus") of mobility; any center, then, is always a little-off; whatever solidity can be discerned sits in the middle of a ravenous vortex. The pullulating pools with their elements in tow are stops along a spiral whose point is perpetually un-fixed; Mercator's portal, at last, has us focus on the asymmetrical propensity to go off-balance contained within any configuration of symmetrical ecological order. Here is where the "magical Arte" of science meets that "Arte" of the imagination. The circle is broken because the maelstrom remains incomplete: we are unsure into what worlds the brumal "bowels" lead, if they terminate at all.

At the same time that its disequilibrium jars familiar arrangements of concentric circles aligned in neat cartographic form, the swirling Arctic also helps to overlay parallel sites of nature and culture in the real world to the south it purports to preside over: in other words, the "Whirl-pool" of/as Arctic flux is not a disorder that needs to be set aright but a realization of living in a world whose spatial symmetries are ephemeral (at best) and divisive (at worst). Put simply by multiple climate scientists, "What happens in the Arctic does not stay in the Arctic."[9] It means deserting the sturdiness of Robert Recorde's *The Castle of Knowledge* (1556), for instance, or eschewing the clean curves of William Cuningham's *Cosmographical Glass* (1559), to rethink subject-object symmetry not as a measurable proportion of equanimity (at a distance) but as an ontological pairing (in proximity). Remember Mercator's channels that both "divide" and "round" at once; pressing up to the glass that "filter[s]" as it "funnel[s]" is what the French theorist Michel Serres has in mind when he describes the passage of time as "percolation," noting that *passoir* ("sieve") should be closer to *pass*: "one flux passes through while another does not" (Serres, with Latour 1995: 58). But in his temporal musings he also makes a messier Mercatorial map as well: "It's better to paint a sort of fluctuating picture of relations and rapports—like the percolating basin of a glacial river, unceasingly changing its bed and showing an admirable network of forks, some of which freeze or silt up, while others open up" (105). Within the mixtures of turbulence, things pass and do not pass along passages that are frequently being un/made, their sifts obeying the liminal physics of a glacial rock.

Glimpsed through a gelid glass differently, the "sky" otherwise known as the "pole" should feel familiar to us in these funnel-shaped ways. Despite the reintroduction of the term into North American vocabularies in 2013 to

2014, the "polar vortex"—the band of low pressure and cold that sits at the earth's two poles—is not a climatic aberration but a chronic condition that, like all weather, is susceptible to extremes. True to its spiraling form, the vorticular pole may constrict (by its "Indrawing") as well as expand—it always connects, and vexingly so. Although the earliest adventurers did not claim to be in what is now called the Little Ice Age (*c.* 1300–1850), they certainly pondered why climates at equal latitudes were different (White 2017: 9–27), and furthermore, how the frigid atmosphere of Thule could possibly stretch across the sea and enter subarctic England. Thus William Strachey (1572[?]–1621) thought the cold weather "Virginia Britannia" experienced in 1607 was indicative of the "the extraordinary frost … felt in most parts of Europe" (Major 1849: 179), while Raphael Thorius (d.1625) poeticized London's bitter winters of the early seventeenth century by asking, "Who now can travell? scarcely in the town / A man can walk with safety up and down, / So furious doth the North-wind swagger, / The wals, unless I reel, do seem to stagger … In a sad case is he that opes his dore, / Unless the whirlwinds wings be clipt before" (1651: 7). The temperature of the north from where these boreal blasts originated remained hotly contested. The Flemish astronomer-cartographer Petrus Plancius (1552–1622), for example, argued that the degree of cold actually decreases as the pole is neared, corroborated by Henry Hudson's (d.1611) experience at the high latitudes of Greenland and Novaya Zemlya from 1607 to 1608:

> [He] confirms this by scientific reasons, and says, that near the pole the sun shines for five months continually; and, although his rays are weak, yet on account of the long time they continue, they have sufficient strength to warm the ground, to render it temperate … He compares it to a small fire, which is but lighted, and then immediately extinguished. (Asher 1860: 246–7)

But even without a causal explanation, is clear that the "whirlwin[d]" carried both fears and fascinations, wrought damages and worked delights; whenever the Thames froze, it provided opportunities for bringing the city onto the ice (and vice versa), from the first "frost fair" of 1608 to the lavish festival held in 1683 to 1684 during one of the city's worst winters on record. The circles of the boreal and the urban coincided, then as now, illustrating not only the complexities of climate but also the complicated idea of "climate" itself. While Mercator's mercurial map at first glance might make his insights seem outmoded or unscientific in our era of greater meteorological understanding, upon closer inspection it underscores a still-swirling Arctic (the air and water currents called the atmosphere), guaranteeing that, while the oceanic vortex has been historically reconfigured, its whirring has never truly halted—and yet it spins.

THE ARCTIC IS AN ARCHIPELAGO OF STORIES

Sometime between 1390 and 1400, and not long before Mercator illuminated the Arctic Ocean as a whirlpool, two Venetian brothers named Nicolò (*c.* 1326–1402) and Antonio Zeno (d. *c.* 1403) supposedly skirted the Arctic Circle. Under the patronage of Zichmi of Frislanda (whom some have postulated as Henry Sinclair of Scotland), Antonio, if it is to be believed, ventured as far as America ("Estotiland" and "Drogeo"). A descendent of his, also named Nicolò Zeno, published the brothers' letters in 1558 along with a map of the various places they visited. The authenticity of their account has been controversial amongst scholars since the mid-nineteenth century, to say the least, and "the debate … has never really ceased" (di Robilant 2011: 6, 193): the island of "Icaria" does not exist, which is most damning to their credibility, and court records locate Nicolò in Venice at the time of their legendary expedition. Whether or not one completely spurns the Zeni family as frauds putting on an elaborate hoax or finds faint (because inaccurate) traces of truth in their north Atlantic adventures, one aspect of their legacy cannot be contested: the seascape they portrayed remained influential for centuries thereafter. Their notoriety far succeeded them; explorers expected "Frislanda" (Faroe), "Eslanda" (Shetland), "Engronelanda," "Estotilanda," and "Icaria" to come into view on the journey west. ("Frislanda" sits in the sphere to the upper left in Hondius's chart.) Rather than debating—or merely deploring—the inauthenticity of their travels, the Zeni map is better appraised for purposefully letting its surveyors drift into the realm of fabrication. By not striving to convey the Arctic perfectly as it is (or was) in favor of Arctics of various perspectives, and thereby underscoring the impossible verifiability of premodern Arctic maps, the brothers sketch for us the process (or phenomenon) of redesigning possible worlds. Being "the last imaginary place," as Robert McGhee (2005) believes it is, the Arctic's creative powers endure for those who wish to express them.

In his edition for the Hakluyt Society, Richard Henry Major appears sympathetic to the Venetians' inventiveness; one of his reasons for supplying a hundred-page introduction is the "vindicat[ion]" of an imaginative man who "indulged in the glowing fancies and diction of his sunny country" (1873: cii), which acts as much as a defense of topological poesy ("diction") as it does of the younger Nicolò's skills at compiling. Even though "the book," he assures us, "which has been declared to be 'one of the most puzzling in the whole circle of literature' will henceforth be no puzzle at all" (cii), the "puzzle" of the Circle remains perplexing. As it was centuries before, the Arctic seafloor, "the last new land" (Hayes 2003: 183), constitutes one of the few uncharted territories left on the planet, even as its surveyable swaths are either claimed or coveted by intergovernmental group members comprising the Arctic Council. What is more, northern worlds are constantly being remapped on the shores of advancing and withdrawing land- and sea-ice; due to the mutable quality of the ice-filled waters, any line separating land from ocean, by nature of its liminality, is necessarily being redrawn by hands (humans) as well as oceanic bodies (ice). The Circle, broken and remade in these ways, is what the farfetched Zeni map of 1558 ultimately pictures: an archipelago of fragments without a whole, splintered lands and seaways that are not just multiple but multiplying, that grow as the "glowing" vision goes. John Gillis, "correct[ing] history's continental bias," diagnoses this mind-altering propensity as "islomania" (2004: 1, 4). Rhizomatic in nature, having neither boundaries nor center, the Arctic has both indulged and engendered "fancies" even as its areas have never been completely circumscribed, its puzzles pieced together, or its problems solved: it is an insular but never-isolated world at risk in uncertain outline, and, in its unfinished composition, it stays a catalyst for experimental ways of environmental being, knowing, and doing.

Back to "the book": the world-ing process in which the Zeni participate reveals the archipelago's propensity to story Arctics on the page in words as much as illustrate them on the map in pictures. Its seas crispen characters—invite (do not stultify) tales. In her study of the "spatial, social, and material specifics" of Arctic disasters of the Victorian era, Adriana Craciun takes a "recursive" approach to accounts penned around John Franklin's 1845 expedition: following Bruno Latour (via Michel de Certeau), she identifies "the complexity of interpretive and imaginative work within cycles of knowledge accumulation," a metanarrative she envisions as "a line of circles" (2016: 18–19). As it accrues knowledge in the present while also retroactively retracing the archives of the past, a given exploration moves forward in non-teleological space and time. By evaluating process over progress, we may glimpse the writing process physically at work while at sea: "Fictional and nonfictional voyages and their texts are promiscuously entangled in the model, where the cultural turn in history and the historicist turn in literature meet in the commons of the ocean" (18). I want to linger on the transtemporal approach to the networked "commons" Craciun crucially lays out. Confronting the "epistemological delirium" that the "New Climatic Regime" (also known as the Anthropocene) generates on a daily basis, writes Latour, "is not a matter of learning how to repair cognitive deficiencies, but rather how to live in the same world, share the same culture, face up to the same stakes, perceive a landscape that can be explored in concert" (2018: 25). A concerted effort to plumb the public pools ("commons") labeled "Arctic" means looking for the nonhuman actors who challenge anthropocentric claims to the Circle by loosening humanity's authoritarian grip over its aqueous realms. If it is true that "when you enter Arctic narrative, you enter every narrative of the Arctic ever written," to quote John Moss (1994: 105), the combined effort for which I am advocating becomes clearer on the basis of bibliography; nonetheless, Craciun's remarks on the "archipelagic Arctic"

(2016: 204) of early modernity differ slightly from mine in that I seek to address the active role the oceanic environment plays in the Arctic Circle's spiraling "line" (lines) of stories, how it spins sagas across an ice-"field of dispersion" and a liquid "landscape of forking paths" (21, 31). The Zeno brothers, indeed, obey a "fractal logic" inherent to the "archipelagic fluidity" (208) of the time, one that subtended and fueled a "culture of chaotic empiricism" (Mayhew 2011: 30)—a "culture," I wager, that is fed by archipelagic entities of northern seas no matter how spurious their reports may be. A material mixing that manifests in the imagination and pours onto maps: such messy matrices host ontological hybridity as well as harbor epistemological mishap, rendering the authorship of other worlds as a more-than-human endeavor.

Fractious encounters with the cold (be they calamitous or not) compel the creativity necessary for world-making as well as resist the author's world-controlling urges. The presence of "uncolonizable" space, whether provided on the map or insinuated at its margins, can also counter empiricist impulses that too often stem storying. Siobhan Carroll calls these spots "atopias: 'real' natural regions falling within the theoretical scope of contemporary human mobility, which, because of their intangibility, inhospitality, or inaccessibility, cannot be converted into the locations of affective habitation known as 'place'" (2015: 6).[10] Predictably, the random acts of *poiesis* that a fractured seascape occasioned were seldom seen as imperative to a country's imperialist agenda. When considering the "probabilitie of a passage" to the northwest in 1625, Samuel Purchas (1577–1626) laments that "painters and poets are not always the best oracles" before lambasting the "learned-unlearned Mariner and Mathematician" ([1625] 1906: 14:411, 413). William Baffin (*c*. 1584–1622) who had failed to produce a navigable route in the previous decade. Sir Dudley Digges (1582/3–1639), politician and shareholder in the Virginia Company and the East India Company, compounded this insult leveled at the untutored in his short treatise from 1611, *Of the Circumference of the Earth*: "*Geographye* depends on the reports of Trauellours (which *Ptolomey* cal's *Historiam Peregrinationis*) and Trauellours be seldome *Mathematicians*, but Merchants, Saylours, Souldiers, men that may vse common Rules and Instruments, not subtilties of nice and curious practice" (1611: 9). (Paint and letters, we may assume, are not included in the list of acceptable "practice[s].") The mathematician Henry Briggs (1561–1630) wrote in 1616 that "Gerardus Mercator, a very industrious and excellent geographer, was abused by a map sent unto him, of four Euripi meeting about the North Pole" (Purchas [1625] 1906: 14:424). We cannot blame the likes of Briggs for his desire to supply facts and correct faults (his meaning of "abused"), just as long as we do not give in to the myopias of Purchas and Digges that banish uneducated inquisitiveness: the realms of fact and mystery may productively coincide (even in our present "post-truth" moment) when we realize that what we know is grounded in institutions and produced by scientific practice. Others could be more hospitable; William Goodlad (*c.* 1576–1639), an English whaler, wrote in 1623 that one Arctic journey transitioned into a kind of writing retreat along Spitsbergen's "uncouth Coast, whereto our English Neptunes are now so wonted, that there they have found not onely Venison but Pernassus and Helicon; and have melted a Musæan Fountain out of the Greenland Snowes and Icie Rockes. Whole Elaborate Poems have I seene of Master Heley, as also of James Presson, there composed: but we have harsher Discoveries in hand" (Purchas [1625] 1906: 14:107). What vistas melted onto the pages of Heley and Presson? What coastal and "uncouth" world piqued their interests enough to give them pause, and, greater still, to poeticize? A puzzle; and that is perhaps precisely the power of the Arctic font: a muse to "elaborate" upon, whose circumstances "nice" and "hars[h]" sponsor further speculation, "subtilties" awaiting to be penned, and thereby put, into "practice."

THE ARCTIC IS A PASSAGE, NOT A DESTINATION

While the mythic qualities of the "Northwest" and "Northeast Passage" summon plottable courses or emplaced things—traceable routes to be traversed and rare prizes, like a "grail" (Berton 1988), awaiting acquisition—the northern ocean was a passage through which things multidirectionally passed: a trip (from the Latin verb *passus*, "pace") that rejects teleological paths running from commencement to terminus, a thing in transit whereby things transition, an Arctic "actor-network" (Duckert 2017: 125–9). Accidental discoveries of sea-routes through the Arctic Ocean to Europe were widely known: in his *Pilgrimes* (1625), Purchas printed Thomas Cowle's 1579 testimony concerning Martin Chacke of Lisbon's successful navigation from the Portuguese East Indies to northwestern Ireland across the North American continent in 1567, separated from his company after being "driven … with a Westerly winde … through a gulfe of the New found land" ([1625] 1906: 14:414). Hopes for finding this "fretum Anian" that set North America apart from Asia were emboldened shortly thereafter by the Greek pilot Juan de Fuca's 1596 discovery, as reported by the investor Michael Lok, of a strait (that now bears his name) just above California and Nova Spania (Purchas [1625] 1906, 14:415–19). The most famous account, perhaps, is of "Indians" arriving on the shores of Roman France, set down by Pliny the Elder in his *Naturalis Historiae* (first century CE). Peter Martyr d'Anghiera's *Decades of the New World* (translated by Richard Eden in 1555/77) repeats the account:

> To sayle from India to Caliz by the other parte of the north by a clime and regions of extreme coulde, shulde bee doubtlesse a difficult and dangerous thynge, whereof is no memory amonge the owlde autours sauynge onely of one shyppe as Plinie and Mela doo wryte, rehersynge the testimony of

Cornelius Nepos who affirmed that the kynge of Sueuia presented to Quintus Metellus Celer Lieuetenaunt of Fraunce, certeyne Indians dryuen by tempest into the sea of Germanie. (Arber 1895: 347)

Something similar happened "in the days of the Emperoure Fredericus Barbarossa, [when] certeyne Indians were browght in a Canoa from the citie of Lubec" (347). Inadvertently or not—note the language of "driven," again, this time by a storm—peoples of eastern Asia were imagined to have completed a northerly route from the east to west centuries before Chacke's achievement (or blusterous blunder) in the opposite direction.

Regardless of the abovementioned journeys' historical veracity, the Arctic was considered to be a passage linking disparate cultures since antiquity; moreover, if Pliny's unverifiable account is taken at face value, Europe was actually the *first* "otherworld" met at the opposite side of the Arctic Ocean: to these "certeyne Indians," we may surmise, the German court represented the "New found land" before upper North America assumed the moniker of "New World" for Eden's readers, prior to John Cabot's expedition (1497) under Henry VII to Newfoundland and Labrador, and even earlier than the eleventh-century Norse settlements in Vinland. Their accomplishment tested the patience of Europeans who wished to similarly pass years later. If "Indians" could manage a feat "difficult and dangerous," so could they; dwelling on the "Indians ... fortune" as well as the Portuguese success, for instance, the ambassador to Moscow, "restynge a whyle in maner astonysshed in his secreate phantasie, he toke great pleasure therin, and sayde ... why shulde wee not certeinely thynke that the lyke maye bee done abowt this parte of the north withowt feare of coulde, especially to men borne and brought vp in that clime?" (286). In essence, the earlier encounter was held out with the promise of newer, more fortunate (fortune-filled) ones for those were climatically disposed to conquer. Few writers evince this logic better than Sir Humphrey Gilbert (1537–83), whose *Discourse of a Discoverie for a New Passage to Cataia* (written 1566, printed 1576) dedicates three of its ten chapters to the famous landing: "So that it plainly appeareth, that those Indians (which, as you have heard, in sundrie ages were driven by tempest, upon the shore of Germanie) came onely through our Northwest passage" ([1576] 1940: 1:154). "Our" is arresting: the seeds of Arctic colonialism were no "phantasie"; the arduous passage across the ocean and (they hoped) beyond it could be possessed and protected, its original inhabitants, if necessary, kidnapped or expunged.

If my reinterpretation of the far-northern Atlantic Ocean as "passage" evokes the "middle passage" of the succeeding centuries' slave trade, I do so on purpose. Where hierarchies of race, gender, and ethnicity enter the passage, the intersectional flows are restricted. The "other" who lived in "other worlds," in short, could too easily be used as a pejorative accusation and a pernicious instantiation of difference. Review the mottoes of The Company of the Merchants Discoverers of the North-West Passage (chartered 1612): "Juuat ire per altum" (He delights to go upon the Deep) and "Tibj seruiat ultima Thule" (The uttermost Thule shall serve thee) (Christy 1894: 2:648). Or one of the "motiues Inducing a Proiect" (presumably enumerated by Digges) that configures "the North pole terrestriall a Magnificent and pure Virgine yet vndiscouered" (2:641). For whom does the Arctic serve and whom does it delight? Regimes of power protect the Arctic actor-network—but only for some passengers. Enslavement had always been a lucrative option since the earliest expeditions: Portuguese captain Gaspar Corte-Real (1450–1501), who had reached "Terra Verde" in 1500, sent home "seven natives, men and women and children" the year after, "and in the other caravel, which is expected from hour to hour are coming fifty others" (Williamson 1962: 229). As I insinuated earlier with "certeyne" east Asian visitors, the Arctic is not the "other" world to Indigenous others—warmer Europe provided that—but a home. What Jace Weaver (2014) calls the "red Atlantic," then, certainly applies to its polar waters. Confronting this masculinist obsession with white hues that persists to this day—roving the pre- to the modern passage of time—demands returning to the early modern experiences of Indigenous peoples of color.

A public desire for novel forms of amusement helped ensure that others' oceans became "our[s]." Published portraits of the Inuit date as far back as 1567, the year when a woman and child were put on display in Augsburg. These individuals were unfortunate prequels to James I's African entertainers who died after dancing in the snow in 1589, commanded to do so, arguably, to establish the threshold for English bodies exposed to extreme temperatures. Inuit in the flesh likewise proffered an unapparelled chance to understand the physiological effects of foreign "clime," all the while sponsoring the pseudo-scientific racism of the Arctic explorer George Best (c. 1555–84) who sought to explain how darker skins could exist in the low light of northern lands. The first Inuit transported under English command came from Frobisher's forays into Baffin Island (now Nunavut): a man ("Calichough"), woman ("Ignorth"), and child ("Nutiok") from his second voyage of 1577 were famously painted by John White (fl.1577–93). (All three soon died of disease.) The English pilot James Hall (d. 1612), who sailed for Christian IV of Denmark three times from 1605 to 1607, was sent to reestablish contact with the ancient Norse colonies of Greenland (which had been lost, unbeknownst to the king, in the fifteenth century). His captain, John Cunningham, seized three Inuit in 1605, which he "vsed with all kindnesse" (Gosch 1897: 1:48) on the *Trost*; Captain Godske Lindenow of the *Røde Løve* took two. The following year, Lindenow, now in command, took five more "with their Boates, and stowed them in our ships, to bring them into *Denmarke*, to enforme our selues better, by their meenes, of the state of their Countrie of *Groineland*" (1:70–1). One of these kayaks currently resides at the Schiffer-Gesellschaft in Lubeck (1:70n5). And on Hall's own (and fatal) voyage of 1612, Andrew Barker seized a man whose kayak is now showcased at the Trinity House in Hull (1:111n4). These souvenirs of boats and human beings render the boreal seas as sites of controlled curiosity, its strangers carefully curated and their lives crafted in objectified ways that reinforce northern European hegemony. The two captives Lindenow took in 1605 exemplify the consequences of becoming better "enforme[d]," as the Danish diplomat and editor of the excursion, C.C.A. Gosch evinces: he "succeeded in taming them to some extent, and taught them to run about the ship in obedience to signs from him" (1:xci). Domesticated wonders: the pool of the unknown becomes a display case; the whirlpool is put to rest; its story told; its bestial citizens made tractable.

Tasked with finding old worlds anew, at least in Denmark's case, the voyage from east to west incurs an oceanic time travel as the past (old/Old) is brought into the present (new/New). But whom is "better[ed]" by the European-Inuit exchange, as we just observed, was too often lopsided in the former's favor. Nonetheless, they were startling possibilities for seeing the "other" in/as the "self" in the other worlds of the Arctic, and, in so doing, checking the colonial logic that depends on situating these spheres of identification as utterly separate. The circles, that is, may conjoin "better." Misrecognition, even if immediately disavowed, is one instance of Arctic anxiety of fungible difference: according to Robert Fabyan's *Chronicle* (1516), three men from Newfoundland were brought to England in 1501 to 1502, probably the capital's first Indigenous visitors: "I sawe ij of theym apparaylyd afftyr Inglysh men In westmynstyr paleys, which at that tyme I cowde not dyscern ffrom Inglysh men" (Williamson 1962: 220). Being able to "dyscern" is essential, of course, to the process of essentializing otherness: becoming the "other" of the "other world" must be avoided. The gaze, too, could reverse and work upon English and not just Inuit identity. In his catastrophic quest for the Northwest Passage through Hudson's Bay in 1619 to 1620 (published in Danish in 1624) in which sixty-three of his sixty-five-member crew perished, Jens Munk (1579–1628) notes that one of his men, "who had very swarthy complexion, and black hair" is mistaken by the Inuit as "one of their nation and countrymen," and is embraced, incredibly, because of it (Gosch 1897: 2:14). Attempts at mutual "enforme-ing" did exist, however, at least on the surface; in 1617, before Spitsbergen was deemed valuable for its seas of whale oil, the Muscovy Company (chartered 1555), unable to make reliably profitable in-roads in the area, conjured up a co-colonizing enterprise that included the Indigenous peoples of Russia. Sir John Merrick, ambassador to the czar, was granted a license "for certaine of his subiects called Lappes [Sámi], a people lyveinge in a very cold clymate and a barraine soyle" to dwell with the English there (Conway 1906: 104). While miscegenetic aspirations like these could always be stymied by the language barrier, of course, what often hindered the remapping of kinships were southern governments' desires to commercially exploit septentrional worlds. Those aforementioned five Inuit brought to Copenhagen in 1605, for example, were abducted so that "friendly relations [may] be permanently established" (Gosch 1897: 1:xciii) between communities—imprisoned ambassadors urged, ironically enough, to make a deal for peace.

A few cracks can be discerned in this dichotomous logic, however, moments when the icy other(sea)world conjoins with your own in less segregated, more intersectional, terms. Consider the activity of "Calichough," Frobisher's detainee, on the River Avon; the chronicler William Adams writes that on October 9, 1577, "he rode in a little bote made of skinne in the water at the backe, where he killed 2 duckes with a dart, and when he had done carried his bote through the marsh upon his back. The like he did at the weare and other places, where many beheld him" (McGhee 2001: 84–5). For the Bristolian onlookers in attendance, "Calichough" kayaking on the Avon at their mayor's delight bends into spectacle, to be certain, providing a local artist with an image that would become a template for illustrating Inuit life (and which adorned the narrative account of his captor). Would any have noticed, in his relative ease of hunting and transition from one waterway ("backe") to another ("marshe"), the man's almost uncanny familiarity with their own local "places"? If so, the distant and formerly distantiated bays of Frobisher and Bristol transpose onto one another; the Arctic turns out to be in your own "backe"-yard. We cannot be sure, but we may speculate: "Ignorth" and he "died … within a month" (85). The Danish annals are less laconic. The two natives Lindenow "trained" in 1605 performed for the Danish king and queen after the *Røde Løve* entered Copenhagen: according to C.C. Lyschander's *Den Gronlandske Chronica* (1608), he "made the Greenlanders show their prowess in propelling their *kayaks*, on which occasion they held their own in a race against a boat of sixteen oars" (Gosch 1897: 1:xci); Cunningham's three also managed to join in to outpace the Danes. The Spanish ambassador, who had just happened to arrive, was especially taken aback: "three of them, in their boats, performed a kind of dance, cutting figures with their *kayaks* in a wonderful manner" (1:xcii), after which he rewarded them handsomely with money and the fashions of a Danish gentleman (feathers, swords, and spurs). Like their kinsmen who kayaked the Avon, however, Peyrère sees more than merely wonder. His relation is a bit more startling; he caps a lengthy description of the kayak's composition and proportions with hypnotic prose: "they crossed and interlaced with each other with such rapidity, that the eye grew quite confused with looking; and so skillfully was it done, that not one of them touched each other" (1:224). Noting, perhaps, the dangers of "confus[ion]" and the inability to discern the strange from the familiar, they are festooned in a mocking manner and "marched up to the Castle 'like Greenland Grandees.'" The king was so impressed that he ordered a two-man kayak constructed "on the Greenland pattern." Regardless of these political tokens of appreciation and attempts at recreational assimilation (or appropriation), not everything is right in the state of Denmark: the kayakers, most obviously, are still confined. Thus, in the spring of 1606 some of them tried to escape, reaching as far as "Skaane" (Skåneland, or the southern Scandinavian peninsula) before they were apprehended "by the peasants." For Gosch, the flight of the Inuit "runaways" spelled the beginning of the end of the Danish strategy of reintroduction to smooth over any hostile retaliations: "As it was, the fact that none of the captives returning could not but be very prejudicial to the intercourse between the expedition and the natives" (1:xciii). Several of these hopeful intermediaries died on the second voyage that embarked that year, and the third voyage of 1607 (if any were aboard) never reached its destination. Denmark's a literal prison for these Inuit inmates, their oceanic passage a one-way trip terminating in death, but not before their outlandish habits can bemuse others. The "dance" is scripted; the actors' "choreography" set for diplomatic means; they may become European nobility ("Grandees"), but only for play.

Although written almost fifty years later and criticized for its speciousness, Peyrère's account adds seminal emotional details to the fugitives' plight. Seeing from the other's perspective has the power, he proves, to meld supposedly antithetical worlds. Those who fled in 1606 "often looked towards the north, and sighed with so much regret after their own country that their guards, being lenient, those who could seized their little boats and oars and put out to sea to try the passage" (1:223). The Inuit are not merely sneaky in this version: they actually solicit sympathy from their caretakers. Gosch is taciturn about their fate; for Peyrère, however, those who made the first attempt died of illness brought on by their further loss of "liberty." (The exact number is unclear here, as is so often the case when comparing various accounts; presumably, the four abductees who survived Hall's return trip enlarged the group.) After their costumed parade to the castle, moreover—Peyrère places the initial escape before the ambassadors' arrival—two of those on the foiled mission of 1606 "who were less suspected than the others, because it seemed unlikely that they would expose themselves a second time to the perils they had encountered, seized their boats and succeeded in regaining the north" (1:225). Their motives were clear: after their pageant was over, "they relapsed into their usual melancholy [...] they thought of nothing but how they might return to Greenland" (1:225). To "try the passage" is an indefatigable feat; to "regai[n]" the north an endless enterprise, a passage that exists just out of reach. Peyrère allows us to see their north receding before them from their Danish cell. But one of them is ultimately captured; the other "escaped, or, rather, was lost; for it does not seem probable that he ever could have arrived in Greenland" (1:225). For this man now thrice abducted, the sight of children and their mothers or nurses causes him to "burst into tears" (1:225), upon which, his jailers astutely deduce, he bemoaned his faraway family. The lamentations compound; indeed, their grief proves lethal as their pain creates a positive feedback loop of perpetual misery: being guarded even closer simultaneously squashes and stimulates their hopes for free passage, "only increase[s] their desire of returning to their country, and their despair of ever doing so" (1:225). Almost all, save two, die of this "regret." Each of them lives about ten years: the first, recruited as a pearl diver in Kolding, succumbs to exposure after he is forced to go "under the water like a dog" (1:226) in winter. The second, yet again, takes flight, and it unsure if it is the same lachrymose individual from earlier (which would then mark his third try). In any case, he swiftly made it approximately thirty of forty leagues out of the sound and into the open ocean (an astonishing 90–120 nautical miles). Once overtaken, his pursuers "make him understand by signs that he would never have known where to find Greenland, and that undoubtedly the waves would have swallowed him up" (1:226).

To the Danes, the hydrographical distance between oceans proved the best way to suppress Inuit "desire[s]" for going. Hence the improbability of the "lost" man's return; their ignorant internees' lack of mappable knowledge epistemologically shackled them. The boat race will eventually be won if your opponent has superior speed but no sense of direction. Yet this man surprisingly responds with a cosmography of his own: "He answered by signs, that he should have followed the coast of Norway to a certain point, whence he would have crossed, and have been guided by the stars to his country."[11] The chasers might have been chastened; a retort, tragically, is not given: the man, we are simply told, sickens and dies back in Copenhagen soon after. Peyrère's sympathy, one could say, only goes so far: sometimes naming these Indigenous passengers "unhappy Greenlanders," he primarily names them "savages," and while not outright condemning his fellow Europeans' behaviors, he is keen on exonerating them, demonstrating that "the Danes did all in their power to keep them [the last two] alive, and gave them understanding that they would be treated like their friends and fellow-countrymen" (1:225). (Ineffective conversion to Christianity proves an impediment.) But the possibilities of a mesmerizing fusion are perceivable, for instance Peyrère's "confused" eyeball absorbing "pattern[s]" of global-local, Inuit-Danish interweave; he might be reluctant to fuse diametrically opposed worlds too closely, but his enthralled attention invites the imagination to wander into other, potentially "touch[ing]" passages. Much hangs on the ambivalent "or" of the "lost" kayaker. What unsegmented horizons did those paddlers espy, slipping farther away from Copenhagen with every stroke, and what shores might the one who "escaped" have possibly attained? What sea did the pearl fisher of Kolding contact when he dove, over a decade, for a foreign government's bidding, and could he have felt the waters of the far north as he plunged?

THE ARCTIC IS AN OPPORTUNITY

"The problem of London's Indigenous history," writes Coll Thrush, "is an enforced silence, not the hidden-ness of past events" (2016: 6). (The same might be said for Copenhagen and elsewhere.) Their strains are apparent: some make the passage back, while others do not; some are afforded the choice to partake in "islomania," others' efforts at percolation are policed. Such stories of guarded filtration to and fro do not require exposure, only greater attention: "It is not an act of discovery; rather it is an act of *re*covery, of acknowledging the deep entanglements of London's places, people, and histories with Indigenous places, people, and histories, and vice versa" (13). The enmeshment of urban with Indigenous histories creates "domains of entanglement" (23), in his words, and they also provoke opportunities for ecological thought by widening the scope of ensnarement. A seventeenth-century Inuit spear point was found on the same Thames riverbank where the "frost fairs" were once held (256). Pondering these transoceanic moments allows us to escape the traps of competition ("uttermost"), condescension ("serve"), and ownership ("thee")—championed by the first merchant companies—that have hampered conceptions of Arctic sovereignty. (Kalaallit Nunaat [Greenland] fights for increased autonomy from the Danish monarchy to this day.) We may "try" to make "the passage" freer, more negotiable, learning from these worlds that were and facing the worlds to be. As binaries regarding both difference (self and other) and distance (north and south) disintegrate, the burdens borne unequally by affected cultures, however, do not simply disappear. Inuit climate change activist Sheila Watt-Cloutier has been one of the most ardent voices for Indigenous communities' *"right to be cold"*—"to demand that the global community recognize that the well-being of our environment is in itself a fundamental human right"—arguing that "the future of the Inuit is the future of the rest of the world" (2015: xxi–ii). But facing the populous Arctic need not pertain solely to people, she explains, "it refers to the circumpolar environment, the Arctic land and the way of life that depends on ice and snow" (231). The Arctic is one of "the best oracles," to borrow from Purchas, for predicting the planet's fate; for Watt-Cloutier, recognizing the overlay of worlds (the result of which is causing the archipelago's rapid unraveling due to rising temperatures) proves that "fundamental change is not just sound policy but also an *ethical* imperative" (xxi). Far from framing groups such as the Inuit Circumpolar Council (ICC) as hapless victims of corporate whims, the message is meant to be politically empowering on a universal scale: "We all have the right to be protected from climate change" (231). For Craciun, too, the predication is dire and the realities are disastrous, but it is precisely because of the future's uncertainty that rights-based policies are required: "The ethos of the unknown is worth preserving" (223).

And yet, agreeing with Davidson that "almost everything that consoles us [about the Arctic] is false" (2005: 251), the question of how we are to make the world common again remains the same. Preempting this dis/comforting pronouncement by several centuries, and not reluctant to liken his quest across Hudson Bay in the summer of 1631 to an old wives' tale, Luke Foxe's (1586–1635) introduction to *North-west Fox* (1635) compares the interminable, because undiscoverable, stretch of the Passage to the endless, because compounded, passages of story: "but for that the most desire to know what I have done, and how farre I have bin, I answer, as the Old women tells tales, *Further and further than I can tell*" (Christy 1894: 1:7–8). I have hitherto argued in this chapter that the Arctic Circle was a foreseeable horizon for some early modern (icy) ocean-goers. The far northern "horizon"—a word that comes from the Greek *horizōn* (*kuklos*), "limiting (circle)"—certainly delimited their world. But I have also argued that the Circle expanded, spiraled, and spun for others. From pivoting portals (Peyrère) to maelstroms on maps (Mercator), from literary circles (the Zeni) to the near-circular returns of Indigenous peoples (Inuit kayakers), these configurations of a veering and vibrant Circle help us reconceptualize the Arctic as a populated, unmappable place, a sea of inhabited and inscrutable ice-islands that challenge cryo-political strategies that assume the opposite (as trackless wasteland, as indefinitely understood, as continentally bound). Ultima Thule is ultimately unknowable; and, as such, it is infinitely storying. Abandon the Pole of singular, storied, transmission, brought to you by an oceanic, "other" world ontologically opposite from your own. Mutability sparks an impulse to portray alternate pictures; to limn pools around a portable pole; to question how (and whose) stories are put in motion or are immobilized; in short, to try and speak a different "language of future Arctic opportunism," in Craciun's words, telling different legacies than the ones we have inherited, thereby revealing how those prevailing narratives were historically constructed and their contingencies subsequently forgotten: "The more carefully we consider earlier cultures of exploration, the more unpredictable become our histories of Arctic exploration" (2016: 228, 232). I would also add, for our consideration, futures. Appropriating the biogeographical term "Nearctic" (the realm that covers most of North America), this chapter constitutes my own attempt at articulating additional "Nearctics" (from *neo-*, "new") to provide "[f]urther and *further*" opportunities for others to "*tell*." As uncertain and imperfect cartography urges our imaginations onward, it is my hope that it furthers archipelagic communities as well. I have come this "farre" for now: the Arctic is a portal that spins, a passage in which worlds are imagined and their stories exchanged; "*further*," it importantly reminds us that, just as any world cannot be totally known, neither can its fate be truly determined.

NOTES

Preface

1 Cindy Starr, "Annual Arctic Sea Ice Minimum 1979-2015, with graph," NASA Scientific Visualization Studio, released on March 10, 2016, https://svs.gsfc.nasa.gov/4786 (accessed 23 October 2020).

Introduction

1 See Jett (2017).
2 See Mentz (2015: xxix and passim).
3 Recent blue humanities scholarship has included much ecocritical and contemporary scholarship, including the works of Stacy Alaimo, Elspeth Probyn, and Patricia Yaeger. This watery discourse, however, also has deep roots in early modern literary and cultural studies. See, for example, Brayton (2012); Cohen and Duckert (2015); Duckert (2017); and Mentz (2009, 2015). I introduced the phrase "wet globalization" in *Shipwreck Modernity* (2015) and "blue cultural studies" in *At the Bottom of Shakespeare's Ocean* (2009).
4 For a recent economic survey, see Nunn and Quian (2010: 163–88); for a broad popular survey, see Mann (2011); for the paradigm-defining study, see Crosby (2003).
5 Portions of this section of the chapter partly derive from Steve Mentz, *Ocean*, (London: Bloomsbury, 2020) 31–41.
6 See, for example, Price (2007).
7 On Pacific voyaging and disease, see Lamb (2016).
8 See Cohen (2012: xxx); and Mentz (2015: 77–128).
9 See Thornton (1998).
10 For a fuller exploration of hurricanes in history and English literary culture, see Mentz (2017: 257–76).

Chapter 2

1 The earlier works from which Marine Architecture (1739) copied were Edward Bushnell's *Compleat Shipwright* (1664); Thomas Miller's *The Compleat Modellist* (1664); and Henry Bond's *The Boatswaine's Art* (1642).

Chapter 3

1. The celebrated "Blue Marble" photo of the earth generally refers to a photo taken on December 7, 1972, by the astronauts of the Apollo 17 space mission, the last manned lunar voyage. Like "Earthrise," the "Blue Marble" reveals a planetary surface composed of ocean, continents, and cloud formations associated with specific weather patterns and events (including the Tamil Nadu cyclone of 1972, which is visible in the upper-right corner of the 1972 photograph).
2. See Bradford (1971: 28–60); see also Parry (1974: 31–48).
3. A knot is a nautical mile per hour, traditionally measured by stringing a knotted rope behind a sailing vessel and then reeling it in and dividing the number of knots streamed per unit of time. A nautical mile is 6,000 feet; a statute mile is 5,280 feet. Thus, one knot of speed is slightly faster than one mile per hour.
4. See Parry (1974: esp. 149–70). See also Landstrom (1969: 100–1). I am grateful to Rui Santos, Managing Director of *Aporvela Lisboa*, for his informative tour of the replica caravel *Vera Cruz*, and to Captain Joao Lucio for his informative discussions of caravel sailing in July 2014 and 2016. I would also like to acknowledge the wonderful caravel exhibitions at the Museu de Marinha of Belem, Portugal.
5. See Brown (1949: 113–49).
6. For a modern edited collection of Shakespeare's works, please see Greenblatt et al. (1997).
7. See Parry (1974: esp. 193–218). See also Fernandez-Armesto (2006: 153–90).
8. In sailors' parlance "to make easting or westing," or "to run your easting [or westing] down," means to go as far as possible in a particular direction, before changing course, to avoid a navigational hazard (such as a lee shore) (*OED Online*, s.v. "").
9. See Keuning (1949).
10. *The Art of Navigation*, Richard Eden's 1561 translation of the *Arte De Navegar*, by Martín Cortés de Albacar (1510–1582), employs the term "art" in this more technological sense.

Chapter 4

1. Merry Wiesner-Hanks notes that "Economic historians sometimes joke that no matter when or where you look, capitalism always seems to be rising" (2006: 213). For an overview of the global, consequential changes in economics and technology in the early modern period, see Wiesner-Hanks (2006, esp. ch. 6).
2. On humoral medicine and early modern conceptions of bodies as porous and emotions as a sort of "internal microclimate," see Paster (2004: 19).
3. See also Schottenhammer (2012: esp. 79–84).
4. For another example, see Jerónimo Corte-Real, a contemporary of Camões, who wrote *O Segundo cerco de Diu* (1574), a twenty-one-book epic covering topics similar to *Os Lusiadas*.
5. Did Ottoman or Chinese writers create similar mythologies in their literary works? A venue for further research.
6. For more on the *Sejarah Melayu*, see Ng (2019).
7. For an overview of this episode and of Portuguese actions in Southeast Asia, see Lockard (2009 esp. chs. 4–5), as well as Heng (2013).

8 Although the Melakans appear shocked about Portuguese guns and cannons, exclaiming "What may be this round weapon that yet is sharp enough to kill us?" (Brown 1970: 152), Indian and Southeast Asian gun and cannon manufacturing was as good or in some cases better than Portuguese and European attempts. Subrahmanyam and Parker explain: "the explicit reference [in the *Lettera di Giovanni da Empoli*] to gunpowder weapons among the defenders of Melaka contradicts the oft-quoted account in the *Sejarah Melayu*, which stresses the fear and surprise caused by the Europeans' bombardment [...]. However, the *Sejarah* was compiled from oral traditions in 1612, whereas Empolí (an eyewitness) wrote in 1514; moreover, although the defenders of Melaka may have possessed gunpowder weapons, it seems unlikely that they were as effective—or were deployed as effectively—as those of the Europeans" (2008: 40n42). See also Levi (2018).
9 For a detailed discussion of the Sala Regia, see de Jong (2003).
10 On Turks in many more Western paintings and texts, see Harper (2011); for more on Lepanto in particular, see Paul (2011).
11 In 1615, Cervantes published a version of this story in a play called *Los Baños de Argel*, which was never performed. For a discussion of the play's ghost fleet as representing the Holy League, see Botello (2015).
12 On Cervantes's sympathetic views of Muslim identities and cultures, see Fuchs (2009) and Menocal (2002).
13 English troops did not fight with the Holy League, and King James VI was only five when the battle took place, but David M. Bergeron describes how in James's epic poem *Lepanto*—published in *His Maiesties Poetical Exercises at vacant houres* (1591)—he "depicts the Turks as worthy opponents" but also "makes clear that victory belongs to the Christian forces by divine intervention at Lepanto" (2010: 258).
14 Spanish optimism about their chances against the English might be exemplified by the writings of a spy in Philip II's service named Bernardino de Escalante; in his *Discursos*, he draws the Tower of London alongside a map of England, Scotland, and Ireland, with copious notes about how easily the Armada will be able to invade the island. See Soto (1996: 127).
15 Wells-Cole asserts, erroneously in my view, that the Spanish ships in the right-hand window are "all in the process of being consumed by fire or foundering off a rocky shore" (2012: 838).
16 On beauty, race, and Elizabeth's striking whiteness in the portraiture, see Hall (1996a: 465–6). For an art historical overview of representations of Elizabeth I, see Strong (1986). On the role of artistic and literary figurations of the queen in discourses about authority in England, see Eggert (2000).
17 Space does not allow me to explore the First and Second Anglo-Dutch Wars (1652–74), but those conflicts and their cultural representations participate in the same discourses that I have so far sketched. On literary representations of these wars in England and Southeast Asia, see Parry (2014) and Ng (2012).
18 See also Degroot (2018).
19 Angus Konstam spends barely a paragraph on slavery in *Piracy: The Complete History* despite English pirates' key involvement in the development of the triangle trade (2008: 50–1). Even such a meticulous chronicler as N.A.M. Roger, to whose work on the British Navy I am indebted, calls attention to Hawkin's and Drake's participation in "trade" and "plunder" and to the Portuguese exports of "sugar in large quantities," but remains silent about the *people* who were forced to labor to

make that sugar and about the human and environmental costs of these ventures (1997: 239).
20 Fabian compares Sir Andrew to an "icicle on a Dutchman's beard," a nod to Barents (Shakespeare [c. 1601] 2008: 726n4), but the comment could equally have raised memories of Frobisher's earlier voyages in audiences' minds. See also Hadfield (2009). In a similar vein, Camillo in John Webster's *The White Devil*, 1.2.53–6 ([1612] 2002) laments his "cold" relations with his wife.
21 For more on the Lady/Empress's performance of peaceful absolute power—at sea and on land—that nonetheless relies on a great deal of violence to be efficacious, see Taff (2019).
22 Belcher is currently at work on *Early African Literature: An Anthology of Written Texts from 3000 BCE to 1900 CE,* an anthology that will make early African literatures available, in many cases for the first time, to a broader readership. What role do maritime and riverine navigation, commerce, and myth play in these literatures? Another new venue for early modern maritime research.
23 On faults of the philosophical logic of "dehumanization" as an explanation for why people commit rape and other atrocities, see Manne (2018, esp. ch. 5).
24 See Sejas (2014).
25 Castanha draws on doctoral work by Guitar (1998) and Mercado (1978).
26 Castanha challenges the Bering Strait migration hypothesis, and joins several other scholars who are reexamining pre-Columbian oceanic travel. See for example Deloria (1997), Jett (2017), and Rozwadowski (2018).

Chapter 5

1 For studies of these and other representational systems, see Brayton (2012); Mentz (2015); and Ramachandran (2015).
2 See Mentz (2006). See Jowitt (2010), which juxtaposes various genres, including drama and romance, in her study of the pirate. In *The Cultural Geography of Early Modern Drama* (2011), Julie Sanders traces the representation of nautical figures in Caroline drama.
3 See also Eklund (2019), which uses the concept of "littoral" to think about the liminality of islands.
4 Matthew Boyd Goldie and Sebastian Sobecki take Hau'ofa's phrase as the governing principle of their special issue, "Our Sea of Islands," *Postmedieval: A Journal of Medieval Cultural Studies* (2016).
5 Holbein's map appeared in the 1518 edition of *Utopia* published in Basel.
6 For an instance of how fictional islands perform the "contradictory fantasy of total isolation and global all-knowing," see Hogan (2012).
7 For examples of reimaginings of *Utopia,* see *New Atlantis* and Margaret Cavendish's *The Blazing World* (1666). More specifically, for seventeenth-century reformers using utopia as the model of a perfectible place, see Gabriel Plattes's *A Description of the Famous Kingdome of Macaria* (1641) and William Petty's *The advice of W.P. to Mr. Samuel Hartlib. For the advancement of some particular parts of learning* (1648).
8 For the different pulls of utopian literature, see Houston (2014).
9 I am influenced by Gillis's discussion of humans as an *"edge species"* (2012: 9). As an epistemological project, *Utopia* also serves as a prime example of what Roland Greene terms "island logic," the notion that "insularity comes to stand in for a kind of knowledge, a distinctively partial knowledge that counters the totalities of institutions and regimes" (2000: 138).

10 For studies of the relations between practical knowledge and literary works, see Spiller (2004) and Turner (2006).
11 Denise Albanese makes a similar point about the island in another utopian text that adapts More's work, Bacon's *New Atlantis*: "the utopian island precipitates a fantasy, not of the library, but of the laboratory" (1996: 69). For a recent study on how "imagination" more broadly intersects with scientific discourse, see Roychoudhury (2018).
12 For *The Tempest's* relation to utopian literature, see Knapp (1992).
13 For the play's shadowing of contemporary events and locations, see Orgel (1998). There is a rich body of work that studies the play through the lens of postcolonial theory, discussions of the "global," and critical race theory. For representative works, see Brown (1985); Loomba (1989); Singh (1996); Skura (1989).
14 For works that study the play's relation to the Mediterranean, see Brotton (1998, 2000: 132–7); and Hess (2000: 121–30). For the play's connections with the Mediterranean and the Irish colonial context, see Fuchs (1997). For a general study of Mediterranean islands in relation to literary works, see Mallette (2007).
15 For explorations of analogies between early modern theatre and scientific laboratory, see Turner (2009) and Shanahan (2008).
16 For studies of *The Tempest* and early modern science, see Spiller (2009) and Maisano (2014).
17 For an account of shipwrecks as key structural elements of premodern and modern thought, see Mentz (2015).
18 For studies of this motif, see Blumenberg (1997) and Mentz (2009: 21).
19 See Maisano (2014: 181) for a reading of this moment in Lucretius alongside *The Tempest* and Bacon's *The Advancement of Learning* (1605).
20 For a discussion of Miranda's creativity, see Cobb (2007). For Miranda as a poet figure, see Sarkar (2017).
21 This identification of Miranda with nature does not reduce her to an object of knowledge as is commonplace in criticism. See, for instance, Albanese (1996: 59–91).
22 This prose romance is a revision of *Old Arcadia*, believed to be begun by Sidney in the 1570s; this work existed in manuscript form until the twentieth century. Sidney revised and expanded the *Old Arcadia* in the 1580s, but it remained unfinished when he died in 1586. This incomplete version, which ends mid-sentence, was published by Fulke Greville in 1590. Sidney's sister, the author and patron Mary Sidney Herbert, published a different edition in 1593—this version combines Sidney's unfinished text with the *Old Arcadia* to offer a kind of conclusion.
23 See Jowitt (2010: 108) for the language in the 1590 version.
24 Wroth appended the sonnet sequence *Pamphilia to Amphilanthus* to the *Urania*. She attempted to withdraw the romance from circulation because of pressure from noblemen who perceived their lives were being shadowed, often not in a positive manner, in its characters. There is no evidence, however, that the work was actually withdrawn. Wroth continued writing a second part of the *Urania* that existed in manuscript form till the twentieth century.
25 For representative work on the Global Renaissance, see Singh (2009).
26 For Wroth's various models of female authorship, see Roberts (1995: xxxiv–xxxv).
27 Helen Cooper argues that premodern romance is characterized by sets of memes. A meme is "an idea that behaves like a gene in its ability to replicate faithfully and abundantly, but also on occasion to adapt, mutate, and therefore survive in different

forms and cultures. These motifs and conventions grew up with the genre of which they formed a part and which they helped to define" (2004: 3).
28 For an exploration of this place as a site of magic and healing, see Werth (2011).

Chapter 6

1 For the lack of critical attention to Portuguese voyages in favor of Columbus's voyage as a constitutive moment of early modern globalization and global consciousness, see Inglis (2011).
2 Studies of the history of this period of Portuguese voyaging include Herman L. Bennett, *African Kings and Black Slaves: Sovereignty and Dispossession in the Early Modern Atlantic* (2019), Josiah Blackmore, *Moorings: Portuguese Expansion and the Writing of Africa* (2009), and John Thornton, *Africa and Africans in the Making of the Atlantic World, 1400–1800*, 2nd edn. (1998).
3 All three documents are translated into English in Greenlee (1995). The narrative of the pilot was first printed in Italian in *Paesi nouamente retrouati* (Lands Recently Discovered), 1507, edited by Fracanzano da Montalboddo. For another English translation of Caminha's *Letter* and of other documents related to Portuguese voyages in Africa and India, see Ley (2000).
4 "*posto queo capitam moor desta vossa frota e asy os outros capitaães screpuam avossa alteza anoua do achamento desta vossa terra noua que se ora neesta naue gaçam achou. nom leixarey tam bem de dar disso minha comta avossa alteza asy como eu milhor poder ajmda que perao bem contar e falar o saiba pior que todos fazer.*"
5 In an engraving in Jan van der Straet's *Nova reperta* (1638), in which a European explorer encounters the allegorical figure of America as a nude woman reclining in a hammock along a shoreline, a ship is visible on the left side; in his study of the engraving, Rabasa notes that "the entering ship symbolizes the course of history" (1993: 26).
6 Translation is mine. "*aly nom pode deles auer fala nẽ entẽdimento que aproueitasse polo mar quebrar na costa.*"
7 For more on sound and acoustics in Caminha's *Letter*, see Blackmore (2018: 215–19).
8 For studies of modern (Creole) literary and song traditions in regions formerly part of the *Estado*, see Jackson (2005) and Jayasuriya (2008).
9 For a brief discussion of India in Barbosa's *Book*, see Subrahmanyam (2017: 84–5, 89–90).
10 See Disney (2009: 141–2).
11 "*Naturallmemte os homees desejam saber.*" Aristotle thus begins the *Metaphysics*.
12 "*que nenhuũ out° prinçepe no mumdo.*"
13 "*toda afriq^a & asya & parte da europ^a pola bamda do maar oçeano com Jmfinjdade dilhas muy grandes Riquos & muy populosos.*"
14 For overviews of books on nautical science and cartography with a focus on Spain, see Pérez-Mallaina Bueno (1989) and Sandman (2007).
15 The 1991 edition of Oliveira's book is bilingual (Portuguese and English) and includes a facsimile of the manuscript of the *Livro*.
16 "All to no avail did God deliberately separate countries by the divisive ocean if, in spite of that, impious boats go skipping over the seas that were meant to remain inviolate" (Horace 2004: 31).
17 For a discussion of the possibility of Camões in China, see Willis (2010: 212–21).

18 As I argue elsewhere (Blackmore 2012: 312–25), in Camões we find the creation and consolidation of a maritime poetic subject that is, in part, the result of the ubiquitous presence of seafaring in the personal and public domains of Portuguese and Iberian life of the sixteenth century. I explore this further in my forthcoming book, *The Inner Ship: Maritime Literary Culture in Early Modern Portugal*.
19 Also see Klein (2013) for further analysis of the poem.
20 Gama was a *capitão-mor*, or royally appointed commander.
21 In a like vein, Klein notes that a central, structural principle of *Os Lusíadas* is that it "[casts] a seafarer as the principle of action and focalizer of the narrative" (2013: 165).
22 See *Selected Sonnets: A Bilingual Edition* (2005) and *The Collected Lyric Poems of Luís de Camões* (2008) for English translations of this sonnet. Several excellent translations of Camões's lyric poetry are also found in Barletta, Bajus, and Malik (2013).
23 For an English translation of Boscán's poem, see Krummrich (2006: 43–134).
24 For a study of how cartography was instrumental in the understanding of the Pacific in Spain, see Padrón (2009: 1–27).
25 For an English translation of the narrative with accompanying introductory study, see Pigafetta (2007).
26 English translations of some of these narratives are in Boxer (2001) and Theal (1964).
27 See Mentz (2015: 11–18) for a recent analysis of the narrative. For Camões in *Os Lusíadas*, the wreck of the S. João (which carried onboard the returning governor of India Manuel de Sousa Sepúlveda, his wife Leonor de Sá, and their children) was one of the tragically emblematic sacrifices, in human terms, of Portuguese overseas empire.
28 Interestingly, the shipwreck tale did not see the same level of attention in Spain as it did in Portugal. There are, however, notable Spanish examples, such as *Naufragios* (1555) of Álvar Núñez Cabeza de Vaca. For other Spanish writings of maritime peril and shipwreck during the age of empire, see Davis (2006) and Dille (2011).
29 Also see Voigt (2009: 82–3, 222–3); and Blackmore (2002).
30 The original manuscript of the *Itinerário* remained lost until 1947 when it was discovered in Lalim, Portugal (Lobo 1984: xxvi).

Chapter 7

1 Giorgio Vasari's *Birth of Venus* (c. 1555/7) also portrays the goddess standing on a shell, but she is surrounded by mythical figures associated with the sea, notably Teti (to her left) and Neptune (to her right). There is also a menagerie of other creatures in the sea, including Tritons and Nereids, who offer Venus the bounty of the sea: pearls, shells, and other treasures.
2 All biblical references are to *The Bible: Authorized King James Version* (1997).
3 See "painting/hanging scroll," Museum Number: 1881,1210,0.86.CH. Available online: https://www.britishmuseum.org/research/collection_online/collection_object_details.aspx?objectId=270686&partId=1&searchText=Bodhidharma+mo+an+&page=1 (accessed November 3, 2017).
4 See "About this Artwork: Master W with the Key; Netherlandish, active 1464–1485; *Ship with Sails Furled and Arrow Pointing to the Right, 1475/85*" n.d.
5 The work is titled *Vase: Neptune and Amphitrite* (c. 1570), and it is listed as Work #44 in Richelieu, 1st Floor, in Gallery of The Hunts of Maximilian, Room 507.

Available online: http://cartelen.louvre.fr/cartelen/visite?srv=car_not_frame&idNotice=15199&langue=en (accessed November 3, 2017).
6   *Neptune on a Sea-Horse* is in Richelieu, 1st Floor, Henri IV, Room 520, Display case 3. Available online: http://cartelen.louvre.fr/cartelen/visite?srv=car_not_frame&idNotice=7848&langue=en (accessed November 18, 2020).
7   See "bowl," British Museum, Number: Franks.760. Available online: https://www.britishmuseum.org/collection/object/A_Franks-760/ (accessed October 22, 2020).
8   See Loverance 2007. Rep. in Description of plaque/figure, The British Museum Collections Online, #1959,0721.1. Available online: https://www.britishmuseum.org/collection/object/A_1959-0721-1 (accessed October 22, 2020).
9   For more recent scholarship on early modern cartographers, see Van Duzer (2013: 80–119), as well as Padrón (2004); Rosen (2015); and Sutton (2015).
10 See Ovid, *Metamorphoses*, bk XIII, lines 958–68.

Chapter 8

1   Several writers at the time adumbrated an Arctic utopia: when a spring storm stranded the Venetian merchant Pietro Querini and his crew on the Norwegian island of Røst for three months in 1431, for example, he considered himself to be "in the first circle of Paradise." The French philosopher Guillaume Postel (1510–81) likewise described a hyperborean heaven in his unpublished manuscript from 1561, *De Paradisi Terristri Loco* (On the Location of the Terrestrial Paradise). And in *Atland* (1679–1702), the Swedish scientist Olaus Rudbeck (1630–1702) set out to prove that Uppsala was, in fact, Atlantis. See Scafi (2006: 285) and Fjågesund (2014: 47, 106).
2   Dithmar Blefkens (1563) described the "Pigmies" of Greenland (Purchas [1625] 1906: 13: 513–14), Arngrim Jonas (1609) argued at length that "the first inhabitants of the Northerne World, were of the number of Giants" (Purchas [1625] 1906: 13:537–8), while Sir Dudley Digges banished both altogether: "it hath euer been, the Custome of Describers of the World in remote partes, to set downe Land or Sea out of their owne imagination, with Giants, Pigmies, Monsters, and miraculous reportes of fabulous Authors" (1611: 2). Magnus's multivolume encyclopedia, of course, also ensured the survival of such strange sea tales ([1555] 1996: 1:104–6).
3   See "The booke made by the right worshipful M. Robert Thorne in the yeere 1527" in Richard Hakluyt's *Principal Navigations* ([1598–1600] 1903): "But it is a generall opinion of all Cosmographers, that passing the seventh clime, the sea is all ice, and the colde so much that none can suffer it. And hitherto they had all the like opinion, that under the line Equinoctiall for much heate the land was unhabitable. Yet since (by experience is proved) no land so much habitable nor more temperate. And to conclude, I thinke the same should be found under the North, if it were experimented" (2:178).
4   The entire lines are "quam circum extremae dextra laevaque trahuntur/caeruleae, glacie concretae atque imbribus atris" (Round this, at the world's ends, two [zones] stretch darkling to right and left, set fast in ice and black storms). See Virgil (1999: 114–15).
5   For more on the north's "infernal geography," see Poole (2011: 95–135); for the "spectral," see McCorristine (2018).
6   For a modern edited collection of Shakespeare's works, see *The Norton Shakespeare* (3rd edn., 2016).

7   Stacy Alaimo, for one, writes about the trans-corporeal exposure these at-risk beings living and dying in the "violet-black" illustrate for us: "a fleshy posthumanist vulnerability that denies the possibility of any living creature existing in a state of separation from its environs" (2016: 167). See also Alaimo 2013. These pitchy ("blacke") not-dead pools also raise the broader specter of Timothy Morton's "dark ecology" replete with "strange strangers": unanticipated, uncanny, and ever-intimate "others" that "appea[r] in this world, not beyond it," figures to what (or whom) we are "always-already responsible" (2012: 40). All haunt, Hades-like, the resonant phrase "other worlds."

8   In the original: "Pygmei hic habitant 4 ad summum pedes longi, quem admodum illi quos in Gronlandia Screlinger vocant … Haec insula optima est et saluberrimus totius septentri-onis … Oceanus 19 ostiis inter has insulas irrumperat. 4 europos facit quibus indesinenter sub septentrionem fertur: atque ibi in viscera terrae absorbetur."

9   An unattributed and widely used adage: for example, "Through the Eyes of Satellites, Scientists See Changing Arctic" (2015).

10 While Carroll's focus is the long Romantic period, I share her predilection for "portraying the poles as spaces frequently conflated with the imagination" (2015: 14) in a proto-imperialist and settler-colonialist context. The earlier maps suggest that "these spaces were … perceived as challenging imperial ambitions by virtue of their intrinsic resistance to cultivation and settlement, and, thus, to territorial appropriation and state control" (6). See also Fuller (2013).

11 That this answer could baffle the Inuit man's interceptors hits upon the Eurocentricity of northern exploration I have been probing. McGhee (2005), for instance, takes up a historically "discarded" tale mentioned by a French fur trader named Pierre-Esprit Radisson: at some point in the early seventeenth century, a Huron party traveled from southern Ontario to James Bay, canoeing northeast before rounding Labrador and finally reaching the mouth of the Saint Lawrence River. "This rare example of a northern exploration by a non-European people" (202), in its very scarcity, offers but one reason why the narrative hegemony of non-Indigenous viewpoints deserves to be tested.

BIBLIOGRAPHY

"About this Artwork: Master W with the Key; Netherlandish, active 1464–1485; *Ship with Sails Furled and Arrow Pointing to the Right, 1475/85*" (n.d.), The Art Institute of Chicago. Available online: https://www.artic.edu/artworks/27881/ship-with-sails-furled-and-arrow-pointing-to-the-right (accessed October 24, 2020).

Abreu, Lisuarte de (1992), *Livro de Lisuarte de Abreu*, Lisbon: Comissão Nacional para as Comemorações dos Descobrimentos Portugueses.

Acosta, José de ([1590] 2010), *Natural and Moral History of the Indies*, ed. Clements R. Markham, Farnham: Ashgate.

Adams, Thomas R. and David W. Waters, eds. (1995), *English Maritime Books Printed before 1801: Relating to Ships, Their Construction and Their Operations at Sea*, Providence, RI: The John Carter Brown Library; London: The National Maritime Museum, Greenwich.

Alaimo, Stacy (2013), "Violet-Black," in Jeffrey Jerome Cohen (ed.), *Prismatic Ecology: Ecotheory beyond Green*, 233–51, Minneapolis: University of Minnesota Press.

Alaimo, Stacy (2016), *Exposed: Environmental Politics and Pleasures in Posthuman Times*, Minneapolis: University of Minnesota Press.

Albanese, Denise (1996), *New Science, New World*, Durham, NC: Duke University Press.

Allard, Carel (1695), *Nieuwe Hollandse scheeps bouw*, Amsterdam: Carel Allard.

Andrea, Bernadette (2016), *The Lives of Girls and Women from the Islamic World in Early Modern British Literature and Culture*, Toronto: University of Toronto Press.

Anghiera, Pietro Martire d' (1530), *De orbe nouo Petri Martyris ab Angleria Mediolanensis protonotarij Caesaris senatoris decades*, Compluti (Madrid): Michaelem de Eguia. Available online: www.archive.org, call no. b2220440 (accessed November 25, 2018).

Apian, Peter (1553), *Instrument Buch*, Ingolstadt.

Apt, A.J. (2004), "Wright, Edward (*bap.* 1561, *d.* 1615)." *Oxford Dictionary of National Biography*, Oxford University Press. Available online: http://www.oxforddnb.com/view/article/30029 (accessed April 17, 2014).

Arber, Edward, ed. (1895), *The First Three English Books on America*, Westminster: Archibald Constable and Co.

Archibald, E.H.H. (1980), *Dictionary of Sea Painters*. Woodbridge: Antique Collectors' Club.

Asher, G.M., ed. (1860), *Henry Hudson the Navigator: The Original Documents in Which His Career is Recorded*, London: Hakluyt Society.

Auden, W.H. (1940), "Musee des Beaux Arts," in *Another Time: Poems*, London: Faber & Faber.

Auden, W.H. (1950), *The Enchafèd Flood, or The Romantic Iconography of the Sea*, London: Faber & Faber.

Bacon, Francis (1626), *Sylva Sylvarum or A Naturall Historie in Ten Centuries*, London: William Lee. Available online from Early English Books Online (accessed November 9, 2018).

Bacon, Francis ([1627] 2008), *The New Atlantis* in *Francis Bacon: The Major Works*, ed. Brian Vickers, Oxford: Oxford University Press.

Balgrave, John (1596), *Astrolabium Uranicum Generale: necessary and pleasaunt solace and recreation for navigators in their long jorneying, containing the vse of an instrument or generall astrolabe: newly for them devised by the author, to bring them skilfully acquainted with all the planets starres, and constellacions of the heavens …*, London: Thomas Purfoot & William Matts.

Barbosa, Duarte (1918–21), *The Book of Duarte Barbosa; An Account of the Countries Bordering on the Indian Ocean and their Inhabitants*, 2 vols, 2nd ser., vols 44, 49, London: Hakluyt Society.

Barbosa, Duarte (1996–2000), *O Livro de Duarte Barbosa*, ed. Maria Augusta da Veiga e Sousa, 2 vols, Lisbon: Ministério da Ciência e da Tecnologia, Instituto de Investigação Tropical, Centro de Estudos de História e Cartografia Antiga.

Barletta, Vincent, Mark L. Bajus, and Cici Malik, eds. and trans. (2013), *Dreams of Waking: An Anthology of Iberian Lyric Poetry, 1400–1700*, Chicago: University of Chicago Press.

Barlow, William (1597), *The Navigator's Supply, Conteining many things of principall importance belonging to Navigation with the description and use of diverse Instruments framed chiefly for that purpose; but serving also for sundry other of Cosmography in general: the particular Instruments are specified on the next page*, London: G. Bishop, R. Newbery, and R. Barker.

Barreiro-Meiro, Roberto (1985), "Estudio y comentarios," in Juan de Escalante de Mendoza, *Itinerario de la navegación de los mares y tierras occidentales*, 9–15, Madrid: Museo Naval.

Bate, Jonathan (2004), "Shakespeare's Islands," in Tom Clayton, Susan Brock, and Vincente Fores (eds.), *Shakespeare and the Mediterranean*, 289–307, Newark: University of Delaware Press.

Bazán, Don Álvaro de (1582), *Il succeso de l'armada del Re Filippo*, Florence.

Belcher, Wendy Laura (2013), "Sisters Debating the Jesuits: The Role of African Women in Defeating Portuguese Proto-Colonialism in Seventeenth-Century Abyssinia," *Northeast African Studies*, 13 (1): 121–66.

Bellamy, Elizabeth Jane, (2013), *Dire Straits: The Perils of Writing the Early Modern English Coastline from Leland to Milton*, Toronto: University of Toronto Press.

Bennett, Herman L. (2019), *African Kings and Black Slaves: Sovereignty and Dispossession in the Early Modern Atlantic*, Philadelphia: University of Pennsylvania Press.

Benton, Lauren (2010), *A Search for Sovereignty: Law and Geography in European Empires, 1400–1900*, New York: Cambridge University Press.

Bergeron, David M. (2010), "'Are we turned Turks?': English Pageants and the Stuart Court," *Comparative Drama*, 44 (3): 255–75.

Berton, Pierre (1988), *The Arctic Grail: The Quest for the North West Passage and the North Pole, 1818–1909*, New York: Viking.

Beschrreibung von Eroberung der spanischen Silberflotta wie solche von dem General Peter Peters Heyn, in Nova Hispania, in der Insul Cuba im Baia Matanzas ist erobert worden (1628), Amsterdam.

The Bible: Authorized King James Version (1997), Oxford: Oxford University Press.

Binney, Captain Thomas (1676), *A Light to the Art of Gunnery*, London: Andre Forrester.

Blackmore, Josiah (2002), *Manifest Perdition: Shipwreck Narrative and the Disruption of Empire*, Minneapolis: University of Minnesota Press.

Blackmore, Josiah (2009), *Moorings: Portuguese Expansion and the Writing of Africa*, Minneapolis: University of Minnesota Press.

Blackmore, Josiah (2012), "The Shipwrecked Swimmer: Camões's Maritime Subject," *Modern Philology*, 109 (3): 312–25.

Blackmore, Josiah (2018), "Portuguese Scenes of the Senses, Medieval and Early Modern," in Ryan D. Giles and Steven Wagschal (eds.), *Beyond Sight: Engaging the Senses in Iberian Literatures and Cultures, 1200–1750*, 209–24, Toronto: University of Toronto Press.

Blackmore, Josiah (forthcoming), *The Inner Ship: Maritime Literary Culture in Early Modern Portugal*.

Blumenberg, Hans (1997), *Shipwreck with Spectator: Paradigm of a Metaphor for Existence*, trans. Steven Rendall, Cambridge, MA: MIT Press.

Blundeville, Thomas (1589), *A briefe description of universal mappes and cardes, and of their use: and also of Ptolemy his tables*, London.

Blundeville, Thomas (1594), *M. Blundeville his exercises, containing eight treatises, the titles whereof are set downe in the next printed page*, London.

Boazio, Baptista (1589), *The famouse West Indian voyadge made by the Englishe fleet*, London: Thomas Purfoot.

Bodhidharma, (1989), *The Zen Teaching of Bodhidharma*, ed. Red Pine, San Francisco: North Point Press.

Bolster, W. Jeffrey (2006), "Opportunities in Marine Environmental History," *Environmental History*, 11 (3): 567–97.

Bolster, W. Jeffrey (2008), "Putting the Ocean in Atlantic History: Maritime Communities and Marine Ecology in the Northwest Atlantic, 1500–1800," *American Historical Review*, 113 (1): 19–47.

Bolster, W. Jeffrey (2012), *The Mortal Sea: Fishing the Atlantic in the Age of Sail*, Cambridge, MA: Harvard University Press.

Bond, Henry (1644), *The Boat Swaines Art*, London: William Fisher.

Boroughs, Sir John (1685), *The sovereignty of the British seas proved by records*, London: Humphrey Mosley.

Botello, Jesús (2015), "'Una armada figuraron que venía': Lepanto como écfrasis en *Los baños de Argel*," *eHumanista*, 30: 240–51.

Botero, Giovanni (1608), *Relations of the Most Famous Kingdoms*, London: William Iaggard.

Bourne, William (1574), *A Regiment for the Sea*, London: [Henry Bynneman for] Thomas Hacket.

Bourne, William (1578), *A Booke Called the Treasure for Traveilers, devided into five Bookes or partes, contaynyng very necessary matters, for all sortes of Travailers, eyther by Sea or by Lande*, London: Thomas Woodcocke, dwelling in Paules churchyard, at the sygne of the black Bear.

Bowditch, Nathaniel Ingersoll (1832), *Wharf Property: The Law of the Flats; Being the Remarks Before the Judiciary Committee of the Senate of Massachusetts, April 11, 1832*, Boston: John Wilson & Son.

Boxer, C.R., ed. and trans. (2001), *The Tragic History of the Sea*, Minneapolis: University of Minnesota Press.

Boyle, Robert (1667), "Other Inquiries Concerning the Seas," *Philosophical Transactions of the Royal Society of London*, 1 (18) (May 30): 315–16.

Boyle, Robert (1674), *Tracts Consisting of Observations About the Saltness of the SEA: An Account of a STATISTICAL HYGROSCOPE And its USES: Together with an APPENDIX about the Force of the Air's Moisture: A FRAGMENT about the NATURAL AND PRETERNATURAL STATE of BODIES*, London: E. Flesher for R. Davis.

Bradford, Ernle (1971), *Mediterranean: Portrait of a Sea*, New York: Harcourt, Brace, Jovanovich.

Brayton, Dan, (2012), *Shakespeare's Ocean: An Ecocritical Exploration*, Charlottesville: University of Virginia Press.

"Brill, Paul" (2019), Encyclopædia Britannica, January 1. Available online: https://www.britannica.com/biography/Paul-Brill (accessed February 2, 2019).

Brotton, Jerry (1998), "'This Tunis, Sir, Was Carthage': Contesting Colonialism in *The Tempest*," in Ania Loomba and Martin Orkin (eds.), *Post-Colonial Shakespeares*, 24–33, London: Routledge.

Brotton, Jerry (2000), "Carthage and Tunis, The Tempest and Tapestries," in Peter Hulme and William H. Sherman (eds.), *The Tempest and Its Travels*, 132–7, Philadelphia: University of Pennsylvania Press.

Brown, C.C. (1970), *Sejarah Melayu, or Malay Annals*, New York: Oxford University Press.

Brown, Lloyd (1949), *The Story of Maps*, New York: Little, Brown.

Brown, Paul (1985),"'This Thing of Darkness I Acknowledge Mine': *The Tempest* and the Discourse of Colonialism," in Jonathan Dollimore and Alan Sinfield (eds.), *Political Shakespeare: New Essays in Cultural Materialism*, 48–71, Manchester: Manchester University Press.

Browne, Thomas (1646), *Pseudodoxia Epidemica*, London: Thomas Harper.

Bry, Theodor de (1594), *Grand Voyages*, Frankfurt.

Bry, Theodor de (1601), *Petit Voyages*, Frankfurt: Erasmus.

Burchett, Josiah (1720), *A Complete History of the Most Remarkable Transactions at Sea*, London: J. Walthoe.

Burney, William (1815), *Universal Dictionary of the Marine*, London.

Butler, Nathanial (1685), *Six Dialogues*, London: Moses Pitt.

Cadamosto [Cà da Mosto], Alvise (1937), *The Voyages of Cadamosto and Other Documents on Western Africa in the Second Half of the Fifteenth Century*, trans. and ed. G.R. Crone, 2nd ser., vol. 80, London: Hakluyt Society.

Cadamosto [Cà da Mosto], Alvise (1966), *Le navigazioni atlantiche del veneziano Alvise Da Mosto*, ed. Tullia Gasparrini Leporace, Rome: Istituto poligrafico dello Stato.

Caminha, Pero Vaz de (1994), *A Carta de Pero Vaz de Caminha*, ed. Jaime Cortesão, Lisbon: Imprensa Nacional-Casa da Moeda.

Camões, Luís de ([1572] 1997), *Os Lusiadas*, Lisbon: António Gonçalves. Available online: http://purl.pt/1, access provided by Biblioteca Nacional de Portugal (accessed December 15, 2018).

Camões, Luís de (1655), *The Lusiad, or, Portugals HIstoricall Poem*, trans. Richard Fanshawe, London: Humphrey Mosley.

Camões, Luís de (1973), *Rimas*, ed. Álvaro J. da Costa Pimpão, Coimbra: Atlântida.

Camões, Luís de (1997), *The Lusiads*, trans. Landeg White, Oxford: Oxford University Press.

Camões, Luís de (2005), *Selected Sonnets: A Bilingual Edition*, trans. William Baer, Chicago: University of Chicago Press.

Camões, Luís ce (2008), *The Collected Lyric Poems of Luís de Camões*, trans. Landeg White, Princeton, NJ: Princeton University Press.

Campbell, Gwyn (2010), "The Role of Africa in the Emergence of the 'Indian Ocean World' Global Economy," in Pamila Gupta, Isabel Hofmeyr, and M.N. Pearson (eds.), *Eyes Across the Water: Navigating the Indian Ocean*, 170–96, Pretoria: Unisa Press.

Campbell, I.C. (1995), "The Lateen Sail in World History," *Journal of World History* 6 (1): 1–23.

Campbell, Mary Baine (1988), *The Witness and the Other World: Exotic European Travel Writing, 400–1600*, Ithaca, NY: Cornell University Press.

Cano, Tomé (1611), *Arte para fabricar*, Seville.

Caretta, Vincent (2005), *Equiano the African: Biography of a Self-Made Man*, Athens: University of Georgia Press.

Carneiro, Antonio de Maris (1666), *Roteiro da India Oriental*, Lisbon.

Carroll, Siobhan (2015), *An Empire of Air and Water: Uncolonizable Space in the British Imagination, 1750–1850*, Philadelphia: University of Pennsylvania Press.

Casale, Giancarlo (2010), *The Ottoman Age of Exploration*, New York: Oxford University Press.

Casas, Bartolomé de las ([1957] 1979), *Historia de las Indias*, bk 1, ch. 8, pp. 47–9, in D.B. Quinn (ed.), *New American World: A Documentary History of North America to 1612*, vol. 1, *America from Concept to Discovery: Early Exploration of North America*, London: Macmillan Press.

Cassidy, Vincent H. de P (1963), "The Voyage of an Island," *Speculum* 38 (4): 595–602.

Casson, Lionel (1989), *The Periplus of the Erythraenean Sea: The Periplus Maris Erythraei: Text with Introduction, Translation and Commentary*, Princeton, NJ: Princeton University Press.

Castanha, Tony (2011), *The Myth of Indigenous Caribbean Extinction: Continuity and Reclamation in Borikén (Puerto Rico)*, 1st edn., New York: Palgrave Macmillan.

Castro, João de (1968–82), *Obras completas de João de Castro*, ed. Armando Cortesão and Luís de Albuquerque, 4 vols, Coimbra: Academia Internacional da Cultura Portuguesa.

Cavanagh, Sheila T. (2001), *Cherished torment: the emotional geography of Lady Mary Wroth's Urania*, Pittsburgh, PA: Duquesne University Press.

Cavendish, Margaret ([1660] 2000), "The Description of a New World, Called the Blazing World," in Sylvia Bowerbank and Sara Mendelson (eds.), *Paper Bodies: A Margaret Cavendish Reader*, 151–251, Orchard Park, NY: Broadview.

Cavendish, Margaret (1664), *Philosophical Letters: or, Modest Reflections Upon some Opinions in Natural Philosophy, Maintained By several Famous and Learned*

Authors of this Age, Expressed by way of Letters, London. Available online from Early English Books Online (accessed November 6, 2018).

Cavendish, Margaret ([1666] 1992) *The Blazing World and Other Writings*, ed. Kate Lilley, London: Penguin.

Cervantes, Miguel de ([1612] 1999), *Don Quixote*, trans. Burton Raffel, ed. Diana de Armas Wilson, New York: Norton.

Cervantes, Miguel de ([1612] 2004), *Don Quixote de la Mancha*, Brasil: Real Academia Española.

Chakravarty, Urvashi (2016), "More Than Kin, Less Than Kind: Similitude, Strangeness, and Early Modern English Homonationalisms," *Shakespeare Quarterly*, 67 (1): 14–29

Chaplin, Joyce E. (2012), *Round About the Earth: Circumnavigation from Magellan to Orbit*, New York: Simon & Schuster.

Charney, Michael W. (2004), *Southeast Asian Warfare, 1300–1900*, Leiden: Brill.

Chavan, Akshay (2018). "How the Battle of Diu Changed World History!," *Live History India*, October 17.

Christy, Miller, ed. (1894), *The Voyages of Captain Luke Foxe and Captain Thomas James in Search of a North-West Passage, in 1631–32*, London: Hakluyt Society.

Churchill, R.R. and A.V. Lowe (1999), *The Law of the Sea*, Manchester: Manchester University Press.

Cobb, Christopher J. (2007), *The Staging of Romance in Late Shakespeare: Text and Theatrical Technique*, Newark: University of Delaware Press.

Cohen, Jeffrey Jerome and Lowell Duckert, eds. (2015), *Elemental Ecocriticism: Thinking with Earth, Air, Water, and Fire*, Minneapolis: University of Minnesota Press.

Cohen, Margaret (2006), "The Chronotopes of the Sea," in Franco Moretti (ed.), *The Novel*, vol. 2, 647–66, Princeton, NJ: Princeton University Press.

Cohen, Margaret (2010), *The Novel and the Sea*, Princeton, NJ: Princeton University Press.

Colombos, C. John (1967), *The International Law of the Sea*, 6th edn., London: Longmans Green & Co.

Colson, Nathaniel (1676), *The Mariner's new Calendar*, London: W. and J. Mount.

Columbus, Ferdinand (1959), *The Life of the Admiral Christopher Columbus by His Son Ferdinand*, trans. Benjamin Keen, London: Printed by Butler & Tanner for Rutgers, The State University [of New Jersey].

A commission for the well governing of our people … in Newfound-land (1633), London: King Charles I.

Conley, Tom (1996), *The Self-Made Map: Cartographic Writing in Early Modern France*, Minneapolis: University of Minnesota Press.

Consolat de Mar (1494), *Consulate of the Sea*, Barcelona.

Conway, Martin (1906), *No Man's Land: A History of Spitsbergen from Its Discovery in 1596 to the Beginning of the Scientific Exploration of the Country*, Cambridge: Cambridge University Press.

Conway, Martin, ed. (1904), *Early Dutch and English Voyages to Spitsbergen in the Seventeenth Century*, London: Hakluyt Society.

Cook, Harold J. (1996), "Physicians and Natural History," in N. Jardine, J.A. Secord, and E.C. Spary (eds.), *Cultures of Natural History*, 91–105, Cambridge: Cambridge University Press.

Cooper, Helen (2004), *The English Romance in Time: Transforming Motifs from Geoffrey of Monmouth to the Death of Shakespeare*, Oxford: Oxford University Press.

Cortés, Martin de Albacar (1561), *The Art of Navigation*, trans. Richard Eden, London.

Couto, Diogo do (1980), *O soldado prático*, 3rd edn., Lisbon: Sá da Costa.

Craciun, Adriana (2016), *Writing Arctic Disaster: Authorship and Exploration*, Cambridge: Cambridge University Press.

Crone, C.R., ed. and trans. (1937), *The Voyages of Cadamosto*, 2nd ser., no. 80, London: Hakluyt Society.

Crosby, Albert (2003), *The Columbian Exchange: Biological and Cultural Consequences of 1492*, 2nd edn., New York: Praeger.

Crosby, Alfred (2006), *Ecological Imperialism: The Biological Expansion of Europe, 900–1900*, Cambridge: Cambridge University Press.

Curtin, Philip D. (1998), *The Rise and Fall of the Plantation Complex: Essays in Atlantic History*, New York: Cambridge University Press.

Dadabhoy, Ambereen (2020), "Skin in the Game: Teaching Race in Early Modern Literature," *Studies in Medieval and Renaissance Teaching*, 27 (2):1–17.

D'Aguiar, Fred (1997), *Feeding the Ghosts*, London: Chatto and Windus.

Daily Sabah Asia Pacific (2019), "New Zealand Mosque Shooter Names His 'idols' on Weapons He Used in Massacre," March 18. Available online: https://www.dailysabah.com/asia/2019/03/15/new-zealand-mosque-shooter-names-his-idols-on-weapons-he-used-in-massacre(accessed April 30, 2019).

Dassié, F. (1677), *L'architecture navale*, Paris.

Davenport, Frances Gardner, ed. (1917), *European Treaties Bearing on the History of the United States and its Dependencies*, Washington, DC: The Carnegie Institution of Washington.

Davidson, Peter (2005), *The Idea of North*, London: Reaktion.

Davis, Elizabeth B. (2006), "Travesías peligrosas: escrítos marítimos en España durante la Época Imperial, 1492–1650," in Anthony Close (ed.), *Edad de Oro Cantabrigense: Actas del VII Congreso de la Asociación Internacional del Siglo de Oro (AISO)*, 1–13, Madrid: Iberoamericana Editorial Vervuert.

Davis, John (1595), *The Seaman's Secrets*, London: Thomas Dawson.

Day, John [alias Hugh Say] to "the Grand Admiral [Christopher Columbus]" ([1497] 1979), in D.B. Quinn (ed.), *New American World: A Documentary History of North America to 1612*, vol. 1, *America from Concept to Discovery. Early Exploration of North America*, London: Macmillan Press.

De Asúa, Miguel and Roger French (2005), *A New World of Animals: Early Modern Europeans and the Creatures of Iberian America*, Aldershot: Ashgate.

Deacon, Margarct, (1965), "Founders of Marine Science in Britain: The Work of the Early Fellows of the Royal Society," *Philosophical Transactions of the Royal Society of London*, 20 (1): 28–50.

Deacon, Margaret (1971), *Scientists and the Sea, 1650–1900: A Study of Marine Science*, London: Academic Press.

de Jong, Jan L. (2003), "The Painted Decoration of the Sala Regia: Intention and Reception," in Tristan Weddigen, Sible de Blaauw, and Bram Kempers (eds.), *Functions and Decorations: Art and Ritual at the Vatican Palace in the Middle Ages and the Renaissance*, 153–68, Rome: Turnhout/Brepols.

Dee, John (1577), *General and Rare Memorials pertayning to the Perfect Arte of Navigation*, London: John Daye. Available online from Early English Books Online (accessed October 2, 2017).
Degroot, Dagomar (2018), *The Frigid Golden Age: Climate Change, the Little Ice Age, and the Dutch Republic, 1560–1720*, New York: Cambridge University Press.
Degroot, Dagomar (2019), "Did Colonialism Cause Global Cooling? Revisiting an Old Controversy," *Historical Climatology*. Available online: https://www.historicalclimatology.com/blog/did-colonialism-cause-global-cooling-revisiting-an-old-controversy (accessed March 15, 2019).
Delbourgo, James (2017), *Collecting the World: Hans Sloane and the Origins of the British Museum*, Cambridge, MA: Harvard University Press.
Deloria, Vine Jr. (1997), *Red Earth, White Lies: Native Americans and the Myth of Scientific Fact*, Golden, CO: Fulcrum Publishing.
Dening, Greg (1980), *Islands and Beaches: Discourse on a Silent Land: Marquesas 1774–1880*, Honolulu: University Press of Hawaii.
Denys, Nicolas ([1672] 1908), *The Description and Natural History of the Coasts of North America*, ed. and trans. William F. Ganong, Toronto: The Champlain Society.
Dias, J.S. da Silva (1982), *Os descobrimentos e a problemática cultural do século XVI*, Porto: Editorial Presença.
Digges, Dudley (1611), *Fata Mihi Totum Mea Sunt Agitanda Per Orbem*, London: W. White.
Digges, Dudley (1615), *The defence of trade*, London: Iohn Barnes.
Dille, Glen F., trans. and ed (2011), *Misfortunes and Shipwrecks in the Seas of the Indies, Islands, and Mainland of the Ocean Sea (1513–1548): Book Fifty of the General and Natural History of the Indies, Gonzalo Fernández de Oviedo*, Gainesville: University Press of Florida.
di Robilant, Andrea (2011), *Irresistible North: From Venice to Greenland in the Trail of the Zen Brothers*, New York: Alfred A. Knopf.
Disney, A.R. (2009), *A History of Portugal and the Portuguese Empire*, vol. 2, Cambridge: Cambridge University Press.
Domingues, F. Contente and R.A. Barker (1991), "O autor e a sua obra," in Fernando Oliveira, *Liuro da fabrica das naus*, 11–21.
Donne, John ([1624] 1975), *Devotions upon Emergent Occasions*, ed. and commentary Anthony Raspa, Montreal: McGill-Queen's University Press.
Dryden, Robert G (2001), "Unmasking Pirates and Fortune Hunters in the West Indies," *Eighteenth-Century Studies*, 34 (4): 539–57.
Duckert, Lowell (2017), *For All Waters: Finding Ourselves in Early Modern Wetscapes*, Minneapolis: University of Minnesota Press.
Durrell, Lawrence (1953), *Reflections on a Marine Venus: A Companion to the Landscape of Rhodes*, London: Faber & Faber.
Earle, Sylvia A. (2010), *The World Is Blue: How Our Fate and the Ocean's Are One*, Washington, DC: National Geographic.
Eden, Richard (1555), *The Decades of the newe worle or west India … Wrytten in the Latine tounge by Peter Martyr of Angleria, and translated into Englysshe by Rycharde Eden*, London: Guilhelmi Powell. Available online from Early English Books Online (accessed October 2, 2017).
Edwards, Clinton R. (1992), "The Impact of European Overseas Discoveries on Ship Design and Construction during the Sixteenth Century," *GeoJournal*, 26 (4): 443–52.

Egerton, Douglas R., Alison Games, Jane G. Landers, Kris Lane, and Donald R. Wright (2007), *The Atlantic World: A History, 1400–1888*, Wheeling, IL: Harlan Davidson.

Eggert, Katherine (2000), *Showing Like a Queen: Female Authority and Literary Experiment in Spenser, Shakespeare, and Milton*, Philadelphia: University of Philadelphia Press.

Eisenstein, Elizabeth L. (1979) *The Printing Press as an Agent of Change: Communications and Cultural Transformations in Early Modern Europe*, 2 vols, Cambridge: Cambridge University Press.

Eklund, Hillary (2015), *Literature and Moral Economy in the Early Modern Atlantic: Elegant Sufficiencies*, Burlington, VT: Ashgate.

Eklund, Hillary (2019), "Shakespeare's Littoral and the Dramas of Loss and Store," *SEL*, 59 (2): 349–65.

Elizabeth I ([1588] 2000a), "Armada Speech to the Troops at Tilbury, August 9, 1588," in Leah S. Marcus, Janel Mueller, and Mary Beth Rose (eds.), *Elizabeth I: Collected Works*, 325–6, Chicago: University of Chicago Press.

Elizabeth I ([1588] 2000b), "On the Defeat of the Spanish Armada, September 1588," in Leah S. Marcus, Janel Mueller, and Mary Beth Rose (eds.), *Elizabeth I: Collected Works*, 424–5, Chicago: University of Chicago Press.

Elizabeth I ([1588] 2000c), "Song on the Armada Victory, December 1588," in Leah S. Marcus, Janel Mueller, and Mary Beth Rose (eds.), *Elizabeth I: Collected Works*, 410–11, Chicago: University of Chicago Press.

Ellis, Richard (1994), *Monsters of the Sea*, New York: Alfred A. Knopf.

Escalante de Mendoza, Juan de ([1575] 1985), *Itinerario de navegación de los mares y tierras occidentales*, Madrid: Museo Naval.

Fagan, Brian (2006), *Fish on Fridays: Feasting, Fasting, and the Discovery of the New World*, New York: Basic Books.

Fagan, Brian (2012), *Beyond the Blue Horizon: How the Earliest Mariners Unlocked the Secretes of the Oceans*, London: Bloomsbury.

Falconer, Alexander (1954), *Shakespeare and the Sea*, London: Constable and Company.

Falconer, William (1769), *An Universal Dictionary of the Marine*, London: T. Cadell.

Fernandez-Armesto, Felipe (2006), *Pathfinders: a Global History of Exploration*, New York: W.W. Norton & Co.

Fjågesund, Peter (2014), *The Dream of the North: A Cultural History to 1920*, Amsterdam: Rodopi.

Fletcher, John ([1647] 2013) *The Island Princess*, ed. Clare McManus, London: Bloomsbury.

Foucault, Michel (1973), *The Order of Things: An Archaeology of the Human Sciences*, trans. Alan Sheridan, New York: Vintage.

Fournier, Père Georges (1643), *Hydrographie contenant la théorie et la pratique de toutes les parties de la navigation*, Paris.

Fuchs, Barbara (1997), "Conquering Islands: Contextualizing *The Tempest*," *Shakespeare Quarterly*, 48 (1): 45–62.

Fuchs, Barbara (2009), *Exotic Nation: Maurophilia and the Construction of Early Modern Spain*, Philadelphia: University of Pennsylvania Press.

Fuchs, Barbara and Aaron J. Ilika, eds. (2010), *Miguel de Cervantes: "The Bagnios of Algiers" and "The Great Sultana": Two Plays of Captivity*, Philadelphia: University of Pennsylvania Press.

Fuller, Mary C. (1995), *Voyages in Print: English Travel to America, 1576–1624*, New York: Cambridge University Press.
Fuller, Mary C. (2013), "Arctics of Empire: The North in *Principal Navigations* (1598–1600)," in Frédéric Regard (ed.), *The Quest for the Northwest Passage: Knowledge, Nation, and Empire, 1576–1806*, 15–30, London: Pickering and Chatto.
Games, Alison (2008), *The Web of Empire: English Cosmopolitans in an Age of Expansion, 1560–1660*, Oxford: Oxford University Press.
Garcie, Pierre (1567), *The rutters of the sea: with the hauens, rodes, soundings, kennings, windes, floods and ebbes, daungers and coastes of divers regions with the lawes of the Ile of Auleron*.
Gastaldi, Giacomo (1556), *La Nuova Francia*, *Terzo voulume della navigationi et viaggi*, Venice.
Gentilis (1613), *Advocato hispanica*.
Gentleman, Tobias (1614), *England's way to win wealth, and to employ ships and marriners*, London: Nathaniel Butter.
Georgeson, Rosemary and Jessica Hallenbeck (2018), "We Have Stories: Five Generations of Indigenous Women in Water," *Decolonization: Indigineity, Education & Society*, 7 (1): 20–38.
Gil, Fernando (2009), "The Traveling Eye: The Seas of *The Lusiads*," trans. K. David Jackson, in Fernando Gil and Helder Macedo (eds.), *The Traveling Eye: Retrospection, Vision, and Prophecy in the Portuguese Renaissance*, 87–124, Dartmouth MA: University of Massachusetts Dartmouth.
Gilbert, Humphrey ([1576] 1940), *The Voyages and Colonising Enterprises of Sir Humphrey Gilbert*, London: Hakluyt Society.
Gillis, John R. (2004), *Islands of the Mind: How the Human Imagination Created the Atlantic World*, New York: Palgrave MacMillan.
Gillis, John R. (2012), *The Human Shore: Seacoasts in History*, Chicago: University of Chicago Press.
Gillis, John R. (2014), "Not Continents in Miniature: Islands as Ecotones," *Island Studies*, 9 (1): 155–66.
Gilroy, Paul (1993), *The Black Atlantic: Modernity and Double Consciousness*, Cambridge, MA: Harvard University Press.
Glissant, Éduoard (1997), *Poetics of Relation*, trans. Betsy Wing, Ann Arbor: University of Michigan Press.
Goedde, Lawrence Otto (1989), *Tempest and Shipwreck in Dutch and Flemish Art*, University Park: Pennsylvania State University Press.
Goldie, Matthew Boyd and Sebastian Sobecki, eds. (2016), "Our Sea of Islands," *Postmedieval: A Journal of Medieval Cultural Studies*, 7 (4): 471–83.
Gosch, C.C.A., ed. (1897), *Danish Arctic Expeditions, 1605 to 1620*, London: Hakluyt Society.
Gould, Eliga H. (2003), "Zones of Law, Zones of Violence: The Legal Geography of the British Atlantic Circa 1772," *William and Mary Quarterly*, 60 (3): 471–510.
Greene, Roland (2000), "Island Logic," in Peter Hulme and William H. Sherman (eds.), *The Tempest and its Travels*, 138–45, Philadelphia: University of Pennsylvania Press.
Greenlee, William Brooks, trans. (1995), *The Voyage of Pedro Álvares de Cabral to Brazil and India from Contemporary Documents and Narratives*, New Delhi: Asian Educational Services.

Grotius, Hugo (1604), *De Jure Predea*.
Grotius, Hugo ([1608] 1916), *The Freedom of the Seas, or the Right Which Belongs to the Dutch to Take Part in the East Indian Trade*, trans. Ralph Van Deman Magoffin, New York: Oxford University Press.
Grotius, Hugo (1609), *Mare Liberum*.
Grotius, Hugo (1625), *De Jure Belli ac Pacis*.
Guilmartin, John F. (1974), *Gunpowder and Galleys: Changing Technology and Mediterranean Warfare at Sea in the Sixteenth Century*, New York: Cambridge University Press.
Guitar, Lynn A. (1998), "Cultural Genesis: Relationships Among Indians, Africans and Spaniards in Rural Hispaniola, First Half of the Sixteenth Century," PhD diss., History, Vanderbilt University, Nashville, TN.
Gunn, Geoffrey C. (2003), *First Globalization: The Eurasian Exchange, 1500–1800*, New York: Rohan and Littlefield.
Hadfield, Andrew (2009), "The Idea of the North," *Journal of the Northern Renaissance*, 1 (1). Available online: https://www.northernrenaissance.org/the-idea-of-the-northandrew-hadfield/ (accessed November 18, 2020).
Hakluyt, Richard (1589), The Principall Navigations Voiages & Discoveries of the English Nation, London: George Bishop and Ralph Newberie, Deputies to Christopher Baker.
Hakluyt, Richard ([1598–1600] 1903–1905), *Principal Navigations*, 12 volumes, Glasgow: MacLehose and Sons.
Hakluyt, Richard (1598–1600), *Principal navigations, voyages, traffiques, and discoveries of the English nation*, 3 vols, London: George Bishop, Ralph Newberrie, and Robert Barker. Available online from Early English Books Online (accessed October 23, 2020).
Hall, Kim F. (1996a), "Beauty and the Beast of Whiteness: Teaching Race and Gender," *Shakespeare Quarterly*, 47 (4): 461–75.
Hall, Kim F. (1996b), *Things of Darkness: Economies of Race and Gender in Early Modern England*, Ithaca, NY: Cornell University Press.
Haraway, Donna J. (2008), *When Species Meet*, Minneapolis: University of Minnesota Press.
Harkness, Deborah E. (2007), *The Jewel House: Elizabethan London and the Scientific Revolution*, New Haven, CT: Yale University Press.
Harley, Brian (1988), "Silences and Secrecy: The Hidden Agenda of Cartography in Early Modern Europe," *Imago Mundi*, 40: 57–76.
Harley, J.B. (2002), *The New Nature of Maps: Essays in the History of Cartography*, ed. Paul Laxton, Baltimore: Johns Hopkins University Press.
Harper, James G. (2011), *The Turk and Islam in the Western Eye, 1450–1750: Visual Imagery Before Orientalism*, Burlington, VT: Ashgate.
Harrington, Matthew P. (1995) "The Legacy of the Colonial Vice-Admiralty Courts (Part 1)," *Journal of Maritime Law and Commerce*, 26 (4): 581–600.
Harrison-Hall, Jessica (2001), *Catalogue of Late Yuan and Ming Ceramics in the British Museum*, London: BMP.
Hattendorf, John B. (2003), *"The Boundless Deep …" The European Conquest of the Oceans, 1450–1840: Catalogue of an Exhibition of Rare Books, Maps. Charts, prints and manuscripts relating to Maritime History from the John Carter Brown Library*, Providence, RI: John Cater Brown Library.
Hattendorf, John B., ed. (1997), *Maritime History*, vol. 2, *The Eighteenth Century and the Classic Age of Sail*, Malabar, FL: Krieger Publishing Company.

Hattendorf, John B., ed. (2007a), *Maritime History*, vol. 1, *The Age of Discovery*, Malabar, FL: Krieger Publishing Company.
Hattendorf, John B., editor in chief (2007b), *The Oxford Encyclopedia of Maritime History*, 4 vols, Oxford: Oxford University Press.
Hauʻofa, Epeli (1993), *A New Oceania: Rediscovering Our Sea of Islands*, ed. E. Waddell, V. Naidu, and E. Hauʻofa, 2–16, Suva, Fiji: School of Social and Economic Development, University of the South Pacific.
Hayes, Derek (2003), *Historical Atlas of the Arctic*, Seattle: University of Washington Press.
Hayman, Eleanor, Colleen James/Gooch Tláa, and Mark Wedge/Aan Gooshú (2018), "Future Rivers of the Anthropocene or Whose Anthropocene is it? Decolonising the Anthropocene!," *Decolonization: Indigeneity, Education & Society*, 7 (1): 77–92.
Hayward, Edward (1656), *The sizes and lengths of rigging*, London: Peter Cole.
Heng, Derek (2013), "State Formation and the Evolution of Naval Strategies in the Melaka Straits, c. 500–1500 CE," *Journal of Southeast Asian Studies*, 44 (3): 380–99.
Hess, Andrew C. (2000), "The Mediterranean and Shakespeare's Geopolitical Imagination," in Peter Hulme and William H. Sherman (eds.), *The Tempest and its Travels*, 121–30, Philadelphia: University of Pennsylvania Press.
Hill, Jen (2008), *White Horizon: The Arctic in the Nineteenth-Century British Imagination,* Albany: State University of New York Press.
Hirsch, Eric (1995), "Landscape: Between Place and Space," in Eric Hirsch and Michael O'Hanlon (eds.), *The Anthropology of Landscape*, 1–30, Oxford: Clarendon Press.
Hoffman, Richard C. (2001), "Frontier Foods for Late Medieval Consumers: Culture, Economy, Ecology," *Environment and History*, 7: 131–67.
Hogan, Sarah (2012), "Of Islands and Bridges: Figures of Uneven Development in Bacon's *New Atlantis*," *Journal for Early Modern Cultural Studies*, 12 (3): 28–59.
The Holy Bible Containing the Old and New Testaments with the Apocryphal/Deuterocanonical Books, New Revised Standard Version (1989), New York: Oxford University Press.
Homer (1870), *The Odyssey*, Oxford: Clarendon Press.
Horace (2004), *Odes and Epodes*, ed. and trans. Niall Rudd, Loeb Classical Library 33, Cambridge, MA: Harvard University Press.
Hoste, Pére Paul (1697), *L'Art des Armées Navales*.
Houston, Chloë (2014), *The Renaissance Utopia: Dialogue, Travel and the Ideal Society*, Burlington, VT: Ashgate.
Hubbard, Benjamin (1656), *Orthodoxal navigation*, London: William Weekley.
Hues, R. (1617), *Tractatus de Globis*, Amsterdam: Judocus Hondius.
Hulme, Peter ([1985] 1986), *Colonial Encounters: Europe and the Native Caribbean, 1492–1797*, London: Methuen.
Inglis, David (2011), "Mapping Global Consciousness: Portuguese Imperialism and the Forging of Modern Global Sensibilities," *Globalizations*, 8 (5): 687–702.
Jackson, K. David (2005), *De Chaul a Batticaloa: as marcas do império marítimo português na Índia e no Sri Lanka*, Ericeira: Mar de Letras.
Jayasuriya, Shihan de Silva, (2008), *The Portuguese in the East: A Cultural History of a Maritime Trading Empire*, London: Taurus Academic Studies.
Jett, Stephen C. (2017), *Ancient Ocean Crossings: Reconsidering the Case for Contacts with the Pre-Columbian Americas*, Tuscaloosa: University of Alabama Press.

Johnson, Captain Charles (1999), *A General History of the Robberies and Murders of the Most Notorious Pirates*, New York: Carroll and Graf.

Johnson, Samuel ([1735] 1985), *A Voyage to Abyssinia (Translated from the French)*, ed. Joel J. Gold, New Haven, CT: Yale University Press.

Jordain, Sylvester (1610), *A Discovery of The Barmudas*, London: Printed by Iohn Windet.

Jourdain, Michel Mollat Du and Monique de la Ronciere (1984), *Sea Charts of the Early Explorers: 13th to 17th Century*, London: Thames & Hudson.

Jowitt, Claire (2010), *The Culture of Piracy, 1580–1630: English Literature and Seaborne Crime*, Burlington, VT: Ashgate.

Jowitt, Claire and David McInnis, eds. (2018), *Travel and Drama in Early Modern England: The Journeying Play*, Cambridge: Cambridge University Press.

Kayll, Robert (1615), *The trades increase*, London: Walter Burre.

Keuning, Johannes (1949), "Hessel Gerritsz," *Imago Mundi: The International Journal for the History of Cartography*, 6: 1: 49–66.

Kieschnick, John and Meir Shahar, eds. (2014), *India in the Chinese Imagination: Myth, Religion, and Thought*, Philadelphia: University of Pennsylvania Press.

Klein, Bernhard (2004), "Staying Afloat: Literary Shipboard Encounters from Columbus to Equiano," in Bernhard Klein and Gesa Mackenthun (eds.), *Sea Changes: Historicizing the Ocean*, 91–109, New York: Routledge.

Klein, Bernhard (2010), "Mapping the Waters: Sea Charts, Navigation, and Camões's *Os Lusíadas*," *Renaissance Studies,* 25 (2): 228–47.

Klein, Bernhard (2013), "Camões and the Sea: Maritime Modernity in *The Lusiads*," *Modern Philology,* 111 (2): 158–80.

Knapp, Jeffrey (1992), *An Empire Nowhere: England, America, and Literature from Utopia to The Tempest*, Berkeley: University of California Press.

Konstam, Angus (2008), *Piracy: The Complete History*, New York: Osprey.

Krummrich, Philip, ed. and trans (2006), *The Hero and Leander Theme in Iberian Literature, 1500–1800: An Anthology of Translations*, Lewiston, NY: Edwin Mellen Press.

Kusukawa, Suchiko (2000), "The 'Historia Piscium' (1686)," *Notes and Records of the Royal Society of Londoni*, 54 (2): 179–97.

Kusukawa, Suchiko (2016), "*Historia Piscium* (1686) and Its Sources," in Tim Birkhead (ed.), *Virtuoso by Nature: The Scientific Worlds of Francis Willughby FRS (1635–1672)*, Leiden: Brill.

Lamb, Jonathan (2016), *Scurvy: The Disease of Discovery*, Princeton, NJ: Princeton University Press.

Landstrom, Bjorn (1969), *The Ship: An Illustrated History*, New York: Doubleday.

Latour, Bruno (2018), *Down to Earth: Politics in the New Climatic Regime*, trans. Catherine Porter, Cambridge: Polity Press.

Lerner, Isaías (2012), "Lope de Vega y Ercilla: el caso de *La Dragontea*," *CRITICÓN,* 115: 147–57.

Levi, Scott C. (2018), "Asia in the Gunpowder Revolution," in *Oxford Research Encyclopedia of Asian History*, Oxford: Oxford University Press.

Lewis, Martin W. (1999), "Dividing the Ocean Sea," *Geographic Review*, 89 (2): 188–214.

Lewis, Simon L. and Mark A. Maslin (2015), "Defining the Anthropocene," *Nature*, 519 (7542): 171–80. Available online: https://www.nature.com/articles/nature14258 (accessed October 23, 2020).

Lewis, Simon L. and Mark A. Maslin (2018), *The Human Planet: How We Created the Anthropocene*, New Haven, CT: Yale University Press.

Lewis, Martin W. and Kären E. Wigen (1997), *The Myth of Continents: A Critique of Metageography*, Berkeley: University of California Press.

Ley, C.D., ed. (2000), *Portuguese Voyages 1498–1663: Tales from the Great Age of Discovery*, London: Phoenix Press.

Leyden, John (1821), *Malay Annals: Translated from the Malay Language*, ed. Sir Thomas Stamford Raffles, London: Longman, Hurst, Rees, Orme, and Brown. Available online: https://archive.org/details/in.ernet.dli.2015.83132 (accessed October 23, 2020).

Lobo, Jerónimo (1984), *The Itinerário of Jerónimo Lobo*, trans. Donald M. Lockhart, ed. M.G. da Costa, Introduction and Notes by C.F. Beckingham, 2nd ser., vol. 162, London: The Hakluyt Society.

Lockard, Craig A. (2009), *Southeast Asia in World History*, New York: Oxford University Press.

Loomba, Ania (1989), *Gender, Race, Renaissance Drama*, New York: St. Martin's Press.

Lope de Vega (1950), *La Famosa Comedia Del Nuevo Mundo, Descubierto por Christoual Colon: Doze Comedias de Lope de Vega Carpio, Familiar del Santo Oficio*, trans. Frieda Fligelman, Berkeley, CA: Gillick Press.

Loverance, Rowena (2007), *Christian Art*, London: BMP.

Lucretius (2007), *The Nature of Things (De Rerum Natura)*, trans. and with notes by A.E. Stallings, introduction by Richard Jenkyns, London: Penguin.

Macedo, Helder (2009), "The Poetics of Truth in *The Lusiadas*," trans. K. David Jackson, in Fernando Gil and Helder Macedo (eds.), *The Traveling Eye: Retrospection, Vision, and Prophecy in the Portuguese Renaissance*, 15–31, Dartmouth: University of Massachusetts Dartmouth.

Magnus, Olaus ([1555] 1996), *Description of the Northern Peoples*, trans. Peter Fisher and Humphrey Higgens, ed. Peter Foote, London: Hakluyt Society.

Mainwaring, Henry (1644), *The Sea-Mans Dictionary*, London: John Bellamy.

Maisano, Scott (2014), "New Directions: Shakespeare's Revolution—*The Tempest* as Scientific Romance," in Alden T. Vaughan and Virginia Mason Vaughan (eds.), *The Tempest: A Critical Reader*, 165–94, London: Bloomsbury.

Major, Richard Henry, ed. (1849), *The Historie of Travaile into Virginia Britannia*, London: Hakluyt Society.

Major, Richard Henry, ed. (1873), *Voyages of the Venetian Brothers, Nicolo and Antonio Zeno*, London: Hakluyt Society.

Mallette, Karla (2007), "Insularity: A Literary History of Muslim Lucera," in Andnan Husain and K. E. Flemin (eds.), *A Faithful Sea: The Religious Cultures of the Mediterranean, 1200–1700*, 27–46, London: OneWorld Publications.

Mancall, Peter C. (2007), *Hakluyt's Promise: An Elizabethan Obsession for an English America*, New Haven, CT: Yale University Press.

Mancke, Elizabeth (1999), "Early Modern Expansion and the Politicization of Oceanic Space," *Geographical Review*, "Oceans Connect," 89 (2): 225–36.

Mann Charles C. (2005), *1491: New Revelations of the Americas before Columbus*, New York: Vintage.

Mann, Charles C. (2011), *1493: Uncovering the New World Columbus Created*, New York: Vintage.

Manne, Kate (2018), *Down Girl: The Logic of Misogyny*, New York: Oxford University Press.

Marine Architecture (1739), London: William Mount and Thomas Page.
Markham, Albert Hastings, ed. (1880), *The Voyages and Works of John Davis, the Navigator*, London: Hakluyt Society.
Mayhew, Robert J. (2011), "Cosmographers, Explorers, Cartographers, Chorographers: Defining, Inscribing and Practicing Early Modern Geography, c. 1450–1850," in John A. Agne and James S. Duncan (eds.), *The Wiley Blackwell Companion to Human Geography*, 23–49, Chichester: John Wiley & Sons.
McCloskey, Jason (2013), "'Navegaba Leandro el Helesponto': Love and Early Modern Navigation in Juan Boscán's Leandro," *Revista de Estudios Hispánicos*, 47 (1): 3–27.
McCluhan, Marshal (1962), *The Gutenberg Galaxy: The Making of Typographic Man*, Toronto: University of Toronto Press.
McCorristine, Shane (2018), *The Spectral Arctic: A History of Dreams and Ghosts in Polar Exploration*, London: UCL Press.
McDermott, James (2001), *Martin Frobisher: Elizabethan Privateer*, New Haven, CT: Yale University Press.
McGhee, Robert (2005), *The Last Imaginary Place: A Human History of the Arctic World*, Chicago: The University of Chicago Press.
McGhee, Robert (2001), *The Arctic Voyages of Martin Frobisher: An Elizabethan Adventure*, Seattle: University of Washington Press.
Menocal, Maria Rosa (2002), *The Ornament of the World: How Muslims, Jews, and Christians Created a Culture of Tolerance in Medieval Spain*, Boston: Little, Brown.
Mentz, Steve (2009), *At the Bottom of Shakespeare's Ocean*. London: Bloomsbury.
Mentz, Steve (2014), "God's Storms: Shipwreck and the Meaning of Ocean in Early Modern England and America," in Carl Thompson (ed.), *Shipwreck in Art and Literature: Images and Interpretations from Antiquity to the Present Day*, New York: Routledge.
Mentz, Steve (2015), *Shipwreck Modernity: Ecologies of Globalization, 1550–1719*, Minneapolis: University of Minnesota Press.
Mentz, Steve (2017), "Hurricanes, Tempests, and the Meteorological Globe," in Howard Martichello and Evelyn Tribble (eds.), *The Palgrave Handbook of Early Modern Literature and Science*, 257–76, London: Palgrave.
Mentz, Steve (2019), *Break Up the Anthropocene*, Minneapolis: University of Minnesota Press.
Mentz, Steve (forthcoming), *Ocean*, London: Bloomsbury.
Mercado, Loida Figueroa (1978), *History of Puerto Rico: From the Beginning to 1892*, New York: L.A. Publishing Company.
Molloy, Charles (1666), *Holland's Ingratitude, or a serious expostulation of the Dutch*, London: Francis Kirkman.
Molloy, Charles (1676), *De jure maritimo et navali: or a treatise of affairs maritime and of commerce*, London.
Monmonier, Marc (1999), *Air Apparent: How Meteorologists Learned to Map, Predict, and Dramatize Weather*, Chicago: University of Chicago Press.
Montalboddo, Fracanzano da, ed. (1507), *Paesi Nouamente retrouati ...*, Vicenza: Gio. Maria da Ca' Zeno.
Montrose, Louis (2006), *The Subject of Elizabeth: Authority, Gender, and Representation*, Chicago: University of Chicago Press.
Moore, Jason W. (2015), *Capitalism in the Web of Life: Ecology and the Accumulation of Capital*, London: Verso.

More, Thomas ([1516], 2002), *Utopia*, ed. George M. Logan and Robert M. Adams, Cambridge: Cambridge University Press.

Morgan, Edmund (1975), *American Slavery, American Freedom: The Ordeal of Colonial Virginia*, New York: Norton.

Morgan, Jennifer L. (2016), "Accounting for "The Most Excruciating Torment": Gender, Slavery, and Trans-Atlantic Passages," *History of the Present: A Journal of Critical History*, 6 (2): 184–207.

Morison, Samuel Eliot (1974), *The European Discovery of America: The Southern Voyages A.D. 1492–1616*, New York: Oxford University Press.

Morton, Thomas ([1637] 1883), *The New English Canaan*, ed. Charles Francis Adams, Jr., Boston: The Prince Society.

Morton, Timothy (2012), *The Ecological Thought*, Cambridge, MA: Harvard University Press.

Moss, John (1994), *Enduring Dreams: An Exploration of Arctic Landscape*, Concord, ON: House of Anansi Press.

Muldoon, James (2002), "Who Owns the Sea?," in Bernhard Klein (ed.), *Fictions of the Sea: Critical Perspectives on the Ocean in British Literature and Culture*, 13–27, Aldershot: Ashgate.

National Maritime Museum (n.d.), "English Ships and the Spanish Armada, August 1588," Royal Museums Greenwich. Available online: https://collections.rmg.co.uk/collections/objects/11754.html (accessed October 23, 2020).

Newitt, Malyn (2009), *Portugal in European and World History*, London: Reaktion Books.

"News Sent from London to the Duke of Milan, August 24, 1497" and "Raimondo de Soncino to the Duke of Milan, December 18" (1979), in D.B. Quinn (ed.), *New American World: A Documentary History of North America to 1612*, vol. 1, *America from Concept to Discovery. Early Exploration of North America*, London: Macmillan Press.

Ng, Su Fang (2012), "Dutch Wars, Global Trade, and the Heroic Poem: Dryden's Annus Mirabilis (1666) and Amin's Sya'ir Perang Mengkasar (1670)," *Modern Philology* 109 (3): 352–84. Available online: https://www.journals.uchicago.edu/doi/10.1086/663975 (accessed October 23, 2020).

Ng, Su Fang (2019), *Alexander the Great from Britain to Southeast Asia: Peripheral Empires in the Global Renaissance*, Oxford: Oxford University Press.

Nixon, Rob (2011), *Slow Violence and the Environmentalism of the Poor*, Cambridge, MA: Harvard University Press.

Norwood, Richard (1637), *The seaman's practice*, London: George Hurlock.

Nunn, Nathan and Nancy Quian (2010), "The Columbian Exchange: A History of Disease, Food, and Ideas," *Journal of Economic Perspectives,* 24 (2): 163–88.

Ogilvie, Brian W. (2006), *The Science of Describing: Natural History in Renaissance Europe*, Chicago: University of Chicago Press.

O'Gorman, Edmundo (1961), *The Invention of America: An Inquiry into the Historical Nature of the New World and the Meaning of Its History*, Bloomington: Indiana University Press.

Oliveira, Fernando (1969), *A arte da guerra do mar*, Lisbon: Ministério da Marinha.

Oliveira, Fernando (1991), *Liuro da fabrica das naus*, Lisbon: Academia de Marinha.

Oliveira, Fernão [Fernando] de (2000), *Gramática da linguagem portuguesa (1536)*, ed. Amadeu Torres and Carlos Assunção, Lisbon: Academia das Ciências de Lisboa.

Orgel, Stephen (1998), "Introduction," in Stephen Orgel (ed.), *The Tempest*, 1–88, Oxford: Oxford University Press.

Orgis, Rachel (2017), *Narrative Structure and Reader Formation in Lady Mary Wroth's "Urania,"* New York: Routledge.
Outram, Dorinda (1997), "The History of Natural History: Grand Narrative or Local Lore," in John Wilson Foster (ed.), *Nature in Ireland: A Scientific and Cultural History*, Montreal: McGill-Queen's University Press.
Ovid (1977), *Heroides and Amores*, Grant Showerman, 2nd edn. trans. rev. G.P. Goold, Cambridge, MA: Harvard University Press.
Ovid (2010), *Metamorphoses*, trans. Stanley Lombardo, Indianapolis, IN: Hacklett.
Oviedo, Fernandez de and Gonzalo Valdés ([1535] 2016), *Sumario de la Natural y General Historia de las Indias*, ed. Alfredo and Arturo Rodríguez López-Abadía, Madrid: Cátedra.
Owens, Sarah E. (2017), *Nuns Navigating the Spanish Empire*, Albuquerque: University of New Mexico Press.
Ozeki, Ruth (2013), *A Tale for the Time Being*, Edinburgh: Canongate Books.
Padrón, Ricardo (2009), "A Sea of Denial: The Early Modern Spanish Invention of the Pacific Rim," *Hispanic Review*, 77 (1): 1–27.
Padrón, Ricardo (2014), "Sinophobia vs. Sinophilia in the 16th Century Iberian World," *Review of Culture/Revista de Cultura*, 46: 94–107.
Palacio, Diego García de (1944), *Instrucción náutica para navegar*, Madrid: Ediciones Cultura Hispánica.
Parish, Susan Scott (2006), *American Curiosity: Cultures of Natural History in the Colonial British Atlantic World*, Chapel Hill: University of North Carolina Press.
Parker, Patricia (1979), *Inescapable Romance: Studies in the Poetics of a Mode*, Princeton, NJ: Princeton University Press.
Parr, Anthony "'For his Travailes let the Globe witnesse': Venturing on the Stage in Early Modern England," *Travel and Drama in Early Modern England: The Journeying Play*, eds. Claire Jowitt and David McInnis, (Cambridge: Cambridge UP, 2018), 21–38.
Parry, David (2014), "Sacrilege and the Economics of Empire in Dryden's *Annus Mirabilis*," *Studies in English Literature*, 54 (3): 531–53.
Parry, J.H. (1963), *The Age of Reconnaissance: Discovery, Exploration, and Settlement, 1450–1650*, London: Weidenfeld and Nicolson.
Parry, J.H. (1974), *The Discovery of the Sea*, Berkeley: University of California Press.
Pasqualigo, Lorenzo, to "Alvise and Francesco Pasqualigo, his brothers in Venice, August 23, 1497" (1979), in D.B. Quinn (ed.), *New American World: A Documentary History of North America to 1612*, vol. 1, *America from Concept to Discovery. Early Exploration of North America*, London: Macmillan Press.
Paster, Gail Kern (2004), *Humoring the Body: Emotions and the Shakespearean Stage*, Chicago: University of Chicago Press.
Pastore, Christopher L. (2014), *Between Land and Sea: The Atlantic Coast and the Transformation of New England*, Cambridge, MA: Harvard University Press.
Pastore, Christopher L. (2015), "Filling Boston Commons: Law, Culture, and Ecology in the Seventeenth-Century Estuary," in John Gillis and Franziska Torma (eds.), *Fluid Frontiers: Exploring Oceans, Islands, and Coastal Environments*, 27–38, Cambridge: White Horse Press.
Paul, Benjamin (2011), "'And the moon has started to bleed': Apocalypticism and Religious Reform in Venetian Art at the Time of the Battle of Lepanto," in James G. Harper (ed.), *The Turk and Islam in the Western Eye, 1450–1750: Visual Imagery Before Orientalism*, 67–94, Burlington, VT: Ashgate.

Pearl, Jason H. (2014), *Utopian Geographies and the Early English Novel*, Charlottesville: University of Virginia Press.
Pereira, Duarte Pacheco (1937), *Esmeraldo de Situ Orbis*, trans. and ed. George H.T. Kimble, 2nd ser., vol. 79, London: Hakluyt Society.
Pereira, Duarte Pacheco (1991), *Esmeraldo de Situ Orbis*, ed. Joaquim Barradas de Carvalho, Lisbon: Fundação Calouste Gulbenkian.
Pérez-Mallaina Bueno, Pablo Emilio (1989), "Los libros de náutica españoles del siglo XVI y su influencia en el descubrimiento y conquista de los océanos," in José Luis Peset (ed.), *Ciencia, vida y espacio en Iberoamérica*, vol. 3, 457–84, Madrid: Consejo Superior de Investigaciones Científicas.
Peters, John Durham (2015), *The Marvelous Clouds: Toward a Philosophy of Elemental Media*, Chicago: University of Chicago Press.
Petty, William (1648), *The Advice of W.P. to Mr. Samuel Hartlib: For the Advancement of Some Particular Parts of Learning*, London.
Piechocki, Katharina N. (2019), *Cartographic Humanism: The Making of Early Modern Europe*, Chicago: University of Chicago Press.
Pigafetta, Antonio (2007), *The First Voyage around the World, 1519–1522: An Account of Magellan's Expedition*, ed. Theodore J. Cachey Jr., Toronto: University of Toronto Press.
Pimentel, Manuel (1712), *Arte de navegar, emque se ensinam as regras practices*, Lisbon.
Pinto, Fernão Mendes ([1614] 1989), *The Travels of Mendes Pinto*, trans. Rebecca D. Catz, Chicago: University of Chicago Press.
Pires, Tomé (1978), *A Suma Oriental de Tomé Pires e o Livro de Francisco Rodrigues*, ed. Armando Cortesão, Coimbra, Portugal: University of Coimbra.
Plattes, Gabriel (1641), *A Description of the Famous Kingdome of Macaria*, London.
Pontanus, Johanus Isacius (1637), *Discussionum historicarum libri duo*, Harderwijk.
Pontanus, Johanus Isacius (1631), *Rerum Danicarum Historia*, Hondius.
Poole, Kristen (2011), *Supernatural Environments in Shakespeare's England*, Cambridge: Cambridge University Press.
Povey, Captain Francis (1702), *The Sea Gunner's Companion*, London: Richard Mount.
Price, Richard (2007), *Travels with Tooy: History, Memory, and the African-American Imagination*, Chicago: University of Chicago Press.
Purchas, Samuel ([1625] 1905), *Hakluytus posthumus: or Purchas his Pilgrimes*, Extra series, (Hakluyt Society) vols 14–33, Glasgow: James MacLehose and Sons.
Purchas, Samuel ([1625] 1906), *Hakluytus Posthumus, or Purchas His Pilgrimes*, Glasgow: James MacLehose and Sons.
Questa e vna opera necessari a tutti li naviga[n]ti chi vano in diverse parte del mondo (1490), Venice.
Quinn, David Beers (1974), *England and the Discovery of America, 1481–1620*, London: George Allen & Unwin.
Rabasa, José (1993), *Inventing America: Spanish Historiography and the Formation of Eurocentrism*, Norman: University of Oklahoma Press.
Ramachandran, Ayesha (2015), *The Worldmakers: Global Imagining in Early Modern Europe*, Chicago: University of Chicago Press.
Rediker, Marcus (2007), *The Slave Ship: A Human History*, New York: Viking.
Relaño, Francesco (2002), *The Shaping of Africa: Cosmographic Discourse and Cartographic Science in Late Medieval and Early Modern Europe*, Aldershot: Ashgate.
Rivett, Sarah (2011), *The Science of the Soul in Colonial New England*, Chapel Hill: University of North Carolina Press.

Roberts, Callum (2007), *The Unnatural History of the Sea: The Past and Future of Humanity and Fishing*, London: Gaia.

Roberts, Josephine A. (1995), "Introduction," in Josephine A. Roberts (ed.), *The First Part of the Countess of Montgomery's Urania*, xv–civ, Medieval & Renaissance Texts & Studies, Binghamton: State University of New York at Binghamton.

Roberts, Neil (2015), *Freedom as Marronage*, Chicago: University of Chicago Press.

Roger, N.A.M (1997), *The Safeguard of the Sea: A Naval History of Britain 660–1649*, New York: Norton.

Romm, James S. (1992), *The Edges of the Earth in Ancient Thought: Geography, Exploration, and Fiction*, Princeton, NJ: Princeton University Press.

[Rook, Lawrence] (1667), "Directions for observations and experiments to be made by masters of ships, pilots, and other fit persons in their sea-voyages," *Philosophical Transactions of the Royal Society of London*, 24: 433–8.

Roychoudhury, Suparna (2018), *Phantasmatic Shakespeare: Imagination in the Age of Early Modern Science*, Ithaca, NY: Cornell University Press.

Rozwadowski, Helen (2001), "History of Ocean Sciences," in John H. Steele, S.A. Thorpe, and Karl K. Turekian (eds.), *Encyclopedia of Ocean Sciences*, vol. 2, 1206–1210, San Diego: Academic Press.

Rozwadowski, Helen (2005), *Fathoming the Ocean: The Discovery and Exploration of the Deep Sea*, Cambridge, MA: Harvard University Press.

Rozwadowski, Helen (2018), *Vast Expanses: A History of the Oceans*, London: Reaktion Books.

Rubiés, Joan-Pau (2000), *Travel and Ethnology in the Renaissance: South India through European Eyes, 1250–1625*, Cambridge: Cambridge University Press.

Russell, Peter (2000), *Prince Henry 'the Navigator': A Life*, New Haven, CT: Yale University Press.

Russell, Steve (2017), "Early Indigenous Peoples and Written Language," *Indian Country Today*, July 19. Available online: https://newsmaven.io/indiancountrytoday/archive/early-indigenous-peoples-and-written-language-UJ-6AxiE4kmg_ImKwfVLKg/ (accessed February 15, 2019).

Safier, Neil and Ilda Mendes dos Santos (2007), "Mapping Maritime Triumph and the Enchantment of Empire: Portuguese Literature of the Renaissance," in David Woodward (ed.), *Cartography in the European Renaissance*, vol. 3, part 1 of *The History of Cartography*, 461–8, Chicago: University of Chicago Press.

Sahagún, Bernardino de ([1529] 1950), *General History of the Things of New Spain; Florentine Codex*, ed. and trans. Arthur J.O. Anderson and Charles E. Dibble, Santa Fe, NM: School of American Research.

Sanders, Julie (2011), *The Cultural Geography of Early Modern Drama, 1620– 1650*, Cambridge: Cambridge University Press.

Sandman, Alison (2007), "Spanish Nautical Cartography in the Renaissance," in David Woodward (ed.), *Cartography in the European Renaissance*, vol. 3, part 1 of *The History of Cartography*, 1095–142, Chicago: University of Chicago Press.

Sarkar, Debapriya (2017), "*The Tempest*'s Other Plots," *Shakespeare Studies*, 45: 203–30.

Sarpi, Paolo (1676), *Del dominio del mare Adriatico*.

Scafi, Alessandro, (2006), *Mapping Paradise: A History of Heaven on Earth*, Chicago: University of Chicago Press.

Schottenhammer, Angela (2012), "The 'China Seas' in World History: A General Outline of the Role of Chinese and East Asian Maritime Space from its Origins to c. 1800," *Journal of Marine and Island Cultures*, 1: 63–86.

The seas magazine opened: or, the Holander dispossest of his usurped trade of fishing upon the English seas (1653), London: William Ley.
Sejas, Tatiana (2014), *Asian Slaves in Colonial Mexico: From Chinos to Indians*, New York: Cambridge University Press.
Selden, John (1615), *Analecton Britannicon*, Frankfurt.
Selden, John (1635), *Mare clausum seu de dominus Maris*, London: Richardo Meighen.
Selden, John ([1635] 1652), *Of the Dominion, or, Ownership of the Sea*, London: Printed by William Du-Gard.
Seller, John (1669), *Practical navigation; or an introduction to the whole art*, London: William Fisher.
Serres, Michel, with Bruno Latour (1995), *Conversations on Science, Culture, and Time*, trans. Roxanne Lapidus, Ann Arbor: University of Michigan Press.
Shakespeare, William ([1594–6] 2008), *A Midsummer Night's Dream* in Stephen Greenblatt, Walter Cohen, Jean E. Howard, and Katharine Eisaman Maus (eds.), *The Norton Shakespeare: Essential Plays, The Sonnets*, New York: W.W. Norton.
Shakespeare, William ([1597] 2008), *Richard II* in Stephen Greenblatt, Walter Cohen, Jean E. Howard, and Katharine Eisaman Maus (eds.), *The Norton Shakespeare: Essential Plays, The Sonnets*, New York: W.W. Norton.
Shakespeare, William ([c. 1601] 2008), "Twelfth Night, or What You Will," in Stephen Greenblatt, Walter Cohen, Jean E. Howard, and Katharine Eisaman Maus (eds.), *The Norton Shakespeare: Comedies*, 689–750, New York: W.W. Norton.
Shakespeare, William ([1610–11] 2008), *The Tempest* in Stephen Greenblatt, Walter Cohen, Jean E. Howard, and Katharine Eisaman Maus (eds.), *The Norton Shakespeare: Essential Plays, The Sonnets*, New York: W.W. Norton.
Shakespeare, William ([1611] 2016), *The Norton Shakespeare*, 3rd edn., ed. Stephen Greenblatt, Walter Cohen, Suzanne Gossett, Jean E. Howard, Katharine Eisaman Maus, and Gordon McMullan, New York: W.W. Norton.
Shanahan, John (2008), "Ben Jonson's *Alchemist* and Early Modern Laboratory Space," *Journal for Early Modern Cultural Studies*, 8 (1): 35–66.
Sharp, Edward (1615), *Britaines Busse: Or, A computation as well of the charge of a Busse or herring-fishing ship. As also of the gaine and profit thereby. With the States proclamation annexed unto the same, as concerning herring fishing*, London.
Sidney, Philip ([1593] 1977), *The Countess of Pembroke's Arcadia*, ed. Maurice Evans, London: Penguin Classics.
Singh, Jyotsna G. (1996), "Caliban versus Miranda: Race and Gender Conflicts in Postcolonial Rewritings of *The Tempest*," in Valerie Traub, M. Lindsay Kaplan, and Dympna Callaghan (eds.), *Feminist Readings of Early Modern Culture: Emerging Subjects*, 191–209, Cambridge: Cambridge University Press.
Singh, Jyotsna G., ed. (2009), *A Companion to the Global Renaissance: English Literature and Culture in the Era of Expansion*, Malden, MA: Wiley-Blackwell.
Skura, Meredith Anne (1989), "Discourse and the Individual: The Case of Colonialism in *The Tempest*," *Shakespeare Quarterly*, 40 (1): 42–69.
Sleeper-Smith, Susan (2015), "Encounter and Trade in the Early Atlantic World," in Susan Sleeper-Smith, Juliana Barr, Jean M. O'Brien, Nancy Shoemaker, and Scott Manning Stevens (eds.), *Why You Can't Teach United States History without American Indians*, 26–42, Chapel Hill: Univeristy of North Carolina Press.
Sloterdijk, Peter (2011), *Bubbles: Spheres I*, trans. Wieland Hoban, Cambridge, MA: MIT Press. [Original German 1998.]
Sloterdijk, Peter (2013), *In the World Interior of Capital*, trans. Wieland Hoban, Cambridge, MA: Polity Press. [Original German 2005.]

Sloterdijk, Peter (2014), *Globes: Spheres II*, trans. Wieland Hoban, Cambridge, MA: MIT Press. [Original German 1999.]
Sloterdijk, Peter (2016), *Foam: Spheres III*, trans. Wieland Hoban, Cambridge, MA: MIT Press. [Original German 2004.]
Smith, Bruce R. (1999), *The Acoustic World of Early Modern England: Attending to the O-Factor*, Chicago: University of Chicago Press.
Smith, D.K. (2008), *The Cartographic Imagination in Early Modern England: Re-writing the World in Marlowe, Spenser, Raleigh and Marvell*, Burlington, VT: Ashgate.
Smith, John (1627), *A Sea Grammar*, London: Ionas Man and Benjamin Fisher.
Soto, José Luis Casado (1996), *Discursos de Bernardino de Escalante al Rey y sus Ministros (1585–1605)*, Laredo: Universidad De Cantabria.
Spenser, Edmund ([1590, 1596] 2001), *The Faerie Queene*, ed. A.C. Hamilton and text ed. Hiroshi Yamashita and Toshiyuki Suzuki, Harlow: Longman.
Spiller, Elizabeth (2004), *Science, Reading, and Renaissance Literature: The Art of Making Knowledge, 1580–1670*, Cambridge: Cambridge University Press.
Spiller, Elizabeth (2009), "Shakespeare and the Making of Early Modern Science: Resituating Prospero's Art," *South Central Review*, 26 (1–2): 24–41.
Stacke, Sarah (2018), "See the Amazing, Ethereal Creatures Living Under Arctic Ice," *National Geographic Online*, September 12. Available online: https://www.nationalgeographic.com/animals/2018/09/white-sea-arctic-underwater-marine-life (accessed January 1, 2019).
Staden, Hans (1557), *Warhaftige Historia*, Marburg.
Starr, Cindy (2016), "Annual Arctic Sea Ice Minimum 1979–2015, with graph," NASA Scientific Visualization Studio, March 10. Available online: https://svs.gsfc.nasa.gov/4435 (accessed October 9, 2020).
Steinberg, Philip E. (2001), *The Social Construction of the Ocean*, New York: Cambridge University Press.
Strachey, William (1610), *A True Repertory of the Wracke*, London.
Strong, Roy (1986), *The Cult of Elizabeth: Elizabethan Portraiture and Pageantry*, Berkeley: University of California Press.
Strunck, Christina (2011), "The Barbarous and Noble Enemy: Pictorial Representations of the Battle of Lepanto," in James G. Harper (ed.), *The Turk and Islam in the Western Eye, 1450–1750: Visual Imagery Before Orientalism*, 217–40, Burlington, VT: Ashgate.
Subrahmanyam, Sanjay (2007), "The Birth-Pangs of Portuguese Asia: Revisiting the Fateful 'Long Decade' of 1498–1509," *Journal of Global History*, 2: 261–80.
Subrahmanyam, Sanjay (2017), *Europe's India: Words, Peoples, Empires, 1500–1800*, Cambridge, MA: Harvard University Press.
Subrahmanyam, Sanjay and Geoffrey Parker (2008), "Arms and the Asian: Revisiting European Firearms and their Place in Early Modern Asia," *Revista de Cultura*, 26: 12–42.
Sutherland, John (2016), "'Musée des Beaux Arts', 'Their Lonely Betters' and 'The Shield of Achilles,'" The British Library, May 25. Available online: https://www.bl.uk/20th-century-literature/articles/musee-des-beaux-arts-their-lonely-betters-and-the-shield-of-achilles (accessed October 23, 2020).
Taff, Dyani Johns (2019), "Precarious Travail, Gender, and Narration in Shakespeare's *Pericles, Prince of Tyre* and Margaret Cavendish's *The Blazing World*," in Patricia Akhimie and Bernadette Andrea (eds.), *Travel and Travail: Early Modern Women, English Drama, and the Wider World*, 273–91, Lincoln: University of Nebraska Press.

Taylor, E.G.R. (1956), "A Letter Dated 1577 from Mercator to John Dee," *Imago Mundi*, 13: 56–68.

Test, Edward Maclean (2019), *Sacred Seeds: New World Plants in Early Modern English Literature*, Lincoln: University of Nebraska Press.

Theal, George McCall (1964), *Records of South-Eastern Africa*, vol. 1, *1898*, Cape Town: C. Struik.

Thompson, Ayanna (2011), *Passing Strange: Shakespeare, Race, and Contemporary America*, Oxford: Oxford University Press.

Thorius, Raphael (1651), *Cheimonopegnion, Or, a Winter Song*, London: T.N.

Thornton, John (1998), *Africa and Africans in the Making of the Atlantic World, 1400–1800*, 2nd edn., New York: Cambridge University Press.

"Through the Eyes of Satellites, Scientists See Changing Arctic" (2015), National Oceanic and Atmospheric Administration, April 30. Available online: https://www.nesdis.noaa.gov/content/through-eyes-satellites-scientists-see-changing-arctic (accessed October 28, 2019).

Thrush, Coll (2016), *Indigenous London: Native Travelers at the Heart of Empire*, New Haven, CT: Yale University Press.

Traub, Valerie (2002), *The Renaissance of Lesbianism in Early Modern England*, New York: Cambridge University Press.

Turner, G. L'E. (2004), "William Bourne," *Oxford Dictionary of National Biography*. https://doi.org/10.1093/ref:odnb/3011.

Turner, Henry S. (2006), *The English Renaissance Stage: Geometry, Poetics, and the Practical Spatial Arts 1580–1630*, Oxford: Oxford University Press.

Turner, Henry S. (2009), "Life Science: Rude Mechanicals, Human Mortals, Posthuman Shakespeare," *South Central Review,* 26 (1–2): 197–217.

Van der Donck, Adriaen ([1655] 2010), *A Description of New Netherland*, ed. Charles T. Gehring and William A. Starna, trans. Diederik Willem Goedhuys, Lincoln: University of Nebraska Press.

Van Duzer, Chet (2013), *Sea Monsters and Medieval and Renaissance Maps*, London: The British Library.

Virgil (1999), *Eclogues. Georgics. Aeneid: Books 1–6*, trans. H. Rushton Fairclough, Cambridge, MA: Harvard University Press.

Voigt, Lisa (2009), *Writing Captivity in the Early Modern Atlantic: Circulations of Knowledge and Authority in the Iberian and English Imperial Worlds*, Chapel Hill: Published for the Omohundro Institute of Early American History and Culture by the University of North Carolina Press.

Wade, Geoff (2005), "The Zheng He Voyages: A Reassessment," *Journal of the Malaysian Branch of the Royal Asiatic Society*, 78 (1): 37–58.

Waghenaer, Lucas Janszoon (1584), *Spieghel der Zeevaerdt*, Leiden.

Wakely, Andrew (1704), *Mariner's Compass Rectified*, London: Richard Mount.

Walcott, Derek (2007), "The Sea is History," in *Selected Poems*, ed. Edward Baugh, 137–9, New York: FSG.

Watt-Cloutier, Sheila (2015), *The Right to Be Cold: One Woman's Fight to Protect the Arctic and Save the Planet from Climate Change*, Minneapolis: University of Minnesota Press.

Weaver, Jace (2014), *The Red Atlantic: American Indigenes and the Making of the Modern World, 1000–1927*, Chapel Hill: North Carolina University Press.

Webster, John ([1612] 2002), "The White Devil," in David Bevington, Lars Engle, Katharine Eisamen Maus, and Eric Rasmussen (eds.), *English Renaissance Drama: A Norton Anthology*, 1659–748, New York: Norton.

Wells-Cole, Anthony (2012), "Scissors-and-Paste in Two Paintings of Elizabeth I," *The Burlington Magazine*, 154 (1317): 834–8.
Werth, Tiffany Jo (2011), *The Fabulous Dark Cloister: Romance in England after the Reformation*, Baltimore: Johns Hopkins University Press.
Wessing, Robert (2006), "Symbolic Animals in the Land Between the Waters: Markers of Place and Tradition," *Asian Folklore Studies*, 65: 205–39.
White, Adam, ed. (1855), *A Collection of Documents on Spitzbergen and Greenland*, London: Hakluyt Society.
White, Sam (2017), *A Cold Welcome: The Little Ice Age and Europe's Encounter with North America*, Cambridge, MA: Harvard University Press.
Wiesner-Hanks, Merry E. (2006), *Early Modern Europe, 1450–1789*, New York: Cambridge University Press.
Williamson, James A. (1962), *The Cabot Voyages and Bristol Discovery under Henry VII*, Cambridge: Hakluyt Society.
Willis, Clive (2010), *Camões, Prince of Poets*, Bristol: HiPLAM.
Wilson, Jean (1980), *Entertainments for Elizabeth I*, Totowa, NJ: Rowman and Littlefield.
Witt, Ronald (1982), "Medieval 'Ars Dictaminis' and the Beginnings of Humanism: a New Construction of the Problem," *Renaissance Quarterly*, 35 (1): 1–35.
Wood, Peter H. (2004), "Teach, Edward [Blackbeard] (d. 1718)," in Lawrence Goldman (ed.), *Oxford Dictionary of National Biography*, online edn., Oxford: Oxford University Press. https://doi.org/10.1093/ref:odnb/27097.
Wood, William ([1634] 1977), *New England's Prospect: A True, Lively, and Experimentall description of that part of* America, *commonly called New England: discovering the state of that Countrie, both as it stands to our new-come* English *Planters; and to the old Native Inhabitants*, ed. Alden T. Vaughan, Amherst: University of Massachusetts Press.
Wright, Edward (1599), *Certaine Errors in Navigation*, London: Valentine Sims. Available online from Early English Books Online (accessed October 23, 2020).
Wright, John K. (1947), "Terrae Incognitae: The Place of the Imagination in Geography," *Annals of the Association of American Geographers* 37 (1): 1–15.
Wroth, Mary ([1621] 1995), *The First Part of the Countess of Mongtomery's Urania*, ed. Josephine A. Roberts, Medieval & Renaissance Texts & Studies, Binghamton: State University of New York at Binghamton.
Yates, Julian (2003), *Error, Misuse, Failure: Object Lessons from the English Renaissance*, Minneapolis: University of Minnesota Press.
Yazzie, Melanie K. and Cutcha Risling Baldy (2018), "Introduction: Indigenous Peoples and the Politics of Water," *Decolonization: Indigineity, Education & Society*, 7 (1): 1–18.
Yussof, Kathyrn (2018), *A Billion Black Anthropocenes or None*, Minneapolis: University of Minnesota Press.
Zurara, Gomes Eanes de (1899), *The Chronicle of the Discovery and Conquest of Guinea*, trans. Charles Raymond Beazley and Edgar Prestage, 2 vols, London: Hakluyt Society.
Zurara, Gomes Eanes de (1915), *Crónica da tomada de Ceuta por El Rei D. João I*, ed. Francisco Maria Esteves Pereira, Lisbon: Academia das Ciências de Lisboa.
Zurara, Gomes Eanes de (1978–81), *Crónica dos feitos notáveis que se passaram na conquista de Guiné por mandado do Infante D. Henrique*, ed. Torquato de Sousa Soares, 2 vols., Lisbon: Academia Portuguesa da História.
Zell, Michael (2003), "Christ in the Storm on the Sea of Galilee," in *Eye of the Beholder*, ed. Alan Chong, Richard Lingner, and Carl Zahn Boston: Isabella Stewart Gardner Museum and Beacon Press.

CONTRIBUTORS

Josiah Blackmore is Nancy Clark Smith Professor of the Language and Literature of Portugal at Harvard University, Cambridge, Massachusetts. His research and teaching focus on the textual cultures of Portuguese maritime expansion and exploration, the oceanic imagination in literary and historical texts, medieval poetry, and the history of sexuality in Iberia from the Middle Ages to the present. He has also written on nineteenth-century novelistic fiction and the work of Portuguese poet António Botto. His books include *Moorings: Portuguese Expansion and the Writing of Africa* (2009), *Manifest Perdition: Shipwreck Narrative and the Disruption of Empire* (2002), and *Queer Iberia* (coeditor, 1999).

Dan Brayton is Julian W. Abernethy Chair of Literature and Director of the Environmental Studies Program at Middlebury College, Vermont. His articles on early modern natural history, blue cultural studies, Shakespeare, and traditional boatbuilding have been published in such journals and magazines as *ELH*, *Forum for Modern Language Studies*, and *WoodenBoat*. His book *Shakespeare's Ocean: An Ecocritical Exploration* (2012) won the Northeast Modern Language Association Book Prize. In addition to teaching at Middlebury, he has taught for Sea Education Association, the Williams-Mystic Program in Maritime Studies, and Semester-at-Sea on shore and in sailing and motor vessels on the Atlantic, Pacific, Mediterranean, and Caribbean.

Lowell Duckert is Associate Professor of English at the University of Delaware, where he specializes in early modern literature, environmental criticism, and the "new materialisms" (especially actor-network theory). He has published on various topics such as glaciers, polar bears, the color maroon, rain, fleece, mining, and lagoons. He is the author of *For All Waters: Finding Ourselves in Early Modern Wetscapes* (2017) and, with Jeffrey Jerome Cohen, the editor of *Elemental Ecocriticism: Thinking with Earth, Air, Water, and Fire* (2015) and *Veer Ecology: A Companion for Environmental Thinking* (2017).

John B. Hattendorf is Professor and Special Advisor at US Naval War College's John B. Hattendorf Center for Maritime Historical Research Newport, Rhode Island, and Ernest J. King Professor Emeritus of Maritime History. His numerous awards include the Anderson Medal for Lifetime Achievement from the Society of Nautical Research (2017), the US Navy's Distinguished Civilian Service Medal (2016) and Superior Civilian Service Medal (2006, 2016), the American Library Association's Dartmouth Medal (2007), and the Caird Medal of the National Maritime Museum, Greenwich (2000). He is the editor-in-chief of *The Oxford Encyclopedia of Maritime History* (2007).

Steve Mentz is Professor of English at St. John's University in New York City. His most recent book, *Ocean*, appeared in March 2020. He is the author of *Break Up the Anthropocene* (2019) and *Shipwreck Modernity: Ecologies of Globalization, 1550–1719* and editor or co-editor of *The Routledge Companion to Marine and Maritime Worlds, 1400–800* (2020) and *The Sea in Nineteenth-Century Anglophone Literary Culture* (2017). He has written numerous articles on ecocriticism, Shakespeare, early modern literature, and the blue humanities and curated an exhibition at the Folger Shakespeare Library, "Lost at Sea: The Ocean in the English Imagination, 1550–1750" (2010).

Christopher L. Pastore is Associate Professor of History at University at Albany, State University of New York where he teaches courses in environmental history, early America, and the Atlantic world. While composing his chapter, he was a 2018–19 Marie Skłodowska-Curie co-fund Research Fellow at the Trinity College Dublin Long Room Hub Arts & Humanities Research Institute. He is the author of *Between Land and Sea: The Atlantic Coast and the Transformation of New England* (2014) and is currently writing an environmental history of the early modern Atlantic world.

Debapriya Sarkar is Assistant Professor of English and Maritime Studies at the University of Connecticut. She is currently completing a book project titled *Possible Knowledge: The Literary Forms of Early Modern Science*. She has recently co-edited, with Jenny C. Mann, a special issue of *Philological Quarterly* on "Imagining Early Modern Scientific Forms" (2019). Her work appears or is forthcoming in *English Literary Renaissance, Shakespeare Studies, Spenser Studies, Exemplaria*, and in several edited collections.

James Seth is an Assistant Professor of Early Modern Literature in the Department of English at Central Washington University, Washington. His current research explores the intersection of early modern dramatic literature, performance history, and oceanic studies, and he is completing a book on maritime musicians and performers on early modern English voyages. His scholarly work has been published in *The Shakespeare Newsletter, Sixteenth Century Journal, Shakespeare en devenir*, as well as in recent edited collections *The Routledge Companion to Marine and Maritime Worlds, 1450–1750* and *The Metaphor of the Monster: Interdisciplinary Approaches to Understanding the Monstrous Other*.

Dyani Johns Taff is Lecturer in the English and Writing Departments at Ithaca College, New York. Her research and teaching interests include gender studies, environmental and maritime humanisms, ship of state metaphors, romance, piracy, translation, and re/interpretations of biblical narratives. She is the author of essays on Ben Johnson, Shakespeare, Margaret Cavendish, and Chaucer, and is currently writing a book titled *Gendered Seascapes and Monarchy in Early Modern English Culture*, which brings together maritime and gender studies lenses to reexamine metaphors for monarchy, pregnancy, marriage, and political conflict.

INDEX

Adams, William 221
admiralty courts 47–8
Alexander VI, Pope 46
Allard, Carel 65
al-Qazwini, Muhammad 187
Andromeda 184–5
Apian, Peter 63
aquaman myth 200–1
Arctic oceans 205–25
Armada Victory 119–23
art
    mythical sea 181–8
    realism 188–94
    sculptures and objects 194–6
Auden, W.H. 3

back staff 64
Bacon, Francis 106
Barbosa, Duarte 162, 163
Barlow, William 38–9
Battle of Diu 109–15
Battle of Lepanto 115–19
Bazán, Don Álvaro de 71–2
Best, George 219
biblical sea 181–4
Billion Black Anthropocenes or None, A (Yussof) 10–11
Blackmore, Josiah 23, 231, 232
blue humanities 1–2, 156, 226
blue-water chronotope 160
Blundeville, Thomas 59, 64

Boazio, Baptista 72–3
Bodhidharma 186–7
Bond, Henry 55–6
Bourne, William 36
Boyle, Robert 44–5
Brayton, Dan 95, 158, 226, 229
Briggs, Henry 216
Bril, Paul 182, 192
Brito, Bernardo Gomes de 173–5
Bruegel the Elder, Jan 181, 182
Bruegel the Elder, Pieter 185
Bry, Theodor de 56, 63, 66
Buddhist arhat 186–7
Burney, William 54–5
Butler, Nathaniel 55

Cabot, John 30, 35
Cabral, Pedro Álvares 158, 159, 161
Cadamosto, Alvise da 34, 158
Caminha, Pero Vaz de (*Letter*) 158–61
Camões, Luís vaz de (*Os Lusíadas*) 21–3,
    111, 113, 165–7, 170–2
Cano, Tomé 66–7
caravels 32–4, 90
carbon levels 7
Carneiro, Antonio de Maris 60
Carpaccio, Vittore 189–90
cartography *see* maps
Castro, João de 163
Cavendish, Margaret 106–7, 125–6
Cavendish, Thomas 13, 14–15

Cervantes, Miguel de 119
Chart of the Pacific (Gerritsz) 97–100
Christianity 27–8, 30, 31, 125–6, 196
chronotope of the sea 160
Chulan, Raja 113–14
circumnavigation 13–15, 39, 173
coastal navigation 89, 90
Colson, Nathaniel 61
Columbian Exchange 5
Columbus, Christopher 25–6, 40, 86
communication
    message-in-a-bottle 103
    at sea 65
    transocean 102
Consulat de Mar (Consulate of the Sea) 77
Corte-Real, Gaspar 219
cross-staff 64
currents 86–93

D'Aguiar, Fred 3
Davis, John 60, 205
Davis's staff 64
Dee, John 123
de Momper, Joos 191
dictionaries 54–5
Digges, Sir Dudley 69, 216
Diu, Battle of 109–15
Don Quixote (Cervantes) 119
Drake, Sir Francis 14, 72
Dryden, John (*Annus Mirabilis*) 100–2
Duckert, Lowell 124, 217, 226
Dutch realism 190–4

Eden, Richard 107–8
Elizabeth I 119–23
English quadrant 64
Escalante de Mendoza, Juan de 165
Estado da India (State of India) 161–2

Fabyan, Robert 220
Falconer, William 54
Falconetto, Angelo 187
fishing 30, 68–9
flags 65
Fletcher, John 198–9
Fortuna 185
Fournier, Père Georges 60–1
Foxe, Luke 225
Fuca, Juan de 217

Galilee, Sea of 182–4
galleys 67
Gama, Vasco da 167, 169, 170
García de Palacio, Diego 165
Garcie, Pierre 59
Gastaldi, Giacomo 68
Gay, John 203
Gentleman, Tobias 68–9
geographical knowledge 27–32
geology 10–11
Gerritsz, Hessel 97–100
Gilbert, Sir Humphrey 218
Goodlad, William 217
Groot, Hugo de (Grotius) 47, 77–9
guns and gunnery 69–70

Hakluyt, Richard 42, 198
Hall, James 205
Hall, John 219, 220
Hein, Piet Pieterszoon 73
Henry, Prince 158
Hereford, Earl of 122–3
Historia Piscium (Ray) 44
Homer (*Odyssey*) 184
Hoste, Père Paul 73
Hubbard, Benjamin 61
hurricanes 16–17

Icarus 185
Inuit abductions 219–20, 221–3
islands and shores 28–30, 135–8
    islomania 136, 156
    New Arcadia 146–50
    The Tempest 138, 142–6
    Urania 137, 150–6
    Utopia 137, 139–42

Janes, John 205
Janson, Wilhelm 187
Johnson, Charles 202–3
Jonah 181–2
Jordain, Sylvester 198

Kayll, Robert 68–9

language of the sea 54–5, 199
lateen-rigged sails 32–4, 90
legal authority 46–50, 75–81
Lepanto, Battle of 115–19

Leviathan 182
Lewis, Simon L. 4–10, 123–4
Liu Songnian 186
Livro de Lisuarte de Abreu (Book of Lisuarte de Abreu) 168–70
Lobo, Jerónimo 176–7
Lope de Vega 200–1

Magellan, Ferdinand 13–14, 172–3
Magnus, Olaus 196, 206
Mainwaring, Captain Sir Henry 54
manuscripts 21–3, 55, 59, 73, 167, 187, 198
maps 17, 20, 27–8, 31–2, 68, 72–3, 141, 144, 151–2, 182, 187–8, 196–8, 210–12, 214–15
maroon communities (*marronage*) 9
Martens, Frederick 208
Martyr de Anghiera, Peter 42, 107, 217–18
Maslin, Mark A. 4–10, 123–4
Massinger, Philip 199
Mendes Pinto, Fernão 175–6
Mentz, Steve 39, 105, 141, 143, 175, 202, 226, 229, 230, 232
Mercator, Gerhardus 210–12
mermaids 198
message-in-a-bottle 103
Molloy, Charles 80
monsoons 90
More, Thomas (*Utopia*) 137, 139–42
Mount, Richard 61
Mountfort, Walter 199–200
Munk, Jens 220
Münster, Sebastian 181

Native American genocide 7
natural history 39–46
nautical protractor 64
navies 70–3
navigation
    handbooks ("rutters") 36
    instruments 35, 36–8, 62–5
    knowledge 32–9
    practical skills 56–61
Neptune, in art 194–5
New Arcadia (Sidney) 146–50
Newfoundland 30, 35, 69
New Pangea 4–10
North Pole 210–13

Norwood, Richard 61
Nuremberg Chronicle 66

oarsmen 129–30
Odysseus 184
Oliveira, Fernando 163–5
Orbis hypothesis 6–7, 123–4
Os Lusíadas (Camões) 21–3, 111, 113, 165–7, 170–2

papal bulls 46
Pastore, Chris 50, 51
pearl fishing 40
Peeters, Bonaventura 193
Peeters, Catharina 193–4
Pereira, Duarte Pacheco 162
Peyrère, Isaac de la 207–8, 221–3
Philip II 120, 130, 131
physicians 42
physico-theology 44
Pigafetta, Antonio 12, 173
Pimentel, Manuel 64–5
piracy 48, 71
    stage plays 201–3
Pires, Tomé 162–3
Plancius, Petrus 213
plants 17, 40
pole, geographical 210–13
Pontanus, Johanus Isacius 80
Porcellis, Jan 191
Poseidon 184
prayer books 74
print culture 45, 86
privateering 48, 71
Ptolemy (*Geographia*) 28, 86
Purchas, Samuel 42, 173, 216, 217

radical relationality 132
Ramusio, Giovanni 173
Ray, John (*Historia Piscium*) 44
religion 27–8, 30, 31, 74, 125–6, 196
Rembrandt van Rijn 182
Rhodian Sea Law 76
rigging 32–4, 68, 90
Rizo, Bernardino 56
Rolfe, John 198
Roll of Oléron 76
Romanticism 3
rowers 129–30

Royal Society of London 42, 44–5
"rutters" 36

sail plans 32–4, 90
Sànchez, Alonso 130–1
Sarkar, Debapriya 230
Schedel, Hartmann 66
sculptures 194–6
seamanship 55–6
sea monsters 187–8, 196–7
Sea of Galilee 182–4
Sejarah Melayu 113–15
Selden, John 47, 80
Seller, John 61
Senopati, Panembahan 113
Shakespeare, William
    Hamlet 94, 202
    Pericles 94, 202
    The Tempest 95–7, 138, 142–6, 198
    The Winter's Tale 201
    Troilus and Cressida 94
    Twelfth Night 124
Sharp, Edward 69
ship design and shipbuilding 66–8
ship-in-a-bottle 103
ship's log 38
shipwrecks 22–3, 39, 173–5
shores *see* islands and shores
Shou Lao 195
Sidney, Philip (*New Arcadia*) 146–50
sirens 187, 197–8
slave trade 3, 7–8, 15–16, 126–8, 158, 218–19
Sloane, Sir Hans 42
Sloterdijk, Peter 11–13
Smith, John 55
Sokollu Mehmed 116
Sor Ana (nun) 128
sovereignty claims 46–7, 76–7
spherology 11–13
square-rigged sails 34, 90
Sri Tri Buana 113, 114–15
Staden, Hans 74
State of India 161–2
Strachey, William 213

sugar plantations 29–30
sundials 64

Taff, Dyani Johns 229
Tempesta, Antonio 187
theologians 44
Thorius, Raphael 213
tides 89
time measurement 64
tobacco 17, 18
Treaty of Tordesilla 46

Urania (Wroth) 137, 150–6
Utopia (More) 137, 139–42

van der Brugge, Jacob Segersz 206
Vasari, Giorgio 116–18, 187
Venus 179–80
vice-admiralty courts 48
Vivaldi, Ugolino and Vadino 89
Volta do Mar 91
Vroom, Hendrik Cornelisz 191, 192–3

Waghenaer, Lucas Janszoon 63
Walcott, Derek 3
warfare 70–3, 105–6
    Armada Victory 119–23
    in art 188–90
    Battle of Diu 109–15
    Battle of Lepanto 115–19
Welwood, William 47
wet globalization 6–10, 13
Weymouth, George 205
wind-blowers 93–7
winds 86–93, 98–9
women 10–11, 119–23, 126, 128, 132, 151, 152, 193–4
world-making 86
Wright-Molyneux map 17, 20
Wroth, Lady Mary (*Urania*) 137, 150–6

Yussof, Kathryn 10–11

Zeno, Antonio and Nicolò 214–15, 216
Zheng He 109–10
Zurara, Gomes Eanes de 158